Towards a Genealogy of Cosmopolitan Thought

ENCOUNTERS IN LAW AND PHILOSOPHY
SERIES EDITORS: Thanos Zartaloudis & Anton Schütz

This series interrogates, historically and theoretically, the encounters between philosophy and law. Each volume published takes a unique approach and challenges traditional systemic approaches to law and philosophy. The series is designed to expand the environment for law and thought.

Titles available in the series

STASIS: Civil War as a Political Paradigm
Giorgio Agamben

On the Idea of Potency: Juridical and Theological Roots of the Western Cultural Tradition
Emanuele Castrucci

Political Theology: Demystifying the Universal
Anton Schütz and Marinos Diamantides

The Birth of Nomos
Thanos Zartaloudis

Leibniz: A Contribution to the Archaeology of Power
Stephen Connelly

Legal Artifices: Ten Essays on Roman Law in the Present Tense
Yan Thomas

Form of Life: Agamben and the Destitution of Life
Gian-Giacomo Fusco

The Anarchist Against the Law: Law Without Authority
Saul Newman and Massimo La Torre

Towards a Genealogy of Cosmopolitan Thought: Before and Beyond Liberalism
Detlef von Daniels

edinburghuniversitypress.com/series/enlp

TOWARDS A GENEALOGY OF COSMOPOLITAN THOUGHT

Before and Beyond Liberalism

Detlef von Daniels

EDINBURGH
University Press

Edinburgh University Press is one of the leading university presses in the UK. Publishing new research in the arts and humanities, EUP connects people and ideas to inspire creative thinking, open new perspectives and shape the world we live in. For more information, visit www.edinburghuniversitypress.com.

Edinburgh University Press Ltd
13 Infirmary Street, Edinburgh EH1 1LT

Typeset in 10.5/12 Palatino by
Cheshire Typesetting Ltd, Cuddington, Cheshire
Printed and bound in the UK using 100% renewable electricity by
CPI Group (UK) Ltd

A CIP record for this book is available from the British Library

ISBN 978 1 3995 5075 8 (hardback)
ISBN 978 1 3995 5077 2 (webready PDF)
ISBN 978 1 3995 5076 5 (epub)

FSC www.fsc.org MIX Paper | Supporting responsible forestry FSC® C013604

This book is printed using paper from well-managed forests, recycling and other controlled sources

Contents

Preface vii
Abbreviations of Works by Kant xxv

Prelude: Sappho's Calling 1

One: Plato and the Challenge to Cosmopolitanism 12
1. Contemporary Cosmopolitanism 14
2. Which History of Cosmopolitanism? 19
3. A Contextual Reading of the *Politeia* 29
4. The *Politeia* in the Hellenic world 54
5. Plato's Challenge Today 60

Two: Kant and the End(s) of Cosmopolitanism 64
1. Political Context and the Formation of a Philosophical Legacy 66
2. Systematic Unity and the Absence of Politics 81
3. Cosmopolitanism as a Legal Requirement 90
4. Religion as Politics and Ideology Critique 130
5. Heidegger's Resolution? 158

Three: Kelsen and the Twilight of Cosmopolitanism 176
1. Kelsen in Context 179
2. The Pure Theory of Law 185
3. Consequences for Cosmopolitan Thought 191
4. Kelsen's Contestation with Carl Schmitt 201
5. Kelsen's Dispute with Eugen Ehrlich 213
6. In the Eye of the Hurricane 225
7. Two Models of Post-foundational Cosmopolitanism 231

Coda: Hölderlin's Response 244

Postscript 252

Bibliography 255
Index 285

Preface

On 11 November 1989, the Russian cellist Mstislav Rostropovich performed an impromptu concert at the crumbling Berlin Wall, playing Johann Sebastian Bach's *Cello Suites*. He did not play for the Germans or himself but, as he explained in an interview, for God, because he had restored unity to his life. Rostropovich, the cellist of the twentieth century, was deeply embedded in the Russian musical tradition but also a staunch defender of art without borders, freedom of speech and democratic values, resulting in harassment from the Soviet regime. After he fled the Soviet Union in 1974, he was deprived of his citizenship and lived the rest of his life as a stateless musician, symbolising cosmopolitan hope through his work. And yet, even in this moment of joy, Rostropovich gave Bach's Bourrée from the third Cello Suite (a sprightly French court dance) a melancholic note. More than thirty years on, the picture of masses of people taking a defunct border by storm and proclaiming a new unity based on freedom, dignity and self-determination as a model for a peaceful world has a bittersweet note.[1] Has such a prospect ever existed, or was it an illusion from the very beginning?

The hope expressed in this short moment has given way to new realities. The shift of the economic centre of gravity from North America and Europe to other parts of the world, especially East Asia, heralds a polycentric form of modernity, one

[1] The metaphor 'bittersweet' (*glukupikron*, literally 'sweetbitter' as love is first sweet then bitter) was coined by Sappho. Her poetic interventions in the discourse of her time will, in the Prelude, present a specific 'bittersweet' angle on the topic of this essay and reappear throughout the reading of Plato, Kant and Kelsen. Her poetic form of thinking will only at the very end find an echo in Hölderlin.

which questions Western cultural and economic dominance and its mode of governance and development. The wars the United States has fought since then in the Middle East have at least thrown doubt on the commitment of the United States to uphold and further the standards of international law, while Russia under President Putin has shown, by attacking Ukraine, that it is willing to openly disregard international law and resort to pure military might as a means to pursue its interests. In the Israeli–Palestinian conflict, both sides are in the grip of extremist forces that make any kind of lasting reconciliation seem impossible. At the same time, the legacies of colonialism and the continuing exploitation of nature have brought about the peril of increasing mass migration, while the resources for meaningful human life on earth are shrinking. From this perspective, the fall of the Berlin Wall might not just evoke memories of unfulfilled promises but already foreshadow the beginning of the dissolution of the imperial fortress of Western civilisation – as if the moment of victory already contained, in a dialectical irony, the seeds of decline.

In terms of cultural analysis, the story of the inevitable dominance of Western civilisation is often associated with Francis Fukuyama's *The End of History*.[2] History (with a capital H), defined as fundamental social and political change brought about by the clash of comprehensive ideologies, 'ended' in 1990. This historical speculation has not just been challenged by alternative, cultural analyses[3] but served for many scholars in the fields of postcolonial studies as a counter-image to challenge the presumed universality of Western categories and concepts. At the same time, realism has, under the label of 'geopolitics', once again become the standard currency of analysing international relations. The specific 'Western' combination of liberal and democratic values with a global capitalist economy has also come under attack within the West by both populist movements and identity politics which decry 'liberalism' or some of its variants as an ideology from the

[2] Francis Fukuyama, *The End of History and the Last Man* (New York: Free Press, 1992). For his most recent defence of the thesis, see Francis Fukuyama, *Liberalism and its Discontents* (London: Profile Books, 2022).

[3] Samuel P. Huntington, *The Clash of Civilizations and the Remaking of World Order* (London: Touchstone, 1998).

very beginning.[4] In his analysis of the special case of the American creedal national identity, Francis Fukuyama argues the right wants to replace it with one based on race, ethnicity and religion while the left seeks to undermine its legitimacy 'by emphasizing victimization, insinuating in some cases that racism, gender discrimination, and other forms of systematic exclusion are in the country's DNA'.[5] From a vantage point one can only observe the self-destruction of the American public sphere with its institutional safeguards that once served as a pillar and counter-factual reminder of a liberal international system. Analyses of the second Trump presidency must follow each unforeseen turn and can only be written retrospectively, echoing Walter Benjamin's description of the *Angelus Novus*.[6]

Against this background, cosmopolitanism, the view that ascribes ultimate value to individuals and sees primary loyalty as good for humanity as a whole – possibly secured through global institutions – might appear to be helplessly naïve. But is it really? The central question of this book is how cosmopolitanism can be conceived vis-à-vis these challenges and counterforces. My thesis is that it does not require a more refined moral or political theory but a historically situated self-reflection – a genealogy of cosmopolitan thought – since a more profound account of the Western philosophical tradition opens up the path to reflecting on both the contravening tendencies within it and its interrelations to other intellectual traditions. As a conclusion, two models of post-foundational thought are proposed that can help us withstand counterforces in difficult times.

This broad outline calls for further clarification. To achieve this, the method employed throughout the essay is first introduced followed by an explanation of why it is necessary to

4 See Mark Lilla, *The Once and Future Liberal: After Identity Politics* (New York: HarperCollins, 2017).

5 Francis Fukuyama, 'Against Identity Politics: The New Tribalism and the Crisis of Democracy', *Foreign Affairs* 97, no. 5 (2018): 208.

6 According to Benjamin, the Paul Klee monoprint *Angelus Novus* (1920) describes the angel of history who, propelled into the future, gazes helplessly at the accumulating wreckage of the past. See Walter Benjamin, *Illuminations*, ed. Hannah Arendt, trans. Harry Zohn (New York: Schocken Books, 1968), 257–58.

reorient the philosophical tradition for addressing the challenges outlined above. Next, the relation of the ensuing line of reasoning to recent philosophical discussions on cosmopolitan thought is explained. Finally, a summary is provided outlining the overall structure of the essay's argument.

1. A genealogy is not a history of ideas that assumes concepts can be traced linearly through history or constructed using historical templates, as in the formula 'the good into the pot, the bad into the crop'. Instead, genealogies are written when the apparent naturalness of one's upbringing or the official history of a cherished idea begins to crumble. This prompts an inquiry into the official history of remembrance and a search for divergences or paths not taken, enabling the exploration of alternatives. Unlike Nietzsche's or Foucault's genealogies, this inquiry is not concerned with unmasking the hidden operations of power beneath moral or epistemic claims. Rather, it seeks to reflect constellations that still contained open possibilities before they hardened into doctrines or systems.

In the field of intellectual history, Quentin Skinner and the Cambridge School have refined this approach. Rather than taking political concepts and their official histories for granted, they investigate their origins to reveal their initial role as responses to the pressing questions of their time. By doing so, they uncover conceptual and social alternatives. Skinner argues that philosophical texts should be read as interventions in ongoing debates, rooted in specific historical contexts.[7] His leading idea is to demonstrate the contingent and contested nature of fundamental concepts. In his more recent work, Skinner draws on the concept of genealogy to enhance our understanding of historical complexities.[8] Rejecting the simplicity of grand narratives or conventional remembered histories, he upholds the 'veto right of the sources',[9] relying on meticulous historical analysis to

[7] See Quentin Skinner, 'Meaning and Understanding in the History of Ideas', *History and Theory* 8, no. 1 (1969): 3–53.

[8] Quentin Skinner, 'A Genealogy of the Modern State', *Proceedings of the British Academy* 162 (2009): 325–70.

[9] The notion has been introduced by Reinhart Koselleck, 'Standortbindung und Zeitlichkeit. Ein Beitrag zur historiographischen Erschließung der

challenge misinterpretations and normative assumptions in political theory. This method of contextualised analysis – interpreting political theories as context-specific answers to the questions of their time and using scholarship to reveal the latent possibilities within earlier ideas – will be used throughout this essay.

However, when applying the Cambridge School's method to a genealogy of cosmopolitan thought, several challenges arise. Standard histories of cosmopolitanism will feature, at the very least, a brief exposition of Cynic or Stoic roots, Kant's contributions (possibly in the context of German Idealist writers)[10] and the liberal theories that flourished after the 1990s in a post-Rawlsian framework. Other historical periods, such as early modern times or the revival of cosmopolitan ideas after World War I, are usually not mentioned.

The limited timeframe and intellectual tradition considered have a drawback: non- or anti-cosmopolitan positions appear only within a (broadly speaking) liberal framework.[11] The Cambridge School's method, by contrast, was developed primarily to analyse the Anglophone tradition of political thought since early modern times.[12] Moreover, scholars working within this tradition often avoid taking explicit positions on contemporary issues. Skinner even argued that 'to demand from the history of thought a solution to our own immediate problems is ... to commit not merely a methodological fallacy, but something like a moral error.'[13]

geschichtlichen Welt', Reinhart Koselleck, Wolfgang J. Mommsen and Jörn Rüsen, eds., *Objektivität und Parteilichkeit in der Geschichtswissenschaft* (München: Deutscher Taschenbuch Verlag, 1977), 45. On the similarities in Koselleck's and Skinner's approaches, see Kari Palonen, 'The History of Concepts as a Style of Political Theorizing: Quentin Skinner's and Reinhart Koselleck's Subversion of Normative Political Theory', *European Journal of Political Theory* 1, no. 1 (2002): 91–106.

10 A more detailed discussion of the contemporary debate and the origin of cosmopolitan thought will be given in Chapter 1.

11 See, for example, the Gillian Brock anthology, *Cosmopolitanism versus Non-Cosmopolitanism: Critiques, Defenses, Reconceptualizations* (Oxford: Oxford University Press, 2013) and the above-mentioned bibliographies.

12 Quentin Skinner, *Visions of Politics, 3 vols.* (Cambridge: Cambridge University Press, 2002).

13 Skinner, *Visions of Politics*, vol. 1, *Regarding Method*, 89.

This approach may therefore seem ill-suited to contributing to current debates on cosmopolitan thought.

The main challenge is not the expansion of the historical method to other periods or traditions, as this has already been attempted in recent years.[14] Instead, the key question is: how can a historical approach help address philosophical problems relevant to the contemporary world? The distinctive strength of the Cambridge School – its ability to challenge established narratives, uncover complexities and reveal the hidden, as-yet-unfulfilled, potential of traditions – risks being diminished when reframed as merely another variant of a broadly liberal theory. Furthermore, the cultural and geopolitical challenges mentioned earlier may seem far beyond the scope of a traditional Cambridge School analysis. However, by broadening our understanding of political thought, it becomes clear that a historically informed approach remains highly relevant. To illustrate this, a brief reflection may serve to unsettle a prevailing understanding of political philosophy and suggest a reorientation that reckons with Heidegger's subterranean presence. This requires a small detour.

2. One of the most pressing global political challenges is forced migration. Historians remind us that migration, often over long distances, has always been a constant feature of human history, either driven by push or pull factors. Sociologists emphasise that most migration occurs within a country or to neighbouring states. However, in political analysis, especially in political philosophy and scholarship, attention is predominantly directed towards migration from the Global South to the North, such as from Latin America to North America or from Africa and the Middle East to Europe.[15] For cosmopolitan political theory, migration is relevant for two key reasons. First, it raises the question of whether and how borders can be justified from the standpoint of

[14] See the interdisciplinary contributions in Adrian Blau, ed., *Meaning and Understanding in the History of Ideas and Beyond: Proceedings of the British Academy* (Liverpool: Liverpool University Press, 2026).

[15] For an overview of the classical philosophical debate, see Sarah Fine and Lea Ypi, eds., *Migration in Political Theory: The Ethics of Movement and Membership* (Oxford: Oxford University Press, 2016).

egalitarian cosmopolitanism.[16] In the European context, where most migrants before the war in Ukraine came from Muslim-majority countries, public debate has often revolved around whether cultural differences could serve as a legitimate reason for restricting migration. Some scholars argue for a universal right to migration, while others defend, albeit on weak cosmopolitan grounds, the right to national and cultural self-determination.[17] This is not the place to engage in that debate in detail; rather, the following highlights one specific aspect. Many contemporary participants in this discussion adopt a dual role – writing as academic philosophers while also engaging in public debate as intellectuals.

However, in doing so, philosophical discourse assumes a modern liberal Western society as its implicit audience. This limitation is also embedded in a frequently employed metaphor in migration debates: the shipwreck with a spectator.[18] These discussions often presume that we, as political philosophers or citizens of Western liberal societies, are positioned on solid ground, deliberating – sometimes compassionately – about the fate of those shipwrecked and our obligations towards them. But, if we shift perspectives and adopt the viewpoint of the migrants themselves, the metaphor – and the role of philosophy it implies – appears in a different light. From their standpoint, the fundamental existential condition is not standing on solid ground but being cast onto unstable planks, constantly in need of repair while drifting towards an uncertain future, with death constantly looming. Meanwhile, 'solid land' does not appear as an open agora for civilised debate but as an iron fortress of bureaucratic

[16] For a strong case in favour of open borders from an egalitarian point of view, see Joseph Carens, 'Aliens and Citizens: The Case for Open Borders', *Review of Politics* 49, no. 2 (1987): 251–73.

[17] David Miller, *Strangers in Our Midst* (Cambridge, MA: Harvard University Press, 2016).

[18] The common contemporary reference is Peter Singer's 'shallow pond' analogy; see 'Famine, Affluence, and Morality', *Philosophy & Public Affairs* 1, no. 3 (1972): 229–43. Hans Blumenberg has shown how the underlying metaphor of 'shipwreck with a spectator' has been used throughout the history of philosophy in multiple ways to determine the role of philosophy; see *Schiffbruch mit Zuschauer: Paradigma einer Daseinsmetapher* (Frankfurt am Main: Suhrkamp, 1979).

rationality, accessible only through hidden paths and back doors. The philosophical or spiritual guidance offered in the marketplace of ideas is not what 'boat people' seek. Instead, it is often provided by an ancient text – the Qur'an – whose presence is so immediate that it cannot simply be read or interpreted like other texts but must be recited or sung.

These concerns and ideas 'from those at sea', can also be expressed in more explicitly philosophical terms, though only by fundamentally altering the philosophical lens and adopting Martin Heidegger's perspective. According to Heidegger, human beings (*Dasein*) achieve an authentic understanding of themselves through their orientation towards death (*Sein zum Tode*). The search for guidance in ancient, 'pre-philosophical' wisdom – whether in pre-Socratic fragments or poetic utterances – is also central to Heidegger's philosophy. Finally, Heidegger expresses a deep unease with modernity, despite its technical and cultural advances. This is not to suggest that Heidegger was the only critic of modernity, the only existentialist writer or that all migrants are 'natural-born Heideggerians' but rather that his thought offers dormant intellectual resources that remain largely unexplored in the Anglo-American tradition of Western political thought.

Since Heidegger's proximity to National Socialist ideology is well known and extensively documented, any reconsideration of his philosophy requires a critical historical approach.[19] Before examining the relationship between the Cambridge School method and Heidegger's deconstruction of the history of philosophy, it is necessary to further justify why Heidegger might play a role in a genealogy of cosmopolitan thought.

At the outset, I suggested that cosmopolitanism might seem naïve or outdated, given that Western dominance has given way to a polycentric world order and that its claims to universality are increasingly challenged – particularly from poststructuralist and postcolonial perspectives, which denounce such claims as false consciousness. Cosmopolitan theorists themselves acknowledge the need to integrate

[19] The literature on this issue is vast. The latest round concerns the so-called 'Black Notebooks', though they have hardly revealed any new facts. For a useful overview, see Richard Wolin, *Heidegger in Ruins: Between Philosophy and Ideology* (New Haven, CT: Yale University Press, 2022).

non-Western and alternative cultural perspectives.[20] Thus, it is crucial to avoid constructing the Western tradition as a mere straw man.

However, Heidegger is not just any existentialist, culture-weary or anti-Enlightenment thinker but looms as a fundamental challenge and promise in the background of critical discussions at three key junctures. Recognising this subterranean presence is another reason to consider Heidegger's implicit presence in a genealogical reflection. Many critical and postcolonial theories that reject Western universalism ultimately draw on poststructuralist thought, which, in turn, is deeply influenced by Heidegger's critique of 'Western metaphysics'[21] starting with Plato and culminating in Nietzsche.[22] This is not to assign blame to Heidegger for every flaw in poststructuralist thought or its reception, but rather to acknowledge that his ideas already shape contemporary political theory, whether explicitly recognised or not.

When turning to the geopolitical challenges facing the West, particularly in relation to Russia and China, Heidegger may initially seem irrelevant, given his lack of contributions to constitutional theory or international relations. However, his influence resurfaces through Carl Schmitt, a theorist frequently referenced in debates on multipolar world orders[23] or Tianxia orders and alternative forms of cosmopolitanism, such as Tianxia theory.[24] While Schmitt was a thinker in his own right, Heidegger provided his philosophy with a deeper

[20] For a defence of Nussbaum's approach vis-à-vis counter-cosmopolitan positions (particularly Christian and Muslim fundamentalist positions), see Kwame Anthony Appiah, *Cosmopolitanism: Ethics in a World of Strangers* (London: Allen Lane, 2006), 265–94, Kindle.

[21] Heidegger does not use the term 'Western metaphysics' but instead refers to the 'occidental philosophical tradition' to emphasise its origins in ancient Greece while downplaying (among other aspects) the empiricist and liberal traditions. In contrast, both critics and proponents often use the term 'Western philosophy' to underscore its universal or liberal core.

[22] For this diagnosis, see Jürgen Habermas, *The Philosophical Discourse of Modernity: Twelve Lectures*, trans. Frederick G. Lawrence (Cambridge, MA: MIT Press, 1987), 131–293.

[23] Alexander Dugin, *The Theory of a Multipolar World Order* (London: Arktos, 2021).

[24] Tingyang Zhao, *Redefining a Philosophy for World Governance*, trans. Liqing Tao (Basingstoke: Palgrave Macmillan, 2019).

existential foundation. This connection is most evident in Alexander Dugin, who began as a Heidegger scholar but ultimately embraced Schmitt's *Großraum* theory, becoming an ideological supporter of Putin's expansionist policies.[25]

Whether the second Trump presidency follows any coherent script is, as with all moments shaped by disruptive political figures, very much up for debate. Unlike in the case of Alexander Dugin, there is no single intellectual mastermind in the background who defines the ideological trajectory. There are, however, timely men, as Nietzsche would say, and influential individuals who dress up as deep-thinking intellectuals.[26] The relevance of Heidegger (and, to some extent, Carl Schmitt) is therefore of an indirect nature. What we find in Heidegger is, first, an open contempt for liberalism in all its institutional forms; second, an effort to give his political reflections a deeper philosophical gravitas (though in the *Black Notebooks*, this deeper sense often borders on petty nonsense) and third, an uncanny preoccupation with modern technology as the force that determines humanity's destiny. These motifs can also be detected, in scattered and distorted forms, within the ideological rationalisations surrounding Trump's policies. Heidegger thus serves less as a source of direct influence than as a switchboard that connects contemporary political attitudes with metaphysical traditions typically excluded from the liberal narrative. This brief sketch of contemporary debates might suggest a clear divide between enlightened, liberal traditions and antiliberal, anti-Enlightenment currents in Western thought.[27]

[25] On Dugin's political appropriation of Heidegger's quest after another beginning of philosophy through inceptual thinking, see Michael Millerman, *Beginning with Heidegger: Strauss, Rorty, Derrida, Dugin, and the Philosophical Constitution of the Political* (London: Arktos, 2020), 167–212.

[26] For a serious attempt to rethink the prevalent liberal tradition in the United States, see Adrian Vermeule, *Common Good Constitutionalism* (Cambridge: Polity Press, 2022).

[27] See, for a simplistic defence of reason and Enlightenment against counter-Enlightenment tendencies, which originated with Rousseau and were later developed by theologians, poets and essayists such as Johann Hamann, Friedrich Jacobi, Johann Herder, and Friedrich Schelling, see Steven Pinker, *The Better Angels of Our Nature: Why Violence Has Declined* (New York: Viking, 2011), 186–88.

However, such a Manichean framework is misleading and does little to advance understanding. When Heidegger's reception in poststructuralist, postcolonial and critical theory is taken into account, lumping all critiques together under anti-liberal or anti-Enlightenment labels oversimplifies the complexity and interconnections of intellectual traditions. Moreover, Heidegger's philosophy also carries a paradoxical promise: his attempt to conceive of a new beginning for occidental philosophy, unburdened by categorical thinking, and his emphasis on poetry as a medium for insight beyond formal philosophical argumentation, have made his work attractive to non-Western thinkers seeking to establish a genuine intellectual dialogue on equal terms. Ironically, the philosophy most entangled in the peculiarities of the German language and historically linked to one of the most pernicious ideologies of the twentieth century has also become a potential seed for a 'world philosophy',[28] with mutual engagement in reading and criticising across philosophical traditions and academic boundaries.

Thus, Heidegger's implicit presence in Western philosophical discourse represents both a challenge and a promise: a challenge, because his thought underpins both anti-liberal or multipolar visions and poststructuralist critiques of Western universalism; a promise, because liberal traditions remain open to critique and may benefit from a more fundamental comparative reflection. If Heidegger's influence is hidden but significant, and if his method is largely based on a creative reinterpretation of tradition, then the Cambridge School method, initially deemed ill-suited for a genealogy of cosmopolitan thought, gains a new purpose: to provide a specific, contextual historical perspective that can critically engage with Heidegger's peculiar reading of the philosophical tradition.

3. After explaining the method and the need to reorient philosophy, one might ask how these tasks relate to the

[28] The term 'world philosophy' is constructed analogously to Goethe's notion 'world literature', referring to literary works that transcend their country of origin and foster mutual understanding across cultures. Goethe's *West-East Divan* and his openness towards indigenous poetry serve as a model for such encounters.

contemporary philosophical discussion on cosmopolitanism, which has flourished since the end of the Cold War – but which, as a broader political force, seems to have lost its momentum quite abruptly. A fundamental conviction found often in the literature, up to the late 2010s, is that contemporary discussion has reached a 'cosmopolitan plateau',[29] meaning that all the influential approaches to moral and political philosophy provide different interpretations of what it means to treat people with equal respect and concern.[30] Thomas Pogge defines the core conviction of cosmopolitanism in the following way:[31]

> Three elements are shared by all cosmopolitan positions: First, individualism: the ultimate units of concern are human beings, or persons – rather than, say, family lines, tribes, ethnic, cultural, or religious communities, nations, or states. The latter may be units of concern only indirectly, in virtue of their individual members or citizens. Second, universality: the status of ultimate unit of concern attaches to every living human being equally – not merely to some subset, such as men, aristocrats, Aryans, whites, or Muslims. Third, generality: this special status has global force. Persons are ultimate units of concern for everyone – not only for their compatriots, fellow religionists, or such like.

Pogge's definition is said not just to denote a certain position among many, but to provide a framework of the discussion in political philosophy. Held/Maffettone explain that it 'helps us delineate the boundaries of reasonable disagreement within our moral debates in a way that is philosophically consistent'.[32] Those denying, for example, the equal moral status of all human beings are 'beyond the boundaries

[29] David Held and Pietro Maffettone, eds., *Global Political Theory* (Cambridge: Polity Press, 2016), 7–10.

[30] This notion was first introduced by Ronald Dworkin, 'Comment on Narveson: In Defense of Equality,' *Social Philosophy and Policy* 1, no. 1 (Autumn 1983): 25.

[31] Thomas Pogge, 'Cosmopolitanism and Sovereignty', *Ethics* 103, no. 1 (1992): 48–9.

[32] Ibid., 43.

of reasonable disagreement and thus have no standing in the debate about the moral bases of global politics'.[33] In this sense, cosmopolitanism appeared as the core of contemporary political philosophy, and all debates seemed to be internal debates about the proper understanding of its elements.

In this vein, some authors distinguish between weak and strong cosmopolitan positions, depending on whether cosmopolitan principles are a 'source of reasons and responsibilities among others'[34] or an overriding framework of reference that trumps all other moral positions. However, as even strong cosmopolitans have developed ways of dealing with cultural differences, the distinction is not particularly helpful for classifying the various positions. Instead, the distinction between moral, political, legal, intercultural and civic cosmopolitanism is more useful for this purpose and has become standard in the literature on cosmopolitanism. Additionally, this distinction roughly mirrors the historical development of cosmopolitanism.

Accordingly, moral cosmopolitanism is the view that the ultimate units of moral concerns are human beings or people. It is a position that subscribes to universality and generality but does not imply the demand for the global institutions required to achieve these aims. Cynic and Stoic cosmopolitanism are examples of this position. Political or legal cosmopolitanism, on the other hand, builds upon moral cosmopolitanism but envisions the need for some kind of institution on a global level. Kant's cosmopolitanism would be the central case for this view. Finally, cosmopolitanism can also be seen as the maxim of reflecting the repercussions of one's lifestyle from a global, non-Western perspective, along with including such perspectives in one's reasoning. In contemporary debate, Kwame Anthony Appiah stands for this strand of cosmopolitan thought.[35] As the distinction has here only been introduced for classificatory reasons, the terminology need not be explicitly taken up in each position.

33 Ibid.

34 Samuel Scheffler, 'Conceptions of Cosmopolitanism', *Utilitas* 11, no. 3 (1999): 260.

35 Appiah, *Cosmopolitanism*.

Much contemporary discussion focuses on the question of whether and to what extent a Rawlsian conception of distributive justice can be applied on a global level. This would be a case of political or legal cosmopolitanism under the scheme proposed here, as the moral premises are usually taken for granted. Insofar as the position includes the claim that global distributive justice can be justified from a variety of comprehensive doctrines in the form of a global overriding consensus, it would additionally be a case of cultural cosmopolitanism. As the distinction serves to classify approaches, it does not carry in itself much argumentative weight. The crucial question concerns how the specific account is justified – be that in terms of moral principles, human rights, global justice, human capabilities or interests. As the debate on the philosophical foundations of cosmopolitanism is already multiform, more recent contributions have focused on specific applied topics, such as the rationale for a just climate regime, immigration or a tax policy from a cosmopolitan perspective.

4. Given this variety and specialisation, one might fairly ask how a contextual, genealogical perspective can contribute anything valuable to this debate. The poetic framing in the Prelude and Coda is the first response to this question, the more detailed argument in the three chapters is the elaboration. The Prelude starts with a reading of a poem by Sappho, a text that was written before the advent of occidental philosophy. It shows that a kind of 'civic cosmopolitanism' from a female 'queer' (non-heterosexual, non-Athenian and non-male) perspective might have been at the beginning of the tradition. In this way, it derails the common narrative that civic cosmopolitanism or intercultural, feminist, postcolonial and other perspectives on cosmopolitanism have only been conceived recently. Perhaps the story needs to be told in reverse order. Additionally, the more we open ourselves up to an ancient perspective, the more the common taxonomy of cosmopolitanism (a certain cosmopolitan way of seeing and reading the world) becomes questionable, as it prefigures the way of looking at unfamiliar writings and inhibits understanding. However, the Prelude is not an appeal to give up on philosophical distinctions, conceptual analysis or to flee from the harsh realities of politics into 'vague' poetry.

Instead, it reminds us of the full potential and ultimate aims of human existence through a mode of deeply reflective communication that transcends borders and cultures. Sappho's poetic voice echoes through the centuries and will find a response in the Coda with Hölderlin's rendering of some Pindar fragments.

Hölderlin, though also a poet, occupies a very different intellectual position when compared to Sappho. He writes after the unfolding of the occidental tradition with its dialectical synthesis of history and reason in Hegel. And yet, Hölderlin keeps a keen awareness that a higher unity of 'judgement' (in brief: Hegel's entire philosophy) and being is still missing. His interpretation of Pindar's fragment on the law (*nomos*) as 'king of all, mortal and immortal' has been taken up by Carl Schmitt to justify racialised legal orders. I argue, however, that a very different encounter with the Other is more in line with the whole context of Hölderlin's thought that emphasises juxtaposition, recognition and historical openness. Hölderlin's poetic thinking offers a way to engage with history without deconstructing it, preserving historical consciousness and philosophical reflection while allowing ideas to evolve. His cosmopolitan vision sees the Orient, antiquity and modernity in dialogue, while rejecting ossified categories.

The two poetic readings contain the entire genealogy in a nutshell: start before philosophy, engage with tradition and, if necessary, move beyond it. Only through this process can the promises, pitfalls and alternatives of cosmopolitan thought be examined. The immediate presence of pre-Socratic sayings, poetry and, in particular, Hölderlin is more than just a cultural embellishment; it recalls Heidegger's influence and the potential degeneration of the philosophical tradition. The argument advanced here is that the most effective way to engage with sweeping philosophical narratives is to reveal alternatives through detailed, historically situated analyses. Accordingly, in the subsequent in-depth readings of Plato, Kant and Kelsen, Heidegger remains the implicit target. Hopefully, the preceding reflections have clarified why a contextual, genealogical approach nonetheless carries political significance.

The first chapter starts like the beginning of a conventional entry on cosmopolitan thought. After a brief outline of current discussions on cosmopolitan thought, the chapter traces the basic ideas of the discussion back to the pre-Socratic Sophists. This might sound like a daring stretch of an established, if not outworn, discourse. However, it turns out to be its nemesis: Plato, with Socrates as his spokesman, is not the founding father of contemporary philosophy but the first anti- or, to be precise, uber-cosmopolitan philosopher. He conceived metaphysics to silence the philosophers who thought they could give laws to 'Greeks and barbarians alike', as cosmopolitan theorists *avant la lettre*, who, however, according to Plato, lacked true insight into the nature of the good. This is reached by applying the methods of the Cambridge School to the *Politeia*, interpreting it as a text aimed at the political situation in the fourth century BCE, where different historical possibilities, including that of a Greek federal system, were still open. Therefore, I present Plato's philosophy as a challenge then and a challenge now: both to post-Rawlsian cosmopolitanism's specific philosophical narratives and to the Western tradition's self-understanding of its cosmopolitan 'destiny'.

The second chapter on Kant is the implicit heart of the genealogy studied in this work, not only because Kant is often invoked as a key reference for contemporary theories of cosmopolitan thought but also because the philosophy he initiated, from Hegel and Marx up to Nietzsche and Heidegger, shapes our understanding of the modern world in a way that continues to question our philosophical common-sense certainties. Yet the task of such a rereading is not straightforward. In Kant's case, the contextual reading of the Cambridge School pursued here takes time to bring us to the right track. When looking more closely at the political structure of the city of Königsberg and the political discourse of Kant's time, we find ways of coming up with Cambridge-style stories about texts aiming to change the politics of the time, and thinkers actively engaged in typically enlightened concerns, such as denouncing the oppression of free city governments, arguing against the death penalty or favouring women's rights. However, it is not Kant who takes these positions, but other intellectuals from Königsberg.

Kant held conservative views on nearly all matters. So did Kant, as later German idealists would say, only initiate a revolution in thinking? Only after working through Kant's entire thinking, his critical philosophy and his anthropological description of humans as expounded in his popular lectures, will we see that, at a well-chosen moment, Kant practised biopolitics by setting his old but dietary-restricted body against the young but obese body of the king. The political dimension of Kant's writings on religion is often missed, just as the specific crypto-religious tradition it triggered remains outside the canon of liberal thought.

The contextual reading pursued here thus has two upshots. Kant's legal philosophy is shown to be deeply entangled in the inner systematic problems of his thinking and less attuned to contemporary liberal convictions. At the same time, his ultimate practical idea, freedom as autonomy realised through an ethical community, is so radical that every commitment or institution falls prey to an ideology of critical disenchantment.

Most accounts of Kant's political philosophy, and those that concentrate on his cosmopolitan thought in particular, somehow take a courageous 200-year leap to introduce Kant directly into contemporary discussions while studiously ignoring the philosophical discourse in between. As I revisit Kant's thinking contextually, including in regard to his empirical writings and the tensions in his critical programme, a different trajectory into the twentieth century emerges.

The third chapter will reflect upon the twilight of the twentieth century through the lens of Hans Kelsen's thinking. After explaining that Kelsen's thought is shaped by reacting to the 'circumstances of modernity', as encapsulated in the conflicts and ideas virulent in fin-de-siècle Vienna, we will see that he experienced and reflected upon two further fundamental revolutions in the twentieth century, symbolised by the dates 1932 and 1948. By following his contestations with Carl Schmitt and Eugen Ehrlich, we will also encounter a specific anti-cosmopolitan stance and mark the existential limits of Kelsen's approach. A story from Jonathan Littell's novel *The Kindly Ones* serves to support a meditation on the relation of all theorising to (illegitimate) power. This does not mean that after the demise of theory, only existential decisions (like Jägerstätter's, a conscientious objector from WWII, decision to resist, depicted in Terrence Malick's film *A Hidden Life*) are left. Through Kelsen's contestation with Eric Voegelin, two models of post-foundational thought can be gleaned, which might provide an orientation for the future: engaging in critical legal studies and debunking foundationalism.

The Prelude and Coda frame the more technical philosophical arguments in the chapters. The Postscript will relate the genealogy to everyday politics mentioned in the Preface, yet bringing the fruits of the genealogical method to bear upon them, while refraining from any direct normative recommendations.

Abbreviations of Works by Kant

Citations from Kant's works refer to the volume and page numbers of the *Akademie-Ausgabe: Königlich Preußische (later Deutsche) Akademie der Wissenschaften* (ed.), *Kants gesammelte Schriften*, 1900–, Berlin: Georg Reimer (later Walter de Gruyter). References to the *Critique of Pure Reason* are cited by page numbers of the original first (A) and second (B) editions.

List of abbreviations (English titles)

Anth	Anthropology from a Pragmatic Point of View
Br	Correspondence
GMS	Groundwork of the Metaphysics of Morals
IaG	Idea for a Universal History with a Cosmopolitan Aim
KpV	Critique of Practical Reason
KrV	Critique of Pure Reason
KU	Critique of the Power of Judgment
MAM	Conjectural Beginnings of Human History
MS	The Metaphysics of Morals
RL	Metaphysical First Principles of the Doctrine of Right
PG	Physical Geography
RGV	Religion within the Boundaries of Mere Reason
SF	The Conflict of the Faculties
TP	On the Common Saying: 'This May Be True in Theory, but it Does Not Apply in Practice'
Vigil.	Metaphysik der Sitten (Vigilantius lecture notes)
VT	On a Recently Voiced Noble-Minded Tone in Philosophy

VNAEF	Announcement of the Near Conclusion of a Treaty of Perpetual Peace in Philosophy
WA	An Answer to the Question: What is Enlightenment?
ZeF	Towards Perpetual Peace

Prelude
Sappho's Calling

Every genealogy has to start somewhere, and thus disregard unmentioned ancestors. Here is one way to commence: if writing brings logocentrism and its illegitimate offspring into the world, every beginning is already tainted. For those uninitiated in Derridean deconstruction, the following pragmatic resolution would be more familiar: Let's start with Hobbes, as his *Leviathan* is the greatest single work of political thought in the English language.[1] Both lines of thought rely on the presence of established traditions and academic conventions and thrive by being, like a summer hit, catchy though not too original so as to play with audience expectations. Regardless of where we came from, we seem to know where we stand and what to expect, as political philosophy cannot be defined arbitrarily. The aim here is to enliven the conventional approach. As the beginning sets the tone for the end, let us unclench our senses.

When dance has sunk into oblivion; don't say, sing! So sings Sappho:[2]

> ἔστι φύσις θήλεια βρέφη σῴζουσ᾽ ὑπὸ κόλποις
> αὑτῆς, ὄντα δ᾽ ἄφωνα βοὴν ἵστησι γεγωνὸν
> καὶ διὰ πόντιον οἶδμα καὶ ἠπείρου διὰ πάσης
> οἷς ἐθέλει θνητῶν, τοῖς δ᾽ οὐδὲ παροῦσιν ἀκούειν
> ἔξεστιν· κωφὴν δ᾽ ἀκοῆς αἴσθησιν ἔχουσιν.

[1] John Rawls, *Lectures on the History of Political Philosophy*, ed. Samuel Freeman (Cambridge, MA: Harvard University Press, 2007), 23.

[2] Athenaeus, *Dipnosophistarum (The Learned Banqueters)*, ed. and trans. S. Douglas Olson (Cambridge, MA: Harvard University Press, 2006), 10.450e–f, adapted from the translation.

It is a female creature that keeps its
children safe beneath the folds
of its garment. And though they are mute, they raise
a resounding cry
through the sea-surge and the whole mainland
to whichever mortals they wish, and even those who
are not there
can hear them, deaf though their perception is.

The poem is a riddle posed by Sappho in archaic times. On the surface, it resonates with references to the *thiasos*, her educational circle of young women. It alludes to the mother figure who shelters and nourishes, to a poetic voice through which the initiated communicate across land and sea, to the dumbness of those around, and last but not least, Sappho's typical bittersweet tone rings out through the lines. Yet the surface structure doesn't make sense; it is puzzling. An Athenian solves the riddle the way all philosophers do when they are confronted with art: as the young at the bosom must be citizens, it is the state that must be meant! Justice, democracy, natural rights or whatever is fashionable among learned men (the voice is from Athens after all, not Lesbos) can subsequently be forced upon the text. So, our philosopher says:

Yes – because the object you're describing is a
city,
and the children she nourishes inside herself are the
politicians.
They shout and bring the overseas
revenues from Asia and Thrace
to us here. An while they're splitting the money up
among themselves and constantly calling each other
names
the people sit nearby, and don't hear or see anything.

And Sappho laughs: You are but a man, and a philosopher moreover. 'Have you ever heard of a politician who is mute? Unless, indeed, he's been three times convicted'.[3] She solves the riddle herself, as follows:

[3] The last sentence, uttered either by Sappho or the philosopher, refers to the *paranomon graphe*, an Athenian legal procedure that allowed for

The female creature is a writing tablet,
and the children she carries around inside herself are
the letters.
Even though they're mute, they speak to anyone they
want
who's far away. And if someone else happens to be
standing
nearby, he won't hear the man who's reading.

The riddle was incorporated by the late Roman author Athenaeus (second century CE) into his burlesque version of a symposium. He took the lines from a comedy by Antiphanes (fourth century BCE), who bequeathed us Sappho's poem. I assume that the riddle is a genuine poem by Sappho,[4] thus dating back to the seventh century BCE, and that Antiphanes only played on it by adding a comic answer.[5] I have taken the freedom to adapt it for our time. There was, of course, nobody called a philosopher in Sappho's time, let alone a political philosopher.[6] However, the political institutions and concepts that shape our world today were developed at this time (Solon, the legendary 'father of Athenian democracy' was a contemporary of Sappho, a poet himself and admired her songs). Hence the answer the philosopher gives is not bad at all but shows a high degree of political and social awareness. He[7] knows that the relevant political entity is the city, thus not simply one class

the exclusion of people from deliberations if they had been convicted three times for proposing a law contrary to an existing one (so to speak, contrary to the constitution).

4 On the authenticity, see Jesper Svenbro, *Phrasikleia. An Anthropology of Reading in Ancient Greece*, trans. Janet Lloyd (Ithaca, NY: Cornell University Press, 1993), 159.

5 The *paranomon graphe* has only been documented since the fourth century, so at least the interjection must be a later addition.

6 On proto-philosophical aspects of Sappho's lyric and teaching as an alternative to the male-oriented Homeric worldview, see Page DuBois, *Sappho Is Burning* (Chicago: University of Chicago Press, 1995), 77–97, 98–126.

7 For dramaturgical reasons, I contrast Sappho at this point with a male philosopher. Throughout the text I will usually use the singular 'they' when referring to philosophers of human beings in general. The example of Sappho and her circle shows that using gender neutral language is

(aristocrats) or oddly assorted people living under some ruler in a demarcated territory, but a volitional community. The city is moreover based on some form of popular rule, as politicians publicly argue, and people can be exiled. The philosopher is even, unlike many contemporary political theorists, critical of the official ideology and reflects instead the material basis of the political system: the real business of politics is merely idle talk, the citizen-masses are imperceptive and everyone ignores the real economic underpinnings. The city describing itself as a self-sufficient community is in fact an empire dependent on imports of grain and duties from subjugated areas (not to mention enslaved labourers).

Surprisingly, this far-sighted analysis even plays on the analogy of city and soul by presenting a similar one, namely between city and mother. Even more surprisingly, Sappho just laughs at all this. (In Greek literary texts, dumb people are never pitied or educated but always laughed at.) To modern ears, Sappho's solution sounds as if she has read a bit too much of Derrida, reducing all serious philosophy to the dominance of speech over writing. The truth is certainly the other way round: readers of Derrida do not read enough of the ancients and miss what they have to say about us.[8]

I propose that Sappho's poem and its later rewriting can serve as a thread that leads us into our question about a genealogy of cosmopolitan thought. In this short anecdote, we have already encountered several topics that will occupy us throughout the book: questioning the foundations and limits of political and epistemic communities, their socioeconomic underpinnings and their ideologies. At the same time,

not just a contemporary convention but reflects an existing though often repressed or undocumented reality. Even from Sappho, one of the most celebrated poets of antiquity, only a few lines have survived. We know nothing about the teaching or discussions in her circle. It is, however, highly unlikely or would need a special explanation if, at a 'multicultural' gathering in Lesbos, politics were never discussed.

[8] For a creative adoption of a poststructuralist and media-theoretic point of view that is especially attentive to the Greek thinking and Sappho's lyric, see Friedrich Kittler, *Musik und Mathematik*, vol. 1, *Hellas* (München: Wilhelm Fink, 2006), 158–65.

the dialogue appears to suggest that 'political philosophy' is not a special 'philosophical perspective' on a given 'subject matter'; in the end, Sappho laughs at all this. But how can she do this? What does this mean for our understanding, and why should we care? To answer these questions, we have to reflect further on Sappho's answer.

Her solution is that the riddle talks not about the city but about writing, particularly about the bittersweet allure of it. To understand Sappho's fascination with writing expressed in the poem, we have to recall how writing has shaped and permeated Greek culture and civilisation. The innovation of the Greek alphabet, the addition of the vowels to the alphabet, enabled every sound to be reproduced in writing and understood by anyone.[9] Unlike the prior alphabetic systems of writing used in the Mediterranean region – for example, the Phoenician and Aramaic alphabet – texts could be understood without knowing their tradition or context. Moreover, reading and writing was not restricted to a class of official scribes (bureaucrats or priests), but practiced widely among the citizens. Most importantly, Greek writing was a poetic and philosophical practice from the very beginning, not invented for the needs of trade, bureaucracy or religious bookkeeping but – to put it bluntly – for preserving Homer. In any case, the Homeric epics remained the paradigm through which the language and culture flourished.[10]

Given this background, it might appear strange that Sappho describes the characters (the young or unborn) as

[9] On the consequences of literacy in Greece, see Erich A. Havelock, *The Literate Revolution in Greece and its Cultural Consequences* (Princeton, NJ: Princeton University Press, 1982); for a more nuanced assessment of the strengths of other systems of writings in the Middle East, see Jan Assmann, *Cultural Memory and Early Civilization. Writing, Remembrance, and Political Imagination* (Cambridge: Cambridge University Press, 2011), 234–75.

[10] On the specific role of the Greek alphabet, see Jack Goody and Ian Watt, 'The Consequences of Literacy', *Comparative Studies in Society and History* 5, no. 3 (1963): 304–45; for a recent assessment of the ensuing discussion, see Khosrow Jahandarie, *Spoken and Written Discourse: A Multidisciplinary Perspective* (Stamford, CT: Ablex Publishing Company, 1999), 22–30.

mute, since at least the vowels can be sung (most noticeably in Homer's rendering of the seductive songs of the sirens, which sound like a variation on the vowels of the Greek alphabet). However, Sappho has a unique way of writing, reading and understanding minds. True, if someone reads a letter silently, a bystander cannot understand it. If the poem just wanted to refer to the cultural innovation of silent reading, it would have a cheap punch line when compared to the more elaborate interpretation of the philosopher. However, Sappho uses writing to communicate with her followers self-consciously in a way that is nearly ceremonial. This is best expressed in another fragment.[11]

> He seems to me equal to gods that man
> whoever he is who opposite you
> sits and listens close
>   to your sweet speaking
>
> and lovely laughing – oh it
> puts the heart in my chest on wings
> for when I look at you, even a moment, no speaking
>   is left in me
>
> no: tongue breaks and thin
> fire is racing under skin
> and in eyes no sight and drumming
>   fills ears
>
> and cold sweat holds me and shaking
> grips me all, greener than grass
> I am and dead – or almost
>   I seem to me.

This well-known poem is genuine beyond dispute and can be used to further analyse Sappho's understanding of writing. In the first line, she alludes to writing.[12] The man is godlike not because he is beautiful, which Sappho cannot know, or because he is in love, but he is godlike

[11] Sappho, frag. 31, trans. Anne Carson (New York: Vintage Books, 2009), 63.
[12] Svenbro, *Phrasikleia*, 151–6.

in comparison to Sappho. Gods do not write, as for them no time or space exists which they could not overcome. Therefore, they always experience the presence of whoever they like. In the presence of the maid, the young man is godlike. Sappho, on the other hand, has to write and thus admit her mortality. Moreover, writing even dissociates her from her beloved; it is only necessary to write if the beloved is no longer in Sappho's community. For this reason, Sappho envies the man in her company and calls to mind the joys they once shared. This painful jealousy nearly kills Sappho. Like a Homeric hero she chokes on her last breath – or almost.[13] For the poem is not a farewell or expression of desperation, but a declaration of enduring love directed at the reader. She hopes that, while reading the poem, her beloved lends her voice to the lines and thus resuscitates the life and ideas of the *thiasos*, the communal life of Sappho's circle. In this way Sappho can challenge the godlike presence of the man and become, through the memory herself, an immortal voice (the only kind of immortality the Greeks cared for).[14]

This last thought is most clearly expressed in the riddle our reflection started with. The phonetic characters are not dead but only unborn, and the letters even resonate loudly across land and sea – if read by someone who knows how to read. The bystander referred to in Sappho's explanation cannot simply be someone who is literally standing beside the one reading the letter and unable to peek across her shoulder, let alone an illiterate. The hope expressed in the poem is that the reader lends her voice, her soul to the poem and thus brings back to life all this that cannot be transmitted in writing: the music in which the poems were sung, the dance and the presence of the community. For this reason, the female being can speak 'to whichever mortal of their choosing', not because letters have an address field or are sealed, but some letters,

[13] On the theme of the female death through love and the male death as depicted in Homer, see Leah Rissmann, *Love as War: Homeric Allusion in the Poetry of Sappho*, Beiträge zur klassischen Philologie 157 (Königstein: Hain, 1983), 66–118.

[14] See frag. 58a, and on being forgotten as a curse, frag. 55.

Sappho's poems, are more than means of communication for practical purposes: they bring back a life form.[15]

The poem is thus not a simple riddle but contains a theory of writing and a way to overcome its limits. A poem can sound worldwide across land and sea and be read by anyone in principle, though it can only truly be understood by those willing to share a life form which is not exhausted by writing.

Even given this interpretation, it is not clear why Sappho can laugh at the philosopher. Sappho's solution may fit better, but both interpretations appear to be on an equal footing. One might even say they show two different aspects of life: the philosopher is more concerned with public, political life whereas Sappho confines herself to cultivating her private feelings in poems that even philosophers can enjoy as entertainment after work.[16] So how is Sappho's account more fundamental or comprehensive? This question can be answered by reflecting further on the art of writing.

The implicit question that is disputed between the philosopher and Sappho is the *nomos basileus* – which kind of 'law' is 'king' of everything.[17] Solving riddles is the classical way of answering this question. The example was, of course, set by Oedipus. As long as no one solves the Sphinx's riddle, the mythical nomos reigns. Only after Oedipus solved the historical riddle did nomos begin. In this sense, Sappho and the philosopher give an answer to the same question. But how

[15] It is unnecessary to speculate about the exact nature of Sappho's community of girls. On its ritual character with Sappho as leader see Claude Calame, 'Sappho's Group: An Initiation into Womanhood', in Ellen Greene, ed., *Reading Sappho: Contemporary Approaches*, (Berkeley, CA: University of California Press, 1996), 113–24.

[16] This distinction is usually presupposed by liberal political philosophers as the subversive power of the arts, and poetry in particular, is mostly perceivable under oppressive circumstances.

[17] The most famous reference to *nomos basileus* goes back to Pindar's fragment ('The law is the king of all, mortal and immortal'). I use it not as an implicit reference but as a hermeneutic tool. On the manifold usage and transformations of the topos of *nomos basileus* in Greek thought, see Marcello Gigante, *Nomos basileus* (New York: Arno Press, 1979) and Thanos Zartaloudis, *The Birth of Nomos* (Edinburgh: Edinburgh University Press, 2019). The topos of the *nomos basileus* will be taken up again in the Coda via an interpretation of Hölderlin's take on Pindar's saying.

are the answers related, aren't they completely different? The philosopher's answer is straightforward and assumes that nomos is in any case some kind of law, very much in the sense we use it today: we just have to figure out what kind of law we need to observe (city laws, inter-city laws or cosmopolitan law) and then build an appropriate theory on this subject. Depending on our tastes, it can be either a social theory, a realist theory of international relations or a theory of (global) justice.

Sappho also speaks about the nomos but as a writer and lover in a different, more fundamental way. To understand Sappho's answer, we have to consider another aspect of her cultural background: the changes writing brought about once it became a widely shared cultural technique. Social life in such a culture is distinctively different from civilisations with specialised scribes. They were usually occupied either with economic, administrative or religious affairs. The task of the scribe would be to write down orders or record certain units (e.g., taxes).[18] They would also read incoming letters aloud as this was the only way the addressee could understand them. The scribes themselves and the technique of writing were thus mere tools in the hands of others. When reading they would become the author's voice, when writing their master's hand. In any case, the master-voice was outside the text. All this changes fundamentally once the characteristic activity of Greek culture became reading and performing Homer; literacy then became a cultural norm. The effects of these changes can hardly be overestimated.

The intriguing point about Sappho's lyric is that she is very much aware that she takes part in and transcends a practice of poetic communication over her lyrical 'I'. The lyrical 'I' cannot be conceived as an external master voice; it lives through the text. Yet the text on its own is – even if it can be read and perhaps even performed by every literate person – not the whole, as it invokes the transformative experience of Sappho's circle. The poems include therefore not just a

[18] See Jack Goody, *The Logic of Writing and the Organization of Society* (Cambridge: Cambridge University Press, 1986) and Jack Goody and Ian P. Watt, 'The consequences of literacy', *Comparative Studies in Society and History* 5 (1963): 304–45.

theory of writing (the point Derrida would focus on), but also of the art of reading and its transformative power through *eros*-inspired teaching and communal singing (a perspective completely missing in Derrida).[19]

Turning back to the dispute about the *nomos basileus*, we realise now why Sappho's answer is more fundamental and comprehensive. The theories the philosopher alludes to are not simply mistaken – he fails to reflect on his own position. In his speech, he assumes the traditional master voice which treats all topics as external objects that can be manipulated according to one's own tastes. Sappho's mockery is that the philosopher assumes the stimulus–response model of a simple (male) machine. Reflecting on the position of the writer is not only the more fundamental thought because it includes a reflection on her lifeworld but also more comprehensive as the limits of writing become apparent.

The agonistic, intertextual writing culture that Sappho practices can be seen as the root of the unfolding occidental philosophical tradition.[20] Sappho's reflection of the pragmatic presuppositions of this very culture is, however, an insight that was explicitly formulated only 2,400 years later. In *The Oldest System Program of German Idealism*,[21] it is stated in the following way: 'mythology must become philosophical in order to make the people reasonable, and philosophy must turn mythological in order to make the philosophers sensuous.'[22] The first part of the sentence takes up the usual

19 On the role of choral singing for Sappho's circle, see Anton Bierl, 'Ich aber (sage), das Schönste ist, was einer liebt!' Eine Pragmatische Deutung von Sappho Fr. 16 LP/V', *Quaderni Urbinati di Cultura Classica* 74, no. 2 (2003): 91–124; on the central role of the chorus in Plato's *Nomoi*, see Julia Pfefferkorn, *Platons tanzende Stadt* (Leiden: Brill, 2023).

20 See Assmann, *Cultural Memory*, 274.

21 This is a sketch written in the handwriting of the young Georg Wilhelm Friedrich Hegel, presumably with the participation of his Tübingen friends Friedrich Hölderlin and Friedrich Wilhelm Joseph Schelling. The bibliotheca augustana provides access to the digitalised manuscript: http://www.hs-augsburg.de/~harsch/germanica/Chronologie/18Jh/Idealismus/ide_frag.html. For the translation, see 'The Oldest System-Program of German Idealism' in *Friedrich Hölderlin: Essays and Letters on Theory*, trans. Thomas Pfau (New York: State University of New York Press, 1988), 154–5.

22 Ibid., 155–6.

developmental history 'from mythos to logos'. (It can even be traced in critical or queer readings of Sappho that presuppose different sets of logos.) The second part of the sentence is more challenging as it contains the germ of the best and the worst of the modern philosophical tradition. The author explains:[23]

> We need a new mythology; however, this mythology must be at the service of the ideas, it must become a mythology of reason. Until we render the ideas aesthetic, that is, mythological, they will not be of any interest to the populace, and vice versa: until mythology has become reasonable, the philosopher has to be ashamed of it.

The development of the occidental tradition with its inherent dialectics of enlightenment has shown that the mythology of reason can evolve into attempts to popularise enlightenment ideas (Greek, Islamic, European, Jewish enlightenment, etc.); the new mythology can, however, also be a bricolage,[24] a deconstruction and rearrangement of old myths for ideological purposes, and give rise to spectres hovering over the killing fields of the twentieth century.

23 Ibid., 154.

24 In coining the term 'bricolage', Claude Lévi-Strauss refers to Richard Wagner as 'originator of structural analysis of mythology'; see Claude Lévi-Strauss, *The Raw and the Cooked: Introduction to a Science of Mythology: I*, trans. John and Doreen Weightman (London: Jonathan Cape, 1970), 15.

One

Plato and the Challenge to Cosmopolitanism

In the Preface, I argued that global geopolitical realities and ideological challenges to Western cultural and economic dominance require more than just a slight adjustment of moral or political theory, namely a genealogy of cosmopolitan thought. As with psychoanalysis, this means going back to the level of unconsciousness. A genealogy, therefore, is a combination of archaeological discoveries and reflection on the reception history. The prelude inspired by Sappho's songs was a first exploration of this thesis. What initially seemed to be a simple riddle about politics turned out to be a meditation on writing and its limitations in omitting communal practices like dance and performance – and the power of eros (overpowering love).

However, after the polyphonic opening, one might also wonder whether the implicit invocation of the grand metaphysical tradition with Heidegger as doyen and the transgression of boundaries with Sappho as muse will ever lead to an answer to what we ought to do in today's globalised world. Even worse, the grand metaphysical tradition might even lend support to immoralist stances, while poetry and murky historical evidence might lead to ad hoc judgements without normative scrutiny. Therefore, one might ask: why not leave all this metaphysical baggage behind and start out from 'post-metaphysical' grounds or political liberalism with a straightforward, normative question? Shouldn't we simply take equality, human dignity and moral rights as a given and treat the planet as a whole as the ultimate basis of assessment? Has the global justice debate since the late twentieth century not shown that, in spite of common assumptions, there are still a wide variety of reasonable positions one might take? Furthermore, do the pressing moral and political problems – global poverty, climate change, ongoing mass migration – not urge us to concentrate on practical issues and strive for feasible and timely practical results?

The thesis of this chapter is that the dinner party at Cephalus's house, which Plato recounts in his *Politeia*, is such a transformative experience for cosmopolitan theory. I thus propose that the very beginning of political philosophy[1] provides an answer to the kind of questions asked today in cosmopolitan theories. This bold assertion requires some explanation. The aim is not to present a 'reading' of two texts that are arbitrarily connected to deconstruct their respective logic. (Derrida's side-by-side interpretation of Hegel's philosophy and Jean Genet's autobiography in *Glas*, where the text is distributed into two columns on each page to allow for unforeseen interferences, is the most extreme form of this kind of reading). Instead the chapter shows that the historical and philosophical situation Plato reacted to in the fourth century BCE resembles, in some respects, the current situation. In any case, the similarities should suffice to invite the contemporary global ethicist to Cephalus's party. I propose that ordinary political discourse was marked by cosmopolitan sentiments similar to those encountered nowadays, and that Plato, while establishing philosophy as a specific kind of inquiry, became, in effect, the first anti-cosmopolitan philosopher. However, I will argue that Plato does not just present an 'anti-cosmopolitan argument' to weigh the pros and cons of cosmopolitanism but instead, through the form of his dialogues, demonstrates that this kind of debate – though a necessary beginning – is insufficient ('sophistic') and must be overcome.

In this way, I hope to revive the philosophical tradition as a legitimate participant in contemporary discourse. There is, however, one caveat that makes the visit to Cephalus's house a lopsided affair. The contemporary cosmopolitan ethicist might be inclined to bring along a copy of their most beloved modern ethical treatise, let's say the *Groundwork of Morals*, and describe our world, with its existing international

[1] Thinking about the various ways to organise a polis or a new colony, however, started much earlier in Greece; the *Politeia* is the first major philosophical treatise.

institutions. However, since the party lasts only one night it is not permitted to read all three Kantian critiques aloud,[2] nor to take the contemporary world as a given. To assure the contemporary cosmopolitan ethicist: the fundamental change modern philosophy and contemporary institutions have brought about will be discussed in the two subsequent chapters.

1. Contemporary cosmopolitanism

1.1 The transformation of political philosophy into cosmopolitanism

As a first step, it is necessary to obtain a clear grasp of cosmopolitan theory as a contemporary phenomenon. The term cosmopolitanism is used here as a generic term, or 'title word'[3] for all those liberal political theories that were developed or became prominent in the last decades of the twentieth century and which apply principles and ideas previously developed for national societies on a global scale. The most prominent are various Rawlsian schemes of global justice; however, utilitarian theories and theories that contain a mixture of various strands also belong to this class. Since the definition carries a time stamp, it excludes classical authors like Kant (i.e., his whole philosophy ranging from his theoretical philosophy to the philosophy of religion) but includes theories inspired by Kant that defend a specifically contemporary interpretation of Kant's cosmopolitanism.[4]

2 In the next chapter, we will see why Kant's moral and political philosophy presupposes not only his critical philosophy but also his empirical science of knowing as expounded upon in his popular lectures.

3 In philosophy, title words, such as being, language, subjectivity and so on, are never 'well defined' as they stand for a kind of fundamental question. On the logic of title words in general, see Pirmin Stekeler-Weithofer, 'Autonome Vernunft und Normbefolgung des Verstandes. Wie Hegel eine Unterscheidung Kants präzisiert', *Hegel-Studien* 48 (2015): 13–36.

4 Thomas Pogge explicitly reinterprets Kant's theory in the framework of Rawlsian theory as being political but not metaphysical. Thomas Pogge, 'Is Kant's Rechtslehre Comprehensive?', *Southern Journal of Philosophy* 36 (1998): 161–87.

One may question this definition as too general and too broad: too general, since apparently all liberal political theories apply some principles on a global scale, and too broad, since it includes many different theories, arguably even some theories that consider themselves to be explicitly anti-cosmopolitan. It might thus appear that the definition delineates not cosmopolitanism but contemporary political philosophy as such. However, we should recall two aspects. First, the extension of moral and political principles on a global scale under the heading of cosmopolitanism is a recent phenomenon of the post-Cold War era. The 1964 edition of the *Encyclopaedia Britannica* does not even have an entry on 'Cosmopolitanism', and under 'International Relations' only refers to related articles on Empire, Hegemony, Imperialism, Mandate, Protectorate, Spheres of Influence and Suzerainty.[5] In official Marxist terminology, on the other hand, 'cosmopolitanism' was regarded as a camouflage strategy on the part of US imperialism.[6] Therefore, left-leaning political theories that kept an eye on official Marxism, such as the Frankfurt School in Germany, did not pursue this line of thought before 1989.[7] It is easy to imagine the kinds of criticism Rawls's distinction between liberal, decent and outlaw regimes (under the presumption that they all must yield to a liberal notion of human rights) would have provoked under Cold War premises. Cosmopolitanism might appear today as the default way to do political philosophy. However, in hindsight, the very premise that political philosophy applies as a matter of course to the whole globe is a specific historical formation of thought.

[5] Previous editions had a short entry on stoic cosmopolitanism but not on Kant, let alone the cultural cosmopolitanism of German Romanticism.

[6] The *Great Soviet Encyclopedia* recounts the history of cosmopolitanism beginning with the stoics, including the teachings of the Catholic Church and continuing all the way to German idealism and explains: 'Cosmopolitanism is an inseparable part of the ideology of imperialism, such as in bourgeois political science. … Proletarian internationalism is opposed to bourgeois cosmopolitanism'. *Great Soviet Encyclopedia*, vol. 13, trans. of the third edition (New York: Macmillan, 1973), 190.

[7] See Sigrid Thielking, *Weltbürgertum. Kosmopolitische Ideen in Literatur und politischer Publizistik seit dem achtzehnten Jahrhundert* (München: Fink, 2000), 242–51.

1.2 Characteristics of contemporary cosmopolitanism

The historical contingency of the rise of cosmopolitanism as a dominant discourse formation is usually not mentioned in contemporary theories, as it apparently restates the default stance to do normative political philosophy. However, questioning that establishes hierarchies, distinctions, or institutional discourse-formations is the first step in any genealogical analysis as it reveals the cracks in theoretical brickwork through which critique can slip in.[8] Still, for acquiring a hermeneutic understanding of the contemporary cosmopolitanism, it is also necessary to appropriate its internal view. In an early programmatic formulation, Thomas Pogge identifies three core elements of contemporary cosmopolitanism – individualism, universality and generality.[9] Similar characterisations can also be found in other authors.[10]

At this point, it would be possible to further differentiate between different strands of cosmopolitanism within the contemporary debate, distinguishing, for example, between moral, legal, cultural and political or institutional cosmopolitanism, according to how much power and which kinds of institutions are theoretically assigned to the global level. Expanding on various modalities of cosmopolitanism would be helpful for answering specific criticisms, such as neglecting the importance of national identities or overestimating the transformative power of administrations with regard to the economics of cultural forces. It would also allow a rough differentiation between strong and weak cosmopolitan approaches in political theory, for example, grouping Pogge, Singer and (the early) Nussbaum on one side, and Nagel, Miller, Rawls and (the late) Nussbaum on the other.

However, these additional finely tuned distinctions would cloud a premise that is taken for granted by all cosmopolitan

8 Sappho's songs served as a poetic reminder that the Western framework isn't as solid or unified as sometimes presumed.

9 Pogge, 'Cosmopolitanism and Sovereignty', 48–9; see also the discussion in the Preface, xviii.

10 See, for example, Held and Maffettone, *Global Political Theory*, 43 or Simon Caney, *Justice Beyond Borders: A Global Political Theory* (Oxford: Oxford University Press, 2005), 3–5.

approaches: they are all egalitarian theories. Once again, this may sound unsurprising, since we are told that 'every plausible political theory has the same ultimate source, which is equality.'[11] Yet, when reflecting on the premise of equality by imagining alternative historical positions, it becomes obvious that the premise is specific to contemporary cosmopolitanism. In contemporary discourse, the value of equality is usually taken as a given,[12] a 'rock-bottom ethical premise … [that] cannot be derived from anything else'[13] or a human end that 'cannot be defended or justified, for it is itself which justifies other acts'.[14] As long as the aim is to defend a certain conception of equality within a society that considers itself to be liberal, the more interesting debate is, indeed, explicating what it means to treat citizens as equals (the 'equality of what?' question). However, in cosmopolitan debates egalitarianism becomes a more prominent premise, since cosmopolitan theories aim not only to be acceptable by liberal societies but also by others, by decent societies[15] or collectivistic moralities.[16] The fundamental problem of contractarian approaches is that the 'international contract' only includes liberal peoples and decent non-liberal peoples. This strategy presupposes that certain regimes are illegitimate, even though this is precisely

[11] Will Kymlicka, *Contemporary Political Philosophy: An Introduction* (Oxford: Clarendon Press, 1990), 4–5.

[12] With regard to the question of how to justify equality in human rights, the same observation has been made by Allen Buchanan, 'Equality and Human Rights', *Philosophy, Politics, and Economics* 4 (2005), 69–70. On the 'groundlessness' of egalitarian theories in various authors, see John Kekes, 'A Reasonable Alternative to Egalitarianism', in Thomas Christiano and John Christman, eds., *Contemporary Debates in Political Philosophy*, (Oxford: Blackwell), 179–94. Kekes, however, uses his observation to serve a one-sided political agenda.

[13] Brian Barry, 'Equality', Lawrence C. Becker and Charlotte B. Becker, eds., *Encyclopedia of Ethics* (New York: Garland, 1992), 324.

[14] Isaiha Berlin, 'Equality', in Henry Hardy, ed., *Concepts and Categories* (London: Hogarth Press, 1978), 102.

[15] John Rawls, *The Law of Peoples with 'The Idea of Public Reason Revisited'* (Cambridge, MA: Harvard University Press, 1999), 59–62.

[16] Allen Buchanan, *The Heart of Human Rights* (New York: Oxford University Press, 2014), 249–73 shows against Rawls that human rights are acceptable by collectivistic moralities. However, instead of arguing with a real collectivist moralist such as Lenin, he constructs his own cardboard figure.

the question that is at stake. Relying on the notion of reasonableness is no way out of the quandary, as long as reasonableness is defined in terms of what people (who are taken to be free and equal) would consent to. However, the point here is not to criticise egalitarian approaches but to draw attention to a characteristic premise of cosmopolitanism.

Nonetheless, there may be a reason that this premise cannot be or need not be explicitly defended, which leads us to a final characteristic of contemporary cosmopolitanism. One might think that all non-egalitarian theories depend on some 'metaphysical views' that cannot be defended within the limits of a 'reasonable empiricism'. Pogge alludes to this argument by suggesting that all approaches that do not share the values of cosmopolitanism must presume a 'metaphysical' view of arbitrary differences, such as those between men and women, commoners and aristocrats, blacks and whites, compatriots and foreigners, and so on.[17] Contemporary cosmopolitanism, on the other hand, is characterised by taking a strictly non-metaphysical attitude. This attitude may be defended in a variety of ways, either as a requirement of reasonableness within political theories or as an (empirical) result derived from human experience.[18] In any case, the theory is presented as being based on very lean, easily acceptable premises, for which 'non-metaphysical' may be the label.

Taken together, these three features are sufficient to characterise contemporary cosmopolitanism. Given certain historical and philosophical narratives about our time, faith in egalitarianism and an anti-metaphysical attitude, cosmopolitanism appears to be the logical consequence of political thinking. The definition is broad, as it is meant to capture both sides of a particular debate. Thus, Nagel, Rawls, Miller or the (late) Nussbaum would not dispute the fact that cosmopolitan developments are in line with contemporary political theory but would only question certain exaggerated

[17] Pogge, 'Cosmopolitanism and Sovereignty', 48.

[18] Martha Nussbaum claims that her account of human capabilities 'is articulated in terms of freestanding ethical ideas only, without reliance on metaphysical and epistemological doctrines'. See Martha Nussbaum, *Frontiers of Justice: Disability, Nationality, Species Membership* (Cambridge, MA: Harvard University Press, 2006), 163.

normative claims. One might be concerned that it is not possible to arrive at interesting insights by reflecting on such very general characteristics, but instead, it is only possible by engaging in this debate and promoting some aspect of global justice, or instead taking a historical point of view by discovering some antecedents of this noble aim. However, I will show how it is possible to reformulate the terms of this debate.

2. Which history of cosmopolitanism?

2.1 The origin of cosmopolitan thought

Conceiving contemporary cosmopolitanism as a specific historical discourse formation is only a first step; history itself needs to be 'historicised', that is, recognised as a creative process, both at the time it happened and later on, as interest-based re-writings. The history of cosmopolitanism is a good example in this regard. However, the official history of cosmopolitanism as it is found in dictionaries and encyclopaedias seems, at first glance, to offer few revealing insights.[19] Cosmopolitanism was coined by Diogenes,[20] while the first fully-fledged theory was arguably formed in the third century BCE by Chrysippus.[21] He might have been a pupil of Diogenes, who elaborated upon the frugal, kynic[22] side of Socrates' life and teachings. Thus, there is a direct line from Socrates and the early sophists to cosmopolitan theory. Chrysippus holds that all people on the earth share a common

[19] For an overview of ancient usages of the term cosmopolitanism, see David Konstan, 'Cosmopolitan Traditions', in Ryan K. Balot, ed., *A Companion to Greek and Roman Political Thought* (Malden, MA: Wiley-Blackwell, 2009), 473–84.

[20] Diogenis Laertii, *Vitae philosophorum*, vol. 1, ed. Miroslav Marcovich (Stuttgart: Teubner, 1999–2002), VI 63.

[21] *Stoicorum veterum fragmenta*, vol. 2, ed. Hans von Arnim (Stuttgart: Teubner, 1964) II, 32, 328.

[22] I use the spelling kynic instead of cynic to indicate that Chrysippus and Diogenes challenged the Athenians not with materialistic explanations of normative vocabulary in the way that the modern word 'cynic' might suggest but rather by showing, like the later Mendicant Friars, ostentatious contempt for ease and pleasure.

humanity and that the wise man is not a citizen of a particular polis but of the earth. Therefore, he should show 'cosmopolitan concern' for others and work to benefit human beings as far as circumstances allow. Details of this account, particularly the ascription of these views to Chrysippus or earlier authors, are a matter of historical dispute, since we mostly know about them from later Stoic reconstructions.[23] Thus, when tracing only the notion cosmopolitanism and looking for theories that are explicitly labelled as such, one is quickly deflected from the beginning of political philosophy into late Roman sources, written at a time when philosophy and public debate had lost all relevance to political life.

From the perspective of contemporary cosmopolitanism, ancient cosmopolitanism may be patronised as informative but also philosophically deficient. In her account, Martha Nussbaum makes this point most forcefully. According to Nussbaum, ancient cosmopolitanism cannot serve as a source of inspiration as it fails to fully spell out principles and arguments and reflect on institutional requirements. Moreover, the Stoics can be accused of favouring a quietist attitude towards injustice, failing to develop fundamental political alternatives to existing imperial regimes and especially for being silent about the most unjust institution of the ancient world, namely slavery.[24] This perspective reveals much about the contemporary perspective on ancient cosmopolitanism. Even if earlier influences are patronisingly granted, history is reduced to mere history, bits and pieces that can be artfully assembled and reconstructed according to the values of the historian. It seems inconceivable that any historical position could be on the same plane as cosmopolitan theory, let alone derail any of its convictions.

23 See Eric Brown, 'Die Erfindung kosmopolitaner Politik durch die Stoiker', in Matthias Lutz-Bachmann, Andreas Niederberger and Philipp Schink, eds., *Kosmopolitanismus. Zur Geschichte und Zukunft eines umstrittenen Ideals* (Weilersvist: Velbrück, 2010), 9–24.

24 For criticism, see Martha Nussbaum, 'Kant and Stoic Cosmopolitanism', *The Journal of Political Philosophy* 5, no. 1 (1997): 14.

2.2 The origin of the cosmopolitan question

In the Preface, we saw how ancient spectres mediated through Heidegger still haunt us in contemporary debates and conflicts but can also be a source of inspiration or of challenges to our fondest presumptions. For igniting the debate on a genealogy of cosmopolitan thought I will propose a daring thesis: Plato was the first anti-cosmopolitan philosopher to react against the cosmopolitan discourse of his time. This may seem difficult to defend, given the historical account of ancient cosmopolitanism just presented. How can Plato react to cosmopolitan theory if it only evolved 100 years after his death? In his history of cosmopolitanism, Eric Brown writes apodictically that there is no reliable evidence for programmatic cosmopolitan claims before the early Stoics.[25] He even rejects the idea that Alexander the Great (already a generation after Plato) was driven by a cosmopolitan impulse.[26] Thus, cosmopolitanism seems not to even be close to Plato's time. However, it is worth reflecting further on the role Alexander the Great played in intellectual memory, as it reveals a missed opportunity of the Hellenic world. It is a truism that Alexander's campaign dramatically changed the entire ancient world, not only in terms of political change but also in terms of how people thought about politics.[27] One might think that only after Alexander was it possible to imagine a Hellenic empire ruling the whole world, or any other form of global political order. However, Alexander's campaign not only brought about the age of Hellenism but also destroyed something else, the idea[28] of cosmopolitanism in terms of a

[25] See Brown, 'Die Erfindung kosmopolitaner Politik', 23.

[26] This claim has been advanced by W. W. Tarn, 'Alexander the Great and the Unity of Mankind', *Proceedings of the British Academy* 19 (1933): 123–66. For a comprehensive critique see Ernst Badian, 'Alexander the Great and the Unity of Mankind', *Historia* 7, no. 4 (1958): 425–44.

[27] On the broader political transformations of the fourth century BCE, see P. J. Rhodes, *A History of the Classical Greek World: 478–323 BC* (Oxford: Blackwell, 2006).

[28] The term *idea* is used here in a non-technical sense. From Plato's perspective, a federation (*koinon*), like all forms of government, would belong to the realm of *doxa* rather than *ideas*.

peaceful confederation of free and autarchic[29] cities. In the fourth century BCE, and thus at the time when Plato wrote his major works, this idea was the real alternative, situated between the out-dated ideal of a small and autarchic polis and the Persian model of a more comprehensive empire.[30]

Before proceeding, a brief methodological reminder is necessary. Even though the word 'cosmopolitanism' had not yet been coined in Plato's time, it can be shown that a corresponding political practice, including speeches about it, did exist. It is therefore appropriate to introduce the term as a heuristic device, insofar as it captures the spirit of those practices. When rediscovering hidden traditions, the Cambridge School does not cling to words either, since its inquiry focuses on how words are employed in historical contexts and the practices they help establish. Later philosophical theories sometimes obscure these practices and therefore need to be deconstructed.

Greek federalism as proto-cosmopolitanism

Since Greek federal states and the ideas and practices related to them are often not mentioned in treatises about ancient political philosophy,[31] it is necessary to recap some historical details. The aim here is not to present new historical facts of findings. There are ample accounts of Greek federal states in the writings of ancient historians. Montesquieu and the Federalists have already drawn on the accounts Greek historians gave to justify certain claims about federalism in general. Recent archaeological findings allow for the understanding of the federal systems of several smaller poleis. Therefore,

[29] It is commonly thought that the freedom of the ancients was not the same as modern freedom. However, the same applies to the notion of autonomy, and the ancient catchphrase was not *autonomia* but *autarkeia*. As this idea channels our thinking in a specific way, the phrase 'free and autarchic city' will be used from time to time. See Mogens H. Hansen, 'The Autonomous City State. Ancient Fact or modern Fiction?' in Mogens H. Hansen and Kurt A. Raaflaub, eds., *Studies in the Ancient Greek Polis* (Stuttgart: Franz Steiner, 1995), 21–43.

[30] These were the only alternatives at this time. The Roman solution of combining city state structure with an imperial form of governance was developed only later.

[31] Federalism, for example, is not mentioned at all by Stephen G. Salkever and Ryan K. Balot, eds., *The Cambridge Companion to Ancient Greek Political Thought* (Cambridge: Cambridge University Press, 2009).

modern historians generally try to reconstruct a more comprehensive picture of the fourth century BCE.[32] The only systematic aim that guides the following account is highlighting that history is an open and contingent process for participants in which different venues are possible, whereas greater narratives, such as 'the Greek's fixation on the polis' or 'the Greek's failure to build a nation', are only written later on.[33]

In this respect one can say that the fourth century BCE, at the time when Plato wrote his dialogues and was politically active, bore the possibility of cosmopolitanism in the form of a federation of free and autarchic poleis. Even though most institutional innovations were – like always in Greek culture – not invented theoretically but tried out in practice, some theoretical elements that contributed to this form of panhellenic or proto-cosmopolitanism can be found particularly in the writings of two authors, Isocrates and Xenophon.[34] Both men were famous contemporaries of Plato, and their thoughts were prominent at this time, though neither presented a complete theory of cosmopolitanism comparable to modern day theories. Yet, if we combine elements from both writers with other ideas around at this time, we can surmise that such a theory, or such thoughts, were possible or, so to speak, in the air. Thus, Isocrates and Xenophon are not read strictly philologically, as sources; rather, the question is what kind of philosophical theory one could assemble from their thoughts and those of their contemporaries. Panhellenism is then not necessarily a proto-nationalistic idea erected to oppose the 'inferior race of barbarians',[35] but can instead

[32] On the general problems of writing a history of the fourth century and new approaches, see the introduction in John Buckler and Hans Beck, eds., *Central Greece and the Politics of Power in the Fourth Century BC* (Cambridge: Cambridge University Press, 2008).

[33] See, for a contemporary reading of Greek political thought against the background of the crisis of polis autonomy, Ryan K. Balot, *Greek Political Thought* (Malden, MA: Wiley-Blackwell, 2006), 177–91.

[34] See Karl Popper, *The Open Society and its Enemies*, 2nd ed. (London: Routledge, 1995), 153. Popper relies on nineteenth and early twentieth century German scholarship that discovered implicit references to Antisthenes throughout Plato's texts.

[35] It is to be noted that even though the distinction of Greeks vs. Barbarians was widely used by poets and rhetoricians and often carried same chauvinist overtones, Persians and Egyptians were not considered to

be interpreted as having been inspired by cosmopolitan considerations.

In the early fourth century BCE, Isocrates[36] was the head of the most famous school in Athens[37] and an ardent promoter of Panhellenic cosmopolitanism.[38] In his speeches, he clearly analyses the perils the Greek world faced in the fourth century BCE. After its victory in the Peloponnesian war, Sparta could not establish a position of permanent supremacy but became despised as a tyrannical city due to its harsh treatment of defeated enemies. Athens had earlier lost its reputation as a defender of Greek freedom, and its numerous hostile expeditions in the best imperialistic fashion did little to restore it. Meanwhile, other cities tried to step in whenever a power vacuum emerged. No power was ashamed to accept help from the Persian king or to employ mercenary forces. Constant civil strife – often fuelled by third-party interests – and countless wars between cities and coalitions threatened to destroy the prosperity, peace and culture of the Greek commonwealth. When reading Isocrates, one has the impression that he describes a situation like that at the end of the European Thirty Years War, a devastated country plagued by mercenaries wandering in strange lands in search for employment.[39] Many actors pursued incompatible interests

be culturally or racially inferior. Thus, the Greek distinction does not yield the same implications as the modern distinction between civilised and uncivilised peoples. For a detailed account of the changing role of this distinction, see Jacob Burckhardt, *Griechische Kulturgeschichte*, vol. 1, ed. Felix Stähelin (Berlin und Leipzig: Deutsche Verlagsanstalt, 1930), 297–313.

36 His speeches are collected in *Isocrates*, trans. and ed. G. Norlin, 2 vols. (Cambridge, MA: Harvard University Press, 1928).

37 Isocrates claims to have had 'more pupils than all the rest together who are occupied with philosophy'. *Antidosis*, 41. Plato's Academy, on the other hand, had a rather shaky beginning. The ridicule by Gorgias 'the philosopher talks in a whisper with three or four pupils' (*Gorgias* 485d) can be read as a description of the early days of the Academy.

38 For the following, see especially his speech *On the Peace*. Aristotle rendered it in his *Rhetoric* III, 17 under the title *On the Confederacy*. Isocrates has changed his view according to historical circumstances. However, the main point is not to pinpoint a specific view to a specific date but to show the kind of theory which Plato was opposed to.

39 See *Isocrates* 4, 186 and *To Philip*, 96. For a detailed analysis of the historical background, see Alexander Fuks, 'Isokrates and the Social-Economic

in constantly shifting coalitions while no traditional solution seems feasible. As an alternative to the constant civil strife of his time, Isocrates proposed forming a confederation of free and autarchic cities: a brotherhood of culture, transcending the bonds of race.[40]

He argued that peace, not only among Greeks but with all of mankind, would be the precondition for striving for true aims, namely being respected by others and raising the standards of living for all.[41] He criticised realist principles of power politics as unjust and serving only short-term interests.[42] In the long run it would be in everyone's interest to uphold peace, end the suffering among Hellenic people and support burdened societies (i.e., refugees from destroyed cities).[43] Insisting that these principles are in 'everyone's interest' was, for Isocrates, not just a *façon de parler* but is specifically addressed to Athens, a relatively strong player. Isocrates also criticised the common enemies of mankind, the mercenaries who commit atrocities that make peace impossible.[44] Thus, simple, solid political judgment based on a fair assessment of effects should convince Athenians and everyone else to pursue this worthy cause.[45]

It is noteworthy that Isocrates was not just a lofty theoretician or a soapbox orator but a highly visible and influential public figure. As a result, the idea of a peaceful federation among free and autarchic cities was well known in Athens and the intellectual circles of the ancient world.[46] Moreover, it was not seen as an exercise in ideal theory or an exaggerated fantasy. Some evidence that it was instead at some

Situation in Greece', *Ancient Society* 3 (1972): 17–44.

40 Isocrates, *Panegyricus*, 50.

41 Isocrates, *Peace*, 20.

42 Ibid., 17.

43 Ibid., 24.

44 Ibid., 41.

45 Ibid., 133–9.

46 Whether federal regimes actually did promote social stability is a different question. The positive evaluation by Montesquieu and the Federalists has been refuted by contemporary historical scholarship; see Hans Beck, *Polis und Koinon. Untersuchungen zur Geschichte und Struktur der griechischen Bundesstaaten im 4. Jahrhundert v. Chr.* (Stuttgart: Franz Steiner, 1997), 251–4.

time thought of as a feasible path history could have taken can be found in the writings of the historian Xenophon. In his *Hellenica*, he recounted the formation of the Chalcidian League and suggested that it was on the brink of becoming the most powerful federal state in Hellas (circa 385–383 BCE).[47] However, he did not favour Panhellenism. Instead of stating his view openly, he puts the warning of forming such a powerful state in the mouths of the envoys from two states that felt threatened by the League. An interesting point from this episode is that the Chalkidian communities had not merged into a new political body or been subjected to a powerful state but had instead retained their local, autonomous identity, since the League was based on the principle of dual citizenship (*sympoliteia*). Therefore, the envoys warned that Olynthus, the head of the League, would become even more powerful as the states had granted each other reciprocal rights of intermarriage and property, and other communities would soon realise the advantages of belonging to this League. It is unnecessary to decide whether Panhellenism at this time was actually a camouflage strategy for imperialism or a feasible path towards peace and prosperity (similar principles were, in the twentieth century, employed in the formation of the European Union). The relevant point is that speculations about new kinds of federal regimes based on dual citizenship and reciprocal economic and social rights were not confined to grand speeches but were grounded in actual political developments.[48] It is, however, more difficult to articulate the philosophical foundation underlying these considerations.

[47] Xenophon, *Hellenica, Books I–V*, trans. Carleton L. Brownson (Cambridge, MA: Harvard University Press, 1921), V, 2, 11–19.

[48] The actual history of the Chalkidian League is less glorious: it lost a bitter war against Sparta and was then dissolved. Arnold Toynbee refers to this episode to speculate whether, instead of the reactionary monarchical model of Macedonia, the federal city state model of Olynthus could have prevailed in Hellas and, as a consequence, Olynthus could have become the Rome of Hellas. On this reading focusing on federalism as the unfulfilled promise of Greek history, see Arnold J. Toynbee, *A Study of History*, vol. 3 (Oxford: Oxford University Press, 1934), 481.

Elements of a proto-cosmopolitan theory

Even though federal regimes were well-known and widespread in the fourth century BCE, and some proto-cosmopolitan ideas were pronounced, there was no fully-fledged cosmopolitan theory. Nevertheless, some elements that bolster Panhellenic cosmopolitanism can be assembled. For both Isocrates and Xenophon, the negative part of the theory can easily be asserted. They each invoke Socrates as a founding figure but go on to advocate (and ascribe to Socrates) a strict anti-metaphysical attitude. Isocrates holds that education should have only a practical value and that all sciences should serve this end. Therefore, abstract theory or philosophy would only be useful as 'gymnastics for the soul', but should not be studied in their own right. These lines are obviously directed against the Platonic Academy.

Xenophon similarly portrays Socrates as someone who gives good and well-reasoned practical advice, for instance that Athens should invest in a proper cavalry trained not by politicians or philosophers but by experienced cavalry-men. In addition, he depicts Socrates as being ignorant or hostile with regard to metaphysical speculation about the good itself. Xenophon's Socrates says: 'I know of no good (*agathon*) that is not good for something, and I do not wish to know it either.'[49] Again, Plato is implicitly accused of forgery: the 'real' Socrates never discussed 'metaphysics' or ideas that are not good for any practical end.

It is more difficult to ascertain the specific philosophical principles underlying this form of cosmopolitanism. This is part of the general problem that no major philosophical treatise apparently existed that promoted Greek democracy.[50] Popper attempts to solve this mystery by

[49] Xenophon, *Memorabilia*, III. 8, 3.

[50] This assessment was widely shared among historians and philosophers up to the middle of the twentieth century. See Moses I. Finley, 'Athenian Demagogues' in Moses I. Finley *Studies in Ancient Society* (London: Routledge, 1974), 9. However, Kurt Raaflaub shows that having one major treatise may not be necessary, as the democratic theory prevalent at this time can be reconstructed by drawing on various sources. Kurt A. Raaflaub, 'Contemporary Perceptions of Democracy in Fifth-Century Athens', *Classica et Mediaevalia* 40 (1989), 33–70.

attributing a cosmopolitan political theory to the early generation of sophists, whom he calls the 'Great Generation'.[51] In his reading, the school of Gorgias – Antisthenes, Alcidamas and Lycophron – held egalitarian theories and believed in a brotherhood of all men.[52] He particularly credits Antisthenes as the only true pupil of Socrates on the grounds that he defended egalitarian and cosmopolitan principles. Popper argues that Antisthenes is the implicit target of Plato's scorn at many places in the *Politeia* and in other works.[53] In trying to find a positive counter image to Plato, Popper arguably overshoots the mark, such as when he portrays Xenophanes as a critical rationalist,[54] Lycophron as a libertarian[55] and claims that fifth century cosmopolitanism was linked to an 'anti-slavery movement'.[56] Plato's representation of the sophists as swindlers and the real corrupters of the youth is obviously one-sided, but simply reversing the negative value judgment does not do justice to the movement.[57] What can be said is that the sophists questioned traditional authority, favoured education over noble origin and appeared in Athens at a time when egalitarian and democratic principles were widely held.[58] All of them shared the optimistic belief that success is based on individual effort and can be taught. At least some defended the political principles on

[51] Popper, *Open Society*, 185.

[52] Ibid., 152.

[53] Ibid., 614–15.

[54] Ibid., 572.

[55] Ibid., 114.

[56] Popper frequently refers to an 'anti-slavery movement' that was 'well on the way' (Ibid. 562, 573), but he never quotes any sources. He may have had the remark of Gorgias's pupil Alcidamas in mind, that God has freed all people and nature has not enslaved anyone. Aristotle alludes to it in *Rhetoric*, I 13, 1373b.

[57] Hegel was the first to reevaluate the sophists as a form of Greek enlightenment. On the subsequent nineteenth and early twentieth century debate on the role of the sophists, see W. K. C. Guthrie, *The Sophists: A History of Greek Philosophy, vol. 1*. (Cambridge: Cambridge University Press, 1969), 10–16.

[58] Oddly enough, the best-known documentation for widespread democratic beliefs is the anti-democratic pamphlet by the so-called Old Oligarch. For a reconstruction of democratic political theory, see Raaflaub, 'Contemporary Perceptions', ibid.

which Athens was based, legal and political egalitarianism (*isonomia*), the equal right to address the assembly and bring charges (*isegoria*), equal representation in government by lot (*isokratia*) and the freedom of speech (*parrhesia*).[59]

3. A contextual reading of the *Politeia*

I have painted Panhellenic cosmopolitanism in broad strokes in order to show the kind of theorising that Plato faced. At this point, it would be possible to use historical and philological studies to elaborate on the variety of views held by different sophists and try to determine how people in various places reacted to political changes and how social life evolved in the fourth century. However, even when concentrating on Athens, it is difficult to integrate Plato into a historical narrative of this kind. On the one hand, he is the founding father of philosophy and has shaped the whole of Western culture, but on the other he is an exceptional figure of his own time. The ensuing question is neither historical nor exegetical but philosophical, and it emerges from today's perspective.[60] The idea of history as social and moral progress culminating in the culture of Athens,[61] the prevailing anti-metaphysical attitude, the celebration of equality and last but not least the general proto-cosmopolitan spirit appear like a mirror image of contemporary cosmopolitanism. We might ask, then, how the development of philosophy as a discipline related to this historical context. How is it possible that ideas and principles that seem self-evident today and characteristic of our age actually pre-date the formation of philosophy as an academic discipline in Plato and Aristotle? And why has political philosophy in the tradition of Plato and Aristotle ignored

59 On the field of words surrounding *isonomia*, see Mogens Herman Hansen, *The Athenian Democracy in the Age of Demosthenes: Structure, Principles, and Ideology* (Norman, OK: University of Oklahoma Press, 1991), 81–4.

60 Pursuing a 'two-tiered outlook' is also the leading idea of Ryan K. Balot, ed., *A Companion to Greek and Roman Political Thought* (Malden, MA: Wiley-Blackwell, 2009).

61 Hansen argues that most people at the end of the fifth and the beginning of the fourth century held a progressive view of history. Of course, Plato is an exception. See Mogens H. Hansen, 'Solonian Democracy in Fourth-Century Athens', *Classica et Mediaevalia* 40 (1989), 71–99.

these cosmopolitan roots and instead taken a very different route than the one outlined by the sophists, rhetoricians and historians?

3.1 Plato's letters: An epistolary novel about his life

The question of how Plato's philosophy is situated within its own historical time is not a new one. Indeed, it emerged along with the beginning of academic philosophy at around the time he was alive. Even though we have no source that posed the question in precisely this way, we can find a response to this question in the letters handed down under Plato's name. These letters were known and discussed in antiquity but only received closer attention again since the late nineteenth century. Ulrich von Wilamowitz-Moellendorf was the first to argue that the letters were like a building block that had been thrown away but became the cornerstone of the new interpretation of Plato.[62] However, von Wilamowitz-Moellendorf overstates his case by presenting all of Plato's dialogues in a strictly chronological order that reflects Plato's life. Additionally, some Nietzschean-inspired philosophers have employed the biographical method to recast Plato as a proto-fascist defender of occidental civilization against the 'Asiatic'.[63] As a result, this tradition of inquiring into Plato's historical context has been largely

[62] Ulrich von Wilamowitz-Moellendorf, Platon, vol. 2 (Berlin: Weidmann, 1919), 299. On Wilamowitz and the debate since the nineteenth century over the biographical interpretation of Plato, see E. N. Tigerstedt, *Interpreting Plato* (Uppsala: Almquist & Wiksell, 1977), 36–51. A contribution published in 1906 by a high school teacher in his school's yearbook remains a very incisive interpretation of all the letters and their authenticity: Rudolf Adam, 'Über die Echtheit der platonischen Briefe', *Wissenschaftliche Beilage zum Jahresbericht des Falk-Realgymnasiums zu Berlin* 110 (1906), 3–29. On the current debate, see arguing against their authenticity Ludwig Edelstein, *Plato's Seventh Letter* (Leiden: Brill, 1966); in favour, the critical review of Edelstein's book by Friedrich Solmsen, *Gnomon*, 41, no. 1 (1969): 29–34, and again bluntly rejecting its philosophical value, Myles Burnyeat and Michael Frede, *The Pseudo-Platonic Seventh Letter* (Oxford: Oxford University Press, 2015).

[63] See especially Kurt Hildebrandt, *Platon: Der Kampf des Geistes um die Macht* (Berlin: Georg Bondi, 1933).

ignored in Anglophone scholarship.[64] This has the unfortunate consequence of portraying Plato as a philosopher completely detached from his own lifetime. Consequently, the Cambridge School's guiding principle – namely, to read philosophical treatises as arguments in a contested political field – is undermined by the premise that Plato's biography and historical circumstances are irrelevant. In what follows, it will be shown how biographical data, especially the seventh letter, can be used in a manner that avoids these interpretive pitfalls.

The seventh letter is the longest and the most central, in which the author, presumably Plato or someone speaking in Plato's name, defends him(self) against accusations of befriending a tyrant, accusations that were evidently widespread in Athens. The nature of the accusation becomes clearer upon reading the thirteenth letter, which was written in close proximity to Plato's lifetime (all the details about Plato, his family and friends are correct) but drafted with the aim of discrediting him. In the letter addressed to Dionysius II, Plato asks for money for himself, his family and his friends, and implicitly offers to work as an informant about affairs in Athens in return. The thirteenth letter 'reveals' Plato as a self-serving, unpatriotic, tyrant-friendly charlatan.

Most of the other letters elaborate on topics mentioned in the seventh letter, but do not offer any new philosophical arguments (and sometimes even confuse events or people, which can be taken as a sign of forgery). As a result, they are often ignored in philosophical interpretations. However, they are an important source for the reception of Plato.

The seventh letter recounts Plato's journeys to Sicily but also reflects in more general terms on the relation of philosophy to politics, the importance of friendship, trustworthiness of politicians and on Plato's motives. The other letters also touch upon these topics, but in addition they stress certain aspects that are not central in the seventh letter. When we

64 See Malcolm Schofield, 'Plato and Practical Politics', in *The Cambridge History of Greek and Roman Political Thought* in Christopher J. Rowe and Malcolm Schofield, eds., (Cambridge: Cambridge University Press, 2000), 293–302.

read the letters together like an epistolary novel,[65] a specific picture of Plato emerges. He appears to be a very practical-minded political advisor, someone with a broad knowledge of different constitutions who proposes constitutions specifically appropriate for various local circumstances.[66] The overall aim of his engagement in Syracuse was establishing peace[67] throughout Sicily by striking a compromise between different factions and setting up an arbiter for settling disputes.[68] Plato's proposal is based on the rule of law, stressing equality of all,[69] aiming at securing Greek freedom[70] and benefitting all people. It is notably a constitution not just for the city of Syracuse but for all the cities of Sicily.[71] Their union should not be achieved in an imperial fashion,[72] but by establishing bonds between friends in various cities.[73] Yet the regime Plato proposes is not just a *modus vivendi* but intends, for the first time in history, to realise the unlikely union of philosophy and political power.[74] For this reason, the events in Syracuse are carefully observed not only in Athens but by people all over the world.[75] The Platonic Academy plays a central role in this narrative. Plato is depicted as sending and receiving letters to different areas and places in the Hellenic world (to Perdiccas, King of Macedonia,[76] to friends of the academy in Asia Minor,[77] to Archytas of Tarent, a Pythagorean philosopher king[78]) and establishing friendships between

65 For the idea of reading the letters as a whole, see Hartmut Längin, 'Erzählkunst und Philosophie in den Platon Briefen', *Grazer Beiträge* 22 (1998): 101–44.

66 Plato, *Epistles*, trans. R. G. Bury (Cambridge, MA: Harvard University Press, 1929), 8.356d. All references to Plato's works are given by Stephanus pagination; translations of the *Epistles* are based on Bury.

67 Epistles 8.356c.

68 Epistles 8.353e, 8.356d, 7.337c.

69 Epistles 7.337c, 7.336d.

70 Epistles 7.336a.

71 Epistles 3.315d.

72 Epistles 7.351b.

73 Epistles 7.332b.

74 Epistles 7.328d, 7.335d, 4.320a, 2.310c.

75 Epistles 4.320d.

76 Epistles 4.

77 Epistles 6.

78 Epistles 9.

philosophers and politicians.[79] Plato's Sicilian adventure is therefore not an isolated event or a misstep but can be read as a geopolitical strategy for all of Hellas. The danger looming on the horizon is that if Platonic justice is not realised, Greek language and culture could vanish from the world after a 'barbarian' (Carthaginian) conquest.[80]

The subtext of the letters is thus that Plato was the spiritual centre of a wide-ranging intellectual community that tries to foster the Panhellenic cause as an intellectual and well-reasoned military and political alliance through practical advice.[81] However, the letters in which this idea is most evident (Epistles 4, 5, 8, 11) are those most scholars consider not to be genuine.[82] Nevertheless, they are germane, since they were written around Plato's lifetime, arguably in the context of the Academy, and thus by people who supported (or intended to support) Plato's cause. We might imagine that people in Plato's lifetime thought 'this is what he should have written: constant civil strife is destroying our civilization and Panhellenic cosmopolitanism (and possibly, peace with Persia) is the obvious solution.' But this is not what Plato actually wrote in his philosophical dialogues. On the contrary: the rhetorical, historical and sophistic tradition I have just described, which appears to be a mirror image of contemporary cosmopolitanism, is precisely what Plato opposed. We are confronted here with a *renversement des alliances*. The tradition of political philosophy that started with Plato has turned out not to be a natural ally of contemporary cosmopolitanism at all, but may actually be its archenemy.

[79] See especially Epistles 6.

[80] Epistles 8.353e.

[81] It is to be noted that this is the storyline of the letters. Some people believe that this actually describes the influence of Plato and the Academy. From a historical point of view, Kai Trampedach shows that no such influence can be confirmed. See Kai Trampedach, *Platon, die Akademie und die zeitgenössische Politik* (Stuttgart: Franz Steiner, 1994), 278–83.

[82] Authenticity is claimed mostly for the seventh letter, sometimes also the eighth.

3.2 The *Politeia* as a dialectical intervention

In a more detailed interpretation of the *Politeia*, it will now be shown how Plato managed to silence these cosmopolitan voices by inventing philosophy as dialectical endeavour. In this way, I propose to read the Platonic dialogues as conscious interventions in the discourses of his time.[83] The question is not simply 'historical' (which of the sophists could be correctly categorised as cosmopolitan) nor merely 'systematic' (thereby presupposing our philosophical premises and historical views as the only correct ones). Rather, it is genealogical in the sense described. A reconstruction of historical circumstances is used to read Plato's philosophy as an answer to the political questions of his time. This allows a new understanding of Plato and also challenges our certainties. To create a level playing field – we mostly know Plato's answers, but hardly the less developed questions –, Plato's cosmopolitan opponents can be given all sorts of support from today's mainstream of cosmopolitan thought.

Plato's philosophy is particularly well suited to this kind of systematic discussion through a historical lens since he uses the same method himself. Like most of his other early and middle dialogues, the *Politeia* is clearly set in the past. However, the *Politeia* is neither a piece of historical scholarship nor a historical novel. Instead, Plato shows that philosophy can be enacted through various voices in different historical settings. This not only separates positions and arguments from people, but also allows historical time to become a variable.[84] Thus, there is no natural necessity to speak in one's own name, like the rhetoricians, or to speak only about present people, and the present time. These are all variables that need to be taken up in the dialectical reflection.

[83] Here I differ from the standard developmental reading that sees the *Politeia* as the culmination of Plato's early 'ideal theory' before his political thought took a more pragmatic turn in the *Laws*; see George Klosko, *The Development of Plato's Political Theory*, 2nd ed. (Oxford: Oxford University Press, 2006).

[84] It is most obvious in the *Menexenos*, Plato's parody of Pericles's funeral speech, where historical events are freely mixed up.

One might object that this line of interpretation confronts an apparently insurmountable difficulty from the outset. Apart from a few strategic remarks,[85] Plato barely addresses the problem of inter-polis relations, nor does he deal directly with Isocrates's Panhellenic ideals or make use of Xenophon's histories in his speculations. This has led philosophers to conclude that Plato (and Aristotle) were simply unaware of or uninterested in these questions, that they were not anti-cosmopolitan but utterly un- or simply pre-cosmopolitan.[86]

Against this common assumption I will show that it is still possible to read Plato with these questions in mind, either in their ancient or contemporary forms. Moreover, I will suggest that Plato played with these kinds of expectations from his audience. Thus, the dialogue is not directed at Glaucon and Adeimantus, who were both dead by the time the dialogue was written,[87] but at readers and listeners in the fourth century BCE who were concerned about political affairs in Hellas.[88] The political questions on people's minds were whether Sparta could maintain its supremacy, whether Athens could rise again (or perhaps another city) and what part the powers at the periphery, and the Persians, would

85 *Politeia* IV 422a-423b, V 471b-c and *Nomoi* III 684a-b.

86 See Pauline Kleingeld and Eric Brown, 'Cosmopolitanism', in *The Stanford Encyclopedia of Philosophy*, Winter 2019 ed., ed. Edward N. Zalta, accessed 20 June 2025, https://plato.stanford.edu/archives/win2019/entries/cosmopolitanism. Leo Strauss is a notable exception. He frequently states that a world state would be the greatest tyranny and credits Plato for this insight. However, he does not specify his notion of the world state and takes no notice of the historical context of Plato. See Leo Strauss, *On Tyranny* (London: Collier-Macmillan, 1963), 206.

87 Allan Bloom argues that the dialogue shows how Socrates cures Glaucon from the desire to rule. However, Bloom does not bother to reflect on the meaning of the dialogue in the fourth century BCE, a time when Socrates was dead, 'dialogues of Socrates' was a well-established literary genre and everybody knew that Glaucon had left no impact on political or cultural life in Athens. So 'having saved Glaucon from politics' is a non-starter. See Allan Bloom, 'Response to Hall', *Political Theory* 5, no. 3 (1977): 315–30.

88 The question of what audience Plato had in mind is a complicated one. In any case, the *Politeia* cannot easily be read by ordinary citizens let alone recited like a Homeric epos, as understanding the *Politeia* requires profound philosophical schooling and elaborate discussion.

play in their future. To put the expectations of Plato's likely audience in a nutshell, we could say: the prize is Hellas. What is the future of the Hellenic world, and how will we fare in it?

The opening scene: Diverting expectations

Plato's opening scene plays with these expectations. It has often been remarked upon how the first few sentences foreshadow the structure of the dialogue, first grabbing Socrates (the archetype of the philosopher), playfully forcing him to come back (and rule), then offering additional arguments to support the quest, to which Socrates gives in for his own reasons.[89] However, the setting of the dialogue also carries a clear political message. The first meeting takes place on the way from Piraeus to Athens, literally in the shadow of the long walls built as part of Pericles's grand strategy to secure Athens's position as a land power. Moreover, Piraeus, the scene of the dialogue, is the cosmopolitan harbour city of Athens, a meeting place for people from all parts of the civilised world, the stronghold of the democratic party and the place where resident aliens (Metics) were allowed to settle. In this setting, Cephalus, the representative of tradition, has the first say. One has to keep in mind that, at the time of the dialogue, the prevailing tradition was already the democratic tradition. Given this context and Cephalus's standing as a respected elder of his community (albeit a Metic), the reader might expect something like Pericles's funeral speech, or in any case a speech about the wealth and honour of the city, how they reflect on each man living in the city, and how the

[89] See, on this aspect, the detailed interpretation by Thomas A. Szlezák, *Platon und die Schriftlichkeit der Philosophie. Interpretation zu den frühen und mittleren Dialogen* (Berlin: Walter de Gruyter, 1985), 271–83. Harold Bloom takes up another motif. He argues that the introduction of a new goddess by the Athenians themselves is an oblique reference to the accusations against Socrates. However, this does not reflect the charge and would sell Socrates' teachings short. Socrates did not just introduce any new god or goddess but, according to the charge, dismissed the existence of the city gods and set his own god (which Socrates called his *daimonion*) above all. See Plato, *Republic*, 2nd ed., trans. Allan Bloom, with notes and an interpretive essay (New York: Basic Books, 1991), 311. All references to Plato's *Politeia* are given by book and Stephanus pagination (e.g. VI 494c) and are based on Bloom's translation.

personal grace of being rich and having sons contributes to a good life.[90]

As he so often does, Plato plays with the reader's expectations only to disappoint them. Cephalus talks instead about sex life in old age and his personal salvation. In this way, Plato demonstrates from the outset that ordinary expectations regarding the proper subject of a book about the *Politeia* – something along the lines of the historical development of institutions, their functions and benefits for people living under them – completely misses the mark.[91] Instead, Plato starts with a highly introspective discussion about justice as a way to gain personal salvation and never gets back to the question of Athens's place in the Hellenic world.

Thus, Plato's first move is to irritate the cosmopolitans by introducing the representative of the traditional democratic elite of Piraeus and letting him ask a question that shatters their self-assurance of the traditional way of life. Cephalus's question recalls Martin Luther's justification of his stubborn heretical stance: 'For what does it profit a man to gain the whole world and forfeit his soul?'[92] Cephalus's question is similarly heretical if we read it from the foil of cosmopolitan sentiments. Cephalus responds to these political considerations as follows: 'The rise of democratic Athens to greatness, its leadership by example rather than force and its mission of uniting Greek cities to a civilized commonwealth[93] – all

90 Herodotus reports that, when questioned by Croesus who the happiest man on earth is, Solon answered: Tellus of Athens. He lived at a time when the city flourished, saw his sons and grandsons grow up and died as a hero on the battlefield. Herodotus, *Histories*, trans. A. D. Godley (Cambridge, MA: Harvard University Press, 1926), 1.29–33.

91 Arguably, the genre of writing books on constitutions (*politeiai*) had already been established at Plato's time. Usually, these treatises were about Sparta or Spartian constitutions but nothing like Plato's *Politeia*. See Malcom Schofield, *Plato. Political Philosophy* (Oxford: Oxford University Press, 2006), 4.

92 Luther quotes Matthew 16: 26. His German translation 'Was hülfe es, wenn ich die Welt gewönne und nähme doch Schaden an meiner Seele?' has become an emblem of Protestantism and arguably also transfigured into German idealism.

93 This alludes to the delusive self-image of the Athenians, which Thucydides recounts in his *History of the Peloponnesian War*. See especially Pericles' funeral oration, *History of the Peloponnesian War* 2.34–2.46. In

this is meaningless to me if my soul would suffer.' The same metaphysical theological question about personal salvation and life after death reappears at the very end of the *Politeia* in Book 10. This indicates that Cephalus's question is not merely an introduction, preparing us for the 'real' question of the *Politeia* about 'what the best regime is', but instead reveals the ultimate dimensions of the question after justice: it culminates in the idea of a last judgment.[94] If the question were limited from the outset to the 'political domain', Cephalus's question ('What's in it for me, for my soul?') would still loom in the background and might justify withdrawing from the discussion altogether. However, Cephalus is not interested in personal salvation alone, but prepares the discussion by presenting (together with his son Polemarchus) the traditional view of justice as 'saying the truth and giving back what is due', a position that is then disputed by the sophist Thrasymachus.

Thrasymachus's challenge: Justice as power relations between men and cities

In the dialogue, the sophist Thrasymachus intervenes directly after the traditional defence of justice. Implicitly, Plato casts the sophistic movement in a specific way, namely as something that ruins the tradition. However, in historical terms, that is, in terms of the historical progression of philosophical theories, one would have to say that the first sophists questioned the tradition but generally supported a democratic and cosmopolitan lifestyle.[95] Only the second generation of sophists challenged morality and developed realist or immoral theories of the kind we know from

Kagan's contrafactual speculations, Athens could indeed have become the 'leader of the free world' if it were not for Pericles' strategic mistakes – and, one might add, if the ancient world could be more easily convinced than the contemporary world to be led by the champions of freedom. See Donald Kagan, *The Fall of the Athenian Empire* (Ithaca, NY: Cornell University Press, 1991), 423–5.

94 On the origin of this idea in the Orphic tradition, see Werner Jaeger, *Paideia: The Ideals of Greek Culture, vol. 2: In Search of the Divine Center*, trans. Gilbert Highet (Oxford: Oxford University Press, 1947), 365–73.

95 On the history, see G. B. Kerferd, *The Sophistic Movement* (Cambridge: Cambridge University Press, 1981).

Callicles and Thrasymachus. One reason that Plato presents the sophists as immoralists is obviously to give them a bad name and reserve the notion of philosophy for the good side, or at any rate, the side opposed to the immoralists.[96] It would have been much harder for Plato to argue directly against a democratic cosmopolitan who, at the time which the *Politeia* was set (around 423 BCE), still had the rise of Athens as an economic and cultural power on his side to support his claims. Instead, Plato uses the historical setting and the characters to present a systematic argument applicable to his own time. The force and method of this argument are best assessed by considering the cosmopolitan consequences of the positions attacked by Plato, that is, by imagining a fourth century reader familiar with the sophistic tradition, the teachings of Isocrates and, like Xenophon, interested in contemporary politics.

Over the course of the argument in books I and II, Plato essentially presents three different views regarding justice: (1) justice means speaking the truth and giving back what is due (Cephalus and Polemarchus), (2) justice is a convention that emerges out of fear (Glaucon as advocatus diaboli) and (3) justice is what serves the stronger (Thrasymachus). The argument need not be repeated in all its intruiging details. Instead, two aspects can be singled out.

First, all of the principles presented could also govern relations between various poleis. It is notable that, at this point of the dialogue, justice is discussed in a general way but not yet restricted to the analogy of city and soul. Plato proposes a definition and then tests it by using different examples ('Is it just to return a sword to a madman?') or by putting it in context ('Has every art a specific end or is earning money the end of every art?'). In principle, one could also ask, for instance, whether circumstances exist in which no city owes anything to another,[97] whether just behaviour of cities is merely conventional, a sign

[96] Plato largely succeeded in discrediting the sophists. Only in the nineteenth century, starting with Hegel, were the sophists recovered from Plato's shadow.

[97] The term for 'owing' *apodidomi* is also used in a monetary sense, so 'giving back what is owed' is an undifferentiated blend of a moral and economic principle.

of fear or simply illusion or stupidity. (One might think of the famous Melian dialogue, in which these questions are raised). The Panhellenic or cosmopolitan dimension of the discussion is even mentioned explicitly. Thrasymachus explains his definition of injustice as wisdom and virtue by arguing that those who practice it can 'subjugate cities and tribes of men to themselves' (I 348d), thus bringing up a regime that comprises not just different cities but even different peoples. He is thereby arguably alluding to the Persian Empire, which usually serves as the archetype of an (unjust) tyranny in Greek literature.[98] However, as a good sophist, Thrasymachus turns the value judgement around by arguing that this kind of regime is indeed a prudent one. Thus, Thrasymachus's thinking is not confined to the world of independent cities. Instead, Thrasymachus argues as a realist, and contends that an imperial regime will be the future of Hellas and might even, at some time, be called 'just'. (In hindsight he was right. The flourishing Hellenic commonwealth of free and politically independent cities turned out to be only a brief episode.)

However, such cosmopolitan implications are not explicitly spelled out. Socrates even cloaks this dimension by using examples mostly taken from the sphere of personal ethics or human behaviour. While disputing with Thrasymachus, however, he does cite the example of a city that attacks or oppresses another without justification (I 351c). This example is important, for it shows that Socrates does not restrict the term 'justice' to individuals or to the order of a polis but uses it instead as a general term also applicable to relations between poleis and other groups. Of course, this does not mean that Plato had anything like a theory of 'Hellenic justice', let alone 'global justice' in mind; it is quite the contrary (as we will see later). It is merely evidence that, in terms of the ordinary, pre-philosophical or sophistic discussion Socrates is engaged in at this stage, inter-poleis relations are not a special case, only to be discussed in a 'second step' after justice is

[98] The Persian Empire was, however, not demonised but to some degree even admired. Arguably Athens learned the imperial techniques it employed from Persia. See Kurt A. Raaflaub, 'Learning from the Enemy', in John Ma et al., eds., *Interpreting the Athenian Empire* (London: Duckworth, 2009), 89–124.

established in the polis, but rather a part of the broad range of examples one talks about.

The second aspect concerns the nature of the discussion in Book I and at the beginning of Book II. One might think that Plato sells the different sophistic theories of justice short, that somehow principles such as truthfulness and reciprocity (mentioned by Cephalus) must feature in the definition of justice, that a social contract theory (mentioned by Glaucon) is a useful explanatory or justificatory device, and finally that Plato appears to be turning a blind eye to the central quality of justice, namely equality.[99] It is certainly possible to pursue any of these lines. The way Plato presents the discussion, however, shows that he has something quite different in mind. At the end of the discussion with Thrasymachus (I 354b–c), Socrates declares that no conclusion has been reached, and moreover, that no positive conclusion could ever be reached in this way. This confession by Socrates should be taken seriously. The innovative idea or milestone achieved by the *Politeia* is precisely to show that all 'sophistic' discussions, even those of Socrates,[100] are aporetic and that real inquiry (which later turns out to be philosophy) consists of something else.

Socrates: Against the Sophists

The follow-up question, of course, concerns what the additional insight provided by philosophy is and why Socratic inquiry is insufficient. After all, it seems to help unmask false generalities, and even comes up with some positive principles, such as 'doing harm can never be an act of justice as no art makes its subject worse.' It would appear that Socrates suggests that real philosophy only begins at a later stage. However, he does not state, in terms of a 'theory', the difference between 'real philosophy' and 'sophistic arguing'.[101]

[99] Political equality (*isonomia*) is only brought up in VIII 563b as something 'we almost forgot to mention'. Popper argues that Plato malignantly concealed it in the previous discussion. See Popper, *Open Society*, 89–93.

[100] The Socratic discussion is only pointless for sophists or people with an incorrect mindset. 'Good philosophical natures' like Glaucon and Adeimantus will realise its insufficiency and pursue the inquiry further.

[101] On the role of the definition of philosophy (V 476c–480a), the section 'Silencing the Interlocutor: Philosophy as Wissenschaft' below.

After the aporetic result in Book I, Socrates has to be 'held on to' and 'forced' to continue developing his argument in response to the challenges brought forward by Glaucon and Adeimantus. What can be said is that, in terms of content, the question is now posed in a more demanding way: Socrates is asked to show that justice is one of the aims that is pursued for its benefits and for its own sake (II 367b–d) and that the just man is the happiest man. In terms of method, a superficial reading would suggest that Socrates gives up the dialectical or discursive style of argumentation after Book I since he no longer engages in discussions with strong-minded interlocutors but mainly presents his view monologically. The question of what kind of inquiry Socrates wants to turn his attention to remains unanswered. At this point, it is only a promise: real philosophy will come later.

Yet Socrates' promise has repercussions on the cosmopolitan perspectives implied by the setting of the initial arguments. If the overall argument is that sophistic argumentation is a deficient kind of argument, then spelling out cosmopolitan consequences and defending them in the same sophistic or traditional way would do little to promote the course of the cosmopolitan. If all sophistic arguments end up in an *aporia* regardless of whether they pursue the 'good' cosmopolitan or the 'evil' immoralist course, then the most important task is to pursue the single course that promises a way out of the quandary and not to expand upon the details of wishful thinking. In this first set of arguments, similarly to the opening scene, Plato plays with the cosmopolitan expectations of his audience but does not refute them by presenting 'anti-cosmopolitan arguments'. Instead, he silences them by posing a question more radical than any posed by the sophists (is justice good in itself?) and by demanding a more fundamental theory (is the just man the happiest man, even in unhappy circumstances?).[102]

[102] This point is, especially for the modern reader, troubling, as a consequence of taking Plato's question seriously, is that even contemporary answers are insufficient, according to this standard. See, for a formulation of the worry, Bernard Williams, 'The Analogy of City and Soul in Plato's Republic', in Edward N. Lee, Alexander P. D. Mourelatos and Richard Rorty, eds., *Exegesis and Argument: Studies in Greek Philosophy Presented to Gregory Vlastos* (Assen: Van Gorcum, 1973), 196–206.

The implicit cosmopolitan interlocutor

A possible criticism of this line of interpretation might be to claim that the setting of the dialogue in a cosmopolitan context and some scattered hints about other cities are insufficient evidence for the claim that cosmopolitan theory functions as an implicit counter position. A further objection might insist that Socrates, by presenting ideas about the best city over the various stages, excludes the question of a cosmopolitan order from the outset. However, I will show that a cosmopolitan interlocutor is a useful device throughout the entire dialogue to elicit the consequences of Plato's position and is even explicitly presumed by Plato himself. In other words, one has to be careful not to read too much Aristotle into Plato.

Plato develops the idea of a just city as an analogy to the soul in order to observe justice as something written in large letters (II 368c–d). Even though he starts with a description of human relations (II 369b–d), he doesn't start with the idea of a 'society' (let alone a closed society of the free and equal), nor does he presume the polis to be the natural aim of man. Instead, he argues it is more convenient for people if everyone specialises in what they do best (369e–370a). Thus a 'loner', someone who lives entirely on their own, would have a difficult life but is not ruled out.[103] Plato then shows that the various professions emerge from the needs people have for each other (II 369e–371e). The city of bare necessity, or the healthy city that evolves in this way, is often quickly dismissed in discussions of Plato to focus, over the intermediate step of the feverish city, exclusively on the complete city. However, the first two models of the city are important, even with respect to the subsequent ideal models (the guardians' city and the philosophers' city). Both the healthy city and the feverish city can be read as implicit responses to cosmopolitan pretensions. The model of the healthy city would even be (to use an anachronistic idea) universalisable.

If all peoples on earth lived the 'healthy lifestyle' prescribed by Socrates for people living in the healthy city, and

[103] Otherwise, Plato would have been an easy target for ridicule by Antisthenes, the kynic pupil of Socrates, who took pride in demonstrating his autarchic lifestyle.

complied with some form of traditional ethics, including provisions for hospitality, the main causes of war, poverty and large-scale migration would be absent.[104] Plato does not specify any provisions regarding traditional ethics, including hospitality; however, the desire for the arts suggests that people are civilised.[105] This model vaguely recalls Rawls's society of liberal peoples[106] who all practice justice but never go to war. The difference here is that in Plato's healthy stage of mankind, political institutions seem to be absent. One can only speculate whether decisions that need to be made are arrived at unanimously, as in some tribal primitive or stateless societies. In any case, Plato's spokesman, Socrates, does not say that this kind of life is impossible. It is Glaucon who denounces this life as a 'city of sows' (II 372d) or, as one may translate loosely, rules for keeping livestock of the human kind.[107] It is also Glaucon and not Socrates who demands more luxuries to satisfy his human desire for luxuries. Plato argues that the need for conquest, an army and all the sciences that deal with human ills emerge from the spirited desire of wanting-to-have-more. His argument is not meant as an exhaustive explanation of the origins of wars and illnesses; there may be an indefinite number of additional causes.

The more interesting question is how this development appears to the eye of the philosopher. The people living in healthy circumstances[108] practice justice as 'minding one's

[104] According to John Rawls, these are still the great evils of human history. See Rawls, *The Law of Peoples*, 6–7.

[105] The only uncivilised characteristic is that the citizens do not eat meat (372b), which means that they do not sacrifice properly to the gods. Since sacred meat was distributed equally, the vegetarianism practiced in the healthy city could be considered an example of antidemocratic hubris. On the relation of formation of the city and public feasts, see N. Loraux, 'La cité comme cuisine et comme partage', *Annales. Économies, Sociétés, Civilisations* 36, no. 6 (1981), 614–22.

[106] Rawls, *The Law of Peoples*, 54–8. Unlike Kant, Rawls never addresses the question of why people should seek each other's company and not choose to live in the splendid isolation growing out of the original position.

[107] With the help of the Human Development Index, such rules could be formulated in an even more sophisticated way today.

[108] The term 'city' is avoided here, as it has not yet been introduced in the dialogue; strictly speaking, communities other than the ideal should not be called 'city' but by 'more splendid names' (IV 422e).

own business' and maintain a moderate lifestyle that would certainly please Socrates. They actually have more luxuries than Socrates' kynic pupils would grant themselves (figs for dessert) (II 372c). One could ask whether Socrates would be satisfied with this state of affairs. Could this be a home for a philosopher? It is Glaucon who states the philosophical problem about this primitive form of cosmopolitanism (or 'cosmo-anarchism'): justice and injustice is not seen 'unless it's somewhere in some needs these men have of one another' (II 372a). Justice happens behind these people's backs, so to speak, but its principle is not obvious to them. For this reason, there can be no philosophy in this place, and it is arguably also for this reason that Socrates gives in so quickly to Glaucon's demand, instead of trying to teach him (like Xenophon's Socrates) to have only 'reasonable' desires or to cultivate his feelings.[109] One interesting aspect of this argument is that, indirectly, even the philosopher would have an interest in the evolution of the healthy city into the feverish city, because only after this change do the social conditions of justice as 'minding one's own business' become institutionalised in such a way as to become discernible.[110]

Of course, the story Plato tells of the development of the healthy city into the feverish city is a story of degeneration, and the miseries faced by the feverish city set the stage for the purging of the city by the guardians. Still, it is worth noting that the feverish city is not merely an intermediate step but also expresses one variety of cosmopolitanism, which becomes the constant counterfoil for the rest of the dialogue. It is not out of evil intentions but practical necessity that the feverish city practices something we might call economic cosmopolitanism. This form of cosmopolitanism is easily paired with an imperialistic strategy. One may object that imperialistic cosmopolitanism is a *contradictio in adjecto*, as every variety of cosmopolitanism is opposed to aggressive

109 See the depiction of Socrates in Xenophon, *Memorabilia*, II.

110 For the Greeks, this materialistic genealogy of morals was arguably less surprising, since Greek mythology lacks the notion of an 'ideal' or 'innocent' beginning. Even the 'good and innocent' Horae (Eirene, Eunomia and Dike, i.e. peace, good order and justice) are fathered by Zeus, a god with questionable character and motives.

wars or violent takeovers. However, in these short passages, Plato presents a materialistic theory of the development of societies. Presumably, the feverish city will not regard itself as imperialistic but will sail under false colours, like Rome, thinking of itself as a republic with nothing more in mind than the moral improvement of the world. In terms of policy and outlook, this city resembles and satirises the politics of fourth century BCE Athens. Even modern historians have trouble keeping up with the many wars Athens fought or financed abroad, most of them arguably launched out of purely economic calculations. Nevertheless, the feverish city represents a precondition for the emergence of a warrior class that can subsequently be used to purge the city of all its ills. It is notable that Plato explicitly reserves the term polis, in the true sense of the word, for the purified city of warriors. Thus, the construction of the ideal polis can truly be seen as a response to two kinds of cosmopolitan pretensions, the 'healthy' cosmopolitanism of self-sustaining egalitarian communities and the 'feverish' cosmopolitanism of expanding empires.

Silencing the interlocutor: Philosophy as Wissenschaft

At this point, one might still think that exploiting possible cosmopolitan consequences of Plato's presentation is a far-fetched argument and that in presenting his ideal of the closed city, Plato did not overcome the cosmopolitans but simply ignored them. One might further reason that the model of a closed society has shaped philosophical discourse ever since, and Plato's theory has been an endlessly recurring subject of study for many generations of young students. However, this is not the way that the *Politeia* was always received over the course of the history of philosophy,[111] nor was it Plato's

[111] In modern times, reading the *Politeia* only became a part of classical education again in the nineteenth century. For the Anglophone world see Frank M. Turner, *The Greek Heritage in Victorian Britain* (New Haven, CT: Yale University Press, 1981), 369–446. For a more comprehensive perspective of the reception of Plato throughout the nineteenth and twentieth centuries, see Tigerstedt, *Interpreting Plato* and on 'Classics' as an academic discipline forged by 'radical liberals' in nineteenth century Britain, Christopher Stray, *Classics Transformed: Schools, Universities, and Society in England, 1830–1960* (Oxford: Clarendon Press, 1991).

aim to propose an 'ideal theory' of a closed society that can then be applied to 'non-ideal circumstances'. The model of the city is only one part of a dialogue that is, once again, filled with implicit references to other ideas and to other Platonic dialogues.

So, what can we make of Plato's construction of the ideal city? One way to approach this is to ask why anyone, especially his cosmopolitan contemporaries, should be convinced by Plato's construction. In the dramatisation of the argument, it is striking that Socrates repeatedly takes pleasure in upsetting his interlocutors by piling one apparently 'absurd' detail upon another (e.g., men and women practicing together naked, V 457b), yet his interlocutors remain silent for the rest of the dialogue. Could they not have responded to Socrates' suggestions or, in their best sophistic manner, let the weaker case appear stronger? In what sense, then, is the *Politeia* intended as a philosophical exploration of justice in distinction to a sophistic shortcut?

These questions can be answered by following the course of the dialogue. Socrates complains jokingly that he has to overcome three waves of attacks: first justifying the equality of men and women, second the community of men and women, and third the philosopher's rule (V 473c). Before he started with this line of argument, he had to be forced to continue in a way that echoed the introductory scene. The question is: what do these stages, so clearly marked, signify? This is a far-reaching question, since Socrates would seem to have already finished his task of explaining the analogy of city and soul at the end of Book IV. What do these additional elements – the equality and community of men and women, and especially the education of philosophers – tell us?

One way to evaluate Plato's theory would be to ask whether the analogy of city and soul is convincing, taking the fully developed city as Plato's definite model.[112] However, this reading would not explain the function of the argument with regard to other 'sophistic' approaches. The *Politeia*

112 See Williams, 'The Analogy of City and Soul', 196–206 and for a detailed defence of Plato's idea, Otfried Höffe, 'Zur Analogie von Individuum und Polis', in Otfried Höffe, ed., *Platon. Politeia* (Berlin: Akademie, 1997), 84–93.

would then appear as just one theory among many, and, due to its complicated multi-layered structure, not even a particularly convincing one. It is thus easy to imagine that neither the modern-day reader nor the reader in Plato's world would be ready to buy into the argument. If Plato's aim was to propose the ideal of a constitution for a city with oligarchic tendencies, then why did he present his claims in this way? Furthermore, what is the source of his confidence that there is nothing a sophist could say against it?

We find the answer to the second part of the question, the basis for Plato's confidence, in the form of an assertion: unlike the sophist, the philosopher is defined as the one who can distinguish between mere opinion and (true) knowledge (V 476c–480a). Thus, Plato is confident that he is the first person to practice philosophy as a *Wissenschaft*[113] (i.e., to seek knowledge in a comprehensive and systematic way; VI 486e). The philosopher is the person who realises that everything that has been presented thus far is connected and who doesn't stop their quest before grasping the truth entirely (VI 485b).

However, providing a specific definition of philosophy does not prove that such a thing really exists. Anyone could make the same claim, including Plato's opponents, and state that their view is *Wissenschaft* as well. We should recall that the sophists were not just political journalists and orators but also taught science (e.g., astronomy, mathematics or musical theory), and some, like Protagoras, had ideas about linguistics as well. It is particularly instructive to realise that Plato concedes this point, not only that such a dispute exists, but also that philosophy as *Wissenschaft* has no conclusive means to stop this discussion. In the *Politeia*, the dispute is referred to in Book VI, just before the allegories that culminate in the ascent from the cave are presented. Here, there are oblique references to all of Plato's contemporary opponents, including the cosmopolitans, and it is at this point in the dialogue that the distinctive feature of Plato's philosophy is introduced, enclosed in the allegory of the cave.

113 The German term *Wissenschaft* is used since it is a generic term for the natural and social sciences plus humanities (*Naturwissenschaften* and *Geisteswissenschaften*), including theology as one of the *Geisteswissenschaften*.

After refuting the sophists, and after developing the analogy of city and soul, Socrates still concedes that 'the many' will be unable to distinguish the true philosopher from false sophists. On the contrary, the many will falsely blame philosophers for pupils who turn out badly (VI 487c–d), when in fact those pupils were taught by sophists. Moreover, Socrates points out that there are teachers or intellectuals (easily identified as Gorgias and Isocrates) who claim to be philosophers and even use a technique of argumentation that resembles philosophical practice, although it consists only of hair-splitting, stubbornness and pointless quarrels (VI 498e–499a). Even Thrasymachus is briefly mentioned as a possible opponent, though not allowed to speak for himself (VI 497d). Of course, Socrates' assurance that 'Thrasymachus has become his friend' and is therefore only listening obsequiously is ironic. In real life, Thrasymachus would join the cosmopolitan-minded sophists while attacking the philosopher from the other side. At this point, Plato also explains that even the very best philosophical nature can go astray by trying to mind the business of 'both Hellenes and barbarians' (VI 494c). Plato thus explicitly introduces a cosmopolitan opponent, even granting that they might have a good philosophical nature, but insisting that, like all the sophists, rhetoricians and historians, they are fundamentally mistaken.

It is pointless to speculate about exactly whom Plato had in mind as this opponent. It may not even be a real person, and Plato may simply be raising the systematic possibility of a cosmopolitan position that is characterised by 'minding the business of Hellenes and barbarians'. Thus, after having presented his 'theory', Plato grants someone could respond to it in the style of a 'liberal' cosmopolitan – but they would not be counted among the philosophers.

However, we are still left with the problem of how to explain the distinction between the true *philosophous* and false *philodoxous* (V 480a). Plato's claim is that philosophy is a fundamentally different kind of endeavour. Therefore, what Plato develops is not an anti-cosmopolitan theory; this would presume that there are two kinds of theory, one cosmopolitan and one anti-cosmopolitan, and that both can argue for their claims on an even playing field. Plato takes the discussion beyond this stage, so he is not anti-cosmopolitan but uber-cosmopolitan. How can this position be achieved?

Plato's uber-cosmopolitan turn: The path to metaphysics

This step is again marked by the motif of holding on to the philosopher (VI 505a). Plato shows that the way to get to philosophy as *Wissenschaft* is in the form of a simple question, namely, after justice has been introduced and explained, asking: 'But is it really good?' (VI 506a). This question sounds simple but is in fact very powerful, for it requires digging into the foundations of one's own theory. The question insists on inquiring whether the theory is based only on sentiments we may have at a certain moment in history or on the latest 'score' in an on-going sophistic quarrel. Alternatively, the theory could explain its own relationship to its time and surrounding world in such a way as to let us understand ourselves and others in a more comprehensive (Plato would say dialectical) way. Plato's strategy is to demarcate philosophy from sophistic theories by asking the additional question 'is it really good?' and, while answering the question, providing his theory with a deeper foundation, a foundation that can in retrospect be called 'metaphysical' (VI 506a). But what exactly is this 'metaphysical' foundation that is prompted by the quest for the good? At first, Plato only offers the criterion that there must be some overall systematic interconnection, names a method (dialectic) and then goes on to introduce his famous allegories (the sun, the line, and the cave). What Plato is doing in these examples is not introducing a positive theory of metaphysics but instead demonstrating a practice that has already informed the whole dialogue, albeit subliminally. Plato's allegories provide us with an answer to why Plato presents his theory in this particular way, even though he knows that it will be unconvincing (for sophists). He presents his theory in this way because he wants to demonstrate that, above all, philosophy is something that has to be practiced among like-minded people.

It is notoriously difficult to explain what exactly Plato's 'metaphysical' theory is, in particular, the specific nature of the highest good and how it relates to the theory of ideas, which Plato frequently mentions but never really explains. In the *Politeia*, Socrates remarks incidentally 'let's leave aside for the time being what the good itself is' (VI 506e) (and this time nobody holds him back!). One could, of course, explain Plato's theory of ideas as well as possible, examine the historical critique and ask whether the theory is convincing. However, the same question would appear again: why does Plato present the 'metaphysical' theory in this way? This question is further reinforced when Socrates admits in the dialogue that the highest ideas cannot be grasped by everyone (at least not by Glaucon) or even be fully explained (VI 506b–507a). The Plato of the seventh letter even states explicitly: 'there neither is nor will ever be a treatise of mine on this subject.'[114]

Given our reading up to this point, Plato's confession may seem particularly disappointing. He has omitted a more detailed institutional exposition of the best city and a defence against rival theories by suggesting a deeper foundation – and now, this deeper foundation has turned out to be elusive. However, Plato's metaphysics is not simply an artfully constructed mysticism aimed at concealing his outright oligarchic leanings.[115] Instead, he has introduced us to a certain kind of questioning.

Paideia as incessant exercise

After sketching out the allegory of the cave, Plato presents a second education programme (*paideia*), this time not for all guardians but only for the philosopher. As illustrated by the allegory, the objective is to 'turn the soul around' and 'guide it from becoming to being'. (VII 521c–d). Plato explains that there are different ways that lead to this kind of questioning, and thus the question about the highest good is not the only way into philosophy. Plato starts with arithmetic and

[114] Epistles 7.341c. These passages are central for the claim of the Tübingen school of interpretation, that Plato has an 'unwritten doctrine'. I make the more modest point that within the *Politeia*, a central doctrine is either not elaborated upon or explained in an indirect way.

[115] Hans Kelsen makes this point most forcefully in his meticulous interpretation of the *Politeia*. Unlike Popper, he holds, as a legal positivist, that all accounts of justice are illusions and takes Plato as proof of his thesis. See Hans Kelsen, *Die Illusion der Gerechtigkeit. Eine kritische Untersuchung der Sozialphilosophie Platons*, ed. Kurt Ringhofer and Robert Walter (Wien: Manz, 1985), 335–76.

then proceeds through various disciplines (VII 522b–531c). The main idea is always the same and may be explained by using the example of arithmetic. The technique of calculating numbers for practical purposes was already known in Mesopotamia and Egypt. However, it was the Greek mathematicians who realised that it was also possible to ask purely theoretical questions about arithmetic (VII 525c). We might argue that, with his discussion of arithmetic (VII 522b–526c), Plato suggests that the way we conceive of numbers (in modern terminology: following the logicistic or intuitionistic programme) has consequences for the way we recognise ourselves and our relation to the world.[116] Therefore arithmetic is 'one of those things we are seeking that by nature lead to intellection' (VII 523a). A detailed engagement with the philosophy of mathematics is not required here, but it may be worth pointing out that similar questions were asked again only during the foundational crisis in mathematics that occurred at the beginning of the twentieth century. In any case, the ensuing question of why the physical world is ordered according to mathematical laws in the first place and how we can have access to both worlds has certainly not been 'solved by modern science'.[117]

Plato thus does not make claims based on shaky mysticism but instead provides examples for the kinds of proof and discussion he thinks about. He also offers a criterion for how research ought to be conducted, by looking for systematic coherence among all the sciences that are jointly illuminated by the *agathon*. Systematic coherence is thus a criterion for philosophy as *Wissenschaft*, but coherence is not the sole or principal criterion. If this were so, Plato's theory would be similar to the natural sciences, where the challenge is to assemble different building blocks in the best possible way. The important feature of philosophy as *Wissenschaft* is the

[116] For a reconstruction of Plato's view of mathematics in contemporary terms, see Vittorio Hösle, 'Zu Platons Philosophie der Zahlen und deren mathematischer und philosophischer Bedeutung', in *Platon interpretieren*, ed. Otfried Höffe (Paderborn: Schöningh, 2004), 138–43.

[117] This question has been explicitly asked this way by Kant. Roger Penrose tackles it from the point of view of contemporary physics, see Roger Penrose, *Shadows of the Mind* (Oxford: Oxford University Press, 1994).

practice to which it belongs, namely the dialectical education of the philosopher.

> Only the dialectical way of inquiry proceeds in this direction, destroying the hypotheses, to the beginning itself in order to make it secure; and when the eye of the soul is really buried in a barbaric bog, dialectic gently draws it forth and leads it up above, using the arts we described as assistants and helpers in the turning around (VII 533d).

Instead of presenting a 'theory of everything', Plato demonstrates how philosophy proceeds as a dialectical discipline that has its ultimate end in the *paideia*, the formation or redirection of the philosophical soul.

Summary

I have avoided presenting Plato's 'doctrinal metaphysics' and only briefly discussed his 'political theory' because my main point was to show how Plato first took up the cosmopolitan sentiments and then overcame them. The common assumption of Plato developing a theory of a closed society that became influential has turned out to be overly simple. Even the answer we have now come to, that the clue to Plato's philosophy is providing his political theory with a 'metaphysical' foundation, which in turn serves an educational end, only explains some things but does not answer everything. It explains that Plato's typology of political systems in Book VIII is not intended as a rudimentary form of political science but rather, as indicated through the introduction ('let the Muses tell us'), a playful ironic enactment of how such a science might proceed (VIII 545e). Simply collecting constitutions would be an important task but would not begin to exhaust what philosophy is about. Only if we made it part of a complete system (as an ideal) would it lead us to understand ourselves and others.[118] The Myth of Er at the end of Book X is also a way of opening the text up to a dialogue with religious ways of thought. Finally, the harsh ban on the arts (X 595a–608b) may serve to remind the reader that

[118] This does not mean that philosophy has to be presented as a system.

cultural dispositions can be changed in principle, even if they are deep-seated at a particular historical moment. However, there are also totalitarian tendencies, and the history of Plato's reception and influence reveals that different aspects of his thought have dominated the discussion at different times over the course of the centuries.[119]

4. The *Politeia* in the Hellenic world

4.1 Plato's tragic worldview

The present interpretation raises another question: why did Plato not develop his own 'uber-cosmopolitan' theory, including a 'metaphysical' basis, and explain how it related to the Hellenic world? His openness to influences from other cultures, his awareness of cultural relativity and even the dialectical method all seem to point in this direction. Moreover, he not only addresses Athenians but the learned audience all over the Hellenic world. It was noted earlier that even the writers of Plato's inauthentic letters had this point in mind.

One answer is given by Plato himself: He constantly stressed that only 'the few' would be able to grasp the idea of philosophy (VI 494a). This assumption may in itself result in an oligarchic view, but it would not preclude developing a Panhellenic or cosmopolitan perspective, perhaps by elevating Athens as the 'leader of the free world'. However, in Plato the oligarchic view is sustained by a tragic idea of history. It is best captured in his allegory of the two ages introduced in the *Statesman*.[120]

In this allegory, Plato draws on motifs from different traditions – the reversal of the course of the universe, the golden time, the clash between two gods, and so on – to sketch a dark image of the state of man. In the golden time, people lived lives

[119] The historical awareness that Plato is always 'our' Plato but not the 'real historical one' is already present in Nietzsche's lectures on Plato from his time as a classicist in Basel (1871/72). See Friedrich Nietzsche, 'Plato amicus sed. Einleitung in das Studium der platonischen Dialoge', in *Werke. Kritische Gesamtausgabe*, part 2, vol. 4, ed. Franco Bornmann and Michele Carpitella (Berlin: Walter de Gruyter, 1995).

[120] *Statesman*, 268d–274e.

of paradise under the rule of the gods, didn't have to bother about food, housing or clothes 'for the climate was tempered for their comfort'.[121] They were born asexually as old people and became younger over the course of their lives. When the gods abandoned their reign, the world became like a ship whose steersman had let go of the helm so that the ship was tossed about with no direction and ultimately doomed to be shipwrecked. During this time people began to procreate, were born young and had to work for their food. Our time and our world are thus not the 'natural', or even a good course of the world but are the 'unnatural', reversed course that is doomed.

In this allegory, the contrast between the soul (or the world of ideas) and the body (or the physical world) is pictured as a contrast in time between an earlier state of the world and the present condition. There is nothing in this world or our course of time that is worth preserving, and our only hope is that the gods will take up the helm again to rescue the ship from the surrounding horrors of nature. The allegory depicts Plato's tragic view of the course of the world. It is not just that some people or political regimes are unjust, or some practices should be reformed, it is the trajectory of the world that is wrong. Only if someone with a god-like soul assumed total power over a people and reversed the entire order of things might it become possible to save the world by setting an example.

It should be noted that in Plato's allegory, the backward course of the world could be purposefully changed, and so there is no eternal battle between two principles, nor the view that good and evil are equiprimordial or, as Plato refers to it, that both good and evil are given by the gods (II 389c).[122] In Plato, the 'enlightened' hope that the world can be changed is pushed to its extreme, for even fundamental aspects of the human condition, such as the incest taboo, are depicted as alterable through education.[123] On the one hand,

[121] *Statesman*, 272a.

[122] Plato struggles with how to describe the relation of good and evil throughout his life, see *Theaetetus*, 176a, where evil appears to have an existence of its own.

[123] The speculations about 'totalitarian' transformations of human nature may serve as a reminder that all empirical studies of happiness depend upon some fundamental, though alterable, social concepts.

philosophy presumes an enormous imaginative power and, by its ability to transform the individual soul to go against various bodily leanings, an enormous erotic power as well. On the other hand, it is hard to conceive of philosophy's fundamental activity as being nothing less than the saviour of mankind when its highest aim, conceiving the good, cannot be 'properly' defined, taught as a technique or even written down as a normative guideline. Instead, philosophy appears to be an evasive practice, and even a modern-day reader is never quite certain whether they are in the philosophical mode seeking insight or just caught up in one of Plato's traps.[124]

4.2 The impossibility of a normative theory for the real world

Again, it would be possible to pursue this line of thought further and try to make sense of Plato's critique of writing and elusive presentation of the highest ideas.[125] However, the aim of the inquiry was to show why Plato did not simply state his 'uber-cosmopolitan theory on metaphysical grounds'. Yet reflecting on Plato's presentation of the practice of philosophy draws the reader to the brink of mysticism while revealing a limitation of Plato's philosophy. There is one thing that can be said with certainty about the way Plato conceives of the practice of philosophy: One must have a teacher, and, to be precise, not just any teacher, but Socrates as a teacher. Philosophy is not an activity everyone can practice in isolation, learn from books or from different teachers, but is instead a practice that requires initiation. For the way Plato brought philosophy to the world, it is not an unhappy fact that Socrates was already dead at the time, but a necessary precondition. When Plato wrote his dialogues, no one

[124] To cite but one example: the cast in the *Parmenides* resembles the one in the *Politeia* except that it has no connection to the matters discussed in the dialogue, and instead of Socrates the narrator is Antiphon, an ordinary horse breeder. It is as if Plato wanted to poke fun at my elaborate interpretation of the *Politeia's* opening scene.

[125] *Phaedrus* 278 b8–e4. Plato's critique of writing and his mysticism are explained in the seventh letter. Even if it is not genuine, it shows that there have been, since ancient times, central problems to each Plato interpretation.

could ask the historical Socrates, 'what do you think about this?' or 'Plato wrote this, do you agree with it?' Thus, the Platonic pathway to philosophical education never allows for competing opinions of equal standing. If the dialogues do not end in an aporia, there is always one superior educating the other. Moreover, real insights are often postponed, withheld or, as with Socrates in the *Symposium*, uttered in someone else's name.

In terms of real-world politics, concentrating on one mythical founding figure together with the establishment of an institution to guarantee the authenticity of interpretation can easily be translated into a claim for leadership of the Platonic Academy.[126] Real insight can only be found there and requires secret initiation. However, due to the lack of direct evidence, particularly any evidence from Plato himself, our characterisation of the Platonic Academy must remain vague and is only useful for explaining its historical context. Yet the evasive reverence of an undefined centre is a feature of Plato's philosophy that has consequences for its reception. One could say that, just as there can be only one initiated philosophical practice, there can only be one *Kallipolis*.

This is an important finding for the present interpretation of Plato as an uber-cosmopolitan philosopher. From Plato's point of view, one could grant that the whole Hellenic world serves as a backdrop or sounding board, more explicitly, that Panhellenic or cosmopolitan views are part of that intellectual universe. Plato might even acknowledge that, at some time or in some place, democratic forms of government might turn out to be beneficial or that the formation of federal alliances might be necessary for economic or military reasons. However, from Plato's point of view, all these aspects of Hellenic political life, in which we may recognise

[126] The description of the life of a real philosopher (VI 496b–497a) can be read as alluding to the Academy, with the 'great soul' (Socrates) as founder and Plato himself among those 'coming from another art' (drama). Winspear suggests that 'the Academy was first of all a political organization', Alban Dewes Winspear, *The Genesis of Plato's Thought*, 2nd ed. (New York: Russell, 1956), 306. Kai Trampedach's finding that the Academy did not in fact play this role does not disprove the thesis that it might originally have been conceived this way. See Trampedach, *Platon*, 278–83.

ourselves and our contemporary world, would be completely irrelevant as long as they lacked philosophy. It is for this reason that Plato does not find it necessary to explicitly refute cosmopolitan theories or engage in debates with democratic or cosmopolitan views, since no debates of this kind can ever be on equal terms but at best will only serve as preliminary or educational discussions, leading to the point of view of real insight.

4.3 The internal limits of Plato's challenge

Plato confronts us with the tragic choice of either continuing with sophistic, historical or rhetorical quarrels, which may please our materialistic inclinations and sophistic prejudices, or trying to overcome those prejudices by delving into the very foundations of being (*agathon*). However, in order to do this, we have to first accept the leadership of Socrates. Accepting Socrates' leadership might appear to be a small price to pay, since he never required (qua Platonic personae) blind obedience but demonstrated what philosophical reversion of life through insight means.

Yet, the figure of Socrates reveals a systematic weakness in Plato's position. He uses Socrates as an indispensable intermediary for finding the way through the intricate practice of philosophy, but he never explains how the man, Socrates, could have arisen in the first place.[127] If everyone needs guidance from the initiated, there needs to be a first initiator, someone who initiated himself or who gained insight from himself. We might therefore ask how the Athenian citizen Socrates could ever become the philosopher Socrates, and why self-recognition should be confined to the case of Socrates, who then must serve as a 'medium' for everyone else. Perhaps Plato implicitly acknowledged this problem in his later dialogues, when the younger Socrates or the Athenian stranger led the discussion. However, these figures form at least a literary continuum with the Socrates of earlier dialogues.

It might be at this juncture that one could challenge Plato's illusion that initiation through discipleship with

[127] Socrates' short autobiographical remark in *Phaedo* 96a–102a is not helpful to this end.

Socrates is a necessary condition for practising philosophy. One could imagine a dialogue between Socrates and the Athenian stranger, in which the protagonists have different backgrounds and disagree about some questions. This dialogue would have moved towards and even necessitated a reflection on the self-formation and the relationships between those two. However, a dialogue of this kind is conspicuously missing.[128] In Plato, the *paideia* (philosophical formation of body and soul) is limited to the teacher–pupil relationship and never happens between two people of equal standing who are both philosophers in the best sense. This also has important political consequences, in Plato's terminology, consequences for the way we conceive the individual soul or the individual city.

Plato invented philosophy as a giant vortex that readily draws bits and pieces from all sides into itself. Even though nearly all topics of philosophical discourse are presented dialectically – thus in a way that is not just a statement, position or claim but a short dialogue in its own right – and even though there is a drift towards the good as an unascertainable centre and a corresponding urge to watch the formation of other souls, there is ultimately a strange disregard of individual human beings. For the most part, they are referred to as sheep, dogs or puppets that need to be formed. Similarly, other cities appear only as external threats or resources for practical studies but never as possible philosophical sites in their own right. One could say that the internal limit that precludes Plato from developing the idea of a Hellenic commonwealth of independent cities is a philosophical one. Plato expressed philosophy by dramatising the person of Socrates, thus demonstrating a particular form of philosophical practice, but he failed to develop the underlying principle that would allow us to conceptualise the relationship between different individuals as subjects, or between different autonomous cities in a commonwealth.

[128] Thomas Szlezák makes the same observation but offers a different explanation. He argues that such a debate would have inevitably led to a discussion about first principles, a doctrine Plato wanted to confine to his esoteric teaching. See Thomas Szlezák, *Platon lesen* (Stuttgart: Frommann-Holzboog, 1993), 144.

5. Plato's challenge today

This chapter began by suggesting that current liberal convictions that appear to lead naturally to cosmopolitan theory or a theory of global justice are not as firmly grounded as one might think and that ancient thought might serve as a mirror of the current discourse. The challenge presented in this way – challenge understood as both provocation and trial – is that the fronts have turned around. The ancient philosophical tradition does not merely represent a pre-cosmopolitan junior stage but instead turns out to be a trap for ancient cosmopolitan sentiments. Since ancient thought is not merely history 'over and forgotten' but a constant companion of modern thinking, this reflection shows that political philosophy has lost its innocence and challenges the self-evidence of its alliance with the 'noble cause' of cosmopolitanism. If we want to accept Plato's suggestion that philosophy may show us a way out of sophistic quarrels by providing us with a foundation and a more dialectical or comprehensive understanding of ourselves and others, we must also face up to the totalitarian 'spell of Plato'. We cannot respond to it by simply reaffirming contemporary liberal convictions,[129] but we must tackle the philosophical problems left over by Plato.

Obviously, the aim has not been to provide answers to contemporary problems, let alone offer normative recommendations about how to build a just world but rather to explore the dimensions of the question of a cosmopolitan order. The aim was not to argue in favour of a 'history of the decay of liberalism' or to pinpoint 'the ancients' or 'the true Plato' against 'the moderns' but to open up a new kind of discourse. Plato's 'metaphysics' has not been defended here – no 'way out of the cave', so to speak, has been indicated – but illuminated it in a different light so that a desire to leave it may arise.

Instead, the chapter has sought to bring the philosophical tradition invoked by Heidegger and his descendants from

[129] In a footnote to his chapter on Plato, Popper proves his liberal confidence in social contract theory by claiming that the 'engineering problems' of securing international peace and preventing human rights violations are 'really not so difficult once they are squarely and rationally faced'. Popper, *Open Society*, 113.

various camps into a different dialogue with contemporary discussion on cosmopolitanism. Plato is an obvious starting point when arguing with the philosophical tradition, yet it turned out that he could also reflect and reveal the limits of the contemporary discussion. To this end, a specific interpretive scheme has been employed. Instead of presuming that Plato was the first to establish timeless 'summit conversations', Plato has been contextualised as a political actor along the lines of the Cambridge School. It turned out that in the political developments of the fourth century BCE and the ideas discussed at the time, parallels to the contemporary discussion can be found.

Freedom and equality were the buzzwords of the democratic party, and the formation of federal regimes or broader alliances to secure peace, foster trade and deter the common enemies of mankind (mercenaries) were discussed and (to some degree) realised in some instances. This common-sense approach, which can be detected in the writings of sophists, historians and rhetoricians, has striking similarities to contemporary convictions. That the focus of the Greek authors was not the physical globe but the whole civilised world, with some ambiguities towards Persia, is a minor technicality, but no difference in principle. For this reason, it was possible to invite the global ethicist to Cephalus's dinner party. However, the conversation quickly turned to topics and proceeded in ways that cannot be found in contemporary cosmopolitan debates. Already the first round of questions turned to topics that appear too fundamental or metaphysical to contemporary minds (personal salvation after death), and other propositions are even too radical (that the just man is the happiest man) and some proposals too far-fetched (the dissolution of the primary family and of private property). Most importantly, however, there was little in the form of 'proper' normative arguments about why the institutions are just and not a single global or Panhellenic institution was mentioned. So, the whole endeavour of the *Politeia* might disappoint the expectations of a global ethicist, in particular when realising that, at Plato's time, the proto-cosmopolitan question loomed in the background of Plato's argument.

However, because of the dual perspective from today's expectations and the historical context, Plato's strategy and his account of philosophy becomes decipherable in a new way. The reason Plato did not discuss politics and political institutions in a more detailed way, as one might expect from a treaty about politics, was that his tragic view of history as an irrational occurrence and his ultimate interest in philosophy as *Wissenschaft* were achievable only through self-formation (*paideia*). The global ethicist present at the discussion would have had an uncomfortable position. On the one hand, they would claim to present the only reasonable position that can be defended against all forms of traditional or old moralities, while on the other hand they would refuse to engage with or answer any of Socrates' questions due to their being beside the point or not relevant in contemporary cosmopolitanism. All of Socrates' questions would have to be qualified as inadmissible: personal salvation, radical evil, eschatology (the end of all things), or searching for the ultimate good or knowledge are off-limits in a contemporary liberal philosophical discourse (this displays an uncanny similarity of the contemporary ethicist with the sophists who also accused Socrates of posing false questions). However, after passing through the *Politeia*, the premises of the global ethicist, freedom and equality on a global scale, are anything but self-evident. It could even be the other way round, as freedom and equality do feature in Plato's account but not vice versa. Even worse, Plato could turn the table and claim that for responding to the premises and claims of the global ethicist, he would not have to change or add a single word to the *Politeia* but start the discourse in the way Socrates started it, asking: so how is sex life in old age? If the respondent stays with Socrates as Glaucon did, they will be led into the same abyss and out again.

One might object that the position of the global ethicist has been presented in a reductive way as each of Plato's claims can be refuted, as subsequent philosophy has shown, starting with Aristotle. However, the question raised by pinpointing the global ethicist against Plato cannot simply be outsourced to the history department as if the assignment was to explain the functioning of an intercontinental rocket to the ignorant old Greek. What is at stake is the legitimacy of modernity. This is not a historical but a historicist question, as it is based on the observation that there is no natural progress in the history of ideas but that each epoch can be 'immediate to

God' while the order of time has no special claim. By putting the global ethicist literally in Glaucon's shoes, we can imagine that defending today's presuppositions is not an easy task, especially since the immoralist (and his modern heirs) are on the same plane. We can now also see why a genealogy of cosmopolitan thought is not an enumeration of cosmopolitan positions throughout history. Once the historicist stage has been reached, historical time as a sequence of objective facts is no longer an answer, as we are interested in those aspects of history that form our identity.

That the objective sequence of time does not suffice as an answer is, by the way, also a Platonic insight. He alluded to it by inventing the myth of the wrong turn of the world, thereby showing that everything, including the sequence of time, can be turned around in thinking.[130] So how can we respond to Plato in a way that explains the legitimacy of modernity, and thus also explains contemporary presuppositions? I propose two approaches: first by introducing the principle of modernity – subjectivity – and second by reflecting on the structure of modernity – the modern law. Both of these terms are title words that stand for a cluster of intellectual developments or philosophical traditions. Rather than discuss their central tenets in an abstract way, The analysis returns to the Cambridge School approach and examines how Plato's challenge can be met through a contextualised reading of Kant and Kelsen.

Kant's account is at the heart of most contemporary cosmopolitan theories. But it would be fainthearted to make a bold leap of two hundred years and ignore the philosophical and political developments in between. In Heidegger's reading, Kant's categorical imperative ends in an existential decision. Kelsen (as a post-Nietzschean sceptic) acknowledges this position but shows that a pure theory of positive law is nevertheless possible and can (within limits, as the following discussion will show) have a reconciliatory effect. Kant's philosophy and Kelsen's legal theory are therefore crucial turning points in understanding the predicament in which we find ourselves.

[130] Plato, *Statesman* 268d–274e.

Two

Kant and the End(s) of Cosmopolitanism

> Dulce et decorum est pro patria mori.
>
> (Horace)

> Es ist doch süß, sich Staatsverfassungen auszudenken.[1]
>
> (Kant)

Drawing on Kant in a genealogy of cosmopolitan thought is, from today's point of view, a self-evident point of reference. Yet the path to this conclusion has been far from straightforward. We have embarked on the genealogical reflection after realising that cosmopolitanism has come under pressure not just for the contingencies of history but also intellectually. Through various transformations, the grand philosophical tradition culminating in Heidegger turns out to be its nemesis.

Through a contextualised reading of Plato, we found a way to show how contemporary questions of cosmopolitan justice can have a bearing on the understanding of Plato's *Politeia*. In this way, we found an approach to Plato that is independent of a Heideggerian reading of the metaphysical tradition. Nonetheless, the contextualised approach has even increased our worries, as Plato shows, through his spokesman Socrates, of how the global ethicist can be drawn into metaphysical discussions which they are unwilling to face. Drawing on Kant then becomes a necessity for a different reason. It is not simply for giving contemporary convictions

[1] Horace: It is sweet and glorious to die for one's country (*Carmina* 3.2). Kant: It is so sweet minting constitutions (*The Conflict of the Faculties, SF* 7:929). For Kant, of course, everything 'sweet' is in any case a treacherous temptation.

a deeper or more reflective foundation but is also for deflecting the previous ancient discussion as well.[2]

Therefore, Kant is not just any predecessor in a long line of cosmopolitan authors but needs to be considered with regard to his central place in the discourse of modernity. However, since the dark sides of modernity need to be reckoned as well, and since only the contextual reading of Plato has brought us into the correct vein, Kant will be introduced in a specific way.

We cannot presume that, after a 200-year dogmatic slumber, Kant suddenly appears as an honorary member in today's philosophical discussions on cosmopolitanism while ignoring Plato's challenge or the later transformations of the German Idealist tradition leading up to Heidegger. Neither can we take the liberal tradition from Kant to Rawls and Habermas for granted as the only point of reference, nor the philosophical summit conversation across time and space that, in a liberal disguise, always leads to laudable ends.

Instead, our reading of Kant will be guided by these questions: How can it be said that the legitimacy of modernity can only be explained with Kant? In which respect is he situated, and does he respond to the circumstances of his world? In which respect are these still our circumstances, the circumstances of modernity? And what happened between Kant and the rebirth of political philosophy in 1971?

These questions will be tackled in the following five sections. We will start by asking, following the lead of the Cambridge School, whether the historical-political context can help to explain the political intervention Kant wanted to make, or – to use Collingwood's terminology – to search for the historical question a philosophical treatise is meant to answer. We will see that even though political activism would have been possible in Königsberg, Kant had a different challenge in mind, namely, to respond to a Platonic

[2] On the limits of Stoic cosmopolitanism from a contemporary Kantian perspective, see Martha Nussbaum, 'Kant and Stoic Cosmopolitanism', *The Journal of Political Philosophy* 5, no. 1 (1997): 1–25. For her traditional overview of cosmopolitan positions throughout history see Martha Nussbaum, *The Cosmopolitan Tradition: A Noble but Flawed Ideal* (Cambridge, MA: Harvard University Press, 2019).

revival (1). In order to understand Kant's response, we will delve into his critical philosophy and consider his 'empirical science of knowing' (*Welt- und Menschenkenntnis*) as developed in his popular lectures as a counterpart. In this way, another leading question, besides the one about the political character of Kant's philosophy, will emerge: the question concerning the unity of reason (2). Kant's political philosophy will turn out to be entangled with systematic problems and limited to the role of an applied doctrine of right. This result can be confirmed with the essay *Towards Perpetual Peace (ZeF)* (3). However, in the closely related area of rational theology, we find Kant taking an active political role and envisioning a perspective akin to moral cosmopolitanism. Yet, while Kant develops an ideology critique of all established institutions in his treatise on religion, taking historical churches as a model, Kant turns out to be another nemesis of contemporary cosmopolitanism (4). This challenging reading is underscored by realising that Heidegger proposed, in the 1920s and 30s, a compelling systematic reintegration of the various strands of Kant we have diagnosed (5).

1. Political context and the formation of a philosophical legacy

Even though contextual inquiries along the lines of the Cambridge School have yielded results in the English tradition of political thought, and we have seen that it can be fruitful in discussing Plato, it still might seem misplaced in Kant's case. A closer investigation of the historical and philosophical circumstances of Königsberg will reveal that a political existence would have been available to Kant. However, he rejected it for reasons made explicit in his moral philosophy. Moreover, an unscholarly yet existential assault on critical philosophy urged Kant to take up Plato's question of how to keep philosophy alive as an unearthing and self-critical practice. The contextual reading will not in itself yield results that can immediately be exploited for drawing contemporary lessons or assessing Kant from today's perspective (e.g. condemning him as a racist, sexist or a logocentric imperialist) but instead set the stage for a more comprehensive and fundamental reading along the lines of Heidegger.

1.1 Kant as a political actor

When Kant died in 1804 in Königsberg, it was not necessary to mention in obituaries that he had almost single-handedly established German as a philosophical language and changed the face of philosophy in the world.[3] The contributions of Fichte, Schelling and Hegel in philosophy, and of Hölderlin and Schiller in poetry and literary theory, were already underway, and Kantian ideas dominated not only academic discussions across the German-speaking world but also exerted influence among theologians, public officials and the emerging bourgeois public sphere.[4] Yet this intellectual revolution had begun only in the mid-1780s, when the *Critique of Pure Reason* finally received wider attention and took the German-speaking philosophical world by storm. Only a decade after the first critique's publication, the French Revolution swept away – just as Kant had done in the realm of reason – all traditional institutions, incidentally, undermining the idea of the naturalness of the *ancien régime*. These two revolutions, given their transformative depth and lasting legacy, were improbable and unforeseen in the context of early eighteenth-century Europe.

Since Heinrich Heine's *History of Religion and Philosophy in Germany*,[5] it has become common wisdom to relate both revolutions and continue Heine's narrative: that Kant, in the realm of the spirit, achieved what the French had in the material, practical world. The problem of this line of interpretation is that Kant is taken out of the political and social context of early eighteenth-century Prussia, situated instead in a timeless realm of reason and judged from the basis of modern, liberal, egalitarian premises.

[3] See Friedrich Wilhelm Joseph von Schelling, 'Nachruf Immanuel Kant', in *Sämtliche Werke*, I, 6:3–10 (Stuttgart and Augsburg: J. G. Cotta, 1860). On the reception of Kant's ideas in his last years, see Manfred Kuehn, *Kant: A Biography* (Cambridge: Cambridge University Press, 2001), 415–22.

[4] Jürgen Habermas's account of the genesis of the public sphere is largely modelled on Kant. The relation to Kant's philosophy will be discussed later, in Section 4.2.

[5] Heinrich Heine, *On the History of Religion and Philosophy in Germany and Other Writings* (1835), ed. Terry Pinkard, trans. Howard Pollack-Milgate (Cambridge: Cambridge University Press, 2007).

If we follow the lead of the Cambridge School, according to which political thought should be understood as an intervention in the lived reality, we must examine in greater detail the circumstances of eighteenth-century Prussia and Königsberg. At first sight, however, an apparent obstacle emerges to this project. In all biographies of Kant, his upbringing, professional career, social life and the historical events of his lifetime are dutifully reported.[6] Yet, apart from a brief conflict with state censorship towards the end of his life,[7] Kant appears to have led the unpolitical life of an observer of politics, without engaging in daily political quarrels at all. The question raised by the Cambridge School about intervention in daily politics thus seems misplaced in Kant's case. A possible historical explanation for Kant's apparently unpolitical attitude could be that Königsberg – unlike ancient Athens, medieval Florence, or early modern London – was not a political and economic centre in its own right but rather a provincial town on the edge of Prussia. Moreover, Frederick the Great, the reigning king of Prussia during most of Kant's lifetime, was interested only in French philosophy and unaware of the developing German Enlightenment discourse. This explanation, however, reflects a modern perspective that takes states or nation-states as the sole relevant actors in history. A different story can be told when Königsberg is viewed as an imagined city-republic.

In the seventeenth century, Königsberg was the coronation site of the Duchy of Prussia (originally the name only of a region on the southeast coast of the Baltic Sea) and at the same time a city-republic with considerable autonomy, its own parliament and its own currency.[8] As regal authority over the city shifted frequently between Poland, Sweden and Brandenburg, the city magistrate was accustomed to negotiating with sovereigns over the city's rights and the sovereign's duties. Its citizenry displayed remarkable resistance to foreign domination, while relying on legal means to defend their liberties. One incident illustrates the form of civilian resistance

6 See the summary of earlier biographies in Kuehn, *Kant*, 4–16.

7 This episode will be discussed in more detail in Section 4.2.

8 The most detailed history of Königsberg is still Fritz Gause, *Die Geschichte der Stadt Königsberg in Preußen*, 3 vols. (Köln: Böhlau, 1965–71).

typical for Königsberg.[9] In 1633, the Prussian landed gentry demanded greater powers for their sovereign, the Elector of Brandenburg-Prussia, and attempted to establish an aristocratic republic similar to that in Poland. The city council of Königsberg resisted the gentry's demands, and the citizenry specifically refused to surrender serfs residing within the city to their feudal lords. A petition from 1639 to the Elector of Brandenburg-Prussia attests to the early modern civic spirit.[10]

> In Prussia all farmers enjoy personal freedom, have the right to move wherever they want, to study or learn a profession. ... However the nobility treats them as if they were wild beasts, making even the children work while giving them only poor food. [They behave like] the Pharaoh who had enslaved the children of Israel.[11]

Parallels to the Fugitive Slave Act of 1793 are striking. However, unlike the Fugitive Slave Act, the petition never became a political icon or received much attention from historians and can therefore only be cited as a trace of a political undercurrent in Königsberg.[12]

One might still think that the history of Königsberg is not relevant for an understanding of Kant, since he clearly turned a blind eye to the city's multicultural life. Instead, he had a clear vision of world politics, which remains most relevant to us today. Yet the written accounts by Kant are disappointing even here. An episode from the history of Königsberg might serve to explain this.

During the Seven Years War (1756–1763) fought between Prussia and Austria, with Britain supporting Prussia and

9 Jürgen Manthey, *Königsberg: Geschichte einer Weltbürgerrepublik* (München: Hanser, 2005), 63.

10 At the time, the notion of 'Bürger' (citizen) was associated with the inhabitant of a city.

11 See *Kurmärkische Ständeakten aus der Regierungszeit Kurfürst Joachims II.*, ed. Walter Friedensburg, vol. 1 (München: Duncker & Humblot, 1913), 36. See also Francis Carsten, *The Origins of Prussia* (Oxford: Clarendon Press, 1968), 131–32.

12 Jürgen Manthey has uncovered, in his ingenious intellectual history of Königsberg, the implicit correspondence between philosophers, writers, politicians and lawyers that persisted over centuries until 1933.

France and Russia supporting Austria, Königsberg was occupied for three years by Russian troops. Since the Prussian forces had been pulled out earlier to support campaigns in Silesia, the occupation took place peacefully as an administrative act. Flags, emblems and official portraits in administrative buildings were replaced, and the university professors swore allegiance to the new sovereign, but the rest of civic and social life proceeded normally.

The political significance of this episode is not restricted to the local circumstances of Königsberg. Indeed, the city was like the eye of a hurricane when the Seven Years War raged – the first global conflict to stretch across Europe and the overseas empires in North and South America, the Caribbean islands, the Philippines and coastal Africa (due to later national historiography, each conflict has its own name). Frederick the Great fought against the Austrian Emperor even though Frederick, as Elector of Brandenburg, was part of the German Empire. His aim was to redesign Europe in terms of a balance among the great powers. The British Crown financed Frederick's war as he kept French troops busy on the continent, troops unavailable to defend French territories in the New World and India. The writings of Frederick the Great show that he was well aware that his own pretensions in Silesia were only a small token in the world-historical play of the British Empire.

At this time, Kant was the implicit centre of Königsberg's intellectual circles and frequented the salons where he met officers, magistrates, merchants, aristocrats, fellow academics and private scholars. It is more than likely that world politics and the future of Königsberg were a topic of conversation.[13] However, in all of Kant's writings, including his private notes and letters, there is not a single word about the political circumstances of his own time. Instead, he regularly gave lectures on geography in which he speculated about the role of climate in the evolution of different races across the globe,

[13] We can get a glimpse of such discussions in civic circles through Johann Wolfgang von Goethe's lively account in his autobiography *Truth and Poetry: From My Own Life*, trans. John Oxenford (London: George Bell & Sons, 1884), 22–63.

customs in faraway countries and the hiding places of (as we know migrating) birds during the winter.

Thus, with Quentin Skinner's thesis in mind – that even the most abstract works of political theory are not general systems of ideas but polemical interventions in the ideological conflicts of their time, and never above the battle, but part of the battle itself[14] – Kant's political philosophy does not really fit this description, as it remains at a strange, otherworldly level. However, this is not due to some special character of German philosophy, as Kant's unusual form of unpolitical detachment was also noticed by his contemporaries.

This can best be shown by considering the example of one of Kant's closest associates, the mayor of Königsberg, Theodor Gottlieb von Hippel (1741–1796).[15] As a public official, he was a social reformer and helped transform the corrupt and inefficient city administration into a modern bureaucracy. At the same time, he anonymously published numerous novels, sketches and enlightened political pamphlets. In Emil Doerstling's picture of Kant's dinner table, he is shown as Kant's most prominent interlocutor, placed at the centre of the picture.[16] If we were to look in Königsberg at the time of Kant for someone who took keen interest in feasible social reforms of public administration, analysed the political circumstances of his time and championed enlightened causes in the manner of a modern public intellectual, we would find this person not in Kant but in von Hippel. Early on, he promoted not just a republican form of government but also argued that only actual democracies furthered public spirit and responsible citizens and referred to existing democracies like Switzerland or the newly founded United States as examples. Likewise, it was von Hippel and not Kant who promoted equal rights for women and argued in favour of full social equality including universal suffrage. In

[14] Quentin Skinner, *Hobbes and Republican Liberty* (Cambridge: Cambridge University Press, 2008), xvi.

[15] On von Hippel's life, see Joseph Kohnen, *Theodor Gottlieb von Hippel. Eine zentrale Persönlichkeit der Königsberger Geistesgeschichte: Biographie und Bibliographie* (Lüneburg: Verlag Nordostdeutsches Kulturwerk, 1987).

[16] The picture is not a portrait, but a later reinvention.

a pamphlet about the French declaration of human rights, he fiercely criticised them as not being actual human rights but merely men's rights. His position on the most disadvantaged people in society could be seen in his practical improvement of social welfare as in his anonymous criticism of the injustices of the landed aristocracy with regard to their servants and tenant farmers.

Kant, on the other hand, defended all the traditional powers up to his late *Doctrine of Right* (1797), as he denied anyone the right to a revolution. In the same text, Kant distinguished between degrees of citizenship according to profession, declared the matter of natural law to be the subordination of women to men and reserved a special place for servants as part of the patriarchal family. This very rough account of Kant's legal philosophy serves here only to highlight the apparent differences to von Hippel when judged from the vantage point of a contemporary perspective.

1.2 Kant as moral observer of world history

The question of the Cambridge School regarding the kind of intervention Kant aimed at with his writings remains inconclusive when considering the immediate political context of Königsberg and Prussian politics. Nevertheless, the question helps to reveal possible venues of political intervention and our contemporary prejudices. We tend to think that a liberal philosopher like Kant would care about historical injustices, promote reforms toward local self-determination, stand for egalitarian causes and comment regularly on international politics. When looking for this kind of political intervention, Kant turns out to be an unpolitical philosopher.

At this point, one might object and argue that Kant's main achievement was the creation of a new philosophical method and the laying of firm foundations for morality with consequences for a cosmopolitan political theory. The appropriate question regarding Kant's political intervention would then concern whether his political judgements with regard to major questions – constitution of states, international peace, rights of individuals, and sensitive issues – the rights of women, indigenous peoples, race, colonialism – would live up to his theoretical achievements. This is the framework of many recent writings on Kant's political philosophy,[17] most prominently in Pauline Kleingeld's account.[18]

She carefully situates Kant's cosmopolitanism in the context of philosophical and literary debates in his time and shows how Kant's position differs from Christoph Martin Wieland's more elitist and less egalitarian moral cosmopolitanism[19] and Anacharsis Cloots's idea of a universal world republic without states.[20] She also notes that Kant only introduced the idea of cosmopolitan rights in the mid-1790s, which led him to address topics such as colonialism, the rights of refugees and attributing equal juridical standing to humans on every continent. Her central claim is that only due to the criticism of Georg Forster did Kant abandon his earlier idea of a racial hierarchy, which included an implicit justification of colonialism, and shifted instead to a more consistent and nuanced egalitarian position.[21] Kleingeld holds that together these shifts constitute a 'revolution' in Kant's thinking around the mid-1790s.[22] The key point of her argument is that by attaining an egalitarian moral perspective, Kant's own development can be seen as a story of moral learning, and his shortcomings in respect to the unequal status of men and women can be acknowledged and lamented.[23] At the same time, this perspective seems to mirror the modern principle of equal moral status among all humans. Kleingeld relies on this parallel to show why contemporary Kantian philosophers can still profit from his more nuanced view by acknowledging how a cosmopolitan perspective can be reconciled with special obligations stemming from particular relationships.[24]

17 Katrin Flikschuh and Lea Ypi, eds., *Kant and Colonialism: Historical and Critical Perspectives* (Oxford: Oxford University Press, 2014).

18 Pauline Kleingeld, *Kant and Cosmopolitanism: The Philosophical Ideal of World Citizenship* (Cambridge: Cambridge University Press, 2012).

19 Ibid., 17.

20 Ibid., 44.

21 Ibid., 111–16.

22 Ibid., 5.

23 Ibid., 173–5, 183.

24 Ibid., 26–34, 175.

However, apart from exegetical issues, especially regarding the significance of a 'second revolution' in Kant's thinking,[25] one might wonder why Kant did not try to solidify the lasting and apparently eternal legacy of his thinking, and why it took so long to rediscover this legacy. The thorny question about his legacy is not why moral inertia persisted in the world, but why the subsequent tradition of German Idealists, foremost the triumvirate who studied Kant's writings in the late 1780s and early 1790s (Hegel, Hölderlin, Schelling), somehow missed this insight and why the later 'existentialist' tradition (Marx, Nietzsche, Heidegger) had so few appropriate things to say about it.

These questions about Kant's legacy and later reception fall within the scope of a contextual reading since these are precisely the questions that Kant himself asked. In the mid-1790s, at the very time when Kleingeld was locating the 'revolution' in his thinking, Kant was reflecting in two essays (*On a Recently Voiced Noble-Minded Tone in Philosophy, VT, and Announcement of the Near Conclusion of a Treaty on Perpetual Peace in Philosophy, VNAEF*) on the legacy of critical philosophy, how it might continue to exert a spirited influence and how it might stand up to a conservative revival of the ancients, especially Plato. These essays will be our guide to a different understanding of Kant.

1.3 A new tone of political intervention

It is well known that, due to his advanced age and declining health, Kant did not respond to the multifaceted criticisms that emerged during the 1790s, as he devoted his remaining years to complete his system (*Critique of Pure Reason, KrV* B xliii). However, he made one exception. In a series of two essays, he responded to criticisms raised by Johann Georg Schlosser, a public official and amateur scholar of limited reputation or learning. The reason Kant responded to Schlosser was neither the quality of Schlosser's arguments (they were

[25] For a detailed discussion that questions the stark contrast that Kleingeld draws and the patronising attribution of moral learning to Kant, see Christoph Horn, *Nichtideale Normativität. Ein neuer Blick auf Kants politische Philosophie* (Berlin: Suhrkamp, 2014), 98–106.

mostly insinuations) nor the influence he had on public discourse. Instead, Schlosser sensed potential breaking points in Kant's philosophy. This needs some explanation.

Schlosser was the first to translate Plato's letters into German and used the comment section to contrast Plato's approach to politics with critical philosophy.[26] Schlosser depicted Plato as a figure who justified his engagement with a tyrannical regime in Sicily and his work as an advisor to the young Dion as a way of bringing about a 'higher good' than Athenian democracy, or a means of avoiding foreign occupation and the takeover of cities by unrestrained democrats. (Similarities to feelings, attitudes and anxieties in German states in the 1790s are obvious.)

Schlosser's most upfront criticism of Kant's philosophy is found in a footnote to Plato's seventh letter. Schlosser praises Plato's confession that the highest insight requires intuitive knowledge of a being itself that is only attainable to the initiated few and turns this dense teaching[27] into a critique of Kant's philosophy. According to Schlosser, it is not only wrong for its critical epistemological approach but also responsible for moral degeneration in society and the ossification of philosophy and thus deprives us of the means to resist evil.[28] In Schlosser's terms:

> A criticism that denies reason this [intuitive knowledge] would not purify it, but would emasculate it. ... It would be at risk of soon degenerating into a mere pattern-factory. ... In the next generation thinking would bring back the old scholastic peripateticism. ... Since prejudice and superstition have been stripped of their taming power, the most irregular libertinism would follow, until thinking and acting are lost in barbarism. ... The kind of morality this

[26] Johann Georg Schlosser, *Platons Briefe nebst einer historischen Einleitung und Anmerkungen [Plato's Letters, along with a Historical Introduction and Notes]* (Königsberg: Friedrich Nicolovius, 1795).

[27] This so-called epistemological digression has its own history of interpretations. For an analytical overview, see Andreas Graeser, *Philosophische Erkenntnis und begriffliche Darstellung: Bemerkungen zum erkenntnistheoretischen Exkurs des VII. Briefs*. Sitzungsberichte der Mainzer Akademie der Wissenschaften und der Literatur (Stuttgart: Franz Steiner, 1989).

[28] Schlosser, *Platons Briefe*, 182–3.

> system has retained from the shipwreck of reason has become so subtle that it will hardly be able to withstand the struggle with vice.[29]

Kant responded to Schlosser's accusations by drawing a distinction between the philosopher who has to achieve his results through hard work and the naïve lyrical enthusiast (*Schwärmer*) who believes he has direct access to being itself but bypasses conceptual work, adopting instead a 'noble tone'. By enjoying the fruits of philosophical labour without having to work to attain them, enthusiasts behave like clichéd nobles (who at this time also refused to engage in menial labour such as trade). This distinction settles the dispute with Schlosser but not with Plato. To respond to this challenge, Kant distinguishes between Plato the letter-writer and Plato the academic. With the latter, Kant agrees on many points in principle, such as the dialectical method, conceiving mathematics as an a priori realm and having an overall practical agenda. But he criticises Plato the letter-writer for extending the realm of a priori knowledge into the mystical, and particularly for his critique of writing, thus for withholding important insights in the manner of a 'clubbist'.[30] Endorsing secret teachings or insights runs counter to Kant's view of philosophy as a potentially world-wide public discourse (*An Answer to the Question: What is Enlightenment?*, *WA* 8:35).

There is one more aspect of Schlosser's critiques that alerts Kant to warn of the 'death of all philosophy'. This would occur once the expression of what, according to certain laws, can be discovered and communicated in our inner sense by reason is replaced by a tone that no one can clearly imitate because it expresses nothing determinate (*On a Recently Voiced Noble-Minded Tone in Philosophy*, *VT* 8:405). Again, it is not a specific argument by Schlosser but rather a certain attitude he expresses and a way of reading the ancients that troubles Kant. He calls Schlosser a *Schwärmer* – a naïve lyrical enthusiast (i.e. one who proclaims more than he can actually argue

29 Ibid.

30 The term was often used to refer to the members or the supporters of the political clubs of the French Revolution. Kant, however, probably has the pseudo-religious rituals of Freemasonry in mind here.

for). However, *Schwärmer* are not immoral people; their ideas are only too radical and not well enough thought through, leading them to become either religious zealots or political revolutionaries. Schlosser is to be counted among the peaceful philosophical zealots who, under the pretence of a philosophical education, forget to think for themselves and instead 'elevate now Plato, now Aristotle to the throne' (*VT* 8:392).

The reason this kind of naïve enthusiasm leads to the death of all philosophy becomes clear once one imagines how such an attitude would play out on a larger scale. If everyone evaluated one or the other philosopher as his or her personal hero, philosophy as a common project for the enlightenment of humankind would diminish and philosophy would turn into a learned yet fragmented reverence of old texts. Kant's critique of the noble tone is thus only a humorous rebuke to Schlosser on the surface and calls for an enthusiastic defence of philosophy as a common project of enlightened reason. Moreover, it needs to be defended by working systematically through the entire philosophical tradition and not by elevating first Plato, then Aristotle (or even Kant) to the throne.[31]

From today's perspective, Schlosser's treatment of Plato and his criticism of Kant may seem to be of merely historical or exegetical interest. However, Schlosser was a stubborn and impetuous man who did not know how to stop when on a futile course. So, he responded with a long book entitled *Writings to a Young Man Who Wanted to Study Kant's Philosophy*, in which he attempted to launch a comprehensive critique of Kant's philosophy, though without having studied it in any depth, as he admits at one point.[32] Again, Kant replied with the essay *Announcement of the Near Conclusion of a Treaty on Perpetual Peace in Philosophy* (*VNAEF* 8:411–422), sensing a real philosophical problem behind Schlosser's musings. Kant's efforts suggest that more is at stake here than merely refuting a few superficial misunderstandings. Indeed, some of the claims that Schlosser makes, without ever explaining them in detail, are reminiscent of positions later developed in

31 Obviously, these loose ends in Kant became a welcome bait for Hegel.

32 Johann Georg Schlosser, *Schreiben an einen jungen Mann, der die kritische Philosophie studieren wollte* (Lübeck: bey Friedrich Bohn, 1797).

German Idealist philosophy in response to Kant. One might say, then, that Kant anticipated some possible reactions to his philosophical project. He summed up Schlosser's main criticism, again in a humorous way, by quoting an aphorism by Abraham Gotthelf Kästner:

> Henceforth forever wars shall cease
> By acting as the sage avers;
> And then will all men live in peace
> Except for the philosophers.[33]

If this were true, Kant's project of an eternal peace – the capstone (though not coronation) of his whole philosophical endeavour – would not only fail, but it would be the philosophers who had brought this about, as quarrels in philosophy over practical questions could be used by sovereigns to bolster their legal disagreements.

Instead of taking the easy route and dissecting the various contradictions and shortcomings in Schlosser's commonsense prejudices against critical philosophy, Kant took up the hard systematic questions of how philosophy can flourish or continue, even though the one decisive, critical and laboursome step had already been taken. Kant's solution was to characterise future philosophy not just formally but in terms of content as an ongoing struggle against naïve lyrical enthusiasm (*Schwärmerei*) and to propose a contract among all philosophers. He describes it as a 'peace treaty so constituted that, if only the parties understand one another, it is at once concluded' (*VNAEF* 8:421). Using a different philosophical idiom, one might say that Kant proposes hermeneutic understanding as the future path of philosophy that, though it acknowledges differences, retains the idea of philosophy as a common project.

All proclamations that philosophy has come to an end or reached its final stage can easily be met by ridicule. However, it does not suffice to point out that after the end of philosophy has been proclaimed, people still called themselves

[33] Immanuel Kant, *Theoretical Philosophy after 1781*, ed. Henry Allison and Peter Heath, trans. Gary Hatfield et al. (Cambridge: Cambridge University Press, 2002), 456.

philosophers, as a certain idea of philosophy, even philosophy in its 'true meaning' might indeed have come to an end.

So has philosophy reached, with Kant, the stage of perpetual peace? Aside from grand historical speculations about the course of philosophy, there is also a systematic way to dispute this claim. To this end, it is again necessary to consider a question Plato raised (and was taken up in a distorted way by Schlosser) that Kant himself struggled to answer.

In the seventh letter, Plato argued that only a man who has spent his whole life among philosophers would be fit to serve as an 'enlightened' king. He insinuated that only when coming to power as a young man would he have the charisma and enough time to bring about fundamental reforms.[34] The question of youth and the appropriate time (*kairos*) for political action is thus at the centre of Plato's reflection. Schlosser misinterpreted Plato's letter as advertising an unpolitical petit bourgeois life. However, he implicitly took up the question of how to educate future leaders, as the second reply to Kant is entitled *Letter to a Young Man*. He ridicules Kant for representing 'emasculated reason', to which Kant replied by characterising Schlosser as a 'man of might'. Thus, the theme of youth and youthful erotic power is well established in the discourse, though not explicitly tackled. The underlying systemic questions become clear when asking what youth could expect from critical philosophy. According to Kant, there is no particular calling for youth: all they can do is enlist among the ranks of older critical philosophers and participate in the eternal work of censoring naïve lyrical enthusiasts.

One might think that the greatest dream of every adolescent should indeed be to become a Kant scholar. The reason this prospect is not particularly appealing can be clarified by reflecting on the tone of youth. We can hear it in a short sketch written around 1796 as a response to Kant's thinking and his political philosophy in particular.

> Beginning with the idea of humanity I want to demonstrate that there does not exist any idea of the state, because the state is something mechanical, just as there is no idea of

[34] Plato, Ep. 7.335d, 7.351c.

> a machine. Only that which is object of freedom is called idea. Hence, we must also move beyond the state! For every state must treat free human beings like a mechanical set of wheels; and that it must not; therefore, it shall cease to exist.[35]

These programmatic sentences are of course taken from the so-called *Oldest System-Program of German Idealism*, a sketch written in the handwriting of the young Georg Wilhelm Friedrich Hegel, presumably with the participation of his Tübingen friends Friedrich Hölderlin and Friedrich Wilhelm Joseph Schelling. This assault against Immanuel Kant marks both the beginning of Hegel's re-foundation of the state in moral practices (*Sittlichkeit*) and the beginning of later totalitarian excrescences – mediated in myriad ways by Marxists and right-wing Hegelians.[36]

The interpretation and appropriation of those few lines have become a research field of their own. I have included them at this point to show that Kant, far-sighted, discerned that the real challenge he had to respond to – the endeavour of the critical philosopher in a world-historical perspective – was neither to influence the political discourse in Königsberg or Prussia (as the Cambridge School presumes) nor to presume an absolute moral position by declaring all humans free and equal (along the lines of contemporary political philosophers). It was instead to engage with the unfolding philosophical tradition of modernity by taking up the *Querelle des Anciens et des Modernes*,[37] albeit this time in philosophy. Schlosser, with his

[35] Frank-Peter Hansen, *Das älteste Systemprogramm des deutschen Idealismus. Rezeptionsgeschichte und Interpretation* (Berlin and New York: Walter de Gruyter, 1989). For the translation, see 'The Oldest System-Program of German Idealism' in Friedrich Hölderlin, *Essays and Letters on Theory*, trans. Thomas Pfau (New York: State University of New York Press, 1988), 154.

[36] From a historical perspective, the common determinant throughout all ideological camps can be seen in the increase and totalitarisation of state power, Wolfgang Reinhard, *Geschichte der Staatsgewalt. Eine vergleichende Verfassungsgeschichte Europas von den Anfängen bis zur Gegenwart* (München: C. H. Beck, 1999), 406–79.

[37] The *Querelle* started as a French literary discourse on the exemplary function of antiquity for arts and sciences and was taken up in German idealism in particular by Schlegel and Goethe. See Peter K. Kapitza,

limited understanding, was of course only a 'dummy' for the real contestation to come. However, at least he sensed some of the topics that were in the air at this time, but his conservative attitude spoiled the envisioning of new developments. He was right to look for passion, though unable to develop a passion for theory, right to criticise the mechanical rattling in Kant's philosophy (everyone can hear it in the *Doctrine of Right*),[38] though he missed the need to theorise the underlying morality (*Sittlichkeit*), and right to seek a higher idea modified through Greek thought, though deaf to the arts.

Even his seemingly most outrageous claims – that after Kant 'thinking and acting are lost in barbarism' and that Kantian morality 'has become so subtle that it will hardly be able to withstand the struggle with vice' – have some truth to them, even a truth Kant shares. The discovery of freedom in one's soul is not a one-time insight gained by a philosopher for the whole of humankind but requires continuous work on oneself and, to sustain its social prerequisites, a timely political intervention. Kant was on the right track when he replied to Schlosser as a representative of a new era. What he missed and could have seen in Schlosser was that all the new developments that sprang up at this time had grown out of various parts of his own thinking.

2. Systematic unity and the absence of politics

I have introduced Kant in an oblique way by situating him in the context of Königsberg to show that, at first sight, he does not fit the image of a philosopher intervening in the political affairs of his time. Yet in his confrontation with Schlosser he was very conscious of the contribution that the project of critical philosophy was poised to make in the course of philosophy. Through this reading, Kant is – at least conjecturally – anchored both in the context of his time and in the further development of Idealist philosophy and its aftermath. We will

Ein bürgerlicher Krieg in der gelehrten Welt. Zur Geschichte der Querelle des Anciens et des Modernes in Deutschland (München: Wilhelm Fink, 1981).

38 Nietzsche calls it the garrulousness (*Geschwätzigkeit*) of Kant 'due to a superabundant supply of conceptual formulations'. Friedrich Nietzsche, *The Gay Science: With a Prelude in Rhymes and an Appendix of Songs*, trans. Walter Kaufmann (New York: Vintage Books, 1974), no. 97.

see later how both of these conjectural trajectories can be further strengthened and affirmed.

2.1 The revolution of thinking

However, there remains a problem with this approach. Kant's answer to Schlosser – and, by extension, to all attempts at contextual interpretation – appears to advocate a strictly systematic reading: become aware of the project of critical philosophy and everything will follow from this. Kant states this assertion most explicitly in the introduction to the *Metaphysics of Morals*, where he writes:

> It sounds arrogant, egotistical, and, to those who have not yet given up their ancient philosophical system, derogatory to assert that before the advent of critical philosophy there was no philosophy (*The Metaphysics of Morals, MS* 6:206).

We must understand the rationale behind this claim before considering Kant's contribution to cosmopolitan thought. To this end, it suffices to introduce two turning points – or, in Kant's terminology, the 'revolution of thinking'.

Kant was well aware of the multiple philosophical approaches before him. In his pre-critical phase, he considered himself a *Freidenker*, or eclectic thinker. Even though he was educated in a fairly Wolffian spirit, he recognised the limits of this kind of systematic, metaphysical philosophy and attempted – like many of his generation – to integrate ideas from British empiricists and moral sentimentalists, especially David Hume and Francis Hutcheson, into his lectures. So, what exactly sets critical philosophy apart from all previous philosophy? At the end of the *Critique of Judgement*, Kant summarises his efforts:

> God, freedom, and the immortality of the soul are the problems to whose solution, as their ultimate and unique goal, all the laborious preparations of metaphysics are directed (*Critique of the Power of Judgment, KU* 5:473).

The enumeration of these problems may seem reminiscent of traditional metaphysics – specifically *metaphysica specialis* – in the tradition of Leibniz and Wolff. However, what distinguishes Kant from all previous philosophy is that he asks the preliminary question: how is metaphysics possible as a science at all? With this, Kant takes a standpoint 'wholly outside of the field of metaphysics' (23:57), investigating the possibility of a priori objects in general. Instead of analysing metaphysical objects directly, he first asks whether it is possible to refer to the traditional objects of metaphysics in the same way as to ordinary, empirical objects. This is the guiding question of the *Critique of Pure Reason*. To this end, he examines the sources, scope and bounds of reason (29:756). In investigating the sources – in the Transcendental Aesthetic and Transcendental Analytic – he shows that we do not have direct access to objects but only to appearances. As a result, the scope of reason does not allow cognition of metaphysical objects (God, freedom, soul), since no synthetic judgements a priori can be formulated about them.

The Transcendental Dialectic demonstrates this by revealing the contradictions (antinomies) that reason necessarily entangles itself in when attempting to establish a metaphysical position. However, this investigation is not merely destructive – it also yields a positive, constructive result by delineating the bounds of reason: reason has a logical use as a faculty of inference and a transcendental use in establishing the systematic unity of understanding (*A* 745 / *B* 675).

That reason possesses unity and can be demonstrated in the form of a system is of key importance for Kant. A mere rhapsody of categories, insights or arguments (*B* 159) would not suffice as a definitive, scientific answer to the original question concerning the possibility of metaphysics. For us, the question of the unity of reason might therefore serve as a guide through Kant's thinking.

2.2 The moral law

It is important to note that, despite his systematic approach, Kant did not conceive the critical project as a whole from the outset but revised it throughout his life. While writing the *Critique of Pure Reason*, he was still convinced that the question 'What should I do?' was 'not transcendental, but moral, and thus it cannot be in itself a subject for our critique' (*KrV*, A805/B833). Thus, at the time of the first critique, Kant still excluded morality from the transcendental sphere. Only after the first – and largely uninformed – review of the *Critique of Pure Reason* by the popular philosopher Christian Garve did Kant realise that he had not demonstrated that the moral law constitutes a realm distinct from the laws of happiness. He introduced the strictly reason- or duty-bound account of morality – a defining characteristic of his practical philosophy – only in the *Groundwork of the Metaphysics of Morals (GMS)*, which can therefore be said to prolong the revolution of thinking into the practical sphere.

In the famous opening sentence, Kant states: 'It is impossible to think of anything at all in the world, or indeed even beyond it, that could be considered good without limitation except **a good will**' (*Groundwork of the Metaphysics of Morals, GMS* 4:393).

The reason the will is the appropriate object for moral consideration is that it can remain stable throughout changing circumstances. All other virtues, such as understanding, wit and judgement, can be used for better or worse. Moreover, gifts of fortune (*Glücksgaben*), such as power, riches, honour and even health, can turn out to be a curse rather than a blessing (*GMS* 4:393).

The opening paragraph reveals that two strands of argument are unfolding simultaneously: the quest for the supreme moral principle and the rejection of all alternative accounts. The second strand often remains only an implicit undercurrent in Kant's argument. However, one can accentuate the gulf between the supreme moral principle and other virtues or gifts of fortune by imagining an evil spirit offering any of them as a gift, as in a twisted fairy tale. Whichever one might choose, the spirit would twist virtues and gifts of fortune to win the individual's soul.

However, it is of course not the will as such that is good, but only the good will. Therefore, Kant has to show that the law determining the will is actually good. Kant's argument is that the will cannot be determined arbitrarily but has to be determined by some rule (maxim). Moreover, the will cannot have any external aim as an object, since all such grounds had previously been excluded. Therefore, the only principle left for determining the will is the 'conformity of actions as such with universal law'. The categorical imperative thus reads: 'I ought never to act except in such a way that I could also will that my maxim should become a universal law' (*GMS* 4:402).

It is formulated in the first person, because it is only felt as a duty by sensuous beings who have desires and wishes which may pull in different directions. It is therefore only the subject who, from an internal perspective, can judge whether my motivation is indeed pure – based solely on the moral ought – or whether some other motive operates secretly in the background. The constant questioning of one's own motivation is again an implicit feature of Kant's moral philosophy, yet it is nevertheless important. He calls it the tendency of reason for trifling disputes (*vernünfteln*) and characterises it as 'continuing propensity to transgression or at least impurity, that is, an admixture of many spurious (not moral) motives to observe the law' (*Critique of Practical Reason, KpV* 5:128). Kant's foundation of moral philosophy is thus bound up from the very beginning with critical stances on competing moral conceptions and a self-critical attitude to one's own motivation. Therefore, Kant would never deny that, without a deduction, the existence of a pure principle of morality can be questioned and even disputed as a mere chimera.

The argument so far determines the principle of morality only if morality can be shown to be real – that is, in Kant's terms, given that practical reason contains synthetic sentences a priori. The step from the analytical to the synthetic method is important, as I can never be absolutely sure about the morality of my own actions, and even less so about the motives of others.

> It is indeed sometimes the case that with the keenest self-examination we find nothing besides the moral ground of duty that could have been powerful enough to move us to this or that good action and to so great a sacrifice; but from this it cannot be inferred with certainty that no covert impulse of self-love, under the mere pretence of that idea, was not actually the real determining cause of the will; for we like to flatter ourselves by falsely attributing to ourselves a nobler motive, whereas in fact we can never, even by the most strenuous self-examination, get entirely behind

> our covert incentives, since, when moral worth is at issue, what counts is not actions, which one sees, but those inner principles of actions that one does not see (*GMS* 4:407).

This self-critical stance derails all attempts to give a positive proof of moral freedom – that is, by presuming the existence of certain observable 'good actions'. In the *Critique of Practical Reason*, Kant therefore chooses a different way. He notes that desires (the satisfaction of some lustful inclination) and second-order desires (to avoid immediate and disproportionate grievances resulting from their satisfaction) would never give rise to the idea of freedom. All such calculations would be prudential and thus form part of theoretical reason. This means that, in principle, the action could be explicable by laws of nature. To illustrate that moral freedom is something else, Kant introduces the example of giving false testimony under duress.

> [I]f his prince demanded, on pain of the same immediate execution, that he give false testimony against an honorable man whom the prince would like to destroy under a plausible pretext, he would consider it possible to overcome his love of life, however great it may be. He would perhaps not venture to assert whether he would do it or not, but he must admit without hesitation that it would be possible for him. (*KpV* 5:30).

Kant calls this consciousness of the moral law a fact of reason, 'because one cannot reason it out from antecedent data of reason' (*KpV* 5:31). Instead, it 'forces itself upon us of itself as a synthetic a priori proposition that is not based on any intuition' (ibid.). The consciousness of the moral law presupposes freedom – it is the *ratio cognoscendi* (*KpV* 5:5). The moral law, in turn, gives the idea of freedom, which in theoretical reason is an extravagance of speculation, objective reality – the moral law is the *ratio essendi* of freedom. In this way, the *Critique of Practical Reason* completes Kant's theoretical philosophy. It is, as he writes, the 'keystone of the whole structure of a system of pure reason, even of speculative reason' (*KpV* 5:324). In light of these two revolutions in thinking in theoretical and practical philosophy, we can sketch Kant's entire programme.

He has to carry out both the theoretical and practical parts of the critical project and demonstrate that both form a unity of reason. Only when we have a systematic, architectonic account of reason – rather than a mere rhapsody – can we be certain that we have identified the true moral motive and theory. To put it in more colloquial terms: merely formulating one moral theory among others would, even by Kant's standards, require an ideology-critical examination of that theory and a psychological questioning of the motives of an actor proposing or promoting it. This is as far as the critical programme extends. However, this does not exhaust Kant's entire system.

2.3 Kant's popular lectures on anthropology and geography

We have seen that Kant conceives of moral philosophy as distinct from the laws of happiness. However, the realm of happiness is not absent from Kant's philosophy – it is simply not part of his critical philosophy, since, according to Kant, such laws cannot be determined in a strict rational manner. Instead, regularities related to happiness can only be collected empirically and perhaps presented in a somewhat structured form. Kant addressed this empirical dimension in his lectures on anthropology and geography, which he delivered over the course of thirty years (*Anthropology from a Pragmatic Point of View*, *Anth* 7:122). These lectures were of lesser importance to Kant. Nevertheless, they yield two significant results for our inquiry into the possible political dimension of his philosophy.

He argues that anthropology is presented from a 'pragmatic point of view' (*Anth* 7:119). One might surmise that the *Anthropology* is his applied moral theory under non-ideal circumstances.[39] However, this is not how the text operates.

[39] This is the dominant Anglophone reception that sees Kant's *Anthropology* as a moral supplement to his ethics, most notably Robert B. Louden, ed., *Anthropology from a Pragmatic Point of View* (Cambridge: Cambridge University Press, 2006); Allen W. Wood, 'Unsocial Sociability: The Anthropological Basis of Kantian Ethics', *Philosophical Topics* 19, no. 1 (1991): 325–51. My approach, by contrast, follows Foucault in treating it as a critical part of theoretical philosophy, an empirical 'science of knowing' systematically distinct from his moral philosophy.

Kant describes human behaviour across a range of different cognitive faculties, senses and desires to illustrate how human beings are – as empirical beings. The only one who is free – or who can use these observations to free himself – is the observer.

Thus, the anthropology is written for a human being who is, as an observer, a 'citizen of the world' (*Anth* 7:120) but not a political actor in the world with a moral compass to change it. Everything we read about freedom in the anthropology concerns the 'inclination of freedom', which, together with the 'inclination of sex' and the 'manias for honour', dominance and possession, constitutes the 'cultural passions' that form Kant's bleak anthropology (*Anth* 7:267–8).

The conclusion that a political or active perspective is once again missing in the anthropology can be affirmed by briefly glancing at the *Physical Geography*. These lectures were published posthumously. From today's perspective, it seems easy to point out racial and ethnic stereotypes and notice empirical failings (storks migrate to Africa in winter but do not hide, as Kant claims, in the woods). However, this kind of criticism does not engage with Kant's overall project, which he pursued in the 'empirical science of knowing' (anthropology and geography). It is best explained in his presentation of topics which a completely worked-out physical geography would have to cover (*Physical Geography, PG* 9:164–5). He mentions a 'moral geography' that would deal with different customs and characters of human beings in different parts of the world, a 'political geography' that would relate the constitution of different countries to climate and landscape, and even a 'theological geography' that would study various forms of Christianity and other religions in relation to different soils in various countries.

In our contextual reading of Kant as a citizen of Königsberg and Prussia – and, for some of the Seven Year's War, of Russia – we have noticed that Kant made no reference to the historical and political situation of his time, thus did not write about the history of Königsberg, its specific role in Prussia, the Seven Year's War or Britain's rise to ascendancy in the world. In the introduction Kant explains that 'geography and history cover the entire breadth of our knowledge' (*PG* 9:162–3) and declares that 'geography is the underlying substrate' (*PG* 9:163) as 'history is nothing but continuous geography' (*PG* 9:161).

In the lecture notes, Kant does not further justify his claim. However, given the outline of the empirical science of knowing, one can guess his reasons. 'Geography' is Kant's umbrella term for empirical or social scientific explanations. To be able to give an explanation, one needs events and variables explaining these events (e.g. explaining a war as a way of masking the underlying class conflict). However, historical narratives fall short of giving explanations of this kind, as usually only specific events are described but not analysed from a general point of view (such as class conflict). Thus, one could see, in the quest for an underlying 'substrate', the seeds of a materialistic theory of society. It is not by chance that Kant readily cites foreign customs but hardly discusses any customs or events from his own lifeworld. Generally speaking, Kant faces the problem that the closer a 'geographical' explanation comes to one's own time and more recent history, the less convincing geographical or typological explanations are. In one's own time and lifeworld, it is obvious that customs, laws and political events are not usually necessitated by some 'geographical law' but result from political decisions or human interaction that could have turned out differently. In other words, history as a political history that could have turned out differently – and the present lifeworld as a field of political contestation – are clearly missing in Kant's empirical science of knowing.

This observation is, however, not a fatal mistake but a systematic feature that leads back to Kant's critical philosophy. In terms of critical philosophy, the 'science of knowing' (anthropology and geography) is, strictly speaking, part of theoretical philosophy, as moral freedom – as autonomy – plays no role in it. One might think that this is yet another reason to ignore, together with the historical context, the empirical part of Kant's philosophy and focus right away on his moral philosophy. Yet the journey has equipped us with two questions that will also guide us through his moral and political philosophy and his cosmopolitan thought in particular:

(1) How can the unity of reason be conceived – or, in particular, is there a comprehensive idea of freedom that covers

both moral freedom and the social freedom of free-acting human beings?

(2) Is there a notion of politics as intervention in Kant?

3. Cosmopolitanism as a legal requirement

We started our reading of Kant with the expectation of finding a firm philosophical basis for current cosmopolitan convictions, as some kind of Kantianism is usually invoked to fend off questions that challenge the liberal political orthodoxy. However, the contextual and inner systematic reading of Kant have already shed some doubts on this belief and revealed different trajectories of Kant's thoughts: the demarcation of the critical project against Plato and naïve enthusiasts (*Schwärmer*), on the one hand, and the exploration of the natural conditions of human life (in anthropology and geography) on the other hand.

Yet, all these considerations could be brushed off by claiming that an 'analytical' or 'systematic' reading of Kant's basic moral philosophy – based in particular on the *Groundwork*, the *Doctrine of Right (RL)* and his political essays – would suffice for an answer to the contemporary question of the foundation of cosmopolitan thought, so that 'mere historical' analyses or the consideration of the legacy of Kant's thought can be left aside. Therefore, it is necessary to show how Kant's 'political philosophy' (the term will be defined more precisely along Kant's lines later on) is situated within his entire philosophical project. To this end, I will show that Kant's notion of right is entangled with systematic problems resulting from his way of conceptualising freedom (3.1). In a reconstruction of the *Doctrine of Right*, I will identify cosmopolitan aspects at two unusual places: Kant's notion of (pre-state) private rights and his notion of punishment (3.2). Perpetual peace, however, will prove to be not a political aim but a legal requirement to justify the rightful condition of having something external as one's own.

3.1 The *Metaphysics of Morals* as a synthesis of Kant's practical philosophy?

The *Metaphysics of Morals (MS)*, published in 1797, was the last major work Kant wrote during his lifetime and was clearly intended to give a final synthesis of his moral philosophy as applied to all practical matters. It has two parts, the 'metaphysical first principles of the doctrine of right' and the 'metaphysical first principles of the doctrine of virtue'.[40] Together, they would be the counterpart of a 'metaphysics of nature' as outlined in his *Metaphysical Foundations of Natural Science*. This apparently well-structured, systematic plan conceals the turbulent publication history and the ongoing theoretical problems underlying the account in the *Metaphysics of Morals*. Kant first announced that he hoped to finish a book entitled *Metaphysics of Morals* by the end of 1767, thus 30 years before its actual publication.[41] In the meantime, he developed critical philosophy, completely reversed many of his convictions regarding the foundation of moral philosophy, and was, towards the end of his life in the late 1790s, increasingly caught up in theoretical and political controversies from all sides while he saw his powers decline. Moreover, the first part of the *Metaphysics of Morals*, the *Doctrine of Right*, was printed on the basis of a confused manuscript that contained many misplaced passages.[42] Considering that the *Metaphysics of Morals* was eagerly anticipated by the reading public, the reception of the work was devastating.[43] Famously, Arthur Schopenhauer described it as so weak that he need not spill

[40] Subsequently, I will refer only to the introduction and the first part with the shorthand form *Rechtslehre* (*RL*).

[41] See his letter to Herder from 9 May 1767 (*Correspondence, Br* 10:74).

[42] Bernd Ludwig, ed., *Immanuel Kant. Metaphysische Anfangsgründe der Rechtslehre* (Hamburg: Felix Meiner, 1986), 7–81, presents the detailed arguments and a completely revised edition. Most of the changes are adopted in John Ladd's translation.

[43] All reviews are now collected in *Die Rezensionen zu Kants Metaphysischen Anfangsgründen der Rechtslehre*, eds. Diethelm Klippel, Dieter Hüning and Jens Eisfeld (Berlin: De Gruyter, 2021). On Kant's discussion with his contemporaries, see Reidar Maliks, *Kant's Politics in Context* (Oxford: Oxford University Press, 2014).

any polemic against it but could simply let it die a natural death.[44]

Apart from the poor organisation of the text, at least two explanations can be given for the unfavourable reception of the work. First, it is overloaded with theoretical jargon, since Kant tried to graft his own theoretical categories onto the established discussions in the natural law tradition, and it constantly draws connections to concepts from Roman law. Second, the political landscape and sentiments changed in the 1790s, and even more after the Napoleonic Wars and the German Campaign of 1813 (in German, *Befreiungskriege*, 'wars of liberation'), so that a work conceived in the remote and apolitical circumstances of Königsberg quickly appeared to be out-dated and unrelated to the modern world.[45] It is not by chance that only in the late twentieth century, against the background of an established liberal order, the detailed argumentation of the *Doctrine of Right* gained more attention among Kant scholars. However, the contemporary Kant scholarship that tries to defend Kant's *Doctrine of Right* as a genuine and original approach in political and legal philosophy overshadows the reasons for its overall negative reception, as most contemporary scholars proceed from the premise that beneath the surface of a faulty print edition and the many unnecessary digressions, there must be the

[44] Arthur Schopenhauer, *The World as Will and Representation*, vol. 1, trans. and ed. Judith Norman, Alistair Welchman and Christopher Janaway (Cambridge: Cambridge University Press, 2010), 558.

[45] The reception of Kant's *Doctrine of Right* in German legal academia, *Rechtswissenschaft*, is a problem of its own. Officially, a priori reasoning was denounced as irrelevant after the advent of the Historical School of Jurisprudence, established by Friedrich Carl von Savigny. In practice, however, Kant's a priori concepts were reformulated as 'dogmatic concepts' peculiar to the *Rechtswissenschaften* and used to structure the legal domain. On the details, see Joachim Rückert, 'Kant-Rezeption in juristischer und politischer Theorie (Naturrecht, Rechtsphilosophie, Staatslehre, Politik) des 19. Jahrhunderts, in Martyn P. Thompson, ed., *John Locke and Immanuel Kant: Historical Reception and Contemporary Relevance* (Berlin: Duncker & Humblot, 1991), 144–215. In the Anglophone world a broad reception of Kant's *Doctrine of Right* started only in the late twentieth century from the background of a very different political and philosophical constellation.

one true, systematic Kantian philosophy: the holy grail that redeems itself over time.[46]

The premise of such analytical or systematic readings that take the presuppositions of our time for granted has been criticised throughout this book. Here, it might suffice to point out two systematic consequences of this approach. First, the resistance against Kant's legal philosophy is not limited to superficial readings by second-rate writers but can also be seen as a sign of an insight into some profound problems. Most famously, such a perspective is found in the so-called *Earliest System Program of German Idealism*, which starts with the attempt to overcome Kant's practical philosophy: 'For every state must treat free human beings like a mechanical set of wheels; and that it must not; therefore it shall cease to exist.'[47] Second, Kant did not simply fill out gaps in a predetermined system, but constantly reworked his system and did not shy away from reformulating its foundations. Despite its apparently overly systematic shape, even the *Metaphysics of Morals* is to be seen as an intermediate stage in an ongoing process of establishing firm foundations for philosophy. Both problems will be briefly addressed, as they also pertain to the two leading questions that have guided us through Kant's practical philosophy.

The lack of a unified theory of freedom

In the introduction to the *Doctrine of Right*, Kant takes up the question of a unified theory of freedom that we have thus far been looking for in vain. The reason the problem arose in the first place was twofold. Within his critical philosophy, freedom could only be understood as a form of action out of respect for the moral law. Therefore, Kant fenced off two failings of practical reason: the concealed impulses of self-love that taint the pure idea of duty, and outright immoral

[46] See, for a most candid defence of an ahistorical, systematic reading, Arthur Ripstein, *Force and Freedom. Kant's Legal and Political Philosophy* (Cambridge, MA: Harvard University Press, 2009), ix.

[47] 'The Oldest System-Program', 155. Kant speaks at one point about the 'machinery of constitutions' (*Maschinenwesen der Staatsverfassung*), so this metaphor of the mechanical set of wheels takes up a usage known from Kant (*RL* 6:340).

actions. As the entire realm covered by his anthropology and geography is, according to Kant, only part of theoretical philosophy, moral freedom appears to be unrelated to the real processes of the world. There are thus two problems which Kant needs to address: to give an account of free actions as good or evil, including their traces in the world, and an account of free actions other than moral actions. We will see that the way Kant addresses these two problems also shapes his understanding of cosmopolitanism in a specific way.

In order to realise the full systematic problem Kant has to face, we also have to take into account his treatise on religion, published four years before the *Doctrine of Right*. When Kant first introduced the analytical connection between autonomy and freedom in the *Groundwork*, he distinguished between three kinds of actions: actions of duty, according to duty and (implicitly) against duty. He then spent much effort explaining how generalisable maxims could result in free actions, namely if the motive of the action is respect for the moral law (it is done out of duty), but not for some empirical motive. Only moral actions in the strict sense guarantee that freedom as autonomy is real (i.e. not an illusion, or an excuse to camouflage the real, material motives). From a third-person perspective, an action according to duty can easily be mistaken for one out of duty, especially if the person deceives others about their motives. They could even deceive themselves, and for this reason, need to question their own consciousness.

The problem with this account is not just that it is individualistic, abstract or too demanding,[48] but that it fails at a fundamental level to explain the notion of free action. For, if the will is to be conceived as free, it must be free to choose either good or evil. If, however, only moral actions are free actions, and immoral actions are not free but determined, it becomes questionable on which grounds they could be reprimanded.[49]

[48] These are three broad lines of contemporary criticism that continue to be voiced today.

[49] In the literature it is known as the Reinhold/Sidgwick Problem. In the twentieth century it has been most dramatically pointed out by Gerold Prauss, *Kant über Freiheit als Autonomie* (Frankfurt am Main: Vittorio Klostermann, 1983). For a criticism of recent solutions, see Courtney D. Fugate, 'On a Supposed Solution to the Reinhold/Sidgwick Problem in Kant's Metaphysics of Morals', *European Journal of Philosophy* 23, no. 3

In the *Critique of Practical Reason*, Kant did not address this problem, though he extended his analysis in one direction. For the first time, he defined actions according to duty (*pflichtmäßig*) as lawful (*gesetzmäßig*) (*KdprV* 5:71), showing that they constitute a sphere of their own. However, he did not specify the sense of legality any further, leaving the question of what it means for free actions to be morally good or evil and legally right or wrong – and how these judgements relate to each other – unanswered.

Only in the treatise on religion did he address the fundamental problem: acting freely means being able to choose either a good or an evil course of action. He states the problem most clearly:

> '[The] subjective ground [of freedom] must, in turn, itself always be a deed of freedom (for otherwise the use or abuse of the human being's power of choice with respect to the moral law could not be imputed to him, nor could the good or evil in him be called "moral")' (*Religion within the Boundaries of Mere Reason, RGV* 6:21).

He dismisses the suggestion that evil actions are done out of sensibility as the motive for a free action must not be a cause but a maxim that 'the human being has incorporated' (*RGV* 6:21). Thus, acting out of sensibility would be too little to explain evil actions. Acting out of *disrespect* for the moral law, on the other hand, would be too much, as it would turn the human being into a 'diabolic being' – a being whose *only* incentive for actions would be the disrespect for the moral law (*RGV* 6:35). Kant's solution at this point is that human beings do not repudiate the moral law, but that it 'makes the incentives of self-love and their inclinations the condition of compliance with the moral law' (*RGV* 6:36). In other words, they respect the moral law only hypocritically.

One might ask whether Kant has presupposed the notion of evil in the notion 'hypocritical respect' and thus not given a convincing answer to the question of the subjective ground of freedom after all. Kant admits that the propensity to evil

(2015): 349–73. The approach developed throughout this genealogy may be called an existentialist one.

remains 'inexplicable to us' (*RGV* 6:43). Following this lead, one might continue to inquire whether the ultimate grounds of morality that are the condition of freedom are inexplicable to us as well.

This is indeed what Kant considers in a footnote: the first subjective ground of the adoption of moral maxims cannot be determined out of free power of choice, as the same question about the freedom of this choice will reappear again, so that 'we are endlessly referred back in the series of subjective determining grounds, without ever being able to come to the first ground' (*RGV* 6:21). Given this candid concession, one might even dramatise this specific problem in Kant and claim that it is necessary to clarify the general notion of free action before proceeding further.[50] However, as the problem appears in the context of a longer argument – how the cognition of inner freedom plays out in religious consciousness throughout historical time – it is also necessary to reconstruct the entire field of inquiry, for any 'solution' to the fundamental problem must stand the test of giving a comparably good answer. Thus, any 'theory of action' on its own that cannot account for the inner workings of religious consciousness would fail this test. Therefore, we leave the problem of a general account of action unresolved but marked, thus requiring further discussion.[51]

For our purposes, there is a second reason not to further pursue the inquiry into fundamental problems. We will see later on that the development of the problem of good and evil actions as it unfolds in religious consciousness and religious history also entails critical lessons for the genealogy of cosmopolitan thought.

Moral and legal actions

We have said that, when extending his notion of freedom as autonomy to encompass the entire variety of phenomena, Kant also has to show how legality, that is, non-moral actions,

[50] Gerold Prauss stressed this problem in Kant again and again, only to recommend his own idealist system, see Gerold Prauss, 'Kants Problem der Einheit theoretischer und praktischer Vernunft', *Kant-Studien* 72, no. 1–4 (1981): 286–303.

[51] This is, by the way, Kant's way of writing as well. Often, he considers objections to his theory in footnotes, as if to save them up for later.

can be part of practical reason, indeed a distinguished part (the *Metaphysics of Morals* starts with the *Doctrine of Right*). Thus far, we have only seen how Kant tackles the problem of good and evil actions and the ensuing difficulties. Curiously, Kant appears to retract this solution in his *Doctrine of Right* and proposes yet another account.

In the introduction, he does not explicitly take up the problem of free action as either good or evil, even though criminal actions are a case of free but evil actions. However, he develops another side of freedom. He starts his argument by claiming that 'freedom of choice cannot be defined – as some have tried to define it – as the ability to make a choice for or against the law' (*RL* 6:226). This, however, was exactly his own position in the treatise on religion. Instead, Kant now claims that 'freedom in relation to the internal lawgiving of reason is really a capacity; the possibility of deviating from it is an incapacity' (*RL* 6:227). However, this would mean reducing evil to an incapacity of reason, which amounts to a kind of heteronomy. Kant even underscores this consequence by denying that the will is free, and introduces, as a make-shift term, the 'power of choice' (*Willkür*).

> Laws proceed from the will, maxims from choice. In man the latter is a capacity for free choice; the will, which is directed to nothing beyond the law itself, cannot be called either free or unfree, since it is not directed to actions but immediately to giving laws for the maxims of actions (and is, therefore, practical reason itself). Hence the will directs with absolute necessity and is itself *subject* to no necessitation. Only *choice* can therefore be called *free* (RL 6:226).

However, if the will no longer imposes the moral law out of freedom but leads necessarily to the moral law, it can no longer be the *ratio cognoscendi* of freedom. Conversely, freedom is not the *ratio essendi* of the moral law, but of some necessity.

Therefore, the solution to the problems of non-moral actions Kant presents in the *Doctrine of Right* is not sufficiently grounded in his account of freedom as autonomy and seems instead to explore a separate aspect of freedom. The account of evil actions in the treatise on religion, on the other hand, is so closely connected to the idea of autonomy that it threatens to dissolve the apparently clear and firm moral stance into an 'inexplicable' existential choice (*RGV* 6:43).

The domain of the juridical

The systematic and architectonic problems Kant runs into in his late practical writings have not gone unnoticed. With regard to Kant's political philosophy, there are two lines of interpretation. Some argue that Kant developed in his legal philosophy an independent account of political philosophy.[52] This, however, would not only contradict Kant's claim in the *Metaphysics of Morals* of presenting the applied part of his critical philosophy, but it would also contradict Kant's entire endeavour of finding a firm foundation of morality. The separation thesis is only true insofar as it disproves the misconception that Kant applies his 'individual morality' to a given institutional structure or uses his 'individual morality' to provide a foundation for 'collective morality' in terms of a set of moral rights or a democratic consciousness.[53] Such suggestions naturally come to mind, as during Kant's time (and today) revolutionary political discourse evolved along these lines – for example, when in the *Declaration of Independence* some truths are held to be 'self-evident' or the French National Constituent Assembly 'declared' the *Rights of Man and of the Citizen*.

However, Kant pursues an entirely different strategy. He distinguishes between the juridical and the ethical domain[54]

[52] Julius Ebbinghaus, 'Das Kantische System der Rechte des Menschen und Bürgers in seiner geschichtlichen und aktuellen Bedeutung', in *Gesammelte Aufsätze, Vorträge und Reden* (Darmstadt: Wissenschaftliche Buchgesellschaft, 1968), 161–93 has formulated the strong separation thesis arguing that Kant's legal philosophy is a normativity *sui generis*, which has no connection to the categorical imperative. For a classification of various possibilities of relating the *Groundwork* and the *Doctrine of Right*, see Gerhard Seel, 'How Does Kant Justify the Universal Objective Validity of the Law of Right?' *International Journal of Philosophical Studies* 17, no. 1 (2009): 49–70. Most contemporary interpreters argue for a weak separation thesis, which is also the route taken here.

[53] This line of interpretation was first developed by Ingeborg Maus, *Zur Aufklärung der Demokratietheorie. Rechts- und demokratietheoretische Überlegungen im Anschluss an Kant* (Frankfurt am Main: Suhrkamp, 1992). Jürgen Habermas and the Frankfurt School follow this reading.

[54] The second part of the *Metaphysics of Morals*, the *Doctrine of Virtue*, deals with ethical questions in Kant's terminology.

according to the motives of actions. Juridical laws are 'directed merely to external actions and their conformity to the law' (*RL* 6:14). Ethical laws, on the other hand, require that the laws themselves are the determining grounds of action. One might question whether the distinction between outer action and inner motivation really captures the difference between law and morality, as legal actions are not forced body movements but require some (inner) motivation as well. When it comes to sentencing criminal actions, even very specific motivations are imputed to the criminal – for example, committing a murder means, according to German law, it was a predetermined homicidal act committed out of reprehensible motives.

The basic distinction Kant has in mind can, however, be clarified by referring to H. L. A. Hart's distinction between the internal and the external point of view.[55] According to Hart, ordinary subjects of the law – citizens – can take an external point of view, acting for any motive, as long as the action is in accordance with the law. Whether this is indeed the case is something officials have to judge. They have to take an internal point of view, regarding the law as if they were its authors. However, even officials can distance themselves from the law; they can take a detached internal point of view, judging as if they were its authors while harbouring secret reservations.[56]

These secret reservations are precisely what Kant wants to exclude when he speaks about the moral law as a determining ground of action. This is something only the subject can judge by scrupulously examining their conscience. As Kant notes in the *Groundwork*, we like to 'flatter ourselves by falsely attributing ourselves nobler motives while acting indeed out of covert incentives' (GMS 4:407). From a legal perspective, the publicly declared 'noble motives' can be taken at face value, since only outer actions count in any case.

But is this enough? Shouldn't we expect more from the law? Is the law not the means of bringing about all desirable

[55] H.L.A. Hart, *The Concept of Law*, 2nd ed. (Oxford: Clarendon Press, 1994), 89.

[56] For a more detailed discussion, see Gerald J. Postema, 'The Normativity of Law', in Ruth Gavison, ed., *Issues in Contemporary Legal Philosophy: The Influence of H.L.A Hart* (Oxford: Clarendon Press, 1987), 83.

global institutional changes, the cosmopolitan condition? Are personal motives, for example, in decisions to buy or not to buy a certain product, not an expression of a moral belief? Finally, are not peace, global justice or aims such as the reduction of poverty goods in themselves? In order to answer this question, we have to pursue Kant's constructive argument to the end. Only then will we realise that the legal domain is restricted to a specific constructivist perspective that needs to be supplemented by common moral actions through 'ethical communities'.

3.2 The *Doctrine of Right*: From freedom to coercion

Kant's Notion of Right

Kant's entire legal philosophy rests on his notion of right.[57] In the programmatic second paragraph, he writes that '[the question] "what is *right*?" might well embarrass the jurist if he does not want to lapse into a tautology or, instead of giving a universal solution, refer to what the laws in some country at some time prescribe' (*RL* 6:229) and adds sarcastically that any merely empirical account would be 'like the wooden head in Phaedrus' fable, ... a head that may be beautiful but unfortunately it has no brain' (*RL* 6:230). The general principle of right that Kant then introduces sounds, at first, rather unspectacular: 'Any action is right that in itself or in its maxim is such that the freedom of choice of each can coexist with everybody's freedom of choice in accordance with a general law' (*RL* 6:230). It guarantees each person's 'one innate right' – namely, to 'freedom (independence from being constrained by another's choice), insofar as it can coexist with the freedom of every other' (*RL* 6:237). This is, according to Kant, 'the only original right belonging to everyone by virtue of their humanity' (*RL* 6:237).

For grasping the gist of this 'general principle of right', its components need to be considered separately. When Kant writes about the 'choices' that can be united, he uses the German term *Willkür*. In German, *Willkür* has a mostly

[57] For a detailed account of Kant's various attempts to deduce the principles of right from the concept of freedom, see Paul Guyer, 'Kant's Deductions of the Principles of Right', *Kantian Review* 10 (2005): 118–46.

negative connotation: it is often used to describe the arbitrary, excessive and irrational choices of an unjust ruler (a *Willkürherrscher* is a tyrant).[58] Thus, Kant's starting point for considering legality is individual choices of this kind – irrational, arbitrary, excessive.

Nevertheless, they can together generate law or right. The term 'right' (in German, *Recht*) again refers to a word that has no equivalent in English.[59] It denotes the 'right state of affairs' – *the done thing* – when individual rights, customs and laws are in order. Unlike the Latin word *ius*, it is not associated with a professional juristic apparatus but grounded in social feelings. Therefore, it is possible to use the expression 'Recht und Gesetz' (right and law are in accordance) or to discuss conflicts between *Recht* and *Gesetz*, or *Recht* and *Gerechtigkeit* (right and justice).

The claim that arbitrary choices generate right becomes even stranger when considering that right is, according to Kant, 'connected with an authorization to coerce' (*TL* 6:231). The German verb *zwingen* invokes the association of brute physical force. A *Zwingburg* (forcing-castle) is not a castle to take refuge in or live in but one to physically enforce authority over an occupied territory. Its ruler, the *Zwingherr* (forcing lord), would coerce the population into obedience. Thus, if the *Doctrine of Right* were not overloaded with systematic vocabulary but written in a more colloquial style, like the *Anthropology*, one might again find a Foucault-like vocabulary – a discourse ('rights-talk') grounded in irrationality and force.

The entire 'moral' aspect seems to depend solely on the notion of a 'general law of freedom'. The expression is reminiscent of the categorical imperative, though it denotes something different, as it is not a test for subjective (inner) maxims

58 For details on the development of the connotations since the Medieval times, see the entry 'Willkür' in *Grimms Deutsches Wörterbuch*. The negative connotation that prevails nowadays was not as dominant in previous times. However, it would have sounded wrong or strange if Kant had started the Groundwork by declaring that only *Willkür* could be called good without limitations.

59 The distinction is, however, common in many other European languages, and in this respect the English language is the exception that bewilders our minds, as Wittgenstein would say.

but rather specifies how outer actions can be coordinated. Thus, it is not an a priori, intrinsic or universalistic principle. As a reminder: the categorical imperative does not require following general laws but excludes all possible empirical motives for following a law so that only the form of a law remains as a test for a maxim. Thus, the notion 'general law of freedom' is, for Kant, not a moral framework – as with Rawls's original position – as 'general laws' as such do not guarantee a 'moral' or right state of affairs.

In Kant's time, it was unnecessary to invent a thought experiment to clarify this point, as everyone lived under the general laws of the *ancien régime*.[60] One could say that at the beginning of the argument, the expression 'general law of freedom' serves as an 'empty signifier', as we are not told what exactly this general law entails. What we can say, given this brief outline, is that Kant asks the more radical question of how it is possible that, out of arbitrary choices and coercion, right (*Recht*) can emerge. Although he limits the use of coercion to hindering hindrances to freedom, thus defending one's rights against 'unrightful' interference, a positive answer to the question of whether *Recht* can emerge without running into contradictions is in no way guaranteed. This can be further illustrated by considering the next argumentative step that Kant takes.

Origins of property

Unlike most contemporary political or legal philosophies, Kant continues his argument with a discussion of 'private right', namely the right to property. Again, he employs highly abstract language. Under the title 'how to have something external as one's own', he maintains that 'it is possible for me to have any external object of my choice as mine' (*RL* 6:246). He calls this a 'permissive principle' and claims: 'Reason wills that this hold as a principle, and it does this as practical reason, which extends itself a priori by this postulate of reason' (*RL* 6:247). For a better understanding of this abstract

[60] The political and social circumstances were very different throughout Germany and Europe. The French term *ancien régime* is therefore a derogatory umbrella term for every political order that is not an egalitarian republic.

argument, it is helpful to consider Kant's lecture notes and popular essays.

In one of his lectures, he refers, in the discussion of the origin of property, to Romulus, the legendary founder of Rome (lecture notes by Vigilantius, hereafter *Vigil.* AA 27:514). According to the legend, the twin brothers Romulus and Remus set out to build a city but had a dispute over the most suitable location. Remus ridiculed the city wall Romulus built on one of the hills by jumping over it. Out of rage, Romulus killed his brother. Kant explains in general terms that 'here, too, the basic principle is that, in order to establish a right, force precedes law, according to a law of permission' (*Vigil.* AA 27:516). Previously, he even said that in *statu naturali*, 'force counts as law' (*Vigil.* AA 27:514). He thus sees the fundamental problem that the origin of property is bound up with force.

He makes a similar point when speculating on the transition from the pastoral life of hunters and gatherers to agriculture. In his philosophical reading of the development of humankind, as told in Genesis, he interprets Cain's murder of Abel as symbolising the conflict between sedentary farmers, who have to invest labour to cultivate the land, and migrating shepherds, who can let their flock stray round and easily move them away (*Conjectural Beginnings of Human History, MAM* 8:18–20). Kant speculates that 'it was probably the farmer who used violence against such incursion' (*MAM* 8:19). Again, he does not explicitly justify violence but sees it as an inevitable part of the development of human civilisation. While continuing his philosophical interpretation of Genesis, Kant holds that, with the formation of larger cities, culture, sociability and public justice emerged, though he also concedes that 'with this epoch began also the inequality among human beings, this rich source of so much evil but also of all good – and it increased ever further' (*MAM* 8:119).

This account recalls the opening claim of Rousseau's *Discourse on the Origin and Foundations of Inequality among Men*. Thus, he has Rousseau's warning in mind:

> The first man who, having enclosed a piece of land, thought of saying 'This is mine' and found people simple enough to believe him, was the true founder of civil society. How

many crimes, wars, murders; how much misery and horror the human race would have been spared if someone had pulled up the stakes and filled in the ditch and cried out to his fellow men: 'Beware of listening to this impostor.'[61]

The question 'how to have something external as one's own' that Kant begins with is thus a real and difficult one. How, then, does Kant get out of the conundrum? As a negative delineation, Kant refutes John Locke's theory of property as a fusion of one's own labour with a thing. Kant points out that, at the most basic level, property is a relation between persons – that is, it is a legal or intellectual relationship (*RL* 6:249). Robinson Crusoe (before the arrival of his native companion Friday) could not acquire any property because it would not make sense to hold animals or the natural surroundings accountable for the violation of property. At the very beginning, property is a mere declaration of choice that is backed by force. Thus, one might say that Kant buys into Rousseau's account of violence and even reinforces it by stressing that, in a state of nature, 'no one is bound to refrain from encroaching on what another possesses if the other gives him no equal assurance that he will observe the same restraint toward him' (*RL* 6:307). One does not even have to wait for 'actual hostility' but is always authorised to use force pre-emptively. Thus, without presuming any faults or evil, the mere existence of human beings who, by their nature, are torn between sense and reason leads to the result that, in the state of nature, force cannot be distinguished from mere violence.

At first glance, the rest of Kant's argument might seem predictable, as all state of nature theories are, in a way, question-begging: either in the state of nature it is presumed what is later on deduced (for instance, freedom and equality) or it is depicted as defective in a way that only the state can mend (as in H. L. A. Hart's version of the primitive society without secondary rules).[62] At first sight, Kant's theory shares several features of this argument, as at some point, he adopts the language of enlightened political philosophy, employing

[61] Jean-Jacques Rousseau, *A Discourse on Inequality*, trans. Maurice Cranston (London: Penguin Books, 1984), 57.

[62] Hart, *The Concept of Law*, 91–98.

terms such as general laws, sovereignty of the people, separation of powers and representative government.

However, he develops his argument in a distinctively different way. As a way of evading the paradox that force counts as law, he introduces a permissive principle (*lex permissiva*) of practical reason (*RL* 6:247). This puts others under an obligation to refrain from using certain objects of our choice because we were the first to take them into our possession. Kant calls this a principle that 'extends practical reason a priori' (*RL* 6:247). The status of this postulate is, however, dubious. Kant is not even consistent in his terminology and calls it a law, principle (*Grundsatz*) or postulate.[63] Systematically, Kant is looking for a way to get the 'dialectical' process of cultural development going without giving up a monistic starting point by presuming two distinct basic forces, like constructive and destructive desires.[64] However, even if one were to take this solution for the state of nature, it would not solve all problems, as force or violence reappears as a driving mechanism throughout civilisation – in mythology (Cain and Abel) as well as in history – as evinced in a teleological perspective.

The entire argument is best understood by recognising the comprehensive scope of Kant's notion of private right. He does not, like most state of nature theories, give a rough description of 'primitive societies', only to move on with the introduction of the state.[65] Instead, he deduces the entire

[63] For a defence of the principle as the core of Kant's legal philosophy, see Reinhard Brandt, 'Das Erlaubnisgesetz, oder: Vernunft und Geschichte in Kants Rechtslehre', in Reinhard Brandt, ed., *Rechtsphilosophie der Aufklärung: Symposium Wolfenbüttel 1981* (Berlin: Walter de Gruyter, 1982), 233–85; Joachim Hruschka, 'The Permissive Law: Kant on Freedom and Right', *Archiv für Rechts- und Sozialphilosophie* 84 (1998): 29–42.

[64] Sigmund Freud faced a related problem when realising that the pleasure principle could not explain properly destructive manifestations of psychic life and the collapse of civilisation during WWI. He therefore introduced, besides the (constructive) sex drive, a (destructive) death drive. Sigmund Freud, 'Civilization and Its Discontents', in *Civilization, Society and Religion*, trans. Albert Dickson (Harmondsworth: Penguin, 1985), 310–13.

[65] This is the target of Widerquist/McCall's criticism of state of nature theories. Karl Widerquist and Grant McCall, 'Myths about the State of Nature and the Reality of Stateless Societies', *Analyse & Kritik* 37, no. 1–2 (2015): 233–57.

realm of private right from the notion of right as hindering a hindrance to freedom. The permissive principle serves to bridge the gap between the factual emergence of possession and the a priori concept of right. Thus, the entire body of private right – property law, contract law, domestic law and some special topics (money and why unauthorised publishing of books is forbidden as a matter of right) – is not just a camouflage of violence but can, according to Kant, be deduced a priori from the notion of right. The details of Kant's argument on specific topics need not be discussed. However, two systematic consequences are directly relevant to a genealogy of cosmopolitan thought.

First, because the notion of private right is developed a priori, it is not merely a generalisation of existing bodies of private law: it can be squared with notions of Roman law and, to some extent, with historical developments. It is, therefore, a highly abstract notion that Kant develops to integrate anthropological, legal and conceptual considerations. Reflecting further on the historical status of this notion of private right as it unfolds over the course of history might again suggest a Hegelian perspective. For this reason, this genealogy of cosmopolitan thought is not a project that takes historical positions as a given but one akin to Kant's thinking.[66]

Second, there is an even more direct cosmopolitan implication, again one that is not explicitly found in Kant. As the entire body of private law follows from conceptual considerations a priori and, in principle, can be related to various existing bodies of positive law but is not bound to any particular jurisdiction, it could be regarded as the germ of a transnational or proto-cosmopolitan concept of law. In other words: wherever people interact, associate, trade, marry or publish books, they could adopt the a priori notion of private right. This conceptual claim can be supported by certain historical speculations.

Proto-cosmopolitan consequences of private right

The time and place in which Kant lived could, in contemporary terms, be described as a site of legal pluralism.

[66] The fundamental question of the relation of philosophy to the established legal tradition will be taken up again in the next chapter.

In Königsberg, several peoples, cultures and religions met; merchants traded both to the West and to the East; and, at some time during the Seven Years War, the imperial state administration changed (from Prussia to Russia and back again). Various groups – merchants, religious communities, especially the Jews and, to some degree, the traditional guilds – lived according to their own laws under the umbrella of a 'foreign' or 'imperial' state authority (depending on whom one asked in Königsberg).

In order to characterise these various regimes as law, it is necessary to develop a social-scientific concept of law, either by pointing out certain functions or 'jobs' that the law performs or by describing its typical content. Both avenues were later pursued by legal pluralists and continue to shape contemporary discussions of these issues.[67] However, Kant is never included in histories of legal pluralism. There are two reasons for this. First, his conception of private right is too closely connected to Roman law concepts and, especially in matters of family law, too heavily influenced by the ideas of his time, leaving no conceptual space for any historical or local variations. For the same reason, the proto-cosmopolitan character of Kant's notion of private right is also not taken up in the contemporary debate on cosmopolitanism.

The second reason brings us back to Kant's line of argument. He would agree that, even though his notion of right is based on the power of choice (*Willkür*) and force, it can be developed into a complete body of private right a priori. However, according to Kant, all these regulations do not amount to 'proper law' – they remain provisional and inconclusive as long as public right is missing.

Public right

The transition from private to public right might appear straightforward once one assumes the idea of a state of nature. Yet Kant takes a specific route that has consequences

[67] The first description alludes to K. N. Llewellyn's theory of the 'Law-Jobs', the second to Eugen Ehrlich's notion of legal pluralism, which will be explored in greater detail in the next chapter. See Karl N. Llewellyn, 'The Normative, the Legal, and the Law-Jobs: The Problem of Juristic Method', *Yale Law Journal* 49, no. 8 (1940): 1355–400.

for his account of cosmopolitanism. He holds that there is a 'postulate to leave the state of nature and proceed with it into a rightful condition' (*RL* 6:307). As it is a postulate of practical reason, it is not due to a negative experience of human beings' violent nature or to the observation of feuds among people in a state of nature. Instead, Kant argues that 'in general they do wrong in the highest degree by wanting to be and to remain in a condition that is not rightful, that is, in which no one is assured of what is his against violence' (*RL* 6:307–308).

It is important to note that the expression 'to assure of what is his' is not just a figure of speech, roughly meaning life, liberty and the pursuit of happiness, but denotes precisely the aim of introducing public right: to transfer the previously deduced content of private right into a rightful condition – that is, a public legal order. Kant explains that public right contains 'no further or other duties of human beings among themselves' (*RL* 6:306) than private law. Thus, public right – which in contemporary social contract theory is the starting point for all discussions about distributive justice – plays, for Kant, no role in determining the legal duties that people have among themselves. In terms of social justice, it might even appear 'superfluous', as public right has no say, for instance, in regulating marriage.

Like private law, it is a highly abstract notion that integrates anthropological, legal and conceptual considerations. Kant explains that it consists of the right of the state, the right of nations and cosmopolitan right. He holds: 'so if the principle of outer freedom limited by law is lacking in any one of these three possible forms of rightful condition, the framework of all the others is unavoidably undermined and must finally collapse' (*RL* 6:311).

As public right is introduced as a conceptual idea, Kant is, at first sight, more lenient in accepting non-state or indigenous societies. He is well aware that states have not always existed, but that the earliest communities, as described, for instance, in the Old Testament (or Hebrew Bible), were hunter-gatherer societies and left traces not only in indigenous societies but also in our world. Likewise, he points out that, in the state of nature, there can be 'societies compatible with rights (e.g., conjugal, paternal, domestic societies in general, as well as many others)' (*RL* 6:306). He is also critical of the forceful subjugation of shepherd and hunter societies (*RL* 6:353) and acknowledges that life in such a 'rightful' way even has a certain allure for people from civilised nations (but not the other way around).[68]

However, on closer inspection, his notion of the state carries very harsh consequences, which become apparent only when following his argument in detail. He uses two lines of argument to justify the introduction of public right: first, the necessity to secure property, and second, the necessity to punish wrongdoers. Only the first has been extensively discussed in the literature on cosmopolitanism, whereas the second has hardly been mentioned, though both have a cosmopolitan upshot.

Establishing a rightful condition

Kant begins his argument on a fundamental level. He holds that the abstract notion of property on its own does not necessarily include any conflict, for 'people could be so dispersed that they would not come into any community with each other' (*RL* 6:262). Only due to the 'spherical surface of the earth' does community become a necessary consequence of human existence. The argument rejects Locke's proviso that appropriation of natural resources is unproblematic as long as enough is left for everyone else by pointing out that the notion of right – and hence property – is an ideal (noumenal) one. The spherical surface of the world is the empirical condition that necessarily brings people into contact.

The argument also has a political dimension. Since in the state of nature 'no one is assured of what is his against violence' (*RL* 6:308), the postulate follows to leave the state of nature and proceed into 'a rightful condition'. The key point is that the rightful condition is not realised merely with the

[68] In the *Physical Geography*, Kant speculates that the 'great inclination towards independence among these peoples' seems to be 'the reason why no native American would think of adopting the way of life of the Europeans, even though they often choose the latter' (*PG* 9:433). Current discussions on Kant's racism with regard to indigenous societies often miss the context and systematic place of his reflections. They are genealogies that help to explain the origin of our institutions. They are, so to speak, second order reflections on our practices, but not first order descriptive value judgements.

establishment of a single state but requires the extension of the argument into a right of nations and cosmopolitan right. Since states are, in relation to one another, in a state of nature, as they constantly threaten each other with war, they are under the obligation to proceed into a league of nations.

> States, considered in external relation to one another, are (like lawless savages) by nature in a nonrightful condition. (...) This nonrightful condition is a condition of war (of the right of the stronger), even if it is not a condition of actual war and actual attacks being constantly made (hostilities). Although no state is wronged by another in this condition (insofar as neither wants anything better), this condition is in itself still wrong in the highest degree, and states neighbouring upon one another are under obligation to leave it. (*RL* 6:344).

This does not require establishing a supranational authority but only a voluntary league of nations in the form of an association (*Genossenschaft*) that can even 'be renounced at any time and so must be renewed from time to time' (*RL* 6:344). The upshot of Kant's argument is that, without the cosmopolitan conclusion, 'anything external that is mine or yours' is merely provisional and only with 'a universal association of states ... can rights come to hold conclusively and a true condition of peace come about' (*RL* 6:350).

One can easily overlook that Kant does not give any recommendations as to why it would be good to have states in the first place and, maybe even better, a universal association of states later on. Instead, he makes a purely conceptual argument. Without a final arbiter and enforcer, the rightful condition cannot persist, as the original exercise of one's right in the first place is not something one could 'prove a priori' or explain to everyone but is rather a matter of an arbitrary choice (freedom as *Willkür*) backed by force (of course, within certain limits). The arbitrary, force-backed starting point carries over, so to speak, to the level of the state.

However, it would not suffice to have just one state either. Indeed, the very notion of a state as part of public right requires having several states in association, as only then can disputes, at least in principle, be settled as a matter of right.

A state that does not respect other states as equals but strives continuously to extend its influence over other territories, or respects other entities only as subjugated and tributary powers, could not conclusively guarantee a rightful condition, as it could suffer the same fate of being subjugated. As the notion of public right is a priori, for Kant it is not relevant at this point to discuss the actual fate of states or empires but only to show that the idea of the state can be conceived or constructed without contradictions (*RL* 6:352–54).

At this point, one might consider taking a generous political-liberal perspective on Kant's conceptual argument as long as it leads to the desired result – a league of nations and cosmopolitan right. However, such an approach would misunderstand both the content and the form of Kant's argument. In the *Doctrine of Right*, published after the treatise *Towards Perpetual Peace*, Kant clarifies that 'perpetual peace, the ultimate good of the whole right of nations, is indeed an unachievable idea' (*RL* 6:350). Only the 'political principles' directed toward this goal can be put into practice. As this is one of the few passages in which Kant explicitly refers to political principles, it is instructive to see what they require.

Kant concedes that wars and imperial conquests bring about much suffering. However, his starting point, as throughout the *Doctrine of Right*, is not the perspective of someone experiencing injustice, but an active one. The right of free states in a state of nature to go to war with one another is not a personal privilege of kings or princes. Instead, it results from the duty of the sovereign to the people to sustain their independence (*RL* 6:346). Thus, once a rightful condition in one territory is established – in other words, once people conceive of themselves as a commonwealth, as a *res publica* – the sovereign who acts on their behalf has a duty to defend this state of affairs. The ensuing *jus in bello* does not abolish this right to self-defence but serves only to ensure that wars are conducted in accordance with the principle that they 'always leave open the possibility of leaving the state of nature among states (in external relation to one another) and entering a rightful condition' (*RL* 6:347). Likewise, the various requirements of the *jus post bellum* Kant mentions – not to punish, colonise or exploit a defeated enemy – serve precisely this end.

As the starting point of Kant's argument is the defence of the freedom of a sovereign state against interference, the confederation of states that are called upon to enter cannot be placed under a sovereign authority but 'must be in an alliance that can be renounced at any time and so must be renewed from time to time' (*RL* 6:344). Thus, there is no mandatory membership in the alliance, let alone any transfer of sovereignty.

The 'cosmopolitan right' mentioned only in the concluding paragraph does not serve to underpin this thin account with a 'moral' concept either but is restricted to 'offering to engage in commerce with any other' (*RL* 6:352). It is a right not due to an assumed original ownership of the earth, but because people cannot avoid coming into contact with one another. Moreover, it is a right that needs to be restricted, as it can easily be misused as a pretence for conquests or the subjugation of other civilisations.

This completes Kant's first line of argument to justify a cosmopolitan condition in the *Doctrine of Right*. One might expect that the details of Kant's republicanism or the path towards perpetual peace could now be fleshed out in greater detail, showing why it is desirable or coincides with our contemporary moral sentiments. However, as we have presented Kant's philosophy in a specific contextual way that takes both the circumstances of his time and his entire thinking, including the empirical side, into account, this path is ruled out. Moreover, when concentrating only on the uplifting cosmopolitan outcome, one easily overlooks the realist underpinning of Kant's political philosophy, which also has an unexpected cosmopolitan side.

Obedience and punishment

To recapitulate: the introduction of public right is not – as in Hobbes – the result of the experience of violence in human beings that makes a state necessary, nor – as in the natural law tradition – of the many beneficial institutions that the state allegedly brings about (*RL* 6:312). Instead, the justification is, just as in the case of the categorical imperative in moral philosophy, entirely independent of any considerations of happiness or consequences. The reason for stressing this point, however, is very different from that in moral philosophy. There, the concern for the purity of motivation was the requirement for truly free actions out of respect for the moral law. Right, on the other hand, secures the freedom of arbitrary choice (*Willkür*) under general external laws. Here, the requirement is strict obedience to authority in all circumstances. Kant writes: 'the saying "All authority is from God" ... sets forth an idea as a practical principle of reason: the principle that the presently existing legislative authority ought to be obeyed, whatever its origin may be' (*RL* 6:319).

In a nutshell: in the *Doctrine of Right*, Kant does not develop a theory of justice but a theory of obedience. Since this interpretation goes against most Kantian-inspired political philosophy and also against many Kant interpretations, it needs to be further explained, since only then can the full weight of the consequences be disclosed. Throughout his writings, Kant stresses again and again this doctrine of absolute obedience to the sovereign, and not a single sentence in his published works, letters or even reflections denounces a particular government or law as unjust, or calls for new laws or resistance – let alone a revolution.[69] In the *Doctrine of Right*, he states his position most clearly:

> [A] people cannot offer any resistance to the legislative head of a state that would be consistent with right, since a rightful condition is possible only by submission to its general legislative will. There is, therefore, no right to *sedition* (...), still less to *rebellion* (...), and least of all is there a right against the head of a state as an individual person (the monarch), *to attack his person* or even his life (...) on the pretext that he has abused his authority (...). Any attempt whatsoever at this is *high treason* (...), and whoever commits such treason must be punished by nothing less than death for attempting *to destroy his fatherland*. (RL 6:320)

This apparently quietistic attitude baffled both his contemporaries and later interpreters.[70] How can it be squared with

[69] See, for further references, Thomas E. Hill, *Virtue, Rules, and Justice. Kantian Aspirations* (Oxford: Oxford University Press, 2012), 277–95.

[70] Horn, *Nichtideale Normativität*, 18–24; Bernd Ludwig, 'Kommentar zum Staatsrecht (II)', in Otfried Höffe, ed., *Klassiker auslegen: Kants metaphysische Anfangsgründe der Rechtslehre* (Berlin: Akademie, 1999), 173–94, esp. 189.

the foundation of political philosophy as a project of the Enlightenment, with the overall 'liberal' political philosophy, and with the cosmopolitan outlook? Some interpreters have tried to detect small traces of a different attitude, insinuating a change of perspective in late Kant that is not consistently reflected in all his texts, or, through creative interpretation, find loopholes in Kant's argument.[71] However, this does not explain the overwhelming number of passages in which Kant explicitly states the opposite: the present legislative authority is justified; there is no right of resistance. To gain a better understanding, it is helpful to reflect first on Kant's terminology.

When Kant speaks about authority, he does not use the German term *Autorität*, but *Obrigkeit*. It has nowadays fallen out of use, as it sounds archaic.[72] However, in Kant's times, the term was more frequently used to denote authority of any origin – within the church, the military, the state, or the authority of lords over their subordinates. In other words, it is a term from the feudal era, when *Obrigkeit* ('authority') was ubiquitous.

For understanding the key point of Kant's argument, it does not suffice to recall once again his starting point (right as freedom to make arbitrary choices); his aim must also be taken seriously: the state, belonging to the tripartite structure of public right, is a total idea (idea of reason) – the only political structure that can be deduced a priori and that has an empirical reality at the same time. Kant's main idea is to give the state a foundation that is independent of all considerations of well-being or happiness. His argument is that practical reason has no regard for any empirical ends, as people differ in their thinking about happiness, and happiness does not follow any formal law (*GTP* 8:290). Kant would therefore consider any theory of public goods a violation of

[71] Franco Zotta, *Immanuel Kant. Legitimität und Recht. Eine Kritik seiner Eigentumslehre, Staateslehre und seiner Geschichtsphilosophie* (Freiburg: Alber, 2000), 216–39 disproves all attempts to construct a right of resistance in Kant.

[72] The German *Obrigkeit* nowadays implies an uncritical trust and belief in authorities whose worldly consequences have been denounced in the study of the authoritarian personality. Theodor W. Adorno et al., *The Authoritarian Personality* (New York: Harper, 1950).

this requirement, as the legitimacy of the state would then depend on the performance of this function.[73] Moreover, public goods could be realised under various regimes, so that the a priori structure of right would falter.

As in moral philosophy, the good will must not depend on any external aim, and authority must likewise be pure. Though Kant is not naïve but is, through his studies in anthropology and geography, well aware that not all states would function well in this respect and that many people might even prefer a state of nature to the present conditions. So, what are Kant's arguments for acknowledging the state as a total idea, if it is not to perform some public goods?

There are three distinct arguments. The first and most obvious is that the existence of states is the precondition for overcoming violence in principle and securing perpetual peace as the highest political good. This argument is not merely a fairy tale for the future but has an important place in Kant's political thought. It is, again, not an external good – such as fear of violence – that motivates us, but the possibility of attaining a rightful condition at all. Without this possibility, the entire idea of reason being practical would have no foothold in the world, and states would, in the end, be indistinguishable from bands of robbers.

One might think that this is a highly speculative argument, but it does have a real bearing on the way of viewing world politics. Even though colonialism was, at Kant's time, still in its infancy, the principal problem was already visible. From the point of view of colonised countries, the colonisers were not 'civilising forces' but simply bands of robbers that could be pacified, like all robbers, with booty on a regular basis. If this were the ultimate end of states – everyone trying to grow bigger, as only the biggest get rewards in the form of colonies – the entire idea of statehood or a system of states would turn out to be a bad ideology, a poorly disguised scheme of exploitation. However, this does not mean that the mere idea suffices to temper the behaviour of states. In any case, the precondition for regulating states in the first place is that their authority

73 Thomas Pogge, *John Rawls* (München: C. H. Beck, 1994), 189–98 misses this point by ascribing a theory of moral goods to Kant.

is sustained and obeyed at nearly all costs, in order for a republic to finally emerge.[74]

Kant's second argument in favour of the state as an absolute idea builds on the murky origin of all states. He argues that 'the origin of the supreme authority is, from the practical point of view for the people who are subject to it, unfathomable (*unerforschlich*)' (*RL* 6:318). Even though Kant uses a term that characterises God's counsel as 'unfathomable' (*unerforschlich*), his reasoning is not quietistic but, rather, enlightened – though only at the very end. Kant points out that any attempt to find the ultimate authority through historical research would be considered high treason (*RL* 6:320). The underlying reasoning is that there is no original contract of submission: authority is, in any case, a matter of force or power, whether power came first, and law followed afterwards, or the other way round. Thus, in any case, authority is a matter of enforcement, something that no rebellion can change. The only enlightened hope is that citizens, even though they may not resist the authority, may complain about injustices, although it is up to the sovereign to change the laws (*RL* 6:319). In one of his political essays, Kant therefore calls the freedom of the pen the 'sole palladium of people's rights' (*On the Common Saying: 'This May Be True in Theory, but it Does Not Apply in Practice, TP* 8:304).

In the *Doctrine of Right*, Kant seems to take delight in shattering the intuitions of his enlightened audience, who believe that the views of ordinary citizens must in some way play a role in the formation of the will of the sovereign – for instance, in the form of a parliamentary assembly. However, since any separation of powers that grants one branch an independent standing, including a means to enforce it, all moderate constitutions are, according to Kant, an absurdity (*Unding*): 'Instead of belonging to Right, it is only a principle of prudence' (*RL* 6:320).

One might think that Kant has failed to give a convincing argument for the authority of states – let alone absolute authority – and has at best offered us (empty) hopes for a

[74] In his *Anthropology*, Kant distinguishes between four ways of how freedom, law and coercion can be combined, leading to anarchism, barbarism, despotism and republic, but does not speculate on how one evolves into another (*Anth* 7: 330–1).

better future. There is, however, one function the state administers which Kant explicitly calls a requirement of justice: punishing criminals and, ultimately, executing murderers and rebels.

Discussions about the justification of the death penalty – in particular, capital punishment for mothers who had killed their illegitimate children – were widespread in enlightened circles, while most intellectuals tended to call for its abolition, especially in difficult cases.[75] Kant is again an exception. Unflinchingly, he writes: 'If someone has committed murder, he must die. Hence there is no substitute that will satisfy justice' (*RL* 6:339). It is telling that, only when talking about 'the right to punish', Kant employs – with emphasis – the moral terminology that one might have expected all along. He proclaims: 'The law of punishment is a categorical imperative' (*RL* 6:332), explaining its measure as 'none other than the principle of equality' (*RL* 6:333) and calling the court that administers the death penalty the 'public justice' (RL 6:335). To add further discomfort for high-minded Kantians, as the state can call on convicted felons to do penal work, they are (legitimately) 'reduced to the status of a slave for a certain time, or permanently if the state sees fit' (*RL* 6:333).[76]

The rationale Kant refers to is the well-known principle of retribution. Punishment can, according to Kant, not serve the public, as this would mean treating a human being as 'a means to the purpose of another' (*RL* 6:331) but must be something required by the criminal himself. Kant underlines this point by giving the example of a true-hearted insurgent who is condemned either to death or to penal labour. Even in this extreme case, Kant proclaims: 'The man of honour would choose death' (*RL* 6:334). The example is telling, as Kant introduces it to change, hypothetically, the perspective.

[75] Kant's close friend Theodor von Hippel discussed a real case in which he was involved in his book, *Nachricht die v. K—sche Untersuchung betreffend. Ein Beytrag über Verbrechen und Strafen*, (1792), ed. Matthias Luserke (St. Ingbert: Röhrig, 2000).

[76] If one wanted to denounce penal labor as a form of modern slavery today, one does not need to look far: prison systems, even in some Western democracies, provide ample evidence of the problematic nature of penal labour.

Nowadays discussions about punishment would be expected to focus either on the rights or dignity of the offender or on the violated dignity of the victim. For Kant, punishment is a right of the sovereign (*RL* 6:331). The example merely shows that there is a corresponding duty on the side of the culprit – which, however, is only realised and accepted by offenders in a few exceptional cases. The sovereign, on the other hand, is not free to exercise the right to punish by arbitrarily granting clemency. Usually, the right to punish is a duty to punish – in the extreme case, a duty to execute. Again, Kant employs a thought experiment to make his point.

> Even if a civil society were to dissolve itself by common agreement of all its members (for example, if the people inhabiting an island decided to separate and disperse themselves around the world), the last murderer remaining in prison must first be executed, so that everyone will duly receive what his actions are worth and so that the bloodguilt thereof will not be fixed on the people because they failed to insist on carrying out the punishment; for if they fail to do so, they may be regarded as accomplices in this public violation of legal justice. (*RL* 6:333)

What can we make of Kant's argument today? Most interpreters are inclined to find ways to alleviate Kant's strict position on punishment, and there is 'barely a contemporary interpreter who will take a stand in favour of this part of Kant's theory of penal law'.[77] Significantly, the topic of punishment is hardly ever mentioned in discussions on cosmopolitanism or global justice. This is unfortunate, as it is the point where Kant adopts an active cosmopolitan stance – effectively putting his theory in action. The archaic formulation he employs for justifying the execution of the last prisoner, 'that each has done to him what his deeds deserve, and blood guilt does not cling to the people for not having insisted upon this punishment'

[77] Jean-Christophe Merle, *German Idealism and the Concept of Punishment* (New York: Cambridge University Press, 2009), 326–27. One of the few to defend the coherence of Kant's account is Benjamin S. Yost, 'Kant's Justification of the Death Penalty Reconsidered', *Kantian Review* 15, no. 2 (2010): 1–27.

(*RL* 6:333), is a perspective all peoples throughout the world could take on the (hypothetically) dispersed people. They can only be respected as fellow Kantian cosmopolitans if they prove they have accepted their burdens as a people. In their name, the last murderer must be executed.

This cosmopolitan perspective presents us with a rather grim outlook on the world. It arises out of the need to justify the rightful condition of having something external as one's own. For having it conclusively, the three-part structure of public right needs to be acknowledged and sustained. The cosmopolitan condition – including the federation of states and cosmopolitan right (right to visit) – is a philosophical history of hope, the hope for a possible course of history that concludes the thought and shows that the highest political good is not a chimera. However, it comes at a high price: the established authorities can claim absolute authority and, in return, adopt the duty to punish wrongdoers, ultimately executing the enemies of the idea of right (murderers and rebels).

One should not underestimate this minimal result. It shows, at least in principle, that the idea of practical reason is not empty or dialectical (self-refuting). At the same time, it is not a form of naïve sentiment or do-gooder mentality (which Hegel later would denounce as the beautiful soul) but reminds us of the grim reality to which even the highest political good is bound. Last but not least, it carries the uneasiness of a productive momentum. It urges us to question Kant's account and look for something beyond it: the highest political good cannot be all philosophy can tell us; it cannot be the highest good as such.

3.3 *Towards Perpetual Peace*: The cosmopolitan dialectic completed

The various explorations of Kant's philosophy have not yet yielded the desired result of providing a firm foundation for contemporary cosmopolitan thought. Instead, they have reasserted concerns that have haunted us along the way. The contextual historical examination of Kant's philosophy has shown how the history of the city republic of Königsberg could have been used as a model of resistance and that many people in Kant's intellectual circle held enlightened views (for instance, equal rights for men and women) or worked for enlightened causes (for instance, the abolition of the death penalty). However, Kant himself did not take part, as one might have suspected, as a public intellectual in such endeavours, but was rather on the conservative side. This does not mean that he was an unpolitical man or had no feel for the subtle shift in the intellectual mood of his time. On the contrary, in his contestation with Schlosser, Kant clearly recognised the upcoming romantic mood and quietist attitude and tried to tackle it on the most fundamental level by taking up Plato again, anticipating the Romantic enthusiasm for the ancients and Plato in particular.

However, the system of critical philosophy that Kant established as a counterforce did not lead us to our contemporary convictions. On the contrary, the prospect of perpetual peace – the keystone of Kant's practical philosophy – came at a high price: the near-total acquiescence to all authority leaves only the faint hope that, one day, some ruler might become enlightened, and, moreover, the unsettling realisation that even in the state of perpetual peace, the relentless machinery of execution will not cease, allowing justice to be endlessly produced.

Since this reading of Kant might be unfamiliar or even distressing for many, I will pursue it through an interpretation of Kant's most famous political essay, *Towards Perpetual Peace: A Philosophical Sketch*. The essay has, in the course of the cosmopolitan revival at the end of the twentieth century, acquired a larger-than-life status and is often cited as the hallmark or founding document of contemporary cosmopolitan thought. The usual assumption is that whatever liberal sentiments one might harbour are prefigured in the essay at the most fundamental level.[78]

[78] Jürgen Habermas, 'Kant's Idea of Perpetual Peace: At Two Hundred Years' Historical Remove', in *The Inclusion of the Other: Studies in Political Theory*, trans. Ciaran Cronin and Pablo De Greiff (Cambridge, MA: MIT Press, 1999), 169–70. For a sharp critique of policy-minded recommendations along the lines of Kant in German scholarly journals on the occasion of the 200th anniversary of the *Perpetual Peace*, see Georg Geismann, 'Nachlese zum Jahr des "ewigen Friedens"', *Logos* 29, no. 3 (1996): 317–45.

In order to show how Kant still poses the more fundamental questions and thus challenges contemporary cosmopolitan sentiments, it suffices to highlight a few selected points. To start with, Kant is often read as someone who shows the path towards perpetual peace – a state of affairs where there is no more violence between republics and justice reigns within the countries so that free human relations can flourish.[79] Kant is also well aware of the Augustinian legacy of this idea, which he refers to as the idea of the 'pastoral life' (*Idea for a Universal History with a Cosmopolitan Aim, IaG* 8: 21).

However, perpetual peace is something else. It is, first and foremost, not an external good to strive for, as this would go against Kant's fundamental conviction that there is nothing good but the good will. Instead, peace is a contingent consequence of rightful relations between states, so that there are no further legal grounds to go to war.[80] Kant's crucial reworking of the Christian tradition is thus a reinterpretation of peace as a legal concept.

Three further consequences follow from this that should be briefly named before being discussed in greater detail. First, the so-called democratic peace thesis, or Kant's philosophy of history, is not a 'political theory' aimed at instructing politicians but a teleological judgement for explaining the course of history by presuming a value judgement. Second, Kant's account is not an 'ideal theory' either, but, on the contrary, extremely realistic, as it is restricted to applying legal concepts (in German: *angewandte Rechtslehre*). Finally, there is little common ground between the historical Kant and various re-appropriations of him, as he vehemently opposes putting any ends – even laudable ones – before duty.

[79] This is the common assumption in the international relations literature on the so-called democratic peace thesis. For a critical assessment of this line of thought, see Seán Molloy, *Kant's International Relations: The Political Theology of Perpetual Peace* (Ann Arbor: University of Michigan Press, 2017).

[80] See, on this point Georg Geismann, 'World Peace: Rational Idea and Reality. On the principles of Kant's political philosophy', in Hariolf Oberer, ed., *Kant. Analysen – Probleme – Kritik*, vol. 2 (Würzburg: Königshausen & Neumann, 1996), 265–319.

Perpetual peace as legal peace

Kant's essay starts, like many of his popular essays in the *Berlinische Monatsschrift*, in a light-hearted tone by offering various interpretations of 'this satirical inscription on a certain Dutch innkeeper's signboard depicting a graveyard' (*Perpetual Peace, ZeF* 8:343). Yet, as it is often with Kant, the playful irony has a deeper meaning as it connects the topic of death – both as the fate of human beings and as a looming danger to philosophy – with the highest political good.

Perpetual peace is not a natural, external good (what Rawls would later term a basic good) that a political moralist might strive to achieve by maximising it through the cunning of politics but 'a juridical condition arising from the acknowledgment of duty' (*ZeF* 8:377). Kant explains that practical philosophy can only be made 'consistent with itself' (*ZeF* 8:376) if it arises from a formal principle (i.e., the categorical imperative). Only then can freedom be shown to have reality, the unity of theoretical and practical philosophy be conceived and the highest political good be understood as a consequence of the principle of right, thus completing the proof that a pure rational foundation and development of the idea of justice is possible.

Here, Kant's entire practical philosophy seems condensed into just two paragraphs. However, it is to be noted that Kant has unfolded in his legal philosophy only the external side of freedom in terms of right. Freedom may also contain aspects of the 'natural good' – it is simply pleasant and feels good to live in peace – but its justificatory basis is solely that states no longer have legal grounds for war.

This limited perspective is especially evident in the preliminary articles for perpetual peace among states. Kant names six conditions but regards three as prohibitive laws 'holding without regard for differing circumstances, which require an immediate end to an abuse' (*ZeF* 8:347). The first three are the following: 1. There shall be no secret reservations in peace treaties, 2. No state shall forcibly interfere with the constitution or government of another state, and 3. No state at war with another shall allow itself such acts of hostility that would make mutual trust impossible during a future peace (*ZeF* 8:343–7).

The second provision clearly shows that Kant speaks only in strictly legal terms. To justify the prohibition of forcible interference, he asks the rhetorical question 'For what can justify it in doing so?' and adds that even in cases of 'great troubles' that come about with people through lawlessness or an ongoing civil war, 'such interference of foreign powers would be a violation of the right of a people dependent upon no other and only struggling with its internal illness' (*ZeF* 8:346). Kant strongly condemns interventions that we might today seek to justify in terms of a 'responsibility to protect' as a 'scandal that would make the autonomy of all states insecure' (*ZeF* 8:346).

When confronted with these remarks, many interpreters either take recourse to a systematic interpretation, condescendingly granting to Kant that he was not yet aware of a collective security system, or speculate that he somehow shrank back from the more 'radical' consequences of his approach – thus surpassing Kant in philosophical radicalism. However, they overlook the specific arguments Kant advances to propose only a limited and voluntary federation instead of a full-blown world state – or a federation of nations with coercive force. Indeed, in the *Essay on the Idea of a Universal History*, published eleven years before *Towards Perpetual Peace*, Kant himself made the argument that only a federation of nations 'where every state, even the smallest, could expect its security and rights not from its own might, or its own juridical judgement, but only from this great federation of nations (*Foedus Amphictyonum*)' could end the lawless condition of savages (*IaG* 8:24). We need to answer the question of why Kant did not simply repeat his earlier argument if it is the more radical, advanced or convincing one.

Intercultural understanding as a precondition

In his earlier essay, Kant introduced the idea of perpetual peace, answering Rousseau's scepticism that civilisation had not brought about moralisation. As long as the last step – the federation of states – has not been taken, Kant agrees with Rousseau's diagnosis, though not with his scepticism in principle about whether civilisation can be achieved. In the later essay, he realised that the method he had proposed earlier entailed a dialectic. At two points, this becomes especially apparent. On the one hand he holds firmly to his thesis that the formation of states out of a state of nature is not just a thought experiment but also a necessary historical development for bringing about civilisation.[81] On the other hand, he is critical of using civilisation as a pretext for subjugating indigenous societies and condemns the injustices and cruelties committed in this course as 'all those supposedly good intentions cannot wish away the stain of injustice in the means used for them' (*ZeF* 6:353). Therefore, he is not univocally committed to the 'Western' or 'Occidental' path to civilisation but grants China and Japan their own path of development (*ZeF* 8:359–60). For contemporary ears, this sounds like a variant of cultural relativism that goes too far – as even basic principles of 'Western civilisation', such as the respect for human rights, seem to be negotiable. Again, Kant has a specific point and way of achieving this aim in mind.

As he explained in his programmatic essay *What is Enlightenment? (WA)*, enlightenment cannot be taught dogmatically (like dogmatic religions teach their doctrines) or introduced by some wise sage who is then venerated as someone with a higher insight, but needs to be achieved through ongoing intellectual self-formation, or as stated in the famous first sentence: 'Enlightenment is the human being's emergence from his self-incurred minority' (*WA* 8:35). The emergence is not a solipsistic endeavour, as a minority has become 'almost nature' to single individuals. Instead, enlightenment requires a public – that is, free and open – space for intellectual discussion. 'But that a public should enlighten itself is more possible; indeed this is almost inevitable, if only it is left its freedom' (*WA* 8:36).

In historical terms, this means that people need to enlighten themselves by addressing specific forms of self-incurred minority. If something can neither be taught dogmatically from the vantage point of a higher morality nor from an objectively more enlightened insight, the 'emergence' has to be achieved by a 'revolutionary' individual – hero or saint – in contestation with a specific audience. Thus, even though Kant has a very strong notion of what can be deduced a

[81] Civilisation is in Kant not a 'moral' term but the process of developing the talents of human beings and is usually advanced by conflicts or wars. See his discussion in the *Critique of Judgement* (KU 5:431-3).

priori – basically the entirety of private and public law – he is reluctant to impose this notion on others and relies on a fragile historical process.

Claiming that some notions are a priori or universal yet not valid universally could be seen as a paradox. Yet Kant gives the argument a specific idealist twist to resolve this apparent paradox. His claims are not, like today's political theory, aimed at policy recommendations but are, first and foremost, a way of interpreting our history by presuming normative ideas. For this reason, Kant makes use of historical facts, such as the forceful Christianisation of German tribes, as well as biblical accounts. His leading question is always how practical reason can be seen as having evolved throughout history, but not how more enlightened ideas of philosophes can be imposed upon the unenlightened rest.

One might again suspect that this kind of historical thinking is rather speculative and, in any case, not very helpful for condemning injustices – especially when the supposed lack of enlightenment in developing states is judged against allegedly 'Western' standards. However, Kant could reply that it is the other way round. The very broad notion of historical developments that includes biblical accounts has an advantage when it comes to dealing with 'non-Western' civilisations. In a long footnote, Kant speculates about the 'ancient community between Europe and Tibet' (*ZeF* 8:359) that can be traced through the Tibetan and Greek words for 'holy peace'. If this historical speculation holds true and could be further supported, it would mean that perpetual peace is not a 'Western' or 'Occidental' tradition that needs to be imposed but was inspired by the 'Oriental' tradition in the first place. In this brief remark, Kant anticipates later discussions on comparable intellectual achievements during the Axial Age.[82]

More important than the actual linguistic or historical findings, however, is the guiding principle behind Kant's reasoning. If reason is a common gift of mankind, and if practical reason has reality, it must be shown to have unfolded

[82] The term was coined by Karl Jaspers in 1949. For an overview of the contemporary discussion, see Hans Joas and Robert N. Bellah, eds., *The Axial Age and Its Consequences* (Cambridge, MA: Harvard University Press, 2012). Sappho, however, is usually not included in these discussions.

throughout history in its various formations. Realising the interdependence and overcoming the various formations of self-incurred minority requires philosophical work – not just of some philosophers acting as wise guardians, but of many generations daring to think for themselves.

The republican peace thesis

Having considered the breadth of Kant's argument about the realisation of practical reason throughout history, it goes without saying that he never formulated the republican peace thesis as a social-scientific law that could be empirically verified or refuted. He introduced the argument among the three guarantees of perpetual peace that the 'great artist nature' (*ZeF* 8:360) provides. The ironic tone indicates that Kant is not making a strict philosophical argument but ventures a teleological judgement by attributing nature within purpose. Kant is well aware that such judgements about the cause of history are only legitimate once the reality of practical reason has been determined independently. Otherwise, history could equally well be told, depending on the underlying values, as a history of decline or ever-changing fate (*SF* 7:8). Therefore, Kant would not be impressed when presented with 'empirical evidence' for the perpetual peace thesis over the last 200 years. He would regard such empirical laws merely as prudent hypothetical imperatives for some worldly external good politicians choose among – a goal that happens to be labelled 'Kantian' perpetual peace.

Thus, for Kant, perpetual peace is not an end in itself, and not every peace is equally good. This is not a stubbornness of Kant but a very realistic account of world politics. Long periods of peace, such as the *Pax Augusta*, could also have been due to the sheer power of an empire that successfully suppressed other people's spirit. The peace Kant has in mind is 'a condition arising from the acknowledgement of duty' (*ZeF* 8:377). Seeing it as an aim, that is, apparently a good in itself, would even be dangerous, as it can be abused by moralising politicians to gloss over political principles contrary to right (*ZeF* 8:373). Again, the rhetoric of the peaceful Roman Empire established by Roman historians and the eulogies found in biographies of emperors would provide ample evidence.

In addition, Kant might also have methodological concerns regarding assessing states on a fixed scale as more or less democratic (republican in Kant's terminology). We have seen that he is reluctant to impose 'occidental' philosophical concepts forcefully on other nations or indigenous societies. In addition, he is also conscious of the historical lessons and aware that evil arises from 'illusions' which moral politicians create by subordinating principles to some ends (*ZeF* 8:376).

This shows that Kant has, in principle, the conceptual means to conceive a dialectics of political forms. And indeed, in his treatise on religion, Kant speculates that historical states have, like human beings, an evil disposition striving to aggrandise themselves by subjugating others. Eventually, he speculates, a despotic universal monarchy emerges that disintegrates through rebellion and factionalism into many smaller states – and the same game begins all over again (*RGV* 6:35). This cyclical or dialectical view of constitutions is closer to Kant's line of argument than recent social-scientific conceptualisations, since the cyclical view could be based on a metaphysical principle, which is typically lacking in social-scientific accounts.

Perpetual Peace as an ideal theory?

The last extension of Kant's argument already makes clear that *Towards Perpetual Peace* is not an essay in 'ideal theory'. However, in spite of the many realistic (anthropological) explanations, Kant's theory is not 'realist' in the conventional sense either. Instead, the significance of Kant's approach lies in the way in which the various aspects are related to each other, or in its synthetic – not to say dialectical – power. This requires some explanation.

Kant's essay has, since its publication in 1795, remained in circulation, but throughout the nineteenth and early twentieth centuries it was seldom cited.[83] The text did not gain prominence until the mid-1980s, particularly within the field of international relations theory, where it was taken up as

[83] On the reception of Kant's essay in Germany, see Georg Cavallar, *Pax Kantiana. Systematisch-historische Untersuchung des Entwurfs 'Zum ewigen Frieden' (1795) von Immanuel Kant* (Wien: Böhlau, 1992).

a liberal policy recommendation opposed to the dominant realist school.[84]

This understanding of politics and political theory is, however, not Kant's own. He uses the term *politics* in an unspecific, ambiguous way, so that it can fall on either side of the distinction between the legitimate and the illegitimate. Politics can be the twisting and turning of an immoral doctrine of prudence (*ZeF* 8:375). This notion of politics as 'a theory of maxims for choosing the most suitable means to one's purpose' (*ZeF* 8:370) is based on an alleged knowledge of the empirical nature of men and seeks to draw maxims from the way the world is (*ZeF* 8:371). This is, however, precisely what Kant denounces as the illusion of the political moralist, even if the aim is to bring about a condition of peace among human beings (*ZeF* 8:375). Kant condemns this way of politics harshly as it distorts the idea of duty by mixing moral doctrines with prudence. In the first draft, he even overstates his case by writing that 'this tremendous injury (*iniuria atrox*) can neither be forgiven in this world nor in the future world' (23:187).

Kant is certainly aware that such politics are often successful and reach their aim, whatever it may be. However, his reasoning is that these laws can only be based on empirical generalisations and are not necessarily laws about the human condition, as such a law can only be derived from reason a priori (the categorical imperative as law of freedom). Thus, politics in terms of balancing different values and choosing between incentives and orders to achieve the aims which a majority of the people voted for (*ZeF* 8:377) is what Kant not only disapproves of but regards as the counterforce from which all evil arises (*ZeF* 8:376). The only legitimate place for politics, in Kantian terms, is as an 'applied doctrine of rights' (*angewandte Rechtslehre*) (*ZeF* 8:370). This point needs further explanation, as only here does Kant's distinctive notion of politics come into sight.

[84] This reception occurred in two distinct waves. The first was initiated by Michael W. Doyle's influential two-part essay: 'Kant, Liberal Legacies, and Foreign Affairs, Part 1', *Philosophy and Public Affairs* 12, no. 3 (1983): 205–35; and 'Part 2', *Philosophy and Public Affairs* 12, no. 4 (1983): 323–53; the second followed in the early 1990s, notably through Bruce Russett's empirical elaboration in *Grasping the Democratic Peace: Principles for a Post–Cold War World* (Princeton, NJ: Princeton University Press, 1993).

As morality is already 'of itself practical in the objective sense' (*ZeF* 8: 379), Kant claims that there can, in theory, be no conflict between morals and politics – it is only in the mind of the self-seeking political moralist. One might ask how this could be possible, given the apparently ever conflict-prone circumstances of politics. Kant answers this objection and shows once again the specific synthesis of his approach. The moral politician realises that perpetual peace is not a natural good (*ZeF* 8: 377) and that trying to achieve it as if it were one good among others would reverse the order of things. They will therefore obey the duty they have as a head of state by aiming to bring the given constitution in accordance with natural right as an idea of reason (*ZeF* 8: 372), of course never through hasty revolutions but always through moderate reforms, so that 'people gradually become susceptible to the influence of the mere idea of the authority of law' (*ZeF* 8: 372).

Thus, neither citizens, intellectuals nor other kinds of enlightened groups are called upon to further the social change: only the sovereign lawgiver, who ponders the question of whether a people could impose 'law upon themselves' (*WA* 8: 39), so to speak, 'in their head'. Subjects have no right to question, for example, the level of taxes the legislator decrees (*GTP* 8: 297). It is not by chance that Kant describes the guiding principles of such politics in terms that resemble a saying from Scripture (Matthew 6:33): 'Seek ye first the kingdom of pure practical reason and its justice, and your end [the blessing of perpetual peace] will come to you of itself' (*ZeF* 8:378).

Kant can do no more than affirm his trust in the providence of nature, as any attempt to theorise developments in the form of a 'social-scientific democratic peace thesis' would be yet another instance of treating morality as a doctrine of prudence. It would moreover be a doctrine of prudence combined with arrogance, assuming that previous generations were simply not smart enough to trick humankind into constitutions that produce the desired results. To put the argument differently: invoking trust in providence is not a sudden shift of tone but an oblique way of saying that perpetual peace has only moral worth if it is the result of the right kind of reasoning. Individuals have to obey the given law of the land; considering how it can be brought into line with natural right is only for the sovereign to decide, though they are not free either but duty-bound to obey natural right and not dodge their duty by pursuing subjectively desirable consequences.

Kant's 'political philosophy' is, even in *Towards Perpetual Peace*, a philosophy of duty paired with providence that leaves no space for politics in terms of common actions of citizens for the common good – in particular: no right to resistance. Kant explicitly repudiates the argument that people have a right to throw off the oppressive power of a tyrant (*ZeF* 8: 382). His argument is that, even though dethronement would do no wrong to him or her, there cannot be a right to rebellion, as a maxim to wage a rebellion whenever it seems suitable could not be publicly acknowledged. Even a tyrant, on the other hand, has the right to punish rebels severely (*ZeF* 8: 382). It is easy to see how this line of argument destroys all the seeds of political organisation, as every action that consists of more than bringing forward petitions can be demonised as high treason.

Kant's political philosophy is thus only 'ideal' in a very specific sense. The idea that morality is in itself practical is taken more seriously, though not as a direct application of moral considerations to everyday political problems but only as an applied doctrine of right. What we might, from a contemporary perspective, consider moral claims are, for Kant, ideas of reason to be considered by enlightened sovereigns and only implemented, if at all, gradually and in accordance with the increasing enlightenment of society. All we can do is hope that 'the great artist nature' supports the desired outcome while the world proceeds in its usual 'political' manner (relying on twisted doctrine of prudence), which must not be countered by the same means.

4. Religion as politics and ideology critique

We started out to find a firm foundation for contemporary cosmopolitan thought, to avoid the quicksand into which Heidegger's philosophy and Plato had led us. Indeed, Kant announces, self-confidently, that before him philosophy in the proper sense did not exist and that he had found a solid foundation of morality that could lead to perpetual peace. However, upon closer inspection, each of Kant's bold claims is wrapped in numerous qualifications and shielded by a myriad of distinctions, so that the safe path across the quicksand is no highway but, at best, an arcane footpath. At each turning point, we have envisioned dangers looming over the bright path ahead. Instead of a lively future of philosophy, the death of all philosophy might lurk behind one's back, as the noble tone could turn out to be a youthful one.

Contextualising Kant in Königsberg and his intellectual circle did not elevate him to the status of a moral saint, and the systematic reconstruction of the critical system revealed gaps and shortcomings in its most central parts. Even the cosmopolitan upshot proved to be highly restrained, with no room for political action other than a sovereign's reform or a hope for the deeds of providence. These scant results, which apparently carve out only a fraction of the foundation we were looking for, make the call for a stronger moral foundation all the more urgent to the contemporary mind.

It was, of course, John Rawls who led the Kant-inspired renaissance in political philosophy. However, instead of abandoning Kant, I will briefly draw on Rawls's project to motivate our ongoing, contextualised reconstruction of Kant by introducing the problem of evil (4.1). This issue proves to be a key component of Kant's project, since it is only in his writings on religion that he fully emerges as a political actor in his own time (4.2). In these same texts, Kant also outlines another cosmopolitan possibility – grounded in inner moral motivations – through what he calls an 'ethical community'. At the same time, he develops a critique of all historical institutions, which can be read as an early model of ideology critique (4.3).

4.1 A Lacuna in Rawls

After following the intricate line of Kant's argument, Michael Sandel's memorable description of Rawls's project may sound like a relief: Rawls sought to save Kant's system by replacing 'Germanic obscurities with a domesticated metaphysic less vulnerable to the charge of arbitrariness and more congenial to the Anglo-American temper.'[85]

[85] Michael J. Sandel, *Liberalism and the Limits of Justice* (Cambridge: Cambridge University Press, 1982), 14.

Since then, most interpreters of Kant have 'followed Rawls's lead' and regarded themselves as 'reconstituted' Kantians.[86] According to Rawls, it is possible to identify core concepts in Kant and rearrange them as building blocks while disregarding others as non-essential or 'metaphysical'.[87] For this reason, Rawls neglects the entire historical context and theoretical interrelations of Kant's practical philosophy, relying only on a small selection of texts to reconstruct his account.

Would this not be an easy way out of the conundrum in which we have found ourselves? Thus far, it has not become clear why a full reconstruction of Kant's account is helpful for a genealogy. A brief intervention might help to motivate staying with Kant.

When thinking back to Schlosser's deprecating criticism of Kant, one might discern uncanny contemporary resonances, as the same kind of criticism could equally be levelled against Rawls and subsequent Rawlsian theories of global justice: so a contemporary Schlosser would hold that liberalism denies 'intuitive knowledge', 'emasculates reason', 'degenerates into a mere pattern-factory', leads to the 'most irregular libertinism' and is unable 'to withstand the struggle with vice'.[88] By the 2020s, at the latest, we have seen, as if through a burning lens, the global advance of 'masculine reasoning' in politics that presents itself as a lively and forceful alternative to 'irregular libertinism', while it remains open who the forces of vice are – depending on the side of the political divide, either liberalism or its totalitarian counterpart.[89]

[86] Katrin Flikschuh observes that '[m]ost Kant-inspired current cosmopolitans do not regard themselves as un-reconstituted Kantians. Most come to Kant via Rawls'. Katrin Flikschuh, 'Kant's Sovereignty Dilemma: A Contemporary Analysis', *Journal of Political Philosophy* 18 (2010): 470.

[87] See Rawls's claim that Kant's moral conception needs to be 'reformulated within the scope of an empirical theory'. John Rawls, 'A Kantian Conception of Equality', in *Collected Papers*, ed. Samuel Freeman (Cambridge, MA: Harvard University Press, 2001), 264.

[88] Schlosser, *Platons Briefe*, 182–83.

[89] In the preface I have analyzed the current political landscape. For a vehement criticism of liberalism from conservative angles, see Patrick J. Deneen, *Regime Change: Toward a Postliberal Future* (New York: Sentinel, 2023).

We have seen that Schlosser merely voiced deprecating criticisms already 'in the air' and how Kant used the occasion to refine his philosophical legacy. As one aim of the genealogy is to understand the sudden forceful opposition to liberalism, it is helpful to realise why only Kant's fundamental reorientation of philosophy allows for a thorough reply.

Rawls never claimed to be a faithful interpreter of Kant. Instead, he considers his *Theory of Justice* Kantian, as it 'sufficiently resembles Kant's [doctrine] in enough fundamental respects so that it is far closer to his view than to other traditional moral conceptions that are appropriate for use as a benchmark of comparison'.[90] He explains that the main differences to Kant's doctrine are, first, the primacy of the social, 'that is, the first subject of justice is the basic structure of society, and citizens must arrive at a public understanding on a conception of justice for this subject first'.[91]

The second difference is the full publicity condition, which 'provides the social milieu within which the notion of full autonomy can be understood and within which its ideal of the person can elicit an effective desire to be that kind of person'.[92] Thus, Rawls's theory, unlike Kant's, is not an a priori, timeless moral account or 'a conception of justice suitable for all societies regardless of their particular social or historical circumstances',[93] but articulates the shared notions and principles already thought to be latent in the common sense of the public culture of modern democratic society. As Rawls takes the good of political life in a modern democratic society as a given, he claims to reconstruct Kant's moral conception 'within the scope of an empirical theory'.[94] Rawls is also candid about the limits of his moral theory, and how it leaves aside 'questions of justice between societies (the law of nations) and our relations to the order of nature and to other things'.[95]

[90] Rawls, 'Kantian Constructivism in Moral Theory', in *Collected Papers*, 303–58.
[91] Ibid., 339.
[92] Ibid., 340.
[93] Ibid., 277.
[94] Ibid., 264.
[95] Ibid., 311.

It is exactly those limits that Kant questions fundamentally. For Kant, only a system that reflects comprehensively 'the relation to nature and other things' (i.e., critical philosophy) can lead us out of the endless dialectical quarrels, and only an account of practical reason that fundamentally questions all gifts of fortune (*GMS* 4:393) – including the circumstance of being born in a democratic society – can serve as a foundation of practical reason or morality. We have further seen that some parts Rawls excluded from ideal theory, especially the relation to other nations and a theory of punishment, were integral to Kant's legal philosophy from the outset. But are these not mere architectural details which can only be judged as part of a comprehensive theory?

It is unnecessary to rehearse Kant's entire argument in hindsight of Rawls, as one question can serve as a key to unlocking another dimension of Kant's philosophy and to reveal a limit in Rawls: the problem of evil. For Rawls, the problem of evil cannot even be formulated in the ideal part of the theory, as it presumes the inherent goodness of a liberal society and the sincerity of publicly voiced moral claims. Kant, on the other hand, constantly questioned whether the good will really is good and also doubted whether peacefully living together in a (republican) state is merely a 'moral veneer' for underlying barbarism that is 'quite undisguisedly and irrefutably obvious in the external relation of states to one another' (*ZeF* 8:375).

The difference becomes most glaring when Rawls finally considers the problem of evil, notably only in the non-ideal *Law of Peoples*. He holds: 'The great evils of human history – unjust war and oppression, religious persecution and the denial of liberty of conscience, starvation and poverty, not to mention genocide and mass murder – follow from political injustice.'[96] Thus, evil does not follow from a characteristic of human nature, and its effects are not inherent in historical institutions, as in Kant. Instead, 'great evils' are 'mistakes' in the design of political institutions and can therefore be 'fixed' by investing the appropriate intellectual resources – thus more 'intelligence' (*Witz*), an intellectual talent Kant

[96] John Rawls, *The Law of Peoples: With 'The Idea of Public Reason Revisited'* (Cambridge, MA: Harvard University Press, 1999), 6–7.

considers dubious, as it leads to pride and arrogance. Rawls therefore does not consider the entire bleak side of human nature and history we have encountered in Kant's empirical writings. But are these in Kant merely side remarks and, moreover, not part of critical philosophy? We must turn to Kant's writings on religion to realise how he integrates evil motivations and anti-Enlightenment forces in history (in contemporary terms: counterforces to liberalism) into his project.

4.2 Kant's political intervention in Prussia

The problem of evil is the core problem in Kant's *Religion Within the Boundaries of Mere Reason*, published in 1793. By turning to religion, one might think we are shifting the focus from a public, possibly cosmopolitan, political doctrine to a metaphysical or comprehensive one that cannot be reasonably defended by way of public reason. However, we will see that, within the context of Kant's philosophy of religion, we find many answers to the puzzles we have encountered so far – in particular the notions of politics and freedom and, moreover, a critical perspective on the source of morality itself. To realise how religion relates to Kant's thought, we first have to consider again the historical context and become aware of the role the Lutheran Church played in Königsberg during Kant's lifetime. Against this historical background, Kant's treatise on religion will turn out to be a genuinely political one.

Religious life in Prussia

Religious thought and practices in Königsberg differed from those in other German territories for several reasons, though they also shared certain features. The most significant feature of religious life in Königsberg was the presence of various ethnic groups residing in the city – Lithuanians, Russians, Poles, Jews and others – each practising religion according to their own denomination or faith. In this respect, Königsberg displayed a notable degree of tolerance. However, the Protestant Church, aligned with the Prussian monarchy, dominated social and political life. In this sense, Königsberg resembled many German territories, which were de facto ruled by a coalition of Protestant (or Catholic) clergy and the royal government.

Noticing this de facto coalition is also helpful for addressing a misconception about the audience of Enlightenment philosophy in Germany up to the late 1790s. Jürgen Habermas argued in *The Structural Transformation of the Public Sphere* that the basis for the public sphere was laid in the bourgeois salon culture that emerged in the transition from the eighteenth to the nineteenth century – a separate sphere between the state and the market.[97] The distinctive feature of the discourse was that arguments concerning the common good were exchanged on the basis of people considering themselves free and equal. Habermas notes the differences between the French humanistic–aristocratic salon, the English merchant club and the German family-based table societies.[98]

However, since he focuses on political discussions, he disregards two distinctive features of the German table conversation, such as that of the circle around Kant. First, religion – or, to be precise, theological discussion – was not taboo or merely a private matter but a readily accessible language with which everyone was familiar, including the historical and comparative aspects of various criticisms and, of course, its political use and instrumentalisation. In his early writings, however, Habermas held that towards the end of the eighteenth century religion had become a 'merely private matter' and had remained, since then, a pre-rational prejudice.[99] Since Protestant theology and institutions played an important role in public and social life, every citizen (including women and, as beneficiaries of welfare, even the most disadvantaged) had something to say about it – in public and certainly at table conversations.

Second, the public sphere, especially in Königsberg, was not a genuinely bourgeois sphere between market and state but leaned heavily towards the state. The majority of people who took part in Kant's table conversation either held official

[97] Jürgen Habermas, *The Structural Transformation of the Public Sphere: An Inquiry into a Category of Bourgeois Society*, trans. Thomas Burger and Frederick Lawrence (Cambridge: Polity Press, 1989).

[98] Ibid., 28.

[99] Ibid., 66–67 and 349.

positions or aspired to have one. This distinctive characteristic of the German public sphere was already noticed at the time. In the words of Adolph Freiherr Knigge: 'What does the third state consist of [in Germany]? Of princely servants, councillors, secretaries, officials, officers, advocates, doctors and the like who all live more or less on the crumbs that fall from the master's table.'[100] For this reason, a book by Kant on religion was not an exotic topic for a liberal or enlightened philosopher, as it might seem today in political theory circles, but a contribution to a central philosophical and political concern that everyone shared. Kant's biographical involvement with religion and religious teaching is also helpful in uncovering his personal political stance.

After the publication of the *Critique of Pure Reason* in 1781 and the *Foundation of the Metaphysics of Morals*, Kant's reputation grew exponentially, and he was soon recognised (in German-speaking countries) as the most important philosopher of his time. However, due to his advanced age he could not participate in debates about his philosophy (*KrV*, B xliii). Nevertheless, he defined, with each new work, the relevant philosophical discourse. Kant's reformulations of the three metaphysical questions of freedom, God and the immortality of the soul were – as regulative ideas or practical postulates – central to the reception of his ideas. Up to the end of his life, no other part of his philosophy was more vigorously discussed among theologians, philosophers and the public at large than his views on religion.[101] These views were central to the broader reception of his philosophy and its implementation in various institutions (university, state bureaucracy, church, schools and charities). Against this background, the conflict with the censorship is to be understood. Kant later recounts the entire affair in the foreword to his *The Conflict of the Faculties* (1798).

100 See Hans-Ulrich Wehler, *Vom Feudalismus des Alten Reiches bis zur defensiven Modernisierung der Reformära 1700–1815* (München: C. H. Beck, 1997), 212.

101 On the early reception of Kant's treatise on religion, see Rudolf Malter, 'Zeitgenössische Reaktionen auf Religionsphilosophie. Eine Skizze zur Wirkungsgeschichte des Kantischen und des reformatorischen Denkens', in Alexius J. Bucher, Hermann Drüe, and Thomas M. Seebohm, eds., *bewußt sein. Gerhard Funke zu eigen* (Bonn: Bouvier, 1975), 145–67.

All politics is local

After the death of Frederick the Great, his nephew, Frederick William II, became King of Prussia. In writings about Kant, Frederick William II is often depicted as a weak character with limited intellectual insight, who – under the influence of the Pietist-minded minister Johann Christoph Wöllner – initiated a Pietist counter-Enlightenment rollback.[102] The infamous edict of religion from 9 August 1788, along with the subsequent censorship edict from December the same year, seems to support the narrative that freedom of expression had flourished only under Frederick the Great. According to this narrative, a wide variety of newspapers, journals and pamphlets gave way to a wretched, narrow-minded religious censorship aimed at curbing emancipatory and revolutionary movements. As a broad historical summary, this position has some plausibility, as evinced by the many protests criticising the edict.[103] However, it would be too facile and unhistorical to depict Kant as the enlightened liberal philosopher rising above the turmoil of his time, for this picture would fail to notice the various intellectual strands that were virulent at this time and Kant's specific take on religion.

The French Revolution and the subsequent Terror of the Committee of Public Safety under Robespierre certainly strengthened restorative tendencies among traditional sovereigns in Germany but also divided the public into opposing camps. There was no way back to the 'happy times' of enlightened dinner conversations under the agnostic rule of Frederick the Great. However, we also have to be aware that all camps – orthodox Lutherans, Pietists and enlightened philosophers – tried to influence the state's religious policy. Therefore, protest from one group against a certain policy is not necessarily a sign of an anti-Enlightenment rollback but can simply indicate a shift of power.

From a historical perspective, it is to be noted that the edict predated the French Revolution and must therefore be

[102] Kuehn, *Kant*, 338–40.

[103] On the effects of the edict in religious and public life and its reception in various social milieus, see Michael J. Sauter, 'The Enlightenment on Trial: State Service and Social Discipline in Eighteenth-Century Germany's Public Sphere', *Modern Intellectual History* 5, no. 2 (2008): 195–223.

viewed in a different light. Significantly, the edict on religion extended the state's guardianship for the first time to Jews and other religious denominations. It was thus crafted in the spirit of an edict of tolerance. Even though it forbade the public propagation of heterodox rationalist views, its main purpose was not to impose a new religious orthodoxy but 'rather to consolidate the existing confessional structures and thereby safeguard the pluralist compromise struck at the Peace of Westphalia in 1648'.[104] In that respect, it prolonged Prussia's tradition of multi-confessional religious coexistence.

An anachronistic criticism that the edict was a sign of a reactionary turn misses the decisive point that it was a conflict between two different versions of Enlightenment. The edict took a purely instrumentalist view of religion, whereby any religion could serve to secure public order. According to the older, rationalist tradition Kant pursued, it was necessary to find a philosophical or rationalist foundation of religion in the first place. To use a Rawlsian distinction, Wöllner, the author of the edict, assumed the 'modus vivendi view'; Kant, on the other hand, sought 'stability for the right reasons', though notably not in public affairs (as this was the prerogative of the sovereign) but religious ones. This line of argument will be extended later, when discussing Kant's philosophy of religion.

The historical context is important, as it is in this debate that Kant for the first and only time in his life took a political stance in a heated debate. The reason we had previously missed his political involvement was that we had taken our implicit notion of politics, the relevance of certain topics, the functioning of the public sphere and the role of a public intellectual for granted, presuming – following the manner of the Cambridge School – that Kant 'must have' recognised the oppression of 'republican forces' in Königsberg, spoken out against the death penalty or for the equal rights of women and felt contempt for the ruthless military politics of Frederick the Great. Through a more detailed and systematic reading, we realised that, given his notion of politics as an applied

104 See Christopher M. Clark, *Iron Kingdom: The Rise and Downfall of Prussia, 1600–1947* (Cambridge, MA: Harvard University Press, 2006), 270 with further discussion.

doctrine of right and his insistence on obedience, he could not have done all this but had to retreat to the freedom of the pen as the 'sole palladium of the people's rights' (*TP* 8:304). However, in an unexpected area – the interpretation of (Christian) religion – Kant did clash with the authorities and took an explicit political stance.

The religion and censorship edicts did not immediately change the intellectual landscape. They provoked widespread public outcry, but older bureaucrats who had been socialised under Frederick the Great enforced them only reluctantly.[105] Nevertheless, Kant's first attempt to publish his long-awaited treatise on religion as a series of four articles failed, as the first piece did not receive official approval (*imprimatur*).[106] For this reason, he resorted to a trick and submitted the four articles together as a book at the University of Jena, thus outside Prussian jurisdiction. He received approval, and it was published in 1794, with a second edition following that same year.

In the preface to the first edition, he openly criticised the humiliation of the sciences through censorship by authorities and later argued against the anti-revolutionary prejudice that some people are not yet ripe for a revolution: '[O]n this assumption freedom will never come, since we cannot ripen to it if we are not already established in it (we must be free in order to be able to make use of our powers purposively in freedom)' (*RGV* 6:188). This did not sit well with the authorities. Kant received a decree forbidding any further publications that would denigrate Christianity. To the great disappointment of his Enlightenment contemporaries, which is mirrored in many later descriptions of the affair, Kant did not go to the barricades, start a public uprising or – as academics might do today – publish an open petition, but instead, as a faithful citizen, capitulated to the king's demand.

Is this the ultimate proof of his apolitical attitude? Once again, Kant resorted to a trick, which he revealed publicly four years later, after the death of Frederick William II and Wöllner's dismissal. In the preface to *The Conflict of the Faculties*, Kant explained that in his answer he pledged

105 Ibid., 857.

106 Kant recounts the entire affair in the preface of *The Conflict of Faculties* (*SF* 7: 5–12).

allegiance to the king only personally, so he felt free to publish on matters of religion after his death. Kant's cunning was to take the feudal allegiance that was used to reprimand him at face value.

In Kantian scholarship, there is discussion about whether this argument satisfies Kant's own standard of obedience as laid out in the *Doctrine of Right*.[107] The more important point, however, is this: in the entire affair, Kant acted politically in the very way he denounced such conduct in the treatise *Towards Perpetual Peace*. He took advantage of a favourable opportunity (*fac et excusa*) to publish the book, included in his answer to the king a secret provision that could not be made public, and later denied any wrongdoing (*si fecisti nega*). He finally engaged in pure power politics by putting his old, fragile, strictly diet-regulated body against the much younger but obese and unrestrained body of the king. Kant thus wagered that he would outlive his king and engaged in power politics as 'biopolitics'.

This episode confirms the hunch of the Cambridge School: philosophical treatises are written like political pamphlets meant to change the immediate politics of their time. However, in this case, the Cambridge School revelation is apparently neither new nor does it bring us any closer to an understanding of the foundations of cosmopolitanism. It apparently even leads into the uncharted domains of the philosophy of religion, which – *pace* Kant – has neither led to perpetual peace among religions nor proceeded along a scientific path since. However, the long preparation was not in vain. Only now, after this long preparation, can we: first, diagnose the systematic problem Kant tries to solve in the treatise on religion; second, assess the solution he proposed (an ethical commonwealth); and third, recognise the self-critical stance that also applies to our contemporary cosmopolitan appropriation of Kant.

4.3 Realising inner freedom

We have previously seen that the way in which Kant conceptualises freedom as autonomy gives rise to two systematic

107 See Allen W. Wood, *Kant and Religion* (Cambridge: Cambridge University Press, 2020), 1–26.

problems, namely, how to give an account of free actions that are not morally motivated and how to conceptualise evil actions as freely chosen. Kant's solution to the first problem was conceiving legal, or outer, freedom as a matter of regulated power of choice. This led to a specific way of conceptualising the law: starting with private law, viewing public right as an enforcement mechanism and requiring near-absolute obedience from subjects. In this view, the cosmopolitan condition turns out not to be 'what we as free and equal agents ought to do' but the condition under which right (the right state of affairs) can be conceptualised (without running into contradictions) and upheld by the sovereign.

While trying to recast Kant's system in the vein of Rawls by replacing 'Germanic obscurities with a domesticated metaphysics,[108] we realised that Rawls's premises of a closed society and full publicity are fundamentally called into question from Kant's perspective. The underlying scepticism is supported by Rawls's failure to take seriously the ultimate metaphysical question about the origin of evil. Even though Kant addresses this question in a religious context – apparently outside politics – this very historical context turned out to be the place where Kant risked his life and emerged as a political actor. Thus, in the field of religion, we have finally found the politically engaged and freely acting Kant we had long sought in vain.

Morality leads to religion versus a liberal consciousness

From a contemporary perspective, it might, despite the historical and contextual preparation, still sound strange to hear Kant's claim that 'morality ... inevitably leads to religion' (*RGV* 6:6). Even granting that 'German obscurities' might have some value of their own, the entire field of religion seems to lie outside, or even beyond, the scope of an enlightened, that is, secular, philosophical perspective. Even those who agree in principle with the Rawlsian liberal perspective might either move towards a more radically enlightened 'woke' perspective, thus criticising the liberal or cosmopolitan perspective for failing to account for its own unreflective power

108 Sandel, *Liberalism and the Limits of Justice*, 14.

relations and implicit 'metaphysical' presuppositions. Others might instead opt for a more pluralist perspective by further strengthening Rawls's claim that all kinds of philosophical perspectives and comprehensive traditions, including non-Western ones, need to be evaluated equally. The apparent reason why religion, in its own right, is not an appropriate topic for philosophy is that any religion – or, in general, any comprehensive doctrine – seems to be based on a worldview that cannot be rationally explained, perhaps not even reasonably understood, as it rests ultimately on an irrational belief.

Kant, however, employs a very different notion of religion, one that remains 'within the bounds of reason alone', as the title of his treatise announces. He starts his argument as if replying to the uneasiness the contemporary reader feels when hearing that Kant's cosmopolitanism is a very restrictive legal idea and not a progressive project of enthusiastic moral believers. The contemporary global ethicist would typically claim: 'But moral actions, or collective moral actions, must have some impact on the world and be capable of transforming the world for the better.' Certainly, Kant replies, we cannot be sure about our own, let alone others' moral motivations, and historical experience contradicts this hope. As an idea, however, it is necessary and has important consequences.

For Kant, it is essential that morality does not depend upon any other aims. However, it is possible to argue in the opposite direction, to base aims upon morality:

> Yet an end proceeds from morality just the same; for it cannot possibly be a matter of indifference to reason how to answer the question, *What is then the result of this right conduct of ours?* nor to what we are to direct our doings or nondoings, even granted this is not fully in our control, at least as something with which they are to harmonize. (*RGV* 6:5)

But how can ends enter morality without spoiling it? Only by making the fanciful supposition that moral actions actually succeed and are even rewarded by bringing happiness to the moral agent. Kant calls the unity of the purposefulness derived from freedom (morality) and that derived from nature (happiness) the idea of the highest good in the world.

It is realised when happiness is distributed in proportion to the observance of duty.

However, life experience tells us that this is simply not the case. All too often the wicked are rewarded, and happiness – the purposefulness of nature – appears to resemble a vexatious lottery, due to natural miseries such as illness and old age. However, once we presume this idea and want it to be real, we must also presume a highest being who has created the entire world of freedom and nature to bring about this unity. Thus, the idea of God and the physical creation are based on the moral law – the categorical imperative – as the fixed point 'in the sky' (in the noumenal world) Kant uses to 'lift' or justify the creation. From this basic starting point, Kant develops his philosophy of religion.

At this point, there are two ways to proceed with the discussion. One can either ask whether Kant had an adequate grasp of the phenomenon of religion, or of Christian Religion in particular, whether the moralisation of religion is just another case of fetishisation (in religious terms, a violation of the ban on images of God) and how Kant's argument influenced the subsequent tradition of the philosophy of religion. However, this line of argument would presume the gulf between religion and philosophy to be a given. As Kant thinks that morality leads necessarily to religion, and that religion can be unfolded within the bounds of reason, we will take a different line of thought by asking whether Kant's reflection on religion might serve as a sounding board for assessing the limits of his cosmopolitan thought. Kant's basic argument on the extension of morality can be used to show why this is a fruitful perspective.

Throughout the discussion of Kant's *Anthropology* and the *Doctrine of Right*, we have emphasised the modest, nearly cynical view Kant often employs. Nowhere does he say that life, liberty, property and the pursuit of happiness are good things in themselves (basic goods) or that political philosophy, when justifying these goods, is also a valuable or progressive force in the world (since there is only one thing that can be considered good without limitation). In this respect, Kant confounds the expectations of contemporary political philosophers. Only now can we see that Kant's aloofness is not a sign of a weak notion of morality that needs to be 'strengthened' by incorporating more good common sense but the result of a worldview that takes morality extremely seriously. A few points may clarify this claim.

The reason Kant does not speak in a contemporary fashion about political philosophy as applied moral philosophy is that he grounds morality in an inner moral motivation. The idea of duty is a 'brazen voice' (*VT* 8:402) everyone finds in their reason, but it is, notably, an inner voice. Nevertheless, it is possible to entertain the notion that a group of people acted indeed out of duty. However, as we are not even certain about the pure moral motivation in our own case, let alone when judging the actions of others, one would presume that only a *Herzenskündiger* (the one who knows the soul) has this insight, which is, of course, just another name for God. Thus, moral motivation and (possibly) moral actions are, according to Kant, real phenomena.

However, it is not only on the high moral ground that Kant adopts a more radical perspective. He also analyses the other side of human nature – the desire for happiness – in more radical ways. A brief comparison might clarify this point. One typical line of justification for liberalism, and cosmopolitanism in particular, presumes that it makes people in the world happier overall, either by purging the world of greater evils (Rawls), enabling people to live out their capabilities (Nussbaum) or taking their happiness directly as a measure (Singer).

Kant would agree that freedom as non-interference or non-domination is a condition for happiness, as a subject can pursue their choices. However, arbitrary choices and the resulting happiness are not the highest and most complete good one can aspire to. In his moral philosophy (and philosophy of religion), Kant often uses the German term *Glückseligkeit*, which is the traditional German translation of the Greek *eudaimonia*, best rendered in English as bliss or perfect happiness. Obviously, any arbitrary consumer choice does not lead to this kind of happiness. However, nor does it refer to 'higher pleasures' (for instance aesthetic pleasure) either and instead has a moral component, as only proportionate happiness forms part of the highest good. It is, therefore, not an elitist concept but an idea of which everyone can become aware.

The key point is that the idea of perfect happiness can serve as a standard for judging the merits of the pursuit of happiness. In other words, 'liberal happiness' cannot be the ultimate goal at which philosophy can settle. However, perfect happiness is not an 'uber-liberal' idea or value one should strive for but a more complex, 'dialectical' concept, as Kant clearly denotes the downside of this idea as well.

If the ultimate task of philosophy consisted of calling in a high tone for (collective) moral action and promoting perfect happiness, philosophy could rightfully be ridiculed for making unwarranted promises, as we fallible human beings, in the real world, simply do not work this way. Thus, when employing a more radical notion of morality and happiness with Kant, one is automatically led to perceive the world from a more radical perspective – a place dominated by the manias for honour, domination and possession (*Anth* 7:268, *KU* 5:433). This can be observed in those who hold power, either in the literal sense or by dominating public discourse. In other words, the problem of evil reappears as a central stumbling block of a complete moral perspective. In the following four sections, we will explore this self-critical perspective.

Creativity of evil versus banality of good

We have already seen that conceptualising evil actions as free poses a fundamental problem for Kant's notion of freedom as autonomy and that his solution in the treatise on religion is not fully convincing. Instead of trying to complete the system of German idealism once again, we will consider, as we have done with his *Doctrine of Right*, the consequences of Kant's core conceptual decisions. By now it should be evident that a social-scientific reading of Kant's republican peace thesis misses Kant's central idea. A stronger criticism of such a social-scientific appropriation of Kant can be made by showing that, without Kant's moral foundation, his phenomenological analysis of evil in the world would prevail. Thus, Kant stripped of his 'metaphysical obscurities' leaves us with Kant as the cool and nearly cynical observer of history, who analyses human beings' desires and capacity for deceit.

At the beginning of the treatise on religion, he states the central paradox: 'the world lieth in evil' and yet 'all allow that the world began with something good: with the Golden Age, with life in Paradise, or an even happier life in communion with heavenly beings' (*RGV* 6:19). Most religious traditions therefore see the course of the world as a continuous decline (until a redeemer arrives). Kant also notes the opposing heroic notion that 'the world steadfastly (though hardly noticeably) forges ahead in the very opposite direction, namely from bad to better' (*RGV* 6:20). However, he qualifies this view with some despair as an opinion voiced by 'philosophers and pedagogues' (*RGV* 6:20). This indicates Kant's distance from simplistic scientific theories of progress. The fundamental problem is that neither perspective can be based upon scientific experience in the strictest sense. It remains to be explained how human beings can be morally responsible for the better or worse course.

One might think it easy to point out the evils in the world. Yet evil actions are just as difficult to identify as morally good ones, since it does not suffice to point out that the actions are unlawful; the maxims must also be evil. However, we cannot observe maxims in others and cannot even be sure of them in our own case. All we can do is conclude, from the consciousness of evil actions in ourselves, that human beings are 'evil by nature' (*RGV* 6:30). This cannot mean that evil actions are carried out of sensibility or caused by nature, for they would then not be considered free.[109] Kant explains that the human being 'holds within himself a first ground (to us inscrutable) for the adoption of good or evil (unlawful) maxims, and that he holds this ground qua human universally – in such a way, therefore, that by his maxims he expresses at the same time the character of his species' (*RGV* 6:21).

It is no coincidence that at this point Kant sees an immediate connection between an inner observation and the character of the human species, thus between the most subjective 'private feeling' and the most objective public observation. What is missing in all of Kant's anthropological, practical

[109] The same goes for any psychological or ethnological explanation of evil actions due to some psychological or cultural law. If moral freedom is real, then explanations cannot continue endlessly, as the acceptance, refusal, or misuse of the explanation cannot be explained in the same way.

and legal writings – the direct appeal to fundamental moral concepts, to human dignity or the categorical imperative – is found on the dark side. Evil corrupts everything, even reason itself. Therefore, the different dimensions of Kant's thinking that are usually kept apart – the foundation of morality, ethical behaviour, anthropological observations, political analysis and even scriptural exegesis – are intertwined in his treatise on religion. A few aspects suffice to show the consequences for his cosmopolitan thinking.

At the most basic level 'the propensity to evil can only attach to the moral faculty of choice' (*RGV* 6:31). The propensity cannot merely be a subjective determining ground but must itself be a deed – moreover, a deed that corrupts the very highest maxims in us. Kant calls it 'an intelligible deed, cognizable through reason alone' (*RGV* 6:31), as it is the condition for every deed contrary to law. It consists of making 'the incentives of self-love and their inclinations the condition of compliance with the moral law' (*RGV* 6:36). We have already noticed that evil seems to be presupposed in the notion of 'hypothetical respect' so that Kant's answer remains wanting on a conceptual level. However, Kant admits that the final ground for the propensity to evil remains 'inexplicable to us' (*RGV* 6:43). Moreover, he shows the corroborating effects of evil on everything, even reason itself, so that the phenomenology he depicts, including the comparative religious perspective he sketches, effectively constitutes the explanation he gives.[110]

Fundamentally, the propensity to evil is detectable in 'a certain perfidy on the part of the human heart' (*RGV* 6:38) in 'deceiving itself as regards its own good or evil dispositions' (*RGV* 6:38) by only acknowledging the good consequences of one's action and not noting the underlying good or evil maxims. Thus, the perfidy of the human heart includes a fair amount of illusion about ourselves, especially those of which we are not necessarily aware. Sometimes we can even be surprised by the complexity of our moral nature, such as when we suddenly realise that 'in the misfortune of our best

[110] One might add the puzzle that any 'solution' to the problem of evil (in Kant's terms evil acts out of freedom) must presuppose an account of pure uncorroborated reason exemplified through a holy will and life.

friends there is something that does not altogether displease us' (*RGV* 6:33).[111]

Thus, in a phenomenological moral analysis, which Kant presumed all along but developed only in the treatise on religion, we always have to reckon with a double perspective – publicly voiced moral claims (or our official moral self-image) and the actual motivations, both of which are often more tainted than we would like to admit. For this reason, the sudden 'Foucauldian insertion' in a moral treatise is not that surprising.

Not only does the ethical idea of friendship crumble in the phenomenological perspective, the entire tradition of state-of-nature arguments that somehow lead to a desirable cosmopolitan condition may be 'derided as sheer fantasy' (*RGV* 6:34). Kant picks out the Rousseauian image of the state of nature as a state of naïve, uncorrupted peace among human beings by referring to the unprovoked cruelty found in certain indigenous societies. Thus 'civilisation' can neither explain the emergence of evil among human beings nor mitigate its effects. This is most evident in the relation civilised people maintain vis-à-vis one another. In a footnote, Kant even sketches his own perpetual war thesis.

> So long as a state has a neighbouring one which it can hope to subdue, it strives to aggrandise itself by subjugating it. It thus strives for a universal monarchy – a state constitution in which all freedom would necessarily expire, and, together with it, virtue, taste and science (which follow upon freedom). Yet after this monster (in which the laws gradually lose their force) has swallowed up all its neighbours, it ultimately disintegrates all by itself. It divides through rebellion and factionalism into many smaller states which, instead of striving after a union of states (a republic of free federated peoples), in turn begin the same game all over again, so that war (that scourge of the human race) will not cease. (*RGV* 6:34)

[111] Kant quotes approvingly François de La Rochefoucauld, *Réflexions, ou Sentences et Maximes Morales* (Paris: Claude Barbin, 1678), no. 583.

Thus, the propensity to evil is indeed 'the foul stain in our species' (*RGV* 6:38) that goes through everything, starting from indigenous communities and personal friendship to undermining even the highest political aims. Kant uses the account merely as an example to illustrate the general observation that the human being is by nature evil. Nevertheless, this brief phenomenology has a devastating effect on any naïve or purely public reason account of cosmopolitanism that ignores the inner and more inscrutable moral sphere. All this could be part of a self-betraying mindset.

Ethical community versus cosmopolitan society

Given the argument thus far, one could still reply that the moral criticism of cosmopolitanism, couched in religious language, does not reach its target, as it still rests on a Pietist mindset in which the world is somehow saved through individual reversion. Any real political account, on the other hand, must include an idea of collective action, if only to solve coordination problems. As long as this collective or social dimension is not addressed, the criticism remains hollow. Moreover, stressing the distinction between the pure inner moral realm and the depraved outer world of mixed incentives creates an abyss that leads to a moral righteousness which hinders addressing real-world political problems. However, Kant's analysis of religion provides the resources to address this quandary too. Again, it appears only through an analogy to the religious sphere.

To start, Kant escalates the abyss between inner moral life and the outer world. If the individual inner revolution were all a human being could do to break the dominion of evil, they would face nearly insurmountable obstacles. Kant argues that one need not even assume any special temptation; the mere existence among fellow human beings in a society will awaken the manias for honour, domination and possession. As these are anthropological traits of human beings, they will eventually corrupt each other's moral disposition. We have previously seen that, as a cool observer of human history, Kant has used these characteristics to sketch the development of human civilisation. It is only in the context of his philosophy of religion that he names a counterforce – the establishment of a different kind of society:

> Inasmuch as we can see, therefore, the dominion of the good principle is not otherwise attainable, so far as human beings can work toward it, than through the setting up and the diffusion of a society in accordance with, and for the sake of, the laws of virtue – a society which reason makes it a task and a duty of the entire human race to establish in its full scope (RGV 6:94).

Insofar as the community is under public law, Kant calls such a society an ethical community (or commonwealth) and holds that it can exist within a political community and may even comprise all its members or extend across multiple communities.

What does Kant mean by this idea of an ethical community, and how does it relate to his cosmopolitan thought? He develops the idea as an analogy to a political community and states a duty, not towards other human beings but towards the human species, to leave the 'ethical state of nature' and become a member of an ethical community. In the idea of an ethical community, he sees the true moral basis of any historical religion. Establishing a universal republic based on the laws of virtue (*RGV* 6:98) is, according to Kant, the ultimate end of all religions. It is not, however, necessary to follow the religious trajectory of the argument. As Kant develops the idea of an ethical community within the bounds of reason, we can also ask whether the general idea of an ethical community might also take a different historical shape.

Significantly, Kant characterises the ethical community in a way that takes up many characteristics of what is sometimes called moral cosmopolitanism. It is based on public law and thus 'entails freedom from coercion in its very concept' (*RGV* 6:95). Moreover, it is an ideal that is not limited to actual societies or states; it refers directly to 'the ideal of a totality of human beings' (*RGV* 6:96), thus indeed to each and every individual in the world. Its aim is 'to establish an absolute ethical whole of which each particular society is only a representation or a schema' (*RGV* 6:96). Considerations of this kind are usually the starting point for contemporary cosmopolitan theories. The specificity of Kant's account is that it is thought as being under God as the 'soul searcher' (*Herzenskündiger*). Nevertheless, it also contains the utopian elements of political philosophy absent from Kant's philosophy of rights.

The constitution of an ethical community is not bound to any established form (such as monarchy, aristocracy or democracy) but transcends them, best symbolised by the constitution of a household or by a 'free, universal and enduring union of hearts' (*RGV* 6:102). With this idea, Kant alludes to the idea of a Christian parish. The term *Genossenschaft* (fellowship or cooperative society) also has a secular, historical lineage, as much of medieval and early modern social life in Germany was organised through cooperative societies of different kinds.[112] Kant gives the idea an aspirational twist, as the principle that unites the fellows is equality (*RGV* 6:122). Finally, the dominion of the good principle, the ethical commonwealth, 'assures the world perpetual peace' (*RGV* 6:124), which is no longer a legal idea but the result of the moral principle.

Dialectics of institutions versus philosophy of law

At this point of the argument, one might think that the ethical community is Kant's political philosophy we have been looking for as a foundation of contemporary cosmopolitan thought. Instead of cleansing Kant from 'German obscurities', all one needs to do is curb the religious exuberance and maybe give up the notion of enforceable right (*Recht*) altogether and rely on the general idea of law (*Gesetz*), as law can either be ethical (free from coercion) or legal (coercive). It is certainly illuminating, considering the influence of Kant's rational theology on later idealist and revolutionary thinkers. However, in the present context it would not help the cause of contemporary cosmopolitan thought to point out that Kant has with his notion of an ethical community an aspirational idea at his disposal.

The fundamental problem is that this idea is, in Kant, always thought to be under 'an invisible moral father' (*RGV* 6:102). The reference to God is not just a figure of speech

[112] For a complete history of the German idea of *Genossenschaft*, including a nineteenth century adaptation, see Otto von Gierke, *The German Law of Fellowship*, trans. Mary Fischer, ed. Anthony Black (Cambridge: Cambridge University Press, 1990).

for 'moral reason' but has a specific function. As laws in an ethical community are designed to promote the morality of actions, they must be based on true duties and not simply on conformity to external laws or a delusional self-image. Therefore, the lawgiver must be a *Herzenskündiger*, one who knows the heart (*RGV* 6:99). The scrutiny of the heart is, in any case, an inner process that cannot be translated or delegated to any public instance or forum, as it is always doubtful whether this instance or forum is an authentic, truthful expression of the inner maxims.

A subsequent question resulting from Kant's setting up the idea of an ethical community queries contemporary cosmopolitan approaches directly. Again, this requires some preparation. We have seen that Kant developed his thinking along two lines: critical philosophy and empirical science of knowledge. Only in a few places, notably in the *Critique of Judgement* and the historical essays, does he unite both strands through a theological perspective on world history. However, the dark side of history – the history of wars and conquests, domination and the many changing forms of government throughout history – is missing in Kant's *Doctrine of Right*, as only the rightful state of affairs can be laid out in general laws. This could lead to the misconception that political philosophy can only deal with the ideal or normative side and has to leave everything else to the empirical sciences. A similar misconception could apply to Kant's rational theology as presented thus far, namely that it is, apart from musings about the inner propensity to evil, mainly concerned with the laudable idea of the ethical community, and its religious application. However, the battle of the good and evil principle also has an external, institutional side. This is most relevant for the analogical reasoning pursued here.

Kant discussed this in the context of the church's history, which he identifies as a constant battle between pure moral religion and the shifting historical forms of ecclesiastical faith. Again, Kant's historical comparative account of various religions – he discusses mostly Abrahamic religions but refers briefly to Eastern religions as well – can be set aside to glean a general lesson. What Kant develops in the historical shape of church history is a general theory of institutions, moreover, a dialectical theory of institutions that integrates both lineages of his thinking (empirical history and moral philosophy). The significance of the topic is that church history cannot be told as a refined story of progress, as its origin – the teachings of Jesus – already contained the pure (moral) insight, while later church history is all too obviously the story of violence, malaise and greed. Kant does not shy away from strong judgements when describing historical forms of religion or 'ecclesiastical faith'. He faults Judaism for being not a true religion but consisting originally only of 'a collection of merely statutory laws supporting a political state' (*RGV* 6:125). He bases his view on the observations that: first, in Judaism all commands could be formulated as laws but make no claim on the moral disposition; second, there is no belief in an afterlife; and finally, that Judaism makes no universal claims but formulates commands only for one (chosen) people. At the same time, Kant is aware of developments within the Jewish faith up to the point where it became, due to Greek enlightenment and in spite of the burdens of its dogmatic faith, ripe for revolution (*RGV* 6:128). Again, the relevant question is not whether Kant's characterisation of Judaism is appropriate but what it shows about Kant's general theory of institutions.[113]

One could say that the account of Judaism reveals the limits – or dialectics – of legalisation. It is the only place in Kant's work where life under law is disparaged. The reasons Kant gives do not exclusively apply to Judaism but are also characteristic of contemporary approaches in practical or political philosophy, consisting of principles that could be formulated as laws while having no 'metaphysical' (inner) realm and applying only to certain (Western) societies. Thus, when the inner realm, Kant's idea of an ethical community, is lacking, an institution established according to such principles is prone to develop the ills of legalisation – a dogmatic faith held up by *Schriftgelehrten* (scribes).

At this point, one might recall some of the criticisms of liberalism as being 'parochial' or 'Western' that were mentioned

[113] For discussions of Kant's controversial characterisation of Judaism see Wood, *Kant and Religion*, 190–209 and Michah Gottlieb, *Faith and Freedom: Moses Mendelssohn's Theological-Political Thought* (Oxford: Oxford University Press, 2011).

in the Preface. However, it would be a populist and moreover ad hominem form of critique to simply equate current discussions on liberalism with Kant's disparaging characterisation of Judaism. Hinting at such parallels is, however, legitimate when raising the question of the effects that excluding metaphysical elements has on greater philosophical discussion and public culture. The historical retrospection reminds us that the age of religious enthusiasm and secular ideologies did not end with Kant, but could even have started in German Idealism.[114] Here is not the place to discuss this legacy in detail, as the main point is to show that Kant's cosmopolitan thought has a mixed legacy: it cannot simply be cut back to utilise it for contemporary purposes, as other parts might mushroom in unforeseen places and strike back unexpectedly.

Ideology critique versus political philosophy

One might regard this inversion of Kant into a critic of ideology as a mere cardboard figure with no standing in the real world, as there is one feature in Kant's philosophy that makes him immune to all populist or half-baked appropriations: his thorough soberness and scientific (in the sense of *Wissenschaft*) foundation of his thinking that is always bound back to an enlightened, public discourse. Indeed, there is only one part of his philosophy in which Kant (hesitantly) calls something a true wisdom – the commitment 'thou shalt not lie' (*VNAEF* 8:522) – which reveals itself, as Kant explained in his contestation with the lyrical enthusiast Schlosser, through the common or ordinary tone (*VNAEF* 8:422). He also ferociously defends the necessity of a free public discourse and the duty of the sovereign to guarantee it (*RGV* 6:133).

However, this does not mean that he did not realise or could not have analysed the many intricate ways in which a discourse can be censored and how this censorship even

114 Most prominently, John Dewey argued that it was not the 'romantic tradition' of German intellectual life that was primarily responsible for militaristic nationalism (culminating in National Socialism), but the 'enlightened' one. He faults Kant in particular for having created the gulf between the spiritual and the natural world (which Hitler linked again violently, like in a short circuit). John Dewey, *German Philosophy and Politics* (New York: G. P. Putnam's Sons, 1915).

gets hold of an individual's mind, so that it is mistaken for their own doing. Kant uses the example of the religious, in particular Christian, discourse to make this point. However, the underlying observation can be generalised to apply to all kinds of implicit censorship, so that Kant's analysis becomes a model for later forms of ideology critique or discourse analysis. The advantage of Kant's analysis of Christian consciousness is that the political actors and underlying interests can be more clearly detected, whereas in later ideology-critical analysis the powers become increasingly abstract – in the form of the economic system, or the order of the discourse itself.

How exactly is Kant's account of Christianity a path towards discourse analysis? One might surmise that Kant characterised Judaism in a somewhat unflattering way only to show Christianity in a brighter light. Indeed, according to Kant, Christianity is the first religion that bears within 'the germ and the principles of the true and universal religious faith to which it is gradually brought nearer' (*RGV* 6:125) and concedes that it is possible that the early Christians, at the time before the gospels were written, were indeed 'truly improved morally or just people' (*RGV* 6:130).

However, from that time on, Christianity evolved as a historically recorded movement, starting with hermits, monks, early parishes – even more so when it became state religion or organised church – and Kant has nothing but scorn for it. Christianity as 'ecclesiastical faith' therefore fares no better than Judaism in Kant's view. To a certain extent, Christianity is, as a historical church, even more dangerous: precisely because of its universalistic nature, every historical church has an inherent tendency to strive to become the only 'Catholic' one, though in a historical form (like a universal monarchy) – all other churches are then typically delegitimised, which leads to continual religious warfare. Like a supplement to the dialectics of institutions, this shows that the propensity of churches, like the propensity of states or individuals, has pernicious effects. The crucial point here is that because of its inward nature, Christianity poses a special danger for the human mind.

In his anthropological, sober manner, Kant holds that human beings have a 'propensity to a servile faith of worship, to which they are spontaneously inclined [to give] the greatest importance above moral faith' (*RGV* 6:134). The spiritual authorities take advantage of this by installing a discourse that prevents criticism (*RGV* 6:134), and the mechanism of this form of inner self-censorship is not confined to the religious sphere. Kant employs very similar anthropological considerations for explaining why human beings resist enlightenment: out of 'laziness and cowardice', they gladly remain minors for life and set up others as their guardians: 'It is so comfortable to be a minor! (...) I need not think, if only I can pay; others will readily undertake the irksome business for me' (*WA* 8:35).

What makes the religious discourse so pernicious is that it drains the only resource the human being has for emerging from their self-incurred minority. Courage to think for oneself – the one and only sentiment on which enlightenment relies for fostering its cause – is equated with lending an ear to the evil spirit (*RGV* 6:133). Kant also notes that once a servile faith of worship is installed in the religious sphere, clerics will finally also rule the state (*RGV* 6:180). Thus, ideology (in Marxian terms, a false consciousness) is not confined to the sphere of religion but easily wanders into the secular realm.

One might still surmise that Kant's critique of the religious mindset is bound to eighteenth-century circumstances in Prussia but does not apply to the problems of today's world. However, in some respects, Kant is even more radical than later forms of critical theory. Unlike a Marxian form of ideology critique, Kant does not presume to represent a historical force that inevitably fosters historical progress – he is all on his own. Unlike Foucault, he cannot presume to have a linguistic method that sets him apart from his object of inquiry – he speaks in the very same language as they do. Needless to say, Kant cannot rely on a historically situated mindset that elevates the discourse of political liberalism above the contestation of comprehensive doctrines. On the contrary, Kant has to hope that enlightenment takes hold within the comprehensive doctrines. Therefore, Kant seems to take pleasure in dissecting the various schools, practices and sentiments found in Christian confessions.

Again, it would be easy to take up these psychographs in a light-mannered way for describing the establishment of academic traditions and specific schools of cosmopolitanism, including the high priests with all their personal failings.

However, such frivolous musings would not do justice to the underlying movement we have discovered through the analysis of Kant. In short: Kant is not just the father of the contemporary liberal, cosmopolitan tradition of political thought but also the father of a specific German tradition of philosophy, which includes idealistic systems and historical-materialistic and value-critical strands, culminating in Heidegger. This needs some explaining.

5. Heidegger's resolution?

In the Preface, I suggested that, alongside the dominant liberal-cosmopolitan tradition, one must also reckon with Heidegger's subterranean influence. One might think that Heidegger's political thinking is essentially discredited as he lent his support to National Socialism, which, in the form of the Holocaust, left an ineradicable stain on Western civilisation. Nevertheless, Heidegger's thought continues in a transmuted shape to influence discourses and developments until today. Throughout myriad transformations in French philosophy, Heidegger's thinking finally left its mark on identity and postcolonial politics, which dissolved traditional liberal certainties.[115]

In a more blatant and nationalistic vein, Heidegger is also a favourite point of reference among pretentious nationalistic theoreticians. Finally, because of his invocation of the pre-Socratic wisdom-saying tradition, Heidegger invites constructing parallels to the Oriental (especially Confucian) tradition, which is currently weaponised by Chinese authorities in standing up against the Western canon. As these are mostly loose, anecdotal allusions, one might think that the best way to curb intellectual overgrowth is serious, detailed scholarship – so to speak, proper gardening in the field of political philosophy.

However, the detailed, contextual reading of Plato and Kant helped little to solidify a liberal, specifically cosmopolitan

[115] See, for a highly polemic account of the phenomenon, Helen Pluckrose and James Lindsay, *Cynical Theories: How Universities Made Everything about Race, Gender, and Identity – and Why This Harms Everybody* (Durham: Pitchstone, 2020). However, the book relies mostly on anecdotal journalistic reports and can therefore only count as a perceived threat.

strand of thinking. On the contrary, dissecting the various strands and approaches in Kant has revealed an urgent need for new synthesis. Only now, after we have pursued a contextual reading of Plato and Kant through the Western tradition, do we understand why Heidegger's philosophy can be seen as a response to some of the loose ends we diagnosed earlier in Kant. That is, the aim of the following section is to show, with an improved understanding, why Heidegger cannot be easily sidestepped by taking the Kantian project and its appropriation in the twentieth and twenty-first centuries seriously.

To this end, we will show why Heidegger developed, in a brief period after the publication of *Being and Time* but before his 'turn' (*Kehre*), an interest in Kant's practical philosophy. During this time, Heidegger also pursued explicit political activities, and his reading of Kant is not just an intellectual exercise but a political intervention in the political discourse of his time. We will first explain the context of Heidegger's reading of Kant (5.1), then show how it responds systematically to loose ends in Kant's thinking (5.2) and diagnose the limits and failings of Heidegger's appropriation of Kant (5.3).

5.1 The context of Heidegger's reading of Kant

Heidegger's reception of Kant started only after the publication of *Being and Time* and presupposes the framework developed therein. However, in our context, it is possible to bypass it for a moment and focus on Heidegger's lecture *The Essence of Human Freedom* (held in the summer of 1930). This is for two reasons.[116] First, the subtitle is *An Introduction to Philosophy*, so the lecture is meant for an audience with no prior knowledge of philosophy or of Heidegger's work in particular. Second, Heidegger pursues the two questions we have asked throughout our analysis of Kant: the Cambridge

[116] Martin Heidegger, *The Essence of Human Freedom: An Introduction to Philosophy*, ed. Ted Sadler (London and New York: Continuum, 2002), 19; idem, *Vom Wesen der menschlichen Freiheit. Einleitung in die Philosophie. Freiburger Vorlesung Sommersemester 1930*, ed. Hartmut Tietjen, (Frankfurt am Main: Vittorio Klostermann, 1982), 26. Subsequent page numbers refer to the English text, the second number in brackets to the German original.

School's question about the political character of philosophical thinking and the unity of Kant's account of freedom.

When explaining his methodological orientation, Heidegger employs distinctly militaristic language when arguing that philosophy has an 'attacking character' (*Angriffscharakter*).[117] He explains that it emerges 'from the innermost essence of freedom, insofar as the latter stands within the horizon of philosophical questioning'.[118] He goes on to characterise the methodological problem as a tension between 'the quite natural view that philosophy has to do with man himself and should have an influence on his activities'[119] and the leading problem of the great tradition, according to which philosophy has to do with '*theoria contemplatio*, speculative knowledge'.[120] The lecture shows how Heidegger engages with the tradition and transforms it to a specific end.

The lecture has a specific place in Heidegger's oeuvre, as it is part of the project of writing a second part of *Being and Time*, a project he later abandoned. In his later self-interpretation, the question from a young friend ('When are you going to write a book on ethics?') was misguided from the beginning.[121] However, in his writings on Kant in the 1920s and 1930s, Heidegger clearly pursued a distinctly practical and political agenda. It is therefore telling to see how Heidegger makes use of Kant and why he gave up on this project.

In 1929 Heidegger published the book *Kant and the Problem of Metaphysics*,[122] in which he gives a highly original reading of Kant's *Critique of Pure Reason*. For our leading questions

117 Heidegger, *The Essence of Human Freedom*, 19 (26). In Ted Sadler's finer English translation ('challenging character'), this nuance is lost.

118 Ibid.

119 Ibid., 26 (35).

120 Ibid.

121 See Martin Heidegger, 'Letter on Humanism', in *Pathmarks*, ed. William McNeill (Cambridge: Cambridge University Press, 1998), 268; idem, 'Brief über den Humanismus', in *Wegmarken*, ed. Friedrich-Wilhelm von Herrmann (Frankfurt am Main: Vittorio Klostermann, 1976), 353.

122 Martin Heidegger, *Kant and the Problem of Metaphysics*, 5th ed., trans. Richard Taft (Bloomington: Indiana University Press, 1990). Page numbers refer to the latest German edition: Martin Heidegger *Kant und das Problem der Metaphysik* (1929), ed. Friedrich-Wilhelm von Herrmann (Frankfurt am Main: Vittorio Klostermann, 1991).

concerning the political character of Kant's philosophy and the unity of his approach, two fundamental rearrangements made by Heidegger are of particular importance. Heidegger holds that the unity of reason, which Kant famously searched for (*GMS* 4:391) – namely, the unity of both stems of sensibility and understanding – can actually be found in the notion of power of imagination (*Einbildungskraft*). This power is, in turn, rooted in 'original time'. With this notion of 'original time', Heidegger alludes to his own existential analysis of Dasein in terms of being-toward-death. Here, Heidegger pursues two objectives: to give a systematic reading of Kant's critical philosophy and to show that his own analysis of Dasein is more fundamental, as it takes up the ancient question of being.

This rearrangement is telling, as we have come across the very same questions in our analysis of Kant. We have seen that, in spite of his claim to have brought philosophy for the first time onto a scientific track (*MS* 6:206), Kant was drawn into a contestation with Plato. We have also realised that Kant's empirical studies remained mostly unrelated to his critical philosophy. Finally, Kant's notion of freedom as autonomy could not be easily transferred into the legal realm to make space for non-moral but free actions, or to the religious realm to allow for free but evil actions. Our ad hoc solution was to acknowledge these difficulties while analysing the legal realm and the sphere of rational theology on their own terms, as only Kant's attentive analyses of the fields – law and religion – allowed us to question contemporary understandings. Nevertheless, Heidegger's claim to have found a thoroughgoing solution is promising and requires close attention.

In *Kant and the Problem of Metaphysics*, Heidegger refers explicitly to practical philosophy only briefly. He writes that Kant's anthropology remains at an empirical level, one which general experience offers but which 'does not pose the question of transcendence at all'.[123] We have previously seen that, for Kant, studies in anthropology cannot discover any laws in the strict sense, as such studies are ultimately concerned with

123 Ibid., 93, (132–33).

doctrines of happiness, which unlike morality consist only of hypothetical imperatives. With regard to the limits of Kant's anthropology, Heidegger's analysis conforms with Kant. The crucial point at which Heidegger diverges from Kant is not in looking for a transcendental foundation, but in setting the foundation in a sensuous faculty. Heidegger acknowledges the far-reaching consequences of this re-reading:

> How is the baser faculty of sensibility also to be able to constitute the essence of reason? Does not everything fall into confusion if the lowest takes the place of the highest? (...) Will not the *Critique of Pure Reason* have deprived itself of its own theme if pure reason reverts to the transcendental power of imagination? Does not this ground-laying lead us to an abyss? In the radicalism of his questions, Kant brought the 'possibility' of metaphysics to this abyss. He saw the unknown. He had to shrink back. It was not just that the transcendental power of imagination frightened him, but rather that in between [the two editions] pure reason as reason drew him increasingly under its spell.[124]

He accuses Kant of not following the subjective line of argument in the transcendental deduction consistently, as envisioned in the first edition of the *Critique of Pure Reason*, but of choosing instead a more logical mode of argumentation. What Heidegger calls the 'spell of reason' is, of course, the insight into the moral law as a 'fact of reason'. But how is this a spell, and what is Heidegger's alternative? He is well aware that, by laying the ground of metaphysics in general, Kant thought he had '"rod and staff" in hand, in order to wander critically through the region of moral philosophy.'[125]

Significantly, Heidegger does not mention the new insight into freedom as autonomy, which Kant articulated only after the *Critique of Pure Reason*, but refers generally to the 'essential originality of the ontological analyses which alone can situate a metaphysics of morals'.[126] Heidegger likewise

124 Ibid., 117–8 (168).
125 Ibid.
126 Ibid.

does not explain why a priori moral reasoning is misguided. This can only be indirectly deduced through the alternative Heidegger promotes against the metaphysical tradition: taking finitude in human beings seriously. 'The laying of the ground for metaphysics is grounded in the question concerning human finitude.'[127]

In his own ontological analysis of Dasein, it is the experience of time, through anxiety and care, that leads to a new understanding of being. 'Metaphysics is not something that was merely 'created' by human beings in systems and doctrines. Rather, the understanding of Being – its projection and its rejection – happens in Dasein as such. "Metaphysics" is the basic event that occurs with the factical existence of something like man in general.'[128] Heidegger points out the difference from Kant's scientific and abstract foundation of metaphysics. 'This [*Critique of Pure Reason*] itself thus rattles the mastery of reason and understanding. 'Logic' is deprived of its pre-eminence in metaphysics, which was built up from ancient times. Its idea has become questionable.'[129]

But what does this mean for moral or political problems, for the concrete decisions that have to be made? In *Kant and the Problem of Metaphysics* (published in 1929), Heidegger remains silent about these questions. Only in the subsequent lecture *The Essence of Human Freedom* (delivered in summer 1930 but published only in 1982) does he explicitly address Kant's moral philosophy. Again, he situates the question of the essence of freedom so that its connection to philosophy – as 'revealing the whole by means of properly conceived particular problems'[130] – becomes clear. When the question of freedom is not asked in a piecemeal way – that is, whether one particular body movement is free – but broadened to include the question of whether a human being can be free from nature and God, 'everything' is included in the question of the essence of freedom. This is because the world and God together constitute the

[127] Ibid., 152 (217).
[128] Ibid., 170 (242).
[129] Ibid., 170 (243).
[130] Heidegger, *The Essence of Human Freedom*, 9 (14).

totality of what is.[131] Therefore, Heidegger's question also has political significance, as politics is part of the world.

Heidegger starts by reconstructing Kant's account of negative, transcendental freedom. He then concludes that positive freedom is found only in moral action. Moving from Kant's account, he argues: 'Practical action is the way of being of the person. Experience of practical freedom is experience of the person as a person.'[132] Thus, Heidegger reads freedom in a personal, phenomenological way, though one that stresses the strictly individual and existential character (the experience of the person as a person).

We have previously seen that the categorical imperative is not simply an abstract formula but embedded in related discourses in anthropology and in the legal and religious spheres. Kant is aware of the trickeries of the human intellect working against strict duty and acknowledges that the formation of ethical character requires a lifetime, so Heidegger's characterisation of practical action as a way of being of the person is well-founded. However, Heidegger deviates from Kant by stressing exclusively the individual, existential characteristic of moral action while downplaying the many social commitments in which a moral action occurs. Heidegger's rewriting of Kant's practical philosophy is therefore not a new perspective but a 'destructive' reading out of principle.[133] Its 'violence' is most obvious in the reformulation of the categorical imperative.

The *Groundwork* opens with a sentence that already encapsulates the trajectory of Kant's argument: 'It is impossible to think of anything at all in the world, or indeed even beyond it, that could be considered good without limitation except a **good will**' (*GMS* 4:393). Heidegger, however, interprets it as follows: 'Qua will – i.e. insofar as it only wills willing – a good will is absolutely good. Qua absolutely good, a good will is a pure will.'[134] As if drawing a conclusion, he continues: 'We have presented the essence of pure practical reason as pure

[131] Ibid., 5 (7).
[132] Ibid., 186 (272–73).
[133] Heidegger himself characterises his analysis in this vein: 'Philosophical controversy is interpretation as destruction'. Ibid., 198 (292).
[134] Ibid., 189 (277).

will.'[135] Thus, Heidegger's rendering of the starting point of Kant's argument sounds like a Nietzschean will to power, as the will only wills itself. Heidegger strengthens this line of interpretation by arguing that the 'formal' principle to which the will is bound (the conformity of maxims with universal law) is not formal in the sense of empty but that 'the form of the law is precisely the decisive, proper and determining instance in relation to the law. What is generally lawgiving for willing is the actual pure willing itself and nothing else.'[136] Thus, universal law turns into the consciousness of a pure willing of itself.

Heidegger elaborates this thought through a variety of formulations: 'This willing of itself is allegedly empty, but at bottom it is precisely this which is most concrete … while knowing that it should act, it knows how it should act.'[137] 'Such a will determines its own willing unconditionally. It cannot help but be in harmony with itself, its pure essence, that is, it cannot but be good.'[138] In these formulations, it is most obvious that Heidegger identifies pureness in determination and goodness. The formulation is particularly striking, as he explicitly identifies the authentic decision with the (morally) good – an association he vehemently opposes in *Being and Time* and in his later self-interpretation.[139] Despite this, he is not quite so candid when calling inauthentic action evil: 'Even when we avoid decision, even when we dissemble to ourselves about the motives for our actions, we have actually decided to turn away from ought. Indeed, precisely in this turning away do we experience the fact of the ought most vividly.'[140]

Even when granting that Heidegger grasped one aspect of the categorical imperative with the immediate consciousness of moral law, one might wonder how Heidegger can reconcile his interpretation with the general formulation of the categorical imperative, which seems to yield direct moral

135 Ibid.
136 Ibid., 190 (279).
137 Ibid., 191 (279–90).
138 Ibid., 191 (280).
139 Heidegger, *Pathmarks*, 268 (353).
140 Heidegger, *The Essence of Human Freedom*, 9 (13).

consequences reminiscent of liberalism. Heidegger addresses this in two ways. First, he ridicules the idea that the specific wording of the categorical imperative is self-evident, or as Kant writes, 'the common understanding can see it without instruction' (*GMS* 5:49). As Heidegger admits, this is not an exhaustive philosophical argument but a sociological explanation that serves to deflate this specific formulation.

In his own argumentation, Heidegger concentrates on the second, humanity formulation. In Kant it reads: 'Act in such a way that you treat humanity, whether in your own person or in the person of any other, never merely as a means to an end, but always at the same time as an end' (*GMS* 4:429). Heidegger gives it a specific twist once again: unlike most contemporary readers of Kant, he shifts the focus from the relation to the other[141] to an appeal directed at oneself. 'Thus, the categorical imperative says before anything else, in all your actions, always act in your essence. The essence of a person is this self-responsibility: to bind oneself to oneself.'[142] Through these two steps – sidestepping the general formulation of the categorical imperative and rewording the humanity formulation so as to stress its subjective appeal – Heidegger cancels out Kant's liberal legacy. Only in passing does he note that the 'binding character' also has a communal aspect: 'Actual, essentially willing already in itself brings about mutual understanding, and this through the mystery of the actual willing of the individual.'[143] In this way, the categorical imperative becomes an ecstatic self-assertion of the self as part of a 'mystical community' (mutual understanding based on a mystery).

5.2 The systematic strengths of Heidegger's interpretation

It might seem easy to chastise Heidegger for misunderstanding Kant, perhaps even for consciously perverting the moral core of the categorical imperative. This charge could be bolstered with references to his role as rector of the University

[141] Samuel J. Kerstein, *Kant's Search for the Supreme Principle of Morality* (Cambridge: Cambridge University Press, 2002), 174–86.

[142] Ibid., 199 (293).

[143] Ibid., 199 (294).

of Freiburg in 1933 and to his political views, which he expressed more openly in letters to his brother and in the *Black Notebooks*.[144] However, before exploring Heidegger's darker side, we must briefly recall the systematic results of his reading of Kant. Only then can Heidegger's lasting impact and possible responses to it be conceived.

We have already noted that Heidegger took up some of the leading questions we have pursued throughout the genealogy. These include the question of the Cambridge School – how to conceive the political or challenging character of philosophy, what Heidegger calls its 'attacking character' – as well as the question of how to engage with the ancients in a fruitful way, the issue Kant stumbled upon in his contestation with Schlosser. A further question concerns the unity of Kant's notion of freedom. Moreover, one overarching hypothesis, assumed at the very beginning of the analysis of Kant, can only now be dissolved.

When leaping from Plato to Kant, we justified setting aside Stoic cosmopolitanism and the entire history of medieval and early modern conceptions by presuming that with Kant subjectivity – the principle of modernity – was first conceptualised in a comprehensive way. However, in our analysis of Kant's philosophy, the term subjectivity turned out not to play a prominent role. Moreover, instead of finding a systematic unity that Kant promised, we have followed different strands of his thought and realised that this unity proves to be lacking. One explanation for this apparent failure of the hypothesis is that systematic philosophical accounts of subjectivity were only developed later in the German Idealist tradition. Yet the intricate discussions in German idealism are not the only place where Kant's thought is taken up. Heidegger's take on Kant's philosophy is a milestone, precisely because it addresses why the question of unity in Kant's

144 See Martin Heidegger, 'Brief an Fritz Heidegger vom 2. März 1932', in Walter Homolka and Arnulf Heidegger, eds., *Heidegger und der Antisemitismus: Positionen im Widerstreit: mit Briefen von Martin und Fritz Heidegger* (Freiburg: Herder, 2016), 26. From a historical perspective, the *Black Notebooks* should not come as a surprise as the wilful and preemptive submission of the majority of German scholars under the Nazi regime and their later excuses is well-documented.

account remains unresolved and inadvertently reveals why attempts to reconstruct this unity are inherently treacherous.

Heidegger's strength is that he takes subjectivity seriously as a specific human quality and does not, like Hegel, fall into the trap of conceiving it as 'absolute presence'[145] or simply as another word for God.[146] For this reason, Heidegger's pragmatic account of subjectivity continues to provoke discussion until today.[147] Even Heidegger's discussion of Kant's practical philosophy is not totally misguided but comes close to developing a general theory of freedom that, unlike Kant's, is not simultaneously a moral theory.[148]

Following these lines, Heidegger's interpretation of the humanity formulation of the categorical imperative is not merely a sly way to avoid moral commitment. He instead stresses that only a human being that is free in itself, as it realises, through care, that it is an end in itself, can relate to other people out of freedom, whether in a moral or an immoral way. Using contemporary terms, one could say that Heidegger develops a pragmatic account of human freedom, since he does not begin by comparing free actions with physical causality but instead inquires into the pragmatic presuppositions of our life-world commitments. Finally, even Heidegger's existential rewriting of the categorical imperative has a true moral kernel, though one that ultimately eludes theorising.

The claim that there is a true moral kernel in Heidegger is likely to raise alarms, so this thought needs to be introduced

145 Ibid., 77 (110).

146 To formulate this thought in Hegel's words: 'That the True is actually only as system, or that Substance is essentially Spirit, is expressed in the representation of the Absolute as Spirit.' Hegel goes on to argue that the absolute spirit is 'absolute presence'. Georg Wilhelm Friedrich Hegel, *Philosophy of Nature (Part Two of Hegel's Encyclopaedia of the Philosophical Sciences)*, trans. A.V. Miller (Oxford: Clarendon Press, 1970), 35 (§258).

147 For a pragmatist interpretation, see Robert Brandom, 'Dasein, the Being That Thematizes', in *Tales of the Mighty Dead* (Cambridge, MA: Harvard University Press, 2002), 324–47.

148 This is the basic thesis of Gerold Prauss, *Erkennen und Handeln in Heideggers Sein und Zeit* (Freiburg: Karl Alber, 1977). For the contemporary discussion, see Min Seol, 'Ethical Lessons from Heidegger's Phenomenological Reading of Kant's Practical Philosophy: Heideggerian Revision of Kant's Justification of Morality', in *Journal of the British Society for Phenomenology* 51 (2019): 1–17.

with care. To begin with the obvious: Heidegger's lame excuses, small lies and bending of facts after World War II are, on both a personal and an intellectual level, disheartening.[149] However, Heidegger's personal faults – and the inadequate reaction to his silence by many Heideggerians – have thwarted the possibility that the very analysis Heidegger gives could point to a genuine, deeply personal moral stance. Once the behaviour described is presented as a role model, such a description can even serve as a guiding principle, one that transcends philosophical explanation. This becomes most evident in the following cinematic example.

In his historical drama *A Hidden Life*, the director and Heidegger scholar Terrence Malick shows how Dasein is disclosed by standing firm in the storm at an existential crossroads. The movie tells the story of Franz Jägerstätter, a devout Catholic from the small Austrian town of St. Radegund, who refused to swear, as a conscripted soldier, the pledge of allegiance to Adolf Hitler. For 'subversion of national defence', he was imprisoned and executed. Using the landscape of the Alps and the rural setting of family life and daily farming activities to invoke a Heideggerian feel, the protagonist is shown to reach his decision alone, against the advice of local authorities and the church, knowing that his wife will face hardships, and his three daughters will grow up without a father. Thus, Heidegger's categorical imperative: 'before anything else, in all your actions, always act in your essence',[150] can also mean to revolt against any conciliating Nazi endorsement from whatever side (including pretentious philosophers), and the 'mystical community'[151] Heidegger alludes to can turn out to be the community of martyrs.[152] In this systematic perspective, Heidegger's thinking can be

[149] The historian Hugo Ott, who has documented Heidegger's time as a rector and his involvement with National Socialism most thoroughly, has disproved many of Heidegger's later self-justifications. Hugo Ott, *Martin Heidegger: A Political Life*, trans. Allan Blunden (London: HarperCollins, 1993).

[150] Heidegger, *The Essence of Human Freedom*, 199 (293).

[151] Ibid., 199 (294).

[152] In 2007, Jägerstätter was beatified by Pope Benedict XVI, who as a young man had served in the German anti-aircraft corps and presumably took the pledge of allegiance.

saved as it provides a resource for new syntheses and different ethical self-understandings. Therefore, Malick's movie is 'film-philosophy', the perpetuation of philosophy in an artistic genre.[153] However, there is also a systematic ambiguity or weakness in Heidegger's account that leads into the darker side of his thinking.

5.3 Heidegger's failing

We have explained that in Heidegger's reading, subjectivity as a principle of modernity emerged as a possible unified account of Kant's thinking – one that comprises his *Anthropology* and his critical philosophy – and that is potentially, even in a pragmatic way, humanistic. Yet Heidegger did not pursue this line of thought systematically to the end but held firm to a second, countervailing ancient idea, namely that theoretical cognition is unlike practical being in the world of Dasein – it is passive perceiving. This is the leading idea of cognition throughout *Being and Time*:[154] cognition, or the Greek *noein*, is the 'simple awareness of something present-at-hand in its sheer presence, which Parmenides had already taken to guide him in his own interpretation of Being'.[155]

153 For a more systematic reflection on the culmination of German Idealist philosophy in Heidegger and its possible prolongation in film, see Robert Pippin, *The Culmination: Heidegger, German Idealism, and the Fate of Philosophy* (Chicago: University of Chicago Press, 2024) and its sequel; idem, *Robert Bresson: Cinematic Style as Philosophy* (Chicago: University of Chicago Press, 2026).

154 There is a long-standing debate about Heidegger's notion of practice. Some authors regard the concept of practice as fundamental to Heidegger's philosophy. See François Raffoul and David Pettigrew, eds., *Heidegger and Practical Philosophy* (Albany, NY: State University of New York Press, 2002). However, even everyday practice requires knowing things in the first place – such as picking up the right kind of wrench – so elementary cognition is presupposed in every practice. The epistemological question, then, is how to conceptualise this kind of cognition: in a Kantian or in an Aristotelian way.

155 Martin Heidegger, *Being and Time: A Translation of Sein und Zeit*, trans. Joan Stambaugh, revised by Dennis J. Schmidt (New York: State University of New York Press, 2010), 22–23; idem, *Sein und Zeit*, ed. Friedrich-Wilhelm von Herrmann (Frankfurt am Main: Vittorio Klostermann, 1977), 25–26.

Heidegger retreats, in the vein of the phenomenological tradition, from the creative and active aspects of subjectivity and cognition central to Kant's critical philosophy and settles on theoretical cognition as the ancient, passive mode. For this reason, there is a constant tension between the heroic activism of Dasein and the passive suffering of fate inherited from the past. In *Being and Time*, the passive mode is expressed in terms such as the 'simple apprehension of something present-at-hand'[156] or 'the mode of simply lingering with'.[157] In Heidegger's later philosophy, history likewise is not created but 'happens', and is passively recollected 'in a more primordial way'.[158] This tension also has consequences for Heidegger's relation to the technical and historical world.

Even though he realises through his studies of technology after *Being and Time* that theoretical knowledge influences or even dominates our practical lifeworld,[159] he does not change the underlying conception of practice to include, for instance, the maintenance of technology within the pragmatic notion of Dasein.[160] Maintenance need not be the work of a professional mechanic. Everyone who wears glasses or has some other prosthesis knows that these need to be taken care of in order to feel natural. Likewise, the maintenance of one's tools is essential for every hiking trip or – since prehistoric times – for surviving a hunt. Even our everyday bodily awareness needs maintenance and schooling, which shows that cognition is, at a very basic level, practical. Heidegger, however, devalues the entire sphere of the technical world to save an imaginary and allegedly non-technical way of life. The details of Heidegger's discussion of technology (his notion of 'enframing' is the technological counterpart to 'alienation')

156 Heidegger, *Being and Time*, 22 (25).

157 Ibid., 57 (61).

158 Heidegger, 'Letter on Humanism', 255 (335).

159 See Martin Heidegger, 'Science and Reflection', in *The Question Concerning Technology and Other Essays*, trans. William Lovitt (New York: Harper & Row, 1977), 155; idem, 'Wissenschaft und Besinnung', in *Vorträge und Aufsätze* 1936–1953, ed. Friedrich-Wilhelm von Herrmann (Frankfurt am Main: Vittorio Klostermann, 2000), 30.

160 For a creative appropriation of Heidegger's thinking along these lines, see Robert M. Pirsig, *Zen and the Art of Motorcycle Maintenance: An Inquiry into Values* (London: Bodley Head, 1975).

need not concern us at this point. However, this tension also reappears in the historical and political world.

Heidegger presents the individual authentic decision as the expression of the categorical imperative. In his reformulation of Kant's practical philosophy, the consciousness of the freedom of the will is expressed in the imperative: 'before anything else, in all your actions, always act in your essence'.[161] Heidegger even ponders the thought that 'the problem of being in general is in itself a problem of freedom,[162] or, even more emphatically: 'Freedom is the condition of the possibility of the manifestness of the being of beings, of the understanding of being.'[163] These sentences sound as if Heidegger wanted to re-establish a specific variant of 'liberal pragmatism', with freedom as the foundational concept.

At the same time, however, freedom is aligned with theoretical cognition or the quietistic acceptance of happenings for which no one in particular assumes responsibility. In his reformulation of Kant's practical philosophy, both tendencies become interwoven: the heroic emphasis on authentic decision and the passive surrender to historical fate.

> Letting something stand-over-against as something given, basically the manifestness of beings in the binding character of their so- and that-being, is only possible where the comportment to beings, whether in theoretical or practical knowledge, already acknowledges this binding character. But the latter amounts to an originary self-binding, or, in Kantian terms, the giving of a law unto oneself.[164]

In short, 'manifestness of being' requires, from a theoretical or practical perspective, passively acknowledging its binding character. In these sentences, Heidegger aligns the practical perspective with the theoretical, as if there were no difference between recognising something in the world and purposefully changing the world for better or worse. Heidegger's declaration of freedom being 'the condition of

161 Heidegger, *The Essence of Human Freedom*, 199 (293).
162 Ibid., 203 (300).
163 Ibid., 203 (303).
164 Ibid.

the possibility of the manifestness of the being of beings' is not merely amoral in an existential sense but also empty. This kind of freedom carries no subjective trait and does not allow for personal responsibility or guilt. Philosophy becomes the very opposite of what Heidegger claimed at the beginning of the lecture: instead of displaying its 'attacking character', it is turned into an asylum for escapees from the world. Notably, not all refugees are innocent: the innocent flee injustice, the guilty flee re-established justice.

We see that Heidegger had thus reached a crossroads. Instead of rejecting the practical, constructive dimension of subjectivity, the path towards a post-foundational account of subjectivity was open in principle. However, it is futile to speculate about alternative historical or philosophical paths that were not taken. The sobering reality can be stated briefly, since it provides no resources for our question about a genealogy of cosmopolitan thought.

On 21 April 1933 Heidegger was elected rector of the University of Freiburg, and on 27 April 1934 his resignation was accepted by the Ministry of Culture of the Federal State of Baden. He joined the NSDAP on 1 May 1933 and remained a member until the end of the war.

As rector of the University of Freiburg, Heidegger used his prestige and official powers to shut down the remaining spaces for free and open critical discussion, suppress any signs of resistance and streamline the university into an institution serving the 'greater good' of National Socialism. Since the publication of his *Black Notebooks*, the crude Nazi and antisemitic subtext of his grandiose philosophical analysis can also be deciphered.

To give just one example: in 1932 Heidegger made a somewhat cryptic note in the *Black Notebook*: 'But: "People without space" and their most singular individuals without time. What is "space" here? What is "time" here? (...) Space and time not the juxtaposed, which is simply "given," but instead the opening and upsurge of being, which must be strived for.'[165]

[165] Martin Heidegger, *Ponderings II–VI. Black Notebooks 1931–1938*, trans. Richard Rojcewicz (Bloomington: Indiana University Press, 2014), 14; idem, *Überlegungen II-VI (Schwarze Hefte 1931–1938)*, ed. Peter Trawny (Frankfurt am Main: Vittorio Klostermann, 2014), 18.

The expression 'people without space' was a common topic among right-wing ideologues and National Socialist propagandists.[166] Only a few years later, this jargon was employed to justify the attack on Russia to make 'living space in the East for the new master race'.

Apparently, Heidegger tried to connect his most abstract philosophical terms of time, space and being with ordinary political discourse. He did this in a specific way: often, he put terms of political discourse, such as 'people', 'living space', 'struggle' and so on, in quotation marks as a way of distancing himself from the 'inauthentic usage' while pretending to search for the true authentic meaning of these terms.[167]

Throughout the *Black Notebooks*, Heidegger's implicit criticism of abstract modernity can be seen to rest on antisemitic stereotypes. Somehow, liberalism, pacifism, Judaism, Husserl and neo-Kantianism are all enemies that need to be defeated, especially as the 'increasing power of Judaism' is presented as an expression of 'occidental metaphysics'. It is futile to expect anything other than poorly disguised ordinary prejudices and uncritical political slogans in these remarks.[168]

Likewise, Heidegger's attempts in his 1934–1935 seminar on Hegel's *Philosophy of Right* to formulate 'morally fundamental' practical concepts while outright rejecting the entire liberal tradition appear amateurish and unintentionally comical. He disparages the separation of powers as an 'inhibition' that results only in 'mistrust and cleverness'. Instead, legislative and executive powers should no longer

[166] Francis Ludwig Carsten, *Essays in German history* (London: Hambledon, 1985), 309.

[167] Heidegger continues this form of mystifying political concepts, even after the war. Notoriously, he retained the remark 'inner truth and greatness of the National Socialist movement' in the 1953 edition of his lecture *Introduction to Metaphysics*. He only qualifies it for the post-war edition (without noting so in the later addition) with the clause 'namely the encounter between global technology and modern humanity'. See the translators' introduction in Martin Heidegger, *Introduction to Metaphysics*, trans. Gregory Fried and Richard Polt (New Haven, CT: Yale University Press, 2000), xv–xvii.

[168] Martin Heidegger, *Ponderings XII–XV. Black Notebooks 1939–1941*, trans. Richard Rojcewicz (Bloomington: Indiana University Press, 2017), 36–37; idem, *Überlegungen XII-XV (Schwarze Hefte 1939–1941)*, ed. Peter Trawny (Frankfurt am Main: Vittorio Klostermann, 2014), 46.

be separated but 'government as leadership' ought to be grounded in the 'Dasein of the Führer'.[169]

His obstinate refusal to express any regret or shame after the war, and his pernicious attempts to downplay his political role – even portraying himself as both a force of resistance and the true victim – contribute to the impression that philosophy must begin anew.

So was the liberal tradition of cosmopolitan thought right to shun much of the German tradition after Kant and rely instead on a highly selective range of philosophical literature? Perhaps philosophy has found a new home in the Anglophone world, one that can, through English as a lingua franca and the law as an inherently liberal medium, orient the world in a cosmopolitan direction?

[169] Martin Heidegger, *Seminare Hegel – Schelling*, ed. Peter Trawny (Frankfurt am Main: Vittorio Klostermann, 2011), 72.

Three

Kelsen and the Twilight of Cosmopolitanism

Our genealogy has thus far failed to equip contemporary cosmopolitan thought with a more thorough or nuanced self-understanding. Instead, it has led into a thicket of brown mud – a dead end seemingly far from the main road of current political philosophy. However, the genealogy that started with Plato does not have to search for hidden exits from the underlying cave.[1] It may also turn to artificial, technical instruments for orientation: modern law. Hans Kelsen, entangled in the intellectual and political life of Vienna, will turn out to be not just a legal theorist but a pivotal figure who wrestled with the tensions of his century. To see how Kelsen fits into the larger argument, we must recall the twofold response to Plato and the genealogical method that has guided us thus far.

After addressing Plato's challenge to contemporary cosmopolitanism, we outlined two primary modes of response. First, by introducing subjectivity as the principle of modernity, and second, by reflecting on modern law as the structure of modernity. In the early stages of the argument, the notions of the 'principle of modernity' and 'modern law' remained undefined.

Only now, after having dealt with Heidegger's appropriation of Kant, can we resolve this. Throughout the discussion, we have introduced historical events and socio-political contexts to illustrate how philosophers composed their treatises in response to the political questions of their time. However, these historical contexts and political questions often had

[1] For an indirect criticism of Heidegger's appropriation of Plato's Allegory of the cave, see Hans Blumenberg, *Höhlenausgänge* [Exits from the Cave] (Frankfurt am Main: Suhrkamp, 1989).

to be brought in externally, as if they were not inherently part of philosophy itself. In Plato's case, this approach was inevitable: he did not write explicitly about the events of his era, assuming that his readers were already familiar with the Greek world and the fate of Athens. In modern times, by contrast, we can no longer assume a single philosophical lingua franca or a shared base of common knowledge. It is thus striking that Kant's anthropological and historical writings remain, in a peculiar way, detached from the lifeworld of Königsberg and Prussia – as if to refute the Cambridge School's presumption that theorists must be closely studied within their historical milieu.

Nevertheless, Kant emerged as a political actor in an unexpected theoretical register, one who sought to transform discourse through biopolitical intervention. He wagered that he would outlive the obese and unprincipled King Frederick William II and that the rational-theological implications of critical philosophy would shape intellectual life more profoundly than any public address or activist intervention ever could.

Kant's example of indirect yet transformative influence expands the methodological maxims of the Cambridge School in two ways. First, in Prussia (and other Protestant German regions) fundamental changes of the philosophical discourse were first visible in religious discourse. Thus, the space where 'political' questions emerge cannot be determined from the outset. Second, insofar as Kant redefined the Western philosophical tradition by cultivating a specific German idiom, the Cambridge School's implicit belief in a neutral philosophical language from which all others can be judged becomes questionable. Therefore, even when donning the historian's hat, the theorist is drawn into the political-philosophical discourse.

In the case of Heidegger, these methodological maxims appear even more inattentive. His philosophical project was to 'deconstruct' the Western philosophical tradition, for which he crafted a wholly unique idiom.[2] So in a sense, there is after Heidegger no more innocent meta-philosophical or

[2] On Heidegger's aim of phenomenological destruction see *Being and Time*, 17 (19).

historical language. Yet on another level, Heidegger's writings confirm the Cambridge School's intuition that even abstract or fundamental philosophical treatises intervene in the political discourse of their time to a degree that it becomes a truism. The difficulty in identifying Heidegger's political aims lies in his evasion of the methodological expectations set by the Cambridge School. He pursued a political mission while largely disengaging from the polity – from the institutions and everyday life of modernity. But Heidegger cannot be dismissed simply as ignorant, nor can his 'mistakes' be corrected by appending to his writings an introduction to modern constitutional law. We have seen that Heidegger is modern in that he weaves together various strands of Kant's philosophy while 'de-transcendentalising' the self.

For this reason, when we refer to 'modern law' as 'the structure of modernity' in our response to Plato's challenge, we must introduce it in a particular, self-reflective manner, to avoid the suspicion that normative conclusions are being smuggled into our depiction of the modern world.

Accordingly, modern law is introduced as the structural form of modernity through a multilayered approach. First, I argue that a contextual reading of Kelsen's early writings reveals how he developed, from a backdrop of value-sceptical thinking, a legal variant of cosmopolitan thought (3.1–3.3). The analysis then shows how Kelsen's contestations with Carl Schmitt and Eugen Ehrlich, along with his post-war writings, enrich our genealogical understanding in three ways. Through the writings and interventions of Carl Schmitt, it becomes clear how a philosophically grounded anti-cosmopolitan position can emerge as the ideological counterpart – or even the reverse side – of legal cosmopolitanism. At the same time, a historical review identifies venues where both positions have clashed on an intellectual battlefield (3.4). Although Eugen Ehrlich, often regarded as a founding figure of the legal pluralist tradition, may seem to have no direct relevance for cosmopolitan thought, his altercation with Kelsen sheds light on another dimension: the social role of scholarship (3.5). Even scholarly work that merely aims to document communal legal practices can, under certain conditions, become complicit in oppressive, even murderous regimes. This issue is addressed in an indirect manner through a discussion of Jonathan Littell's novel *The Kindly Ones* (3.6). Finally, Kelsen's work is valuable for engaging with some of today's challenges. Unlike many of his contemporaries who, after the war, returned to renewed versions of natural law theory, Kelsen continued to demonstrate the relevance of his sceptical approach. His post-war writings offer insight into two additional models of post-foundational cosmopolitan thought: critical legal analysis and the debunking of foundationalism, as exemplified in his commentary on the law of the United Nations and his critique of Voegelin's grand historical narrative portraying liberalism as a form of Gnosticism (3.7).

1. Kelsen in context

The suggestion that Kelsen might offer a resolution to the layered philosophical discourses we have accumulated may appear surprising. This is largely because Kelsen is primarily known in the Anglophone world as a legal theorist who influenced H. L. A. Hart, only to have his theory ultimately dismissed by Hart.[3] As analytical jurisprudence tends to position Hart as both its starting point and central figure, it often appears disconnected from 'continental' traditions of legal thought and practice. Nevertheless, Kelsen stands at the intersection of these two traditions and may thus function as a bridge between them. To grasp Kelsen's unique position within twentieth-century legal-philosophical discourse and his contribution to a particular strand of cosmopolitan thinking, his work must again be contextualised.

1.1 Living through the turmoil of the twentieth century

Kelsen is not a widely recognised figure among political philosophers. Therefore, it is helpful to revisit the major phases of his life and the scope of his intellectual pursuits. Born in 1881 into a German-speaking Jewish family in Prague (two years

[3] For a criticism along the lines of stressing social normativity as a solution to the intricate problems posed by Kelsen's notion of the basic norm, see Joseph Raz, 'Kelsen's Theory of the Basic Norm', *The American Journal of Jurisprudence* 19 (1974): 94–111.

before Franz Kafka), Kelsen was raised in Vienna, where he experienced the tense but culturally dynamic atmosphere of the late Austro-Hungarian Empire. After completing his studies and producing his initial academic works in Vienna, he was drafted into the Austrian army, serving under the last Imperial Minister of War. In 1919, he became professor of public and administrative law at the University of Vienna. He co-authored the Austrian constitution of 1920 (which remains in force today) and was appointed a judge at the Austrian Constitutional Court. In 1930, he assumed a professorship in international law at the University of Cologne – then home to Carl Schmitt. After the Nazi rise to power, Kelsen was compelled to flee Germany, having been targeted as one of the 'Jewish professors' (despite having converted to Catholicism and identifying as agnostic). He ultimately settled at the University of California, Berkeley, where he taught political science until his death in 1973.

To appreciate the breadth of his philosophical interests, one might observe that the same books and traditions that later influenced Jacques Derrida were also present on Kelsen's shelves. He wrote on Plato, Freud, Marxism, neo-Kantianism and ethnology and examined the political-theological dimensions of juridical thought. The distinct importance of Kelsen's contribution, however, lies not in devising a transferrable method like deconstruction, but in his legal scholarship's engagement with three pivotal historical moments: 1913, 1932 and 1948.

Of these, 1948 is most immediately relevant to the genealogy of cosmopolitan thought: Kelsen produced the first comprehensive commentary on the law of the United Nations.[4] He took seriously the promise that the UN had converted cosmopolitan ideals into a legal framework, thereby setting the terms for future discussions. Yet to fully understand the relationship between Kelsen's legal theory and the structure

[4] Hans Kelsen, *The Law of the United Nations: A Critical Analysis of Its Fundamental Problems* (London: Stevens & Sons, 1951). For a contemporary assessment of Kelsen's view see Jörg Kammerhofer, 'Hans Kelsen's Place in International Legal Theory', in Alexander Orakhelashvili, ed., *Research Handbook on the Theory and History of International Law* (Cheltenham: Edward Elgar Publishing, 2011), 143–67.

of modernity – as well as the existential crisis of the twentieth century – the earlier dates must also be considered.

The Cambridge School's directive to investigate the 'question' to which a theory responds can be straightforwardly applied to the year 1932: how can one respond to the emergence of a populist, authoritarian movement within a liberal democracy? The 'circumstances of modernity', as exemplified by the Austro-Hungarian Empire, resist such simplification. While not reducible to a single query, they may be evoked by recalling some of those who resided in Vienna in 1913; individuals shaped by its tensions and atmosphere, who might well have encountered each other in the City Park. Among them: Sigmund Freud, Oskar Kokoschka, Alma Mahler, Arnold Schoenberg, Ludwig von Mises, Ludwig Wittgenstein and – more ominously – Adolf Hitler, Joseph Stalin and Leon Trotsky. In this sense, the splendour and tragedy of twentieth-century modernity were, for a time, condensed within a single city.

For our genealogy of cosmopolitan thought, it is critical to recognise that modernity was so far introduced only through abstract philosophical notions, such as subjectivity or Heidegger's right-wing appropriation. Considering instead the atmosphere in Vienna in 1913 allows the full complexity of modern developments – across society, politics, the arts and science – to come into view.

1.2 The Austro-Hungarian Empire as a model

For understanding the notion of modern law and Kelsen's specific take on it, we must first consider the particular sociopolitical conditions of the Austro-Hungarian Empire. This is more than a historical aside. In contrast to the political contexts of fourth-century BCE Athens or eighteenth-century Königsberg, the conditions of the Austro-Hungarian Empire may serve as a prototype for examining contemporary postcolonial realities. On one side, the Empire was a feudal remnant, a multi-ethnic, multi-national entity assembled through Habsburg conquest. The ancien régime persisted, with a monarch at the apex, a landowning nobility and a class of aristocrats employed primarily in the military and, to some extent, the bureaucracy. On the other side, the civil law system

(*Bürgerliches Recht*) guaranteed equal subjective rights, and an extensive bureaucracy facilitated modernisation through regulating the industrial revolution and mitigating some of its social ills. The rise of modern developments in the arts and sciences was, however, not a well-executed master plan but rather an incidental outcome of the expansion of the education system.

What makes the Empire particularly instructive from a political perspective is its 'post-colonial situation', or more accurately, its 'pre-national condition'. Ethnically and religiously diverse populations, all undergoing capitalist transformation and exposed to early signs of cultural modernity, coexisted under the Empire's legal regime. At the time, heated debates from all ideological camps attacked the Empire: to clerics, it was too liberal; to liberals, too social; to socialists, too capitalist; to republicans, too feudal; and to the avant-garde, too outdated. Each national group sought advantage by denouncing the Empire's legitimacy. Only one ethnic group consistently supported the common bureaucracy throughout all the various milieus and ethnicities: the large Jewish population. In hindsight, this support appears prescient, as what followed proved disastrous for them.

Maintaining this fragile but peaceful modus vivendi under the rule of law was the fundamental political challenge that Kelsen addressed in his early theory. This is most evident in his pre-World War I writings.[5] Confronted with the question of whether Austrian or Hungarian law held primacy, Kelsen contended that legal science (*Rechtswissenschaft*) could resolve ideological impasses only by refraining from all ideological or value-based arguments and focusing exclusively on its proper domain: the analysis of legal 'ought'. Only then could the law be construed as a coherent, value-free means for social regulation and conflict resolution. From a contemporary liberal perspective – one that assumes the normative primacy of individual liberty and republican governance – this may appear as a 'utopia of legality'.[6] Yet in historical

[5] Hans Kelsen, 'Reichsgesetz und Landesgesetz nach österreichischer Verfassung', *Archiv des öffentlichen Rechts* 32, nos. 1–2, 3–4 (1914): 202–45, 390–438.

[6] Lars Vinx, *Hans Kelsen's Pure Theory of Law: Legality and Legitimacy* (Oxford: Oxford University Press, 2008), 25.

context, the idea of a pure theory of law had strong practical underpinnings.

In his major works of the 1920s and beyond, Kelsen no longer referred to social and political circumstances as exemplifications but relied only on conceptual arguments. As with Kant's critical philosophy, these arguments must first be considered in their own terms before being reconnected with their historical backdrop.[7]

1.3 Law and jurisprudence in contested circumstances

To readers attuned to contemporary political philosophy, Kelsen's arguments may often seem abstract and overly formal, as if detached from the philosophical tradition and the legacy of liberalism. This impression, however, results from a misreading that overlooks both the context of his work and his intended audience. Kelsen wrote as an academic lawyer within the well-established continental discipline of *Rechtswissenschaften* – literally, 'the science of law'. Unlike the British or American traditions, where civil and constitutional law were not formally taught in universities until the mid-twentieth century (Hart himself never studied law), jurisprudence had been a core academic field in continental Europe since the medieval period.

This is not to claim superiority for one tradition over another, nor to suggest that scholars in either context are inherently more socially or morally aware. Rather, it clarifies the audience Kelsen envisioned. By the 1920s, German legal science was intellectually rich but in disarray due to the defeat of Germany and Austria in World War I and the resulting constitutional reorganisation. The moral foundations sought by Kant and other philosophers were discredited, as there were simply too many natural law theories around, each mirroring the convictions of its author. Similarly, the historical school

[7] In his autobiography from 1947, Kelsen pointed out that the pure theory was addressed at the specific social and political situation in Austria and can therefore be seen as 'a specific Austrian theory'. Hans Kelsen, 'Autobiography', in *Hans Kelsen Werke*, vol. 1, *Veröffentlichte Schriften 1905–1910 und Selbstzeugnisse*, ed. Matthias Jestaedt (Tübingen: Mohr Siebeck, 2007), 59–60.

of Friedrich Karl von Savigny, which aspired to uncover the true spirit of Germanic law through historical research, had either dissolved into antiquarianism or been appropriated for nationalist ideologies.[8]

In Austria, these tensions were especially acute. Although the 'national problem' of the Austro-Hungarian Empire had been ostensibly resolved by the Treaty of Versailles, post-war Austria remained ideologically fragmented. In addition to ethnic divisions, the country faced surging antisemitism and deep constitutional disputes. Even the state's territorial boundaries were contested, with significant support for unification with Germany and claims over neighbouring regions. Proposals for future governance ranged from a restored monarchy and corporatist models (*Ständestaat*) to a socialist republic. Divergent visions also permeated debates about economics, social structures, family life and the role of 'the Jews' as construed in contemporary discourse in a future state.

This overview underscores why Austria's situation cannot simply be classified among the 'circumstances of justice', as such frameworks presume shared parameters – territory, legitimate stakeholders, reasonable conceptions of justice – that were themselves under dispute.

Nonetheless, political and legal debates were anchored in the reality of a republican constitution. Kelsen was among the few legal scholars in Germany and Austria who unequivocally supported this liberal constitutional order, albeit in the framework of a pure theory of law. It can best be explained by tracing his career through the turbulent period between 1920 and 1950 as his contestation with other scholars would eventually bring out a specific legal variant of a post-foundational cosmopolitan thought.

8 For a brief history of the various schools, see Mathias Reimann, 'Nineteenth Century German Legal Science', *Boston College Law Review* 31, no. 4 (1990): 837–97.

2. The pure theory of law

2.1 Hierarchy of norms

Throughout his career and across changing political circumstances, Kelsen maintained three fundamental convictions: the thesis of the separation between the domains of the 'ought' and the 'is'; the thesis of a hierarchy of norms; and the thesis that the highest norm, the so-called *Grundnorm* or basic norm, can only be conceived as a (transcendental) presupposition.[9] Since contemporary discussions of these theses – albeit under different labels – largely define the Anglo-American tradition of analytical jurisprudence or legal positivism, Kelsen is typically grouped within this camp. However, contextualising Kelsen's work reveals that his theory warrants a different interpretive focus.

Kelsen's primary objective was not to theorise 'law' as a natural kind,[10] but rather to construct a theory of 'legal science': a framework aimed at refining the German tradition of scholarly and interpretive legal writing (*Rechtswissenschaft*). According to Kelsen, legal science must recognise that there is no necessary connection between law and morality and that its true domain is the analysis of the legal 'ought', which can be worked out by presupposing the basic norm.

We have already outlined the socio-political realities to which this theory responded. Its true strength, however, lies in its conceptual clarity and constructive potential. Kelsen begins by distinguishing the realm of the 'ought' from the realm of the 'is' – a distinction, he claims, we are 'immediately aware of ... and cannot be explained further'.[11] One might say that understanding this basic distinction is part of linguistic

[9] See Hans Kelsen, *Pure Theory of Law*, trans. from the 2nd ed. by Max Knight (Berkeley, CA: University of California Press, 1967), 2, 5, 195. Kelsen has changed his conception of the basic norm several times throughout his writings. On the transcendental account, see Stanley L. Paulson, 'The Neo-Kantian Dimension of Kelsen's Pure Theory of Law', *Oxford Journal of Legal Studies* 12, no. 3 (1992): 311–32.

[10] For an analysis of law as a natural kind, see Joseph Raz, 'On the Nature of Law', *Archiv für Rechts- und Sozialphilosophie* 82, no. 1 (1996): 1–25.

[11] Kelsen, *Pure Theory*, 5.

competence.[12] However, comprehending the difference between 'norms' and 'facts' in the modern world requires awareness of various contextual and discursive levels. Kelsen argues that a legal act derives its normative force not from some undefined sacred norm or a shared moral sense, but from a higher norm. In this way, law becomes self-regulating: it governs its own creation. Thus, the legal order is a 'system of general and individual norms connected in such a way that the creation of each norm of the system is determined by another.'[13]

Since each legal act derives its normativity from a higher norm, which in turn is grounded in yet another higher norm, this structure threatens to become infinite. Kelsen resolves this by asserting that every normative system – moral or legal – must presuppose a basic norm that grounds the objective validity of the system's norms. 'The basic norm is the common source for the validity of all norms that belong to the same order – it is their common reason of validity.'[14] As Kelsen focuses specifically on the legal system, he does not treat legality as a separate problem. Instead, he equates legality with a norm's membership in the legal system, in much the same way that morality is made up of moral norms, or etiquette consists of rules of courtesy within a given social milieu.[15]

2.2 Autonomy of law

The reason this account addresses the question of legal normativity becomes clearer when we examine alternative

[12] This does not mean, however, that normativity is an eternal concept that resides above historical change and philosophical consciousness. For tracing the origins of the distinction between 'is' and 'ought' one would have to consider thinking in mythical times or maybe in indigenous cultures. For an attempt that outlines at least the relevant contexts for approaching this question, see Hans Kelsen, *Society and Nature: A Sociological Inquiry* (Chicago: University of Chicago Press, 1943).

[13] Kelsen, *Pure Theory*, 233.

[14] Ibid., 195.

[15] From a sociological perspective, Niklas Luhmann, *Die Gesellschaft der Gesellschaft* (Frankfurt am Main: Suhrkamp, 1997), has further developed this conceptual separation of the whole of society into different systems.

views. This brings us to another of Kelsen's leitmotifs – often overlooked in analytical jurisprudence – namely, the autonomy of law and legal science. Identifying the basic norm with observable behaviour would be, first and foremost, an epistemic error: an attempt to derive an 'ought' from an 'is'. Yet this critique is not merely a conclusion drawn from an abstract principle; rather, it functions as a strategic move to demonstrate the possibility of an idealist alternative to empiricist approaches. It may be summarised in the following slogan: whenever someone offers an empirical foundation for law – such as a 'social fact' – ask what normative assumptions underlie that fact or why it should be considered binding. More than this cannot be offered for an 'immediate awareness'.

This strategy is well illustrated in Kelsen's response to H. L. A. Hart's critique. Hart argued that Kelsen's notion of a basic norm was a 'needless reduplication',[16] given that normativity could arise from a social fact. He identified the 'practice of officials' as the relevant fact.[17] However, while the term 'practice' may sound empirical, pointing to it does not resolve how a practice can generate normativity, unless one is simultaneously acting (e.g., Romulus building a wall) and invoking a normative interpretation (ordering Remus to respect the wall as a border). Indeed, in the postscript to *The Concept of Law*, written three decades later, Hart clarified that it is not the practice itself but the 'distinctive normative attitude' that underpins normativity. Thus, Hart's notion of 'practice' does not dissolve the 'is/ought' dichotomy; his 'normative attitude' is simply another expression of an 'ought'.[18] The existence of the rule of recognition, which Hart emphasises, ultimately amounts to the presupposition that the normative system is effective, a presupposition Kelsen shares.

Maintaining the epistemic autonomy of a legal system (and, by extension, the purity of legal science) may appear to be an unnecessary complication. In post-Hartian Anglophone

[16] Hart, *The Concept of Law*, 246.
[17] Ibid., 108.
[18] Ibid., 255.

legal philosophy, this concern is often dismissed altogether.[19] However, the perspective Kelsen insists upon is not merely an eccentric variant of contemporary discourse. It stems from a specific and historically grounded view of modernity as a precarious achievement. Modern rationality has not only enabled the rise of modern science and the erosion of mythical worldviews. It has also rationalised the lifeworld, dividing it into distinct functional systems. Consequently, the scientific worldview (understood in an idealist, comprehensive sense) can no longer provide existential meaning or a sense of wholeness.[20]

The precariousness of this modern condition is revealed by the emergence of totalitarianism in the twentieth century. These regimes, while technologically advanced and ideologically potent, reversed many of modernity's functional differentiations. (Contemporary parallels – such as attacks on the judiciary and legal academia in democracies governed by populist regimes – are glaring, though they must be set aside in the context of a historical analysis.)

In this contextual perspective, retaining the autonomy of the legal system is not merely a historical reminder or an abstract epistemic argument, but the recognition of an epistemic achievement that rests upon a specific kind of organisation of society. The criticisms often voiced regarding Kelsen's theory of the basic norm that it is 'utterly sterile',[21] or an

[19] Ronald Dworkin even denies that there is a meaningful distinction between the practice of law, legal theory, moral theory, and metaethics. See Ronald Dworkin, *Justice for Hedgehogs* (Cambridge, MA: Harvard University Press, 2011), 10. Legal positivists typically do not treat 'legal science' as an autonomous, value-neutral discipline in the classical sense. Rather, they understand legal theory as a descriptive or explanatory account of law as a social practice. See Scott J. Shapiro, *Legality* (Cambridge, MA: Harvard University Press, 2011), 19.

[20] This process was described in the 1920s and 1930s by several thinkers, see notably Max Weber, *The Vocation Lectures,* trans. Rodney Livingstone (Illinois: Hackett Books, 2004); and Edmund Husserl, *The Crisis of European Sciences and Transcendental Phenomenology: An Introduction to Phenomenological Philosophy*, trans. David Carr (Evanston, IL: Northwestern University Press, 1954).

[21] Karl N. Llewellyn, *Jurisprudence: Realism in Theory and Practice* (Chicago: University of Chicago Press, 1962), 356.

'exercise in logic and not in life',[22] can then be granted as being the price of modernity.

However, Kelsen stresses the autonomy of law not only for epistemic reasons but also for practical ones. Again, a contextual reading shows that he thereby develops a specific point of view, which is worth retaining. Defending the autonomy of the legal system regarding moral norms requires a more complex argument. Since moral norms are normative as well, it would not be a categorical mistake to derive a legal norm from a moral one; it would only derail the autonomy of the legal system regarding a specific discourse. Therefore, Kelsen develops a specific argument that presupposes the existence of a bureaucratic state and a post-Nietzschean attitude with regard to philosophy.[23] Both assumptions need to be briefly explained.

In contemporary jurisprudential debates, natural law theorists who advocate a 'classical position' often note that natural law traditions typically make space for positive law and acknowledge its normative force, albeit within boundaries set by natural law theory.[24] Kelsen counters this with a historical account. Before the codification of legal materials and the bureaucratisation of the state apparatus, classical natural law theory served to systematise legal content and procedure where no formal framework existed. However, with the centralisation and rationalisation of the legal system, each legal act could be validated only by reference to the legal system itself. Thus, the functional necessity of natural law theory diminished.

[22] Harold Laski, *A Grammar of Politics*, 4th ed. (London: George Allen & Unwin, 1938), vi.

[23] For an explicit formulation of Kelsen's post-Nietzschean stance see his *Secular Religion: A Polemic Against the Misinterpretation of Modern Social Philosophy, Science and Politics as 'New Religions'*, ed. Robert Walter (Wien: Springer, 2011), 199–271. On the basic norm as a post-foundational conception of normativity, see Carlo Invernizzi Accetti, 'The Temporality of Normativity: Hans Kelsen's Overcoming of the Problem of the Foundation for Legal Validity', *Philosophy and Social Criticism* 42, no. 1 (2015): 28.

[24] For a classical position, see John Finnis, *Natural Law and Natural Rights* (Oxford: Oxford University Press, 1980). Finnis acknowledges through sharp criticism Kelsen's influence on legal positivism.

Still, some might argue that natural law remains necessary for other reasons, for example, to offer a morally compelling account of the legal system, to provide standards for critique or to explain why individuals should obey the law.[25] Against this line of reasoning, Kelsen develops a specific form of ideology critique, pointing out when and how a legal practice dissolves into some form of mythical thinking and showing how moral and legal theory try to ignore the post-foundational philosophical stance. If natural law theory is no longer a functional necessity, it works like a law behind the law that can be accessed at will at every stage of the law-creating and law-applying process. This does not mean, however, that it consistently produces positive social outcomes. Historically, Kelsen argues, natural law theory has tended towards conservatism, often legitimising the prevailing power structure.[26]

Importantly, Kelsen does not adopt a stance of cultural relativism. Rather, he acknowledges the historicity of moral and philosophical theories. This perspective was first articulated by Karl Marx, who offered a materialist account of philosophical development. Yet Marx still sought a scientific foundation for historical progress. It was Nietzsche who radicalised this insight by suggesting that every narrative of progress could also be read as a narrative of decline and who rejected the pretensions of philosophy in favour of playful interpretation.[27]

Once this insight is taken seriously, philosophy can no longer provide an ultimate foundation for the legal system and becomes post-foundational. Kelsen illustrates this with examples, such as the contrasting conceptions of property in capitalist and socialist systems.[28] His strategy is not to argue

[25] In the contemporary debate, Ronald Dworkin has made this line of thought prominent again.

[26] Hans Kelsen, *General Theory of Law and State* (Cambridge, MA: Harvard University Press, 1949), 416–18. *Pars pro toto*, Kant's explanation can be named, that the saying 'All Authority is from God' sets forth 'a practical principle of reason: the principle that the presently existing legislative authority ought to be obeyed, whatever its origin' (*RL* 6:319.)

[27] Friedrich Nietzsche, *The Gay Science: With a Prelude in Rhymes and an Appendix of Songs*, trans. Walter Kaufmann (New York: Vintage Books, 1974).

[28] Kelsen, *Pure Theory*, 220.

abstractly for a value-free approach but to show how allegedly neutral legal theories often conceal normative judgements and how moral theories fail to articulate an absolute conception of the good.[29]

Furthermore, Kelsen not only seeks to preserve the autonomy of law from moral philosophy but also resists sociological reductions of law. He often employs epistemological arguments to show that sociological theories – those that frame legal behaviour as a matter of prediction – fail to capture the internal sense of legal obligation and themselves rely on normative assumptions. Still, social theories can be used for another kind of ideological critique: the claim that law merely reflects power dynamics or class relations. Thus, the autonomy of law is challenged from two sides: natural law theory and sociological theory. Kelsen's response is to demonstrate that legal theory can be pursued in a pure and value-free manner.

3. Consequences for cosmopolitan thought

With this apparatus in hand, we can now consider the strength of Kelsen's approach and its consequences for a specific form of cosmopolitan thought. Unlike the approaches discussed thus far, Kelsen tries to distance himself as far as possible from all material theories of justice or implicit value-laden presuppositions. The only sense of justice that is necessarily connected to the notion of a legal order is, according to Kelsen, 'justice, in the sense of legality, … a quality which relates not to the content of a positive order, but to its application'.[30] However, he qualifies his endorsement of justice by explaining that 'justice in this sense is compatible with and required by any positive legal order, be it capitalistic or communistic, democratic or autocratic.'[31] In this

[29] Kelsen's prime philosophical target is Plato, as he sees in him the basis of all philosophical attempts to conceive of the good through thinking (*theoria*). See Hans Kelsen, *Die Illusion der Gerechtigkeit. Eine kritische Untersuchung der Sozialphilosophie Platons*, eds. Kurt Ringhofer and Robert Walter (Wien: Manz, 1985).

[30] Kelsen, *General Theory*, 14.

[31] Ibid.

way, he shows that modern law has a rationality of its own which is independent from ideological conflicts. His analysis of elements of the law – such as sanction, delict, legal duty, legal responsibility and the legal person – and the elements of the legal order – such as the distinction between law and state, private and public law and the relation between various branches of state administration – are dealt with at the most abstract level so that his theory can indeed claim to be a fully general theory of law and state.

One might object that by disregarding all moral and social content of the law, the theory cannot possibly make any contribution to the question after a genealogy of cosmopolitan thought, as it seems to refuse to engage in a meaningful way with the most relevant questions of any cosmopolitan theory, namely – positively – its moral justification and benefits for humanity, and – negatively – its potential paternalistic effects. The mere conceptual or technical analysis of legal norms is apparently a non-starter. However, when reflecting on the development and the ideological context a specific discursive constellation emerges, which Kelsen's theory answers.

To this end, we must briefly consider two conceptual consequences of Kelsen's theory: the unity of national and international law (monism) and the notion of sovereignty as a legal fiction. Both concepts are extensively discussed in law, political science, philosophy and related disciplines. The aim here is not to survey these discussions, but to introduce Kelsen's account as a plausible position within the contemporary debate. Since we are still engaged in the genealogical discussion, we will examine Kelsen's position in relation to the accounts we have encountered thus far. We will then explore how Kelsen was situated in his own time – using the language of the Cambridge School, we seek to understand the (historical) question to which his theory was an answer. The two most radical theoretical alternatives (and alternatives in terms of a possible lifeworld) at the time were formulated by Eugen Ehrlich and Carl Schmitt, respectively.

Ehrlich argued in favour of a pluralist conception of law that embraces multiple co-existing lifeworlds, whereas Schmitt deconstructed legal thinking into a form of naked power-based reasoning. The upshot of this discussion is existential in nature, as revealed in the lives of Ehrlich and Kelsen. The ultimate reflection on the destruction of civilisation from within is so unsettling that it can only be conveyed through literary means.[32]

3.1 Unity of national and international law

The most accessible route to a positivist interpretation of cosmopolitan thought appears to be through Kelsen's thesis on the unity of national and international law, which follows directly from the core assumptions of his theory. He asserts that, from a normative standpoint, national and international law cannot exist as two entirely separate legal systems. Rather, it becomes necessary to identify one as normatively foundational. His central rationale is that, on logical grounds, it is impossible to uphold two potentially contradictory norms simultaneously. Kelsen refers to this as an epistemological postulate: the requirement to understand all law as part of a unified system – that is, from a single vantage point – as a closed, coherent whole.[33] He maintains that if two normative systems aim to govern the same domain, one must be hierarchically subordinate to the other, because one 'contains a norm which determines the creation of the norms of the other, and hence the latter has the reason of its validity in the former. The basic norm of the higher order, then, is also the reason for the validity of the lower order.'[34] Thus, the hierarchy of norms must be preserved up to the basic norm.

The perspective Kelsen presents is fundamentally a purely normative one, articulated through an epistemological

[32] In contemporary discourse, Iris Murdoch is often cited for the thesis that literary texts disclose dimensions of the human condition and moral life that elude deduction from philosophical theory. In a parallel endeavour, Robert Pippin pursues a similar agenda, beginning with *The Culmination* and extending its existential implications in *Robert Bresson*.

[33] Kelsen, *Pure Theory*, 238.

[34] Ibid., 322. Kelsen is fully aware that he presents a strictly legal perspective. Accordingly, he presupposes the autonomy of law, including the thesis of the autonomy of jurisprudence. For an overview of the various discourses on sovereignty that appear across different legal theories, see Samantha Besson, 'Sovereignty', in Rüdiger Wolfrum, ed., *Max Planck Encyclopedia of Public International Law* (online edn).

framework. He is, of course, aware that international law is not as institutionally developed as national law; it lacks a comparable number of specialised organs for norm creation and enforcement. Instead, international law, much like that of stateless societies, historically evolved through custom and treaty, emerging only after the formation of states. For Kelsen, the unity thesis reflects not merely a theoretical proposition, but a requirement grounded in deontic logic.[35] Yet, it is more than an abstract intellectual exercise – it carries significant consequences for how we conceptualise the structure and function of law on a global scale.

3.2 Sovereignty as legal fiction

In advancing the thesis of the unity of national and international law, Kelsen allows for the basic norm to be situated either at the national level – where a specific national constitution becomes the source of international law's validity – or at the international level, which then governs the creation and application of national law. Owing to his strictly value-neutral framework, Kelsen remains formally agnostic regarding which of these hypotheses holds superior normative status. He emphasises that this conceptual positioning does not alter the content of international law.[36]

Even when the basic norm is situated at the national level, international law can still possess extensive authority, functioning as a set of powers delegated from the foundational national constitution. However, the full strength of Kelsen's theory becomes apparent when the basic norm is located at the international level. In this scenario, the concept of sovereignty loses all essentialist or pre-legal connotations and transforms instead into the scope of action permitted under

[35] For a more comprehensive discussion of Kelsen's monism, including the criticisms by H. L. A. Hart and Joseph Raz, and a defence of a pluralist jurisprudence, see Detlef von Daniels, *The Concept of Law from a Transnational Perspective* (Aldershot: Ashgate, 2010), 141–68. For a defence of Kelsen's monism on epistemological and descriptive grounds, particularly in relation to European Union law, see Paul Gragl, *Legal Monism: Law, Philosophy, and Politics* (Oxford: Oxford University Press, 2018).

[36] Kelsen, *General Theory*, 387.

international law.[37] This is not a moral claim, but rather a legal perspective backed by force, that is, the sanctions traditionally associated with international law.[38] In this model, sovereignty belongs solely to the international legal order, not to the national one. Consequently, the only remaining interpretation of a 'sovereign national legal order' is that it is immediately subject to the international legal order.[39]

Kelsen's discussion assumes a somewhat traditional understanding of the international legal order, in which courts and supranational institutions play minimal roles. However, when examined in light of the European integration process – especially the actions of the European Court of Justice, which affirmed the supremacy of EU law, its direct effect and the inclusion of human rights protections – Kelsen's argument becomes clearer.[40] All attempts to define 'essential sovereign competencies' within the EU legal context appear not as theoretical limitations, but as political manoeuvres within an integrated legal system.[41]

Kelsen explicitly acknowledges the cosmopolitan implications of this development. As he writes:

> The entire legally technical movement, as outlined here, has – in the last analysis – the tendency to blur the border line between international and national law, so that as the ultimate goal of the legal development directed toward increasing centralization, appears the organizational unity of a universal legal community, that is, the emergence of a world state.'[42]

[37] Ibid., 385.

[38] On the limits of Kelsen's coercive order paradigm and a reformulation of the theory in line with his later normative order approach, see Jörg Kammerhofer, 'Kelsen – Which Kelsen? A Reapplication of the Pure Theory to International Law', in *Leiden Journal of International Law* 22, no. 2 (2009): 225–49.

[39] Kelsen, *General Theory*, 387.

[40] The first one to notice the constitutionalisation of the EU was Eric Stein, 'Lawyers, Judges, and the Making of a Transnational Constitution', *American Journal of International Law* 75, no. 1 (1981): 1–27. On the application of Kelsen's doctrine to European Union Law, see Gragl, *Legal Monism*, 212–90.

[41] Kelsen, *General Theory*, 387.

[42] Ibid., 328.

Yet this outcome is, for Kelsen, not a moral imperative, but rather the logical result of a quest for epistemological consistency. Only indirectly does he betray his (subjective) preferences, as he associates the primacy of national law with the worldview of solipsism, imperialism and the geocentric view of the universe and the primacy of international law instead with objectivism, pacifism and the heliocentric worldview.[43] Even though he does not see the connections as strict logical ones and states that the pure theory is indifferent to both conceptions, the national one clearly comes out as scientifically inferior. If every state were to assert the primacy of national law, the coherent existence of international law would unravel, rendering such a stance, even within the framework of pure theory, untenable.

3.3 A post-foundationalist perspective

Kelsen's thesis on the unity of national and international law has received substantial attention in legal theory. A key point of contention is the claim that two legal norms cannot conflict – a proposition challenged from the standpoint of deontic logic.[44] However, the present inquiry approaches Kelsen's theory from a different angle: can it offer a pathway out of the conceptual impasse identified in Heidegger's interpretation of Kant? When evaluated through the lens of contemporary cosmopolitan thought, Kelsen's theory may initially appear limited. It articulates cosmopolitanism strictly as a juridical possibility, without engaging with the material conditions that might support a cosmopolitan trajectory – such as Kant's notion of nature's providential guidance – nor does it offer a value-based justification for adopting a cosmopolitan standpoint.

Nonetheless, our genealogical investigation has already cast doubt on the self-assured framework of contemporary liberal political philosophy, demonstrating the feasibility of posing more radical, metaphysical questions through Plato. We also discovered that Kant's philosophy is not timeless but

43 Ibid., 386–87.

44 See, for a comprehensive discussion, von Daniels, *The Concept of Law*, 141–68.

opens into a self-critical and ideology-critical line of questioning, even if cloaked in religious terminology. Heidegger's pragmatic and existentialist appropriation of Kant is a consequence of this lineage. It is precisely here that Kelsen's intervention becomes salient.

Although Heidegger reinterprets Kantian subjectivity pragmatically, he ultimately lacks the tools to meaningfully analyse modern society – including the domain of law – because he dismisses the entire 'technical' dimension of human existence. Kelsen's distinctive insight is that one need not assume traditional material values or a liberal worldview anchored in a particular historical context. Still, it remains possible to reconstruct the internal logic of law independently of ideological presuppositions.

Kelsen's legal constructivism embodies precisely the kind of 'technical world' that Heidegger derides, viewing it either as superficial or as an outgrowth of the Western metaphysical tradition. However, Kelsen's theory is neither: it responds to a post-Nietzschean condition, forgoing claims to ultimate truth while articulating a specific, normative-constructive orientation towards the legal world. Moreover, law is an institutional structure with which all individuals in modern societies must engage, even Heidegger himself.

This becomes evident in Heidegger's own case. As rector of the University of Freiburg, Heidegger issued legal decrees. After the war, his behaviour – distorting facts, evading accountability – revealed his awareness that his actions could be judged within legal frameworks.[45] It is this perspective that Kelsen stresses in a specific legal, post-foundationalist way. For Kelsen, trials such as denazification proceedings do not determine metaphysical guilt or moral depravity but rather state the sanction of a norm of positive law.[46] It is precisely this legally grounded perspective that was lacking in the first chapter, when we sought a way to counter Heidegger's grand yet politically pernicious narrative without merely assuming

[45] For a detailed account of Heidegger's rectorate, his failed attempt to intellectually align himself with the Nazi regime, and his later self-justifications, see Hugo Ott, *Martin Heidegger: A Political Life*, trans. Allan Blunden (New York: Basic Books, 1993), 133–368.

[46] Kelsen, *Pure Theory*, 109–10.

an alternative set of values or reducing his philosophy to a disguise for political ideology. Legal proceedings offer a model for rendering definitive judgments on both individual and collective actions and for confronting the past. A brief examination of transitional justice processes may support this thesis.

In such trials, defendants often adopt the stance of amateur philosophers, denouncing the political nature of the proceedings, questioning the universality of the norms, or impugning the integrity of the judiciary. While such concerns are not entirely unfounded, they assume that the opposing legal framework must necessarily adopt a simplistic moralistic position. From a Kelsenian perspective, it is misguided to assume a strict distinction between political and legal proceedings in the first place since both are fundamentally legal processes. The question of whether an act constitutes law creation (legislation) or law application (jurisdiction) is one of degree; it depends on the extent to which the act-rendering organs – whether parliament or court – are predetermined by the legal order. In either case, it involves the creation of a legal artefact. The quality of that artefact often rests not on its underlying material value but on the care and precision with which it is executed.

Compelling illustrations of this point are the German border guard cases.[47] After reunification, East German guards who shot individuals attempting to cross the border were prosecuted for murder. The defence portrayed the trials as victor's justice, denying guilt based on obedience to orders or duress. However, these trials were not grounded in universal moral principles but in the GDR's own penal code. Through careful reconstruction of the actual range of choices available to the border guards (such as whether to shoot with single or rapid fire) and of the circumstances following the killings of refugees (which were deliberately concealed in official records and where the soldier was quietly transferred to another unit), the awareness of criminal wrongdoing and the personal guilt of the shooters were established.

[47] On the context, see Peter E. Quint, 'Judging the Past: The Prosecution of East German Border Guards and the GDR Chain of Command', *The Review of Politics* 61, no. 2 (1999): 303–29.

Kelsen had long advocated international jurisdiction.[48] Yet, he did not claim to have discovered the ethical value of such trials. International criminal responsibility can be justified in multiple doctrinal frameworks. The specific contribution of Kelsen's legal theory is, therefore, best understood within the broader philosophical debate, so to speak, among the voices that emerged from the imaginary 1913 meeting in Vienna's city park. Kelsen sidesteps ideological confrontation by grounding his work in the relativistic premise that notions of justice are not only multifaceted but also inherently contradictory. Thus, he does not need to claim a higher or more enlightened standpoint. Similarly, he does not need to establish 'apolitical' grounds for legal proceedings, as he openly acknowledges the political and decisionist character of law-making through various institutional organs. The only polemic the pure theory of law undertakes is against essentialist conceptions of the state or of a people, conceptions that allegedly cannot be reconciled with the structural requirements of international law. Kelsen's dialectical manoeuvre is to demonstrate that both nationalist and cosmopolitan perspectives must adopt a unitary legal framework, insofar as they operate through the mechanisms of modern law. In this sense, the post-foundational legal perspective also becomes a challenge – a catch – for any philosopher or theorist engaged in the political world.

Judged by the standards of contemporary cosmopolitan philosophy, this conclusion might appear lacking in substantive discourse on justice. Furthermore, Kelsen's insistence on the purity of legal science may seem to echo a metaphysical remnant of a neo-Kantian worldview, one that implicitly carries the universalist assumptions of modern moral or political theory. Yet, from another perspective, Kelsen can be viewed as the true heir to Kant's cosmopolitanism.

In our contextual reconstruction of Kant's thought, we observed that his work consisted of two strands: the empirical science of knowledge and critical philosophy. Cosmopolitan

[48] Hans Kelsen, *The Legal Process and International Order*, trans. William Horsfall Carter, New Commonwealth Institute Monographs 1 (1935): 2–27.

theory, strictly speaking, played only a modest role within the doctrine of right. The strongest expression of a cosmopolitan duty in Kant, in terms of justice, was the call for criminal punishment, culminating in the demand for the execution of the last murderer of a people that chooses to dissolve itself.

Kelsen adopts this programme in a refined and stripped-down form. He agrees with Kant that human beings, from an anthropological standpoint, are marked by continual struggle. These manifest ideologically, as Kant noted in the religious domain, and extend into the psyche of each individual. Kelsen also maintains that it is largely possible to reconstruct law and the state independently of specific moral theories. However, unlike Kant, he explicitly severs any remaining link between legal theory and a moral or enlightened conception of freedom as autonomy. Instead, he insists on the constructive and non-foundational character of all legal artefacts.

At this point, a deeper concern emerges. One might ask whether Kelsen's particular variant of legal positivism – even when framed as post-foundationalist – truly offers a resolution to the existential deadlock we encountered in Heidegger's reading of Kant. Might Kelsen's pure theory itself reflect the very moral disorientation embodied in the imaginary 1913 meeting in Vienna's city park? And should Kelsen not be held accountable for contributing to the corrosive effects of moral relativism, especially given that his critique of the categorical imperative as 'a meaningless tautology'[49] seems to echo Heidegger's own sentiment?[50]

To answer these questions, we must delve further into the political debates in which Kelsen actively participated. As we shall see, through his engagements with Carl Schmitt and Eugen Ehrlich, an existentialist dimension ultimately emerges as the anchoring force of Kelsen's legal thought.

[49] Kelsen, *General Theory*, 14.

[50] Heidegger, *The Essence of Human Freedom*, 287. Heidegger echoes themes from German neoconservatives in Weimar times.

4. Kelsen's contestation with Carl Schmitt

An all too easy way to redeem Kelsen against the charge of 'pernicious relativism' would be to invoke his personal political convictions, which clearly leaned toward the liberal or social democratic side. However, Kelsen was neither a saint nor a martyr (like Franz Jägerstätter), whose life could serve as a personification of specific values or a particular mindset. Moreover, he consistently insisted on the distinction between his theoretical work and his personal political beliefs, emphasising that different convictions are likewise legitimate and necessary within an agonistic democracy. Thus, the distinction between individual political convictions and actions and the general theoretical level should not be blurred. Nevertheless, it is instructive to observe how the theoretical discussions in which Kelsen engaged revealed the existential dimension of his theory.

From a methodological standpoint, these discussions also illuminate the maxims of the Cambridge School. At the beginning, we have assumed that authors and philosophical critics respond to the specific political questions prevalent in their time. In our analysis of Kant, we had to qualify this thesis: Kant fundamentally altered the underlying philosophical discourse while simultaneously intervening politically in a political-theological context. Although Heidegger's political impulse may now seem all too obvious, at least in retrospect, we could understand its philosophical foundation only after bringing Kant's thinking to its limits. A common feature across these variations of the Cambridge School thesis is that philosophers – or the texts themselves – are assigned an active role. Even Heidegger's later declaration of being merely a 'shepherd of being'[51] can be interpreted as allowing a very specific Zeitgeist to prevail, largely unchallenged. In Kelsen's case, we will observe how the zeitgeist, in the form of the violent terror of the Nazis, infiltrated academia to such an extent that hardly any theoretical refuge remained. Here, theory and theorists become victims of the very 'question' they had sought to address. For a genealogy

[51] For the notion of the 'shepherd of being', see Heidegger, 'Letter on Humanism', 252 (162).

of cosmopolitan thought, it is crucial to consider this darker dimension in order to recognise both the dangers and the potential counter-movements that emerge in response.

4.1 The other side of cosmopolitanism

At this point in the argument, we can finally address the elephant in the room. Through various forms of contextualisation – the shifting of emphasis from political to metaphysical questions (in the case of Plato) and the introduction of 'additional problems' (in the case of Kant) – we have challenged the orthodoxy of contemporary cosmopolitan thought. One might infer that this genealogy amounts, at least implicitly, to a defence of an anti-cosmopolitan or 'nationalistic' approach. However, we have neither defended nor even introduced an anti-cosmopolitan or nationalistic stance. This could even be regarded as a serious methodological flaw, insofar as a 'proper' genealogy would trace both opposing camps, cosmopolitanism and nationalism, across historical development.

Yet the methodological principles of such a traditional history of ideas were already criticised in the first chapter. This does not mean, however, that the abstract opposition between cosmopolitanism and nationalism cannot be addressed within a contextual approach. At a particular moment in history, the debate between cosmopolitan and nationalist thought reached an intellectual climax, responding to a highly specific political question. This crystallisation occurs in the debate between Kelsen and Schmitt over the role of the 'guardian of the constitution'.[52] To understand both the debate itself and the impact of Schmitt's criticism, it is necessary first to explore further the consequences of Kelsen's position.

[52] Lars Vinx, ed. and trans., *The Guardian of the Constitution: Hans Kelsen and Carl Schmitt on the Limits of Constitutional Law* (Cambridge: Cambridge University Press, 2015).

4.2 Kelsen's legal institutionalist theory of democracy

We have seen that Kelsen's legal constructivism addresses a foundational uneasiness concerning the perceived 'shallowness' and 'rootlessness' of modern liberal democracies voiced by Heidegger and other neoconservative writers while simultaneously enabling a unitary, cosmopolitan perspective. Yet Kelsen's theory is not inherently committed to liberal values, as its theoretical framework allows for the basic norm to be posited at the national level. Kelsen draws two further conclusions from his constructivist approach. First, he argues that the (equal) sovereignty of states is not grounded in any natural quality of peoples but is instead a legal notion bestowed by international law. This implies not merely the obvious point that states are the primary subjects of international law but more precisely that they are considered equal only to the extent that international law so stipulates. Consequently, the social-scientific question of whether a population genuinely conceives of itself as a sovereign people plays no normative role.[53]

Kelsen extends this perspective to the national level. He contends that, as the state is identified with the legal order, it cannot be based on a notion of popular sovereignty understood as the actual union of the will of the people. Rather, the concept of popular sovereignty is a legal fiction, while the genuine formation of political will occurs within the organs of the state, particularly within the parliament.[54] This notion requires further exploration, as it leads to a distinctive understanding of liberal democracy.

According to Kelsen, the notion of popular sovereignty is not part of the legal order but precedes it, serving primarily ideological purposes.[55] When understood as the actual and ongoing consent of everyone belonging to one people, it presupposes a self-evident, unquestionable criterion for who constitutes the people, a presupposition that would immediately collapse if even a single individual changed their

[53] Kelsen, *General Theory*, 252–53.

[54] See Hans Kelsen, *Allgemeine Staatslehre* (Berlin: Springer, 1925), 312–14 or, more attuned to an American audience, Kelsen, *General Theory*, 283–92.

[55] Kelsen, *General Theory*, 314.

mind.[56] Thus, most accounts of popular sovereignty inevitably smuggle in some substantive, material definition of who belongs to the people, using the notion to critique decisions made by actual representative parliamentary bodies.

Given his Austrian background and his awareness that a state can encompass a multitude of ethnicities with diverse religious, cultural and linguistic identities, Kelsen regards the idea of popular sovereignty as a fiction, a point of imputation devoid of intrinsic value.[57] At first glance, this may appear to be an ad hoc solution. However, Kelsen reinforces his argument by pointing to a well-established parallel. In a constitutional monarchy, where a queen serves as head of state, all laws, judgments and decrees are issued in her name. Yet no one seriously questions whether the queen personally intended to issue every parking ticket or whether she agrees with the government's general policies. Thus, the practice of treating the ultimate point of imputation as fictitious is already entrenched in political discourse. Whether official acts are ultimately imputed to the queen or to the people is arbitrary in a modern society, given that legal systems are coercive orders. Some individuals will inevitably have to comply against their will, most evidently when subjected to sanctions.

However, unlike the notion of a queen, the notion of popular sovereignty is unavoidable in modern political discourse, as it is intimately bound up with the idea of freedom. Once again, Kelsen develops a constructivist notion of freedom, one that appears only within the framework of the legal process. He concedes that real freedom means self-determination, whether at the individual, existentialist level or as a collective.[58] However, collective freedom can hardly be sustained without an institutional order, as a change of will by a single individual would transform the collective's free will into an imposed, alien will upon that individual. One might think that by presupposing the freedom and

[56] Hans Kelsen, 'On the Essence and Value of Democracy' (1929) in Arthur Jacobson and Bernard Schlink, eds., *Weimar: A Jurisprudence of Crisis*, trans. Belinda Cooper (Berkeley, CA: University of California Press, 2000), 89–93.

[57] Ibid., 94.

[58] Kelsen, *General Theory*, 285.

equality of all individuals, it would somehow be possible to infer acceptance of majority rule.

Kelsen, however, chooses a different line of argument. He does not wish to presuppose freedom and equality as natural, evident or pre-political values. Moreover, in cases where a question has a scientific answer – such as whether the Earth revolves around the Sun or vice versa – requiring acceptance of a majority decision would only add insult to injury. Therefore, Kelsen does not attempt to justify each case of coercion as 'freely chosen' in some higher philosophical sense. Instead, he argues that all one can do is strive to maximise the degree of freedom within the framework of modern society. Thus, the existentialist notion of individual or collective freedom must be transformed into the concept of liberty under law. Democratic elections provide one means of involving, if not everyone, then at least a large number of individuals in the decision-making process. Individuals can consider themselves free and still accept majority decisions precisely because there is no objective, scientific method for resolving political questions. Instead, different views must be heard, allowing today's minority to become tomorrow's majority.[59]

At this point, another feature of Kelsen's legal institutionalist theory of democracy becomes significant. Disagreement over political questions is not solely the result of deep, underlying convictions, but also a consequence of the complexity of modern society. No individual can be an expert in every field, and there is no natural or scientific method for ranking the importance of different fields. Consequently, consultation with experts and the forging of compromises are inevitable tasks for political rulers in modern societies. Parliamentary representation is a way to organise this process and to consolidate, through political parties, relatively stable ideological convictions. The essence of Kelsen's democratic theory is thus to deny that the traditional distinction between monarchy and popular sovereignty is fundamental. Instead, the parliamentary system can be organised to preserve liberty by enabling choices between different positions and fostering the transformation of political convictions through public discourse.

[59] Ibid., 286.

In this framework, a constitutional court is tasked solely with preserving ongoing contestation and protecting the rights of the minority. Although Kelsen's theory is not articulated as a 'theory of global democracy', it carries a distinct cosmopolitan implication: it does not rely on the presupposition of a single homogeneous people – or multiple homogeneous *demoi* – but instead identifies the conditions under which a pluralistic and contested political order can be sustained and further integrated through forging of compromises.[60]

4.3 Schmitt's political activist counter-position

In a traditional history of ideas, Kelsen's legal cosmopolitanism – along with its institutionalist account of democracy as a counterpart – might be included as a minor, intermediate step before arriving at more liberal formulations, particularly in more detailed and extended discussions of contemporary post-Rawlsian cosmopolitanism. However, from the contextual perspective adopted here, it is most striking that at the very time Kelsen was formulating his legal cosmopolitanism, Carl Schmitt was developing a counter-theory that berated Kelsen's account.

Although Schmitt is now infamous for his association with Nazism, it is important to remember that in the 1920s and early 1930s, when he wrote many of his major works, he was working as a constitutional lawyer and presented his agenda as an 'integrative'[61] or value-laden interpretation of the Weimar Constitution.

[60] Kelsen, 'On the Essence and Value of Democracy', 100–4. Kelsen's theory is particularly suited to analysing the multi-level governance system within the European Union, which in turn can be seen as a federal union under international law. For an overview, see Tamara Ehs, ed., *Hans Kelsen und die Europäische Union* (Baden-Baden: Nomos, 2008).

[61] Schmitt's method of 'concrete order thinking' (*konkretes Ordnungsdenken*) is reminiscent of Ronald Dworkin's method of 'integrative interpretation', though the underlying values are certainly different. See Carl Schmitt, *On the Three Types of Juristic Thought* (1934), trans. Joseph Bendersky (Santa Barbara: Praeger, 2004).

Schmitt's core thesis is that 'the genuine political distinction is the one between friend and foe.'[62] This claim does not directly repudiate liberal principles by, for instance, declaring that 'all men are created unequal', but instead subverts the liberal tradition by rejecting its foundational premises. According to Schmitt, the formation of a political community – or a *volonté générale* – cannot be derived from non-political criteria, such as moral, aesthetic or economic values; it arises from an independent and original distinction. By introducing this distinction concretely, as the friend-foe opposition, Schmitt simultaneously asserts that political identity is always shaped by specific historical circumstances. In other words, any actual political 'we' is already built upon a bedrock of past wars, historical injustices and exhausted ideologies. The world Schmitt envisions has no ideal counter-image like Rawls's original position but is instead the actual, historical world, marked by irreducible conflicts.

Through this intervention, the theory of constitutional democracy – as rendered by Kelsen as a resolution to ideological conflict – becomes, in Schmitt's account, part of the problem. Once the aim of fostering peace and reconciliation among values, convictions, classes and ethnicities is no longer seen as the fundamental goal of a constitution but is instead consciously rejected and struggle (*Kampf*) is embraced as the inevitable reality, political theory itself turns into a tool for enabling and intensifying ethnic or ideological conflict. If peace and reconciliation are viewed as merely one side in a larger conflict, there is no higher plane from which to secure them – only struggle, all the way up (or down).

Only with Schmitt do we encounter a fully developed anti-cosmopolitan theory operating on the same theoretical level. His theory is not simply nationalistic in the sense of privileging nations as the primary actors or identifying a particular people as the 'true' people of a nation. Rather, the friend-foe distinction reaches back into history, selectively recognising only some authors as genuinely political. Moreover, it is political by intervening decisively in contemporary debate,

[62] This is the opening sentence of the more radical 1933 edition of *The Concept of the Political*. See Carl Schmitt, *Der Begriff des Politischen* (Hamburg: Hanseatische Verlagsanstalt, 1933), 7.

whether by defining the people in exclusionary (e.g., anti-semitic) terms or by dismissing democratic procedures as 'unpolitical'.

Yet for a specific reason, Schmitt's theory is at cross-purposes with Kelsen's. Although both thinkers were responding to the same constitutional crisis, Schmitt denied the existence of any detached, scientific or scholarly discourse untouched by the friend-foe distinction. His theory is political in the ultimate sense: it demands an existential political commitment. In this respect, one could argue that Schmitt radicalised the contextual and engaged reading of political texts in the spirit of the Cambridge School to its extreme by leaving nothing untouched by the political.

This is not to say that liberal or cosmopolitan thought is entirely disarmed in the face of Schmitt's challenge. But it must reckon with Kelsen's unique contribution – not only as the most thorough response to Schmitt during the Weimar era but also as a model for confronting such destructive interventions. This can be demonstrated by closely examining the intellectual confrontation between Schmitt and Kelsen.

4.4 Theories in action: Kelsen and Schmitt on the guardian of the constitution

Towards the end of the Weimar Republic, Schmitt applied his theoretical distinction to a practical political purpose by arguing that only the president (who happened to be the conservative Hindenburg) represented the 'people as a whole', not the 'pluralistic, dispersed parliament'.[63]

Kelsen responded to this shrewd attack on democratic institutions not by directly criticising Schmitt's implicit values or convictions but by demonstrating through a sharply pointed, meticulous and devastating critique how Schmitt failed on his own terms as a constitutional lawyer.[64] Kelsen showed how Schmitt exploited ambiguities: he would first outline an ideal type, such as the ideal form of

[63] Carl Schmitt, 'The Guardian of the Constitution', in *The Guardian of the Constitution*, 79–124.

[64] Hans Kelsen, 'Who Ought to Be the Guardian of the Constitution?, in *The Guardian of the Constitution*, 174–221.

parliamentarism, only to denounce the actual parliament of the Weimar Republic as a degenerate form. Other constitutional constructs, such as popular sovereignty, were conflated with specific political movements: the will of certain groups (the 'real people') who allegedly embodied the will of the whole. It is this identification of a necessary fiction (popular sovereignty as actual collective will) with a concrete political will that Kelsen exposed as ideological and as a flawed interpretation of constitutional law.

What is decisive here is not the specific details of the argument but the nature of the discussion itself. Kelsen did not engage Schmitt's major oppositions, nor did he counter them with his own system of values. Instead, he traced Schmitt's world-historical dramatisations back to concrete constitutional issues that could be debated – even on Schmitt's own terms.

A further reason why debate was possible at this level is that Kelsen and Schmitt were not opponents on all points; they shared many assumptions. For instance, both acknowledged the ultimately ungrounded character of legal decisions ('decisionism') and sought, through their respective theories, to preserve a fundamental constitutional commitment – though they each emphasised it differently. For Schmitt, it was the preservation of sovereign decision-making power; for Kelsen, it was the preservation of the constitution as an ongoing compromise, encompassing party democracy, the interplay of government and opposition and the federal structure. In both cases, the shared background assumption was that deep-seated pluralism of values and irreducible ideological conflict defined the modern world.

However, their reactions to this diagnosis diverged sharply. Schmitt embraced existential, content-free struggle, fighting opportunistically for the ideology that suited him – even to the point of intellectual self-sacrifice. For Schmitt, factual superiority – or victory – stood in for correctness. By contrast, Kelsen, in an equally existential way, insisted on the ideal of the value-free nature of science and the possibility of a pure (legal) theory.

Yet the story of Kelsen's life, combined with the perversion of law in Nazi Germany, added a blistering warning to this ideal – and a cautionary layer to their altercation. Unexpectedly, the originally theoretical debate between Kelsen and Schmitt spilled into a legal proceeding when the constitutionality of the so-called coup in Prussia (*Preußenschlag*) of 1932 was brought before the *Staatsgerichtshof* (State Court for Constitutional Matters) in Leipzig a few months later.[65] The coup involved the takeover of the Social Democratic–dominated Free State of Prussia by the Reich, under the pretext of restoring order after a series of violent clashes between Nazis and Communists. Conservative Chancellor Franz von Papen used emergency decrees issued by President Paul von Hindenburg to weaken this social-democratic stronghold and undermine the federal structure.

In retrospect, the coup in Prussia was yet another blow to the edifice of the Weimar Republic, laying the groundwork for the *Gleichschaltung* (Nazification) of Germany following Adolf Hitler's rise to power on 30 January 1933. Yet in 1932 the legal framework of the Weimar Republic still functioned, allowing the constitutionality of the decree to be challenged in court.

In his opening plea, Schmitt – now serving as advocate for the Reich – bestowed on it the monopoly on politics 'in the most intensive sense', asserting its right to determine the (internal) enemy.[66] The court ultimately upheld the Reich's intervention in part. More importantly, in these proceedings, the major intellectual representatives of the opposing ideological forces of the Weimar Republic met, albeit indirectly, for a final time on the battlefield of intellectual debate. Crucially, two thoroughly abstract theoretical positions were employed in a legal proceeding at a critical turning point in history. Kelsen's legal cosmopolitanism provoked Schmitt's vortex-like political thinking, leaving no room for a detached, non-political sphere of academic debate. However, the intellectual contestation itself proved fleeting, while the underlying political conflict escalated into an existential threat for one side.

65 On the historical background, see Clark, *Iron Kingdom*, 619–88.

66 Arnold Brecht, *Preußen contra Reich vor dem Staatsgerichtshof* (Berlin: J. H. W. Dietz, 1933), 40.

4.5 The demise of theory

With the Nazi party's rise to power, Kelsen was among the first professors to be dismissed from his university post in Cologne, branded a 'typical communist Jew'.[67] It did not help that Kelsen had written a critique of communism and was a baptised Christian (he considered himself an agnostic). Once again, the dismissal and the surrounding biographical events carry theoretical significance, as they reveal that certain pragmatic presuppositions Kelsen had taken for granted could, in fact, be revoked. Even though Kelsen acknowledged value pluralism, he still assumed that its underlying fundamental beliefs – such as individualism and collectivism – could be understood and reconstructed as respectable philosophical traditions.

However, it is impossible to engage in rational debate with someone who denies their opponent equal standing based on racial prejudice. If whatever a 'Jew' (as defined by racial ideology) says is automatically disqualified or used against them, then the basic precondition for any civilised resolution of conflict is lost. Moreover, when openly racist laws are enacted,[68] irrationality becomes embedded in every dimension of the legal system. As a result, the law loses its claim to function, at least in principle, as a rational order of human affairs. Finally, academia itself – supposedly the battlefield of ideas – proved especially susceptible to political corruption, arguably due to its reliance on careerist networks.[69]

These three factors taken together, (1) a political theory that lends credibility to anti-democratic or non-rule-of-law regimes, (2) the introduction of irrationality into the legal

[67] On the details of this episode, see Rudolf Aldár Métall, *Hans Kelsen: Leben und Werk* (Wien: Franz Deuticke, 1969), 47–57.

[68] One of the first laws the Nazis enacted was the so-called 'Law for the Restoration of the Professional Civil Service', which dismissed all 'non-Aryan' members of the civil service.

[69] For Hannah Arendt, the realisation that not just the Nazis but also friends of her turned against Jews for opportunistic reasons was the most shocking experience of the advent of the Nazi regime. See Hannah Arendt, 'Zur Person', in *Ich will verstehen. Selbstauskünfte zu Leben und Werk*, ed. Ursula Ludz (München: Piper, 1996), 56. For a collection of some juridical theories of this kind, see Jacobson and Schlink, eds., *Weimar: A Jurisprudence of Crisis*, 320–34.

order and (3) a failure of integrity within academia and legal institutions, are sufficient to offer at least a partial account of how a relatively well-functioning republic and vibrant intellectual culture deteriorated into one of the most atrocious regimes in history – backed by the majority of academics. Without hesitation, scholars across all disciplines rushed to demonstrate how Nazi ideology could be integrated into their work by introducing the irrational Aryan/Jewish dichotomy into biology, physics, engineering and beyond.[70]

In the genealogy of cosmopolitan thought, we have reached a turning point with Kelsen's post-foundational legal cosmopolitanism and Schmitt's politically engaged counter-position. After these two possibilities have been laid bare, every civilised debate must proceed under a proviso. However, this does not imply that both positions are of equal standing. Kelsen explicitly denies that a democracy has the right to defend itself by force against a majority whose sole will is to destroy that very democracy. 'A democracy that tries to assert itself against the will of the majority, even by force, has ceased to be a democracy. A people's government cannot exist against the people.'[71] Yet this does not mean that Kelsen passively accepts whatever the majority or the prevailing legal order demands. In an existentialist manner that mirrors Schmitt's, he reaffirms his own values: 'One must remain faithful to one's flag, even if the ship sinks; and can only take with it into the depths the hope that the ideal of freedom is indestructible and that the deeper it sinks, the more passionately it will revive.'[72]

[70] For a 'Hall of Shame' in which representatives of all sciences are assembled, see Konstantin von Neurath, ed., *Deutsche Wissenschaft: Arbeit und Aufgabe. Dem Führer und Reichskanzler legt die Deutsche Wissenschaft zu seinem 50. Geburtstag Rechenschaft ab über ihre Arbeit im Rahmen der ihr gestellten Aufgabe* [German Science: Work and Task. On the occasion of the 50th birthday of the Führer and Reich Chancellor, German science gives an account of its work within the task assigned to it.] (Leipzig: Hirzel, 1939).

[71] Hans Kelsen, 'Verteidigung der Demokratie (1932)', in *Verteidigung der Demokratie. Abhandlungen zur Demokratietheorie*, ed. Matthias Jestaedt and Oliver Lepsius (Tübingen: Mohr Siebeck, 2006), 237.

[72] Ibid.

5. Kelsen's dispute with Eugen Ehrlich

One might think that, with this theoretical turning point, we have reached the – morally speaking – lowest point of the genealogy. However, there is an even deeper level upon which light must be cast: the horror of the Holocaust, which casts a shadow over the debate. Again, insight will be gained through a contextual reading, though not in the form of a conscious intervention by a philosopher but through something that happened to a philosopher – or to their thinking. This requires some explanation.

Thus far, one might argue that we have presented the anti-cosmopolitan counterposition in a lopsided way by linking the national – or, to use more fashionable terms, the communitarian, sovereigntist or conservative – position primarily with Carl Schmitt's thinking, framed in terms of friend and foe. However, Schmitt's thought must be seen as responding to the very same social and political constellation that made Kelsen's legal cosmopolitanism possible in the first place. It is not only Schmitt who would reject the liberal narrative of naturally distinct and peacefully coexisting peoples as a myth. Kelsen, too, would criticise any value-laden account – be it communitarianism, republicanism or cosmopolitanism – for smuggling implicit normative presuppositions into theory or shielding them from public debate.

Yet, from a contemporary perspective, another line of criticism might be raised against Kelsen's juridical constructivism. One could argue – loosely following a Foucauldian analysis of power or governmentality – that all systems of state order are ultimately permeated by (unjustified) structures of power and that genuine resistance arises from marginalised groups. Moreover, it might be claimed that resistance to hidden or unacknowledged power structures constitutes an end in itself, thus exempting critical theories from the obligation to offer a moral account of the 'good' inherent in these groups. This rough sketch of contemporary critical discourse on governmentality and postcolonial studies, outlined in the Preface, is intended here to motivate a further inquiry into the abyss of the twentieth century.

This will be undertaken in an indirect and partly allegorical manner through an examination of Kelsen's discussion with Eugen Ehrlich on the viability of legal pluralism. It will become clear that this provides a way to reflect not only on contemporary critical discourse regarding power and coloniality but also on the catastrophic collapse of civilisation in the twentieth century – the maelstrom of darkness that threatened to absorb every domain of human achievement. Unlike in the previous discussion, Kelsen's and Ehrlich's theories will not be introduced to analyse or react to the events leading up to the Holocaust (where any response other than horror and moral condemnation is unimaginable). Rather, they will be used to observe how even carefully constructed theories could be involuntarily absorbed and shattered by that maelstrom.

5.1 The debate on legal pluralism

Thus far, we have seen how Kelsen's legal cosmopolitanism was challenged by Schmitt's interventionist and activist political theory. The second major theoretical concern for Kelsen was to distinguish pure theory from all material or sociological accounts and to preserve legal theory and the law as a medium of contestation that remains impartial. We have seen that the theoretically unsolvable debates among the various ethnic groups and ideological convictions of the Austro-Hungarian Empire formed the background for this conviction: there is no objective, 'sociological' evidence that transforms a specific group into a 'sovereign' people. Nevertheless, in contemporary terms, Kelsen's preoccupation with the shortcomings of sociological jurisprudence might seem somewhat antiquated, given that the sociology of law is now a well-established and multifaceted field of research. However, one domain where the debate remains very much alive is the enduring tension between analytic jurisprudence and legal pluralism.[73]

The fundamental working assumption of legal pluralism is that we inhabit a world of multiple normative communities, only some of which enforce their norms through officially

[73] For a harsh criticism of analytical jurisprudence from a legal pluralist perspective, see Brian Tamanaha, *A General Jurisprudence of Law and Society* (Oxford: Oxford University Press, 2001).

sanctioned coercive force and formal legal processes.[74] In a global perspective, legal pluralism can be studied everywhere, from the past to the present, in local and global circumstances.[75] Legal pluralists often present themselves as more attentive to the social practices of indigenous peoples or other marginalised groups – particularly in postcolonial settings – whose concerns and interests tend to be ignored by the apparatus of official state law. Since most research in this area is conducted by anthropologists, the focus is usually on the empirical level. However, tracing the debate back to Kelsen and Eugen Ehrlich reveals that theory, in both cases, cannot presume a detached, outsider's perspective but is involuntarily drawn into the conflicts of its time. It is precisely this aspect that must be acknowledged in a genealogy of cosmopolitan thought so as to reflect upon the ultimate existential anchoring of philosophical inquiry.

5.2 Legal pluralism in the Bukovina

Even though the problem of legal pluralism is arguably as old as law itself,[76] the debate over its theoretical significance began with Eugen Ehrlich's studies of 'living law' in Bukovina and reached an early culmination in his dispute with Hans Kelsen.[77] Ehrlich was among the first academic lawyers to recognise that the official law of modern bureaucratic states often bore little relation to the lived experience of communities

[74] For contemporary definitions of legal pluralism, see Robert M. Cover, 'The Supreme Court, 1982 Term – Foreword: Nomos and Narrative', *Harvard Law Review* 97, no. 4 (1983): 4–68; Paul Schiff Berman, 'Global Legal Pluralism', *Southern California Law Review* 80, no. 6 (2007): 1155–1237, with further references.

[75] See Brian Tamanaha, 'Understanding Legal Pluralism: Past to Present, Local to Global', *Sydney Law Review* 30, no. 3 (2008): 375–411.

[76] Every remembered legislation is typically superimposed on previous social practices. The commandment 'thou shalt not covet your neighbor's wife' means you shalt not take her into debt bondage, as it was apparently previously practiced, again a practice that might have reformed even more archaic or cruel forms of retribution. See David Graeber, *Debt: The First 5,000 Years* (Brooklyn: Melville, 2011), 75–87.

[77] The debate is collected in Stanley L. Paulson, ed., *Hans Kelsen und die Rechtssoziologie. Auseinandersetzungen mit Hermann U. Kantorowicz, Eugen Ehrlich und Max Weber* (Aalen: Scientia, 1992).

that continued to follow their own laws and customs, for which Ehrlich coined the term 'living law'. Unlike much of today's legal pluralist scholarship, which focuses on colonial or postcolonial contexts, Ehrlich's example was drawn from the social life of Bukovina, a remote region of the Austro-Hungarian Empire (now located between Ukraine, Poland and Romania). In this culturally diverse setting – home to various ethnicities, religions and national minorities, coexisting under imperial law – Ehrlich observed a semi-autonomous social order. As a professor at the German-speaking university in Czernowitz, the administrative capital of Bukovina, he studied the living law of mostly rural communities with the aim of providing a framework to support more equitable forms of economic and cultural development. His research culminated in the wide-ranging *Fundamental Principles of the Sociology of Law*, where he laid the groundwork for what would later be recognised as the theoretical foundations of legal pluralist studies.[78]

According to Ehrlich, 'living law' should be understood as the normative practices of specific communities or social groups. They exist not because they are enforced by the state but because they are widely accepted within the group itself. He argues that across history and under varying circumstances, a small number of 'facts of the law' (usage, domination, possession, declaration of will) consistently give rise to distinct social orders.[79] Although state law influences social organisation to some degree, Ehrlich contends that 'at the present as well as at any other time, the centre of gravity of legal development lies not in legislation, nor in juristic science, nor in judicial decision, but in society itself.'[80] Because his goal was to understand a broad range of phenomena – not only local communities but also professional communities such as mercantile societies – he employed a correspondingly broad and pragmatic concept of law.

Given this outline, Ehrlich could readily be included among contemporary legal pluralists who study local communities in

78 Eugen Ehrlich, *Fundamental Principles of the Sociology of Law*, trans. Walter L. Moll (Cambridge, MA: Harvard University Press, 1936).
79 Ehrlich, *Fundamental Principles*, 85.
80 Ibid., XV.

postcolonial contexts or examine normative practices within professional groups and who seek to defend the independent legal authority of such norms against the overreaching claims of official state law. However, the full scope – and ultimately the tragedy – of Ehrlich's position only becomes visible when considered in light of the cultural context and the ensuing theoretical debate with his opponents.

Ehrlich implicitly assumed in his writings that the dominant legal outlook of his time was a form of black-letter, state-centred positivism.[81] However, the theoretical debate on legal pluralism was initiated by Kelsen, whose legal positivism was a far more refined theoretical construction. While Ehrlich was conducting his research in Bukovina, Kelsen was already a well-established professor of law at the University of Vienna, the cultural and administrative centre of Austria-Hungary. His scathing review of Ehrlich's book set the tone for subsequent disputes between legal pluralists and legal positivists.[82] Kelsen criticised Ehrlich for failing to provide a clear definition of law as distinct from moral norms or social customs, for conflating the descriptive and prescriptive senses of rules, and – instead of clarifying the concept of law – merely obscuring it further through what he called a methodological mishmash. Ehrlich issued a brief but equally dismissive reply, accusing Kelsen of misinterpretation and of being blinded by idiosyncratic presuppositions. Two further counter-replies only reinforced the mutual lack of understanding.

On the surface, the debate appears to concern the proper definition of law, the correct way to demarcate the domain of jurisprudence – distinct from related disciplines such as sociology or political philosophy – and the appropriate task and method of jurisprudence (*Rechtswissenschaft*). Given that Kelsen, in addition to developing his pure theory of law, would later write ethnological, sociological, political and philosophical works himself, one might conclude that the debate over

[81] The German public lawyer Paul Laband could be seen as representing such a position.

[82] For Kelsen's review and the exchange with Ehrlich, see Paulson, *Hans Kelsen und die Rechtssoziologie*, 839–53.

jurisprudence's proper domain was somewhat overstated.[83] Yet the heated and at times even personal exchange between the two scholars suggests that more was at stake: namely, an underlying fear of ominous developments that could already be felt in the years leading up to World War I, though not yet fully determined. Curiously, both Ehrlich and Kelsen shared this unease and a common concern for something fragile and at risk: the precarious political and social compromise once embodied by the Austro-Hungarian Empire.[84]

As previously noted, Ehrlich's interest in living law was prompted by the coexistence of diverse religious and ethnic groups in Bukovina and his desire to support more equitable paths for economic and cultural development. His ethnological engagement with the legal practices and daily lives of mostly rural, disadvantaged communities in Bukovina – viewed from the standpoint of an academic lawyer – could be seen as embodying the ethos of a legal pluralist. This ethos is also evident in the fact that Ehrlich did not indiscriminately record all customs. Instead, he sought to identify those practices that had crystallised into legal maxims or guiding principles (*Rechtssätze*)[85] and that did not directly contradict state law.[86] For this reason, Ehrlich referred to the living law of such groups as the 'moral forces of society'.[87] However, his own moral convictions remained largely implicit. As a sociologist, Ehrlich was acutely aware of the diversity and often

[83] Since Kelsen is mostly discussed in legal theory there is no monograph that describes the entire range of his theoretical interests and practical work. For a brief analysis of Kelsen as cultural theorist, see Christoph Kletzer, 'Kelsen and Blumenberg: The Legitimacy of the Modern Age', *King's Law Journal* 25, no. 1 (2014): 19–33.

[84] On the weary fin-de-siècle mood in Vienna and Austro-Hungary, see Carl E. Schorske, *Fin-de-Siècle Vienna: Politics and Culture* (New York: Alfred A. Knopf, 1980), 3–23.

[85] See Ehrlich, *Fundamental Principles*, 171–91. The English translation 'legal propositions' is problematic as it does not convey the idea of long-standing, respected rules.

[86] Ibid., 170.

[87] Bismarck's policies, on the other hand, were for Ehrlich a warning example of a purely state- and force-driven idea of law that fails to take account of the moral forces of society. See Eugen Ehrlich, 'Bismarck und der Weltkrieg', in *Politische Schriften*, ed. Manfred Rehbinder (Berlin: Duncker & Humblot, 2007), 107.

conflicting nature of ideas about justice. Therefore, he did not advocate a distinct 'communitarian' conception of justice in opposition to a 'liberal' one.[88] Rather, he emphasised the enduring tension between such ideals:

> Among all of the ideas of justice that have been described until now there is not one that has failed to encounter an antagonist in the course of historical development who, in the deepest chest-tones of genuine conviction, would proclaim the opposite as that which alone is just. This affords a deep insight into the nature of justice.[89]

5.3 Kelsen and Ehrlich at cross purposes

Ehrlich's critique of justice may call to mind Kelsen's post-Nietzschean, value-sceptical attitude. However, unlike Kelsen, Ehrlich does not retreat into a subjective proclamation of his personal ultimate values. Instead, he holds on to one recurring idea of justice that runs as an undercurrent throughout his writings: justice as equity. He consistently condemned indiscriminate or overly abstract legal regulations that failed to account for the needs and customs of the governed. At the same time, he defended equitable solutions practised within social groups, even when these conflicted with official law.[90]

Because Ehrlich wrote little on public law or political philosophy, his appreciation for the admittedly imperfect political compromise represented by the Austro-Hungarian Empire becomes apparent only in retrospect. At the outset of World War I, he joined a peace initiative composed of intellectuals and politicians seeking to explore the conditions for lasting peace in Europe. In a memorandum addressed to

88 The distinction between communitarianism and liberalism was not established at this time. Ehrlich uses instead the terms 'collectivism' and 'individualism' to denote a similar point.

89 Ehrlich, *Fundamental Principles*, 241–42.

90 Ehrlich did not extensively explain or justify this notion of justice. However, the tradition of conceiving 'justice as equity of the wise' could be traced back to Leibniz. See Patrick Riley, *Leibniz' Universal Jurisprudence: Justice as the Charity of the Wise* (Cambridge, MA: Harvard University Press, 1996), 141–98.

an anti-German and anti-Austrian English audience, Ehrlich argued that forcibly dissolving the multicultural and multi-ethnic Austro-Hungarian Empire would not simply 'liberate unjustly incarcerated nations', but would most likely trigger a new wave of ethnic tensions and social conflict.[91] This did not mean, however, that Ehrlich defended the aristocratic regime of the Empire. On the contrary, he held the Habsburg rulers accountable for failing to foster a shared multicultural Austrian identity, for neglecting the social and cultural needs of many of their subjects and for contributing – through sheer incompetence and blind allegiance to a belligerent Germany – to 'the fall of a great empire'.[92]

Since we have already introduced Kelsen's pure theory in its historical context, we can now see that the interests of Kelsen and Ehrlich aligned, even though they approached their shared objective from two very different angles.[93] Ehrlich aimed to preserve the local traditions of various ethnic and social groups by acknowledging them in his research and by providing tools for cautious economic and cultural development.[94] Kelsen, by contrast, sought to establish legal theory – and thereby the law itself – as a consistent and value-free instrument of social regulation and conflict resolution.

91 Eugen Ehrlich, *The National Problems in Austria* (The Hague: Martinus Nijhoff, 1917).

92 See Eugen Ehrlich, 'Das Ende eines großen Reiches', in *Politische Schriften*, 19–80. Ehrlich's own ideas for a peaceful postwar order were more along the lines of the thinking of Austro-Marxists who promoted a federal, social democratic republic with Vienna as cultural capital. See Manfred Rehbinder, 'Aus den letzten Jahren im Leben und Schaffen von Eugen Ehrlich', in Dieter Dölling, ed., *Festschrift Ernst-Joachim Lampe* (Berlin: Duncker & Humblot, 2003), 199. For a contemporary perspective on how the Austro-Hungarian model of legal and political compromise might still offer relevant insights today, see Börries Kuzmany, *Vom Umgang mit nationaler Vielfalt. Eine Geschichte der nicht-territorialen Autonomie in Europa* (Berlin: De Gruyter, 2024).

93 On the shared Habsburg background of Hans Kelsen and Eugen Ehrlich, and its influence on their respective legal theories, see Franz Leander Fillafer, 'Imperial Diversity, Fractured Sovereignty, and Legal Universals: Hans Kelsen and Eugen Ehrlich in their Habsburg Context', *Modern Intellectual History* 19 (2022): 421–43.

94 Ehrlich developed his view indirectly through a critique of socialist ideas. See Ehrlich, 'Die Aufgaben der Sozialpolitik im österreichischen Osten (Juden- und Bauernfrage)', in *Politische Schriften*, 135–44.

To this end, he attempted to purge legal theory of ideological or value-based content and concentrated on its proper domain: the analysis of the legal 'ought'.[95]

Arguably, both men sensed that whatever would follow the fragile, yet at least peaceful and rule-of-law-based modus vivendi of the Austro-Hungarian Empire was likely to be worse – especially for the Jewish minorities across the region.[96] But in theoretical terms, their views were fundamentally at odds. For Kelsen, Ehrlich's approach amounted to a contamination of legal science with unjustifiable subjective value judgments and a confused mix of methods that threatened the law's role as a neutral arbiter. Ehrlich, for his part, might have countered that Kelsen's vision of legal purity was not just an epistemological stance, but a social reality, one that, due to its lack of sensitivity to social context, could effectively serve a state-driven, even imperialist, agenda. Each, in this sense, saw in the other the extreme form of what he most distrusted, even though they implicitly shared an appreciation for the same political ideal: a *sozialer Rechtsstaat* (a social welfare state based on the rule of law) that accommodates diverse identities and competing worldviews. They even shared a belief in the professional ethos of academic lawyers: that value-free, scientific scholarship could help guide and illuminate the work of the state bureaucracy.

5.4 'The Gorgonian head of power stares at us'

So far, in discussing Ehrlich and Kelsen, the night of the twentieth century has not appeared as a topic or a problem within the theories themselves. Yet the rumblings of World War I already formed the backdrop to the academic debate and foreshadowed the tragedies and terrors that would unfold

[95] Kelsen, *General Theory*, 3–15.

[96] The modus vivendi is exactly the kind of stability out of a balance of political forces that Rawls considers as insufficient as it is not supported by a sense of justice. See John Rawls, 'Justice as Fairness: Political not Metaphysical', in *Collected Papers*, ed. Samuel Freeman (Cambridge, MA: Harvard University Press, 2001), 410–11. Ehrlich and Kelsen, on the other hand, both sensed that such a common sense of justice could not be achieved under the given multicultural and multiethnic circumstances of an empire, and striving for it would imperil even the modus vivendi.

in the century ahead. Ehrlich died in 1922, but not before witnessing the dissolution of the multiethnic Habsburg Empire and the rise of xenophobia and resentful nationalism in his native Bukovina. The newly formed Kingdom of Romania incorporated Bukovina under a nationalistic agenda marked by xenophobic sentiments: anti-German, anti-Ukrainian and, last but not least, antisemitic.[97] The German-speaking University of Czernowitz was transformed into an institution explicitly tasked with fostering nationalistic narratives and patriotic consciousness among young Romanians. The 'old-fashioned', multicultural-minded faculty was pushed out. Ehrlich's attempts to return to his home university, where he had served for many years, were thwarted by protests from students and faculty, fuelled by antisemitic and nationalist hostility directed at him.[98]

The exact details of these events need not be spelled out in full here. They played out at the international level (such as the establishment of the principle of self-determination for 'civilised' peoples in the Treaty of Versailles), at the national level (the formation of nation-states in Eastern Europe) and at the local level in Czernowitz. Curiously, the clearest manifestations of what one might call 'evil' are not found at the international or national level, but at the local one.

The peace negotiations following World War I, particularly President Woodrow Wilson's initiative, included noble aims.[99] A restoration of a multiethnic Danube state under

[97] The history of the Romanianisation of Bukovina is still a contested field. See Mariana Hausleitner, *Die Rumänisierung der Bukowina. Die Durchsetzung des nationalstaatlichen Anspruchs Grossrumäniens 1918–1944* (München: Oldenbourg, 2001). For a brief account, see Monica Eppinger, 'Governing in the Vernacular: Eugen Ehrlich and Late Habsburg Ethnography', in Marc Hertogh, ed., *Living Law: Reconsidering Eugen Ehrlich* (Oxford: Hart, 2009), 21–47.

[98] On the history of the university and Ehrlich's role, see Manfred Rehbinder, 'Die rechts- und staatswissenschaftliche Fakultät der Franz-Josephs-Universität Czernowitz. Ihr Beitrag zur Erforschung des Rechts in einer multikulturellen Gesellschaft', in Gerhard Holoch et al., eds., *Festschrift Hans Stoll zum 75. Geburtstag* (Tübingen: Mohr Siebeck, 2001), 327–44.

[99] For a more nuanced view of the political aims of Wilson and his antagonists, see Stephen Wertheim, 'The League That Wasn't: American Designs for a Legalist-Sanctionist League of Nations and the Intellectual

Austrian leadership was, after the inner-ethnic fighting imposed by Habsburg generals, no longer a realistic prospect. The dissolution of the Empire was therefore inevitable. Yet the way Romanianisation was implemented in Czernowitz reveals a darker turn: non-Romanian citizens – especially Germans, Ukrainians and Jews – were harassed, expelled and stripped of homes, farms and university positions. These actions, along with the tacit acceptance of antisemitic violence, foreshadowed even more brutal forms of ethnic cleansing to come. It was, so to speak, the Gorgonian head of power that emerged when the veil of living law was lifted.[100]

One might reason that all of this is irrelevant to legal pluralism, as it occurs outside the immediate scope of Ehrlich's theory. Yet it reveals a crucial gap in his work, which also marks a fundamental problem within the tradition of legal pluralism itself. Ehrlich fails to account for the internal dynamics of living law groups and their potential impact on other groups within a broader social context. He lacks the conceptual tools to explain how living law can outgrow its informal setting, become official state law and then turn oppressive. Although Ehrlich begins with the idea of a dynamic, evolving legal order, he still assumes that various social groups are essentially static and always subordinate to a state bureaucracy that forms a separate, overarching system. In this respect, Ehrlich's thinking remains tied to a nineteenth-century, predemocratic conception of the opposition between state and society, in which the (monarchical) state has its own social foundation (the aristocracy) and a legitimacy independent of civil society (*bürgerliche Gesellschaft*), rather than emerging from it through democratic self-constitution.

Origins of International Organization, 1914–1920', *Diplomatic History* 35, no. 5 (2011): 797–836.

100 The expression 'Gorgonian head of power' was coined by Kelsen in a reply to natural law theorist Erich Kaufmann. The full quote is: 'The question natural law aims at is the eternal question of what lies behind positive law. And whoever seeks the answer, I fear, will not find the absolute truth of some metaphysics nor the absolute justice of natural law. Whoever lifts the veil and does not close his eye, the Gorgonian head of power stares at him.' Hans Kelsen, 'Diskussionsbeitrag', *Veröffentlichungen der Vereinigung der Deutschen Staatsrechtler* 3 (1927): 54–55, author's translation.

Because of this, Ehrlich fails to recognise – or to conceptualise – how, through the influence of a nationalist ideology, one group within a broader society might claim to represent the 'true' society while portraying minorities as internal enemies. This is the vexing problem that a democratic process – or, in Ehrlich's terms, a process grounded in living law[101] – can yield antidemocratic or authoritarian outcomes. Moreover, increasing the awareness of judges and bureaucrats regarding living law may have the unintended consequence of reinforcing xenophobic or nationalist ideologies, especially when certain living law groups come to dominate state institutions.

As a legal pluralist, Ehrlich was especially disheartened to see his hopes for a peaceful modus vivendi for Jews in Eastern Europe irrevocably shattered. In one of his political essays, he analysed how economic, social and ethnic tensions – particularly those affecting Jewish communities – were deeply intertwined, and he argued that the formation of nation-states would not resolve any of them. With a tone of resignation, he noted that he belonged to a generation that had once hoped for the assimilation of Jews into the German-speaking population, particularly in Austria-Hungary. Together, they might have preserved German culture within Eastern Europe's cultural mosaic and contributed to the region's economic development.[102]

In reflecting on the horrors of the twentieth century, it is essential to recognise that, alongside the oft-repeated slogan of the 'Jewish problem'[103] voiced by antisemites across Europe, there had once existed – however faintly – a prospect for a 'multicultural resolution'.

[101] Ehrlich has no elaborated theory of democracy. However, he equals it with living law as only in a democracy 'the forces of society are utilized by the state.' See Eugen Ehrlich, 'Von der Zukunft des Völkerbundes', in *Politische Schriften*, 186.

[102] Eugen Ehrlich, 'Die Aufgabe der Sozialpolitik', 142–3.

[103] In Germany, the historian Heinrich von Treitschke coined in 1879 the infamous slogan 'the Jews are our misfortune' and, because of his reputation, made antisemitism socially acceptable. See Alfred J. Andrea and James H. Overfield, eds., *The Human Record: Sources of Global History*, Volume II: Since 1500 (Boston: Cengage Learning, 2011), 294–5.

Ehrlich personally experienced the double-edged cruelty of antisemitism. Known in Czernowitz as an assimilated, German-speaking Catholic Jew, he was rejected by the new Romanian government. His offer to learn Romanian and teach in the new national language was derided as a sign of 'typical Jewish fickleness and national unreliability'. In the end, his faith in the integrity of legal institutions, the ethos of the academic community and his hope for the progressive enlightenment of society through value-free scholarship was shattered.[104] In his writings, he referred to antisemitism only once, describing it as an 'imprudent student prank'[105] – perhaps suggesting that humour was the last refuge for asserting human dignity amid turbulent times.

6. In the eye of the hurricane

Even though we have teetered, through the debate between Kelsen, Schmitt and Ehrlich, on the precipice of Nazism, one might still argue that it is possible, as an intellectual historian, philosopher or reader, to observe and assess these developments without being implicated in them. The academic discipline itself, along with those who practice it, seems to remain off the hook. We know, and can easily justify, why Nazism is morally wrong. We can study with horror the many atrocities committed under Nazi rule and ask how responsibility or guilt can be acknowledged, or how similar developments might be avoided in the future. In any case, the lessons Nazism appears to offer seem to be entirely detached from our own lifeworld. It is this implicit methodological and existential conviction that will be questioned in the remainder of this chapter.

One example may illustrate how the reversal of meaning within legal institutions did not require a wholesale overhaul of laws and systems, nor the replacement of all officials. Often, small changes sufficed. A typical state law examination in Nazi Germany might feature a case involving a

[104] For a detailed account of the events, see Stefan Vogl, *Soziale Gesetzgebungspolitik, freie Rechtsfindung und soziologische Rechtswissenschaft bei Eugen Ehrlich* (Baden-Baden: Nomos, 2002), 91–107.

[105] Ehrlich, 'Die Aufgabe der Sozialpolitik', 143.

'Jewish' tenant whose lease has been terminated and who then sues his 'Aryan' landlord.[106] (Tenant protection laws were still in effect during this time.) A candidate who merely parroted Nazi slogans in solving the case would fail. However, a candidate who solved the case *lege artis* – in favour of the Jewish tenant – would also fail. The correct approach was to demonstrate competence in the 'fit' dimension of legal reasoning and then, at the last possible moment, invoke the 'justification' dimension, interpreting the law in alignment with the 'appropriate' values.[107] Theoretical frameworks distinguishing these two dimensions were developed by legal academics at the time and after the war were, mysteriously, reformulated by simply changing the underlying values.[108]

This example underscores a general point: the existence of a legal system, value-based theories of interpretation, engagement with 'Western' political theory or even a judiciary trained during republican times (as with many Nazi-era lawyers) did not suffice to shield the law from becoming a pernicious instrument. Even Kelsen's ultimate recourse to rationality – namely, the natural sciences, driven by the inherent logic of discovery – proved to be just as corruptible as law and politics. Without hesitation, representatives

[106] It is not a real but a simplified fictitious case to explain the way the whole legal system worked. A full historical study would have to go into the details of the two exams and the different legal topics dealt with in them and detect the ideological agenda in slight changes of the wordings. For a more detailed account along these lines, see Louis Pahlow, '"Ich verüble dem Verf. weniger einzelne juristische Fehler als das Versagen des Rechtsgefühls". Juristische Staatsprüfungen im Dritten Reich (1934–1945)', in Thomas Gutmann et al., eds., *Von den Leges Barbarorum bis zum ius barbarum des Nationalsozialismus: Festschrift für Hermann Nehlsen zum 70. Geburtstag*, (Köln: Böhlau, 2008), 399–420.

[107] Fit and justification are the two dimensions in Ronald Dworkin's theory of integrative interpretation. See Ronald Dworkin, *Law's Empire* (Cambridge, MA: Harvard University Press, 1986), 225–75. It is easy to see that this theory could also be used in a different context by simply changing the underlying values.

[108] The details of the sweeping transformation of the legal system are of course more complex. For the case of private law, Bernd Rüthers has shown the continuities in his classical study *Die unbegrenzte Auslegung: zum Wandel der Privatrechtsordnung im Nationalsozialismus*, 7th ed. (Tübingen: Mohr Siebeck, 2012).

across all scientific fields rushed to demonstrate how they could integrate Nazi ideology into their disciplines. The irrational Jewish/Aryan dichotomy found its way into biology, physics, engineering and beyond.

The dialectics of political theory are not merely a historical case study of a remote (and fortunately extinct) species. They offer a cautionary warning. Any attempt to secure a neutral stance above political disputes – for example, by adopting only a minimal normative standard – or a neutral position beyond theoretical debate by presuming a pragmatic concept of law – is at risk of being drawn back into the fray by depicting the underlying assumptions as one part of the debate. Especially when the assumptions of law as a means of peaceful conflict resolution or scholarship as a rational and verifiable endeavour are called into question, the dialectic of political theory inevitably extends to meta-theoretical debates as well.

One might believe that the complete collapse of Western scholarship is merely a hypothetical dystopia. However, the increasing fragmentation of the humanities and social sciences into mutually sealed-off discourses and the rise of systematic censorship, both online and in academic forums, by populist or totalitarian regimes already corrodes the infrastructure of a free and open public sphere. Moreover, the assumption that the international practice of scholarship – or the moral integrity of the scholar herself – can always be preserved and remain insulated from turmoil on the ground must be questioned. The existential moment each scholar may face at some point is best captured through a fictitious narrative.

Excursus: Erinyes, the kindly ones

The name 'Auschwitz' has become the symbol of evil in its most monstrous forms. Even its mere mention demands careful effort to avoid using it as a superficial gesture or failing to convey its endless, multifaceted wickedness. At this point, we are not only in the eye of the storm of the twentieth century but also far removed from anything that can be adequately captured by the language of legal pluralism, philosophy or perhaps even abstract theory altogether. Since the Nuremberg Military Tribunals, the Nazi regime's vast bureaucratic killing apparatus – its camp system, its ties to the war machine, the military-industrial complex and segments of civil society – has been thoroughly documented. Victim and survivor testimonies have been assembled to such an extent that Holocaust studies has become a discipline in its own right.

Yet one significant gap in the literature remains that speaks directly to our inquiry into the (often involuntary) entanglement of scholarship with mechanisms of destruction: we possess only a small number of reports, diaries, autobiographical or semi-fictional accounts from within, from the perspective of perpetrators, accomplices and bystanders.[109] This absence – this silence – marks a disturbing void, suggesting that the innermost abyss of the Holocaust remains elusive. The silence, the good conscience or even the 'healthiness of evil' would in itself be worth reflecting upon.[110]

The absence of first-hand reports can, however, be addressed through literature. Jonathan Littell's *The Kindly Ones* is one of the first novels written from the perspective of a (fictitious) SS officer.[111] It invents the voice and inner reasoning of a perpetrator. More than with most novels, it is crucial here to distinguish between the views expressed by the protagonist – a self-obsessed, sexually depraved SS officer and serial murderer – the aesthetic standpoint of the novel itself and the interpretations offered by the author and critics.[112] Because *The Kindly Ones* is not a *roman à thèse*, it does

109 A notable literary exception is Robert Merle, *Death Is My Trade*, trans. Alan Ross (London: Derek Verschoyle, 1954), a novel written in first person based on the life of the commander of Auschwitz, Rudolf Höß. The study on the Reserve Police Battalion 101 is notably a relatively late historical study but not an account written by one of the perpetrators. See Christopher R. Browning, *Ordinary Men: Reserve Police Battalion 101 and the Final Solution in Poland* (London: Penguin, 1998).

110 Strangely enough, the guilt of perpetrators seemed to be hidden, or worse unproblematic, even in psychoanalytic therapy. At least there are hardly any reports of guilt voiced in psychoanalytic sessions. See also Browning, 'The Strange Health of Captain Hofmann', in *Ordinary Men*, 114–20.

111 Jonathan Littell, *The Kindly Ones*, trans. Charlotte Manell (London: Vintage, 2010).

112 After its publication, the novel has been intensely discussed in various countries. See Aurélie Barjonet and Liran Razinsky, eds., *Writing the*

not provide a singular thesis or moral resolution. Instead, it invites readers – despite its harrowing subject matter – into a disquieting 'free play' of imagination and understanding.[113]

The second chapter of *The Kindly Ones* speaks directly to our discussion of the limits of theory. The narrator and main protagonist, a high-ranking SS officer named Dr. Aue, is sent to the Caucasus and tasked with producing a 'manageable' definition of which among the various ethnic groups should be classified as Jewish. One group in particular – the so-called *Bergjuden* (mountain Jews), an ethnic community native to the Caucasus mountains – presents a problem. It does not fit neatly into the simplistic Nazi ideology that all Jews must share a common racial origin and exist as a foreign body within a 'truly' native population.[114] In the course of his investigation, Dr. Aue gathers historical reports, the writings of ethnologists and anthropologists and studies the customs of the local population. In short, he proceeds in the best fashion of a legal pluralist – only in the service of a genocidal regime.

The disturbing insight of the story is that it is not only the protagonist who bears responsibility. All the scholarly writings, scientific reports and ethnographic observations he draws on become entangled in his perverse task. This is exemplified in the character of Dr. Voss, a preeminent linguist who uses the Wehrmacht's advances into the Caucasus to collect data for his studies on undocumented Iranian languages. At the same time, he offers a counter-narrative to the racial logic imposed by Dr. Aue and his SS colleagues. When Aue asks what he makes of the 'problem' of the *Bergjuden*, Dr. Voss replies: 'The way they've put it, it's absurd. The only thing you can say about these people is that they speak an Iranian language, practice the Mosaic religion and live according to the customs of the Caucasian mountain people. That's it.' When Aue insists that they 'must have an origin', Voss shrugs: 'Everyone has an origin, most of the time a dreamed one.'[115] It is tempting to hail Dr. Voss as the voice

Holocaust Today: Critical Perspectives on Jonathan Littell's The Kindly Ones (Amsterdam: Rodopi, 2012).

113 This is Kant's characterisation of the aesthetic experience, see KU 5:218.

114 Littell, *The Kindly Ones*, 299.

115 Ibid.

of reason. But Littell resists assigning any one character the role of moral mouthpiece. The episode ends with two grim twists. First, Voss's counterargument is made only in private: he leaves no paper trail. Second, he does not survive long: he is shot, not by a resistance fighter, but by a local farmer who sees him attempting to seduce his daughter. In his final scene, the polyglot scholar lies dying in a hospital, mourning 'incomprehensible vowels'.

In a later scene – a fictional conference between SS officers, Wehrmacht personnel and a Reich representative – the 'final solution' to the *Bergjuden* question is discussed. Dr. Voss's views do not play any role. The disturbing point is clear: all scholarly activity, regardless of its premises or involvement, is vulnerable to being drawn into the machinery of extermination. The practice of scholarship itself – the systematic collection and categorisation of knowledge – can be co-opted by a perverse administration. The problem that political philosophers, or scholars in general, not only consciously influence political discourse but can also be absorbed by its most pernicious power practices is not merely a theoretical issue, but, as the novel shows, an existential possibility every scholar has to face.

Kelsen's minimalist fallback position, the legal order as a framework for the contestation of different political views, proved untenable once his core assumptions (peace and reconciliation) were swept into the ideological whirlpool. With Ehrlich, we saw how the pluralistic spirits he invoked returned as ghosts. The very groups whose customs he had documented re-emerged as nationalist ideologies, haunting him with their transformed identity. Both scholars witnessed the collapse of a constellation of ideas and pragmatic presuppositions they had taken for granted. Yet evil did not emerge as a theme within their theories; it unfolded around them in moments they had left unaccounted for. At its most unsettling depth, Littell's literary character Dr. Aue illustrates how scholarship itself may rely on, and be propelled by, imperial expansion. It may be absorbed into its machinery, ultimately leaving scholarship itself to rot as a curio in a killing field.

The aim of this genealogy, then, is not moral certainty, but self-awareness. One's favourite subject may become the monster of tomorrow. One's fallback position may become a partisan line in a political conflict. Even one's own research – archived for posterity – may be twisted, repurposed or weaponised. In the end, Mephisto, Faust's nemesis, may have the last laugh.

7. Two models of post-foundational cosmopolitanism

The digression into the abyss tends to captivate all attention and cloud our imagination. In a variation on a dictum by Theodor W. Adorno, one might say that after Auschwitz, writing philosophy – particularly political philosophy – is impossible.[116] Yet ordinary life, and in its more reflective moments philosophy itself, continues and demands our attention. The night of the twentieth century must be included in the genealogy of cosmopolitan thought precisely to prevent any return to a 'self-evident', 'natural' or 'traditional' starting point – as often found in political theory, natural law theory or Aristotelian frameworks. This is not to suggest that all philosophy, all Western philosophy or all forms of thinking (including poetic thinking) have fallen into equal disrepute. But to understand the specific contributions philosophers have made to the discourses of their time – and to assess their guilt or responsibility – we had to present philosophical theories, and the lives of philosophers, in a contextual manner.

The ultimate existential anchoring could be symbolised only through the recounting of saintly acts, as in the case of Franz Jägerstätter, or through storytelling, as in the case of Dr. Aue. Even though the genealogy is thereby contextualised in a specific way, it can still serve – because of its anchoring in the philosophical tradition – as an allegory for other narratives. It is for this reason that the further genealogy of cosmopolitan thought must proceed in a post-foundational manner. This does not mean taking any particular version of the Western tradition for granted but instead remaining mindful of the human and civilisational propensity for evil. But how can this be done without lapsing once again into

116 For this reason, Hannah Arendt insisted in her interview with Günter Gaus on being called a political theorist but not a political philosopher. See Arendt, 'Zur Person', 44.

hypocrisy masked by grand speech?[117] As this task involves assuming existential responsibility for the future, it cannot be captured in a theory – though certain models may offer guidance. Once more, Kelsen provides two pathways for post-foundational cosmopolitan thought that may still hold relevance for today.

7.1 Critical legal analysis

Given Kelsen's life experiences and his broad philosophical interests, one might expect that, after the war, he would have turned to making sense of the rupture of civilisation, especially since he had been personally targeted and represented an Austrian legacy that was also formative for Hitler.[118] Yet he took a very different path. Rather than celebrating the defeat of Nazism as a milestone in human progress or promoting, like many post-war intellectuals, the cause of liberalism (or communism), Kelsen turned his attention to writing a detailed commentary on the law of the United Nations.[119] This was not conceived as a 'third way' meant to mediate between the clashing post-war ideologies. Rather, Kelsen approached the UN Charter as a legal document, a 'constitution' stripped of solemn declarations or ideological embellishment. Here again, his Viennese background offers insight into his approach. (Notably, Kelsen had previously co-authored the Austrian Constitution of 1920.) The drafting of the UN Charter and the Universal Declaration of Human Rights was a remarkable collaborative achievement and deservedly praised by contemporaries.[120] But for Kelsen, no value commitment, however noble, could ultimately resolve

117 To quote Kant again: 'This dishonesty, by which we throw dust in our own eyes and which hinders the establishment in us of a genuine moral disposition, then extends itself also externally, to falsity or deception of others' (*RGV* 6:38).

118 Brigitte Hamann, *Hitler's Vienna: A Portrait of the Tyrant as a Young Man*, trans. Thomas Thornton (Oxford: Oxford University Press, 1999) traces the anti-modern, anti-cosmopolitan and antisemitic prejudices of the petite bourgeoisie in Vienna of the time of the fin de siècle.

119 Kelsen, *The Law of the United Nations*.

120 See Mary Ann Glendon, *A World Made New: Eleanor Roosevelt and the Universal Declaration of Human Rights* (New York: Random House, 2002).

deep-rooted value conflicts, particularly in an international charter with global aspirations. Its effectiveness could only be measured by the quality of its legal form.

His harsh critique of the League of Nations' inadequate legal framework serves as the background to his interpretation of the UN Charter. As he put it:

> If one wants to serve peace, it is better to speak of international law than – as unfortunately happens all too often – to declaim about a nebulous justice and thereby neglect the further development of international law, which is only in its infancy. If the Covenant of the League of Nations had used the proud word 'justice' less often, but had taken more care in its legal-technical formulation, it would have fulfilled its task better.[121]

To avoid a second failure of international law, Kelsen did not hesitate to issue harsh criticisms where needed. For him, the ability to endure such contestation was itself a sign of good law. A few select examples may suffice to illustrate Kelsen's approach, for what matters most is not the particular arguments but the kind of legal mindset he modelled.

Kelsen begins his analysis by stating that the book is 'a juristic, not a political, approach to the problems of the United Nations'.[122] Thus, it is not an 'integrative interpretation' in the manner of Ronald Dworkin, in which particular value commitments are advanced to justify a specific moral reading of the Charter. Kelsen assumes that, despite certain underlying proclamations, there is no genuine international consensus on such moral values. Instead, he takes the separation of law and politics as a given.[123] Nevertheless, a juridical commentary still serves a specific function. It is not to offer the true or authentic interpretation of a legal document – that task belongs solely to the organs formally empowered to interpret it. Rather, its function is 'to find, by a critical analysis, the possible meanings of the legal norm undergoing

121 Hans Kelsen, 'Die Technik des Völkerrechts und die Organisation des Friedens', *Zeitschrift für öffentliches Recht* 2 (1934): 240.

122 Kelsen, *The Law of the United Nations*, 13.

123 Ibid.

interpretation; and then, to show their consequences, leaving it to the competent legal authorities to choose from among the various possible interpretations the one which they, for political reasons, consider to be preferable, and which they alone are entitled to select'.[124] This may even include presenting interpretations 'which are politically undesirable and those which permit the conjecture that they were not intended by the legislator .... [as to] induce him to improve his technique'.[125]

Kelsen's analysis, then, is a candid assessment of the strengths and weaknesses of the Charter seen as a legal text, that is, as a contested, coercive order. For this reason, Kelsen draws a sharp distinction between the political ideals expressed in the preamble, which he views as 'rather of ideological than legal importance',[126] and those provisions of the Charter that are enforceable by sanction. Likewise, he cautions against the inclusion of natural law language in the Charter (e.g., 'all human beings are born free and equal'), since such philosophical doctrines are far from universally accepted.[127]

Kelsen, as a scholar, is not 'for' or 'against' human rights as a matter of principle, that is, on philosophical, metaphysical or ideological grounds. Instead, he examines how human rights are conceptualised in the Charter and points out inconsistencies that make certain notions less effective as legal tools. Often, Kelsen's critiques may seem pedantic or overly severe, for instance, when he notes that 'the formula "human rights and fundamental freedoms" is incorrect, since "freedoms" are human rights: rights to be free from restrictions imposed by the government'.[128] Yet his aim is not to applaud noble goals but to lay the groundwork for a functioning legal framework. Accordingly, he focuses closely on the organisational parts of the Charter: how membership is determined, whether it is compulsory, whether withdrawal is possible, what the rights and duties of the various organs are (General Assembly, Security Council, Secretary-General) and how

124 Ibid., xvi.
125 Ibid.
126 Ibid., 9.
127 Ibid., 40.
128 Ibid., 29.

disputes can be settled. He also evaluates the mechanisms for enforcing decisions and the sanctions available to the UN, as these are critical for assessing the Charter's viability as a coercive legal order.

Today, the book is clearly dated. This is a development Kelsen himself would have welcomed, given that authentic interpretation belongs to the designated organs, especially the General Assembly, the Security Council and the courts. Yet as a model of analysis, Kelsen's account remains instructive precisely because it is post-foundational. He does not purport to present a universally accepted philosophical foundation but acknowledges the limited and fragile role that international law can play in a fragmented world. Even a charter based on universal principles, he reminds us, is a human creation and subject to decay, just as the League of Nations was.

Still, this is not merely a sociological analysis of power relations, what we might today call a Foucauldian perspective. Kelsen maintains the normative character of law as something that can be scientifically analysed and reconstructed. The strength of this model becomes clearest when contrasted with paths not taken: we can imagine Kelsen's voice responding to the lofty pronouncements of the imaginary 1913 meeting in Vienna's city park. In this role, Kelsen serves as a switchboard between divergent ideas – between early twentieth-century ideological battles and the sober, post-war legal perspective.

He was not simply a jurist with a narrow specialisation but a thinker who lived through the three great crises of the twentieth century and addressed many of their ideological dimensions in his writings. Kelsen was a friend of Ludwig von Mises, attended Freud's seminars and authored books on Plato, Freud, Marxism, neo-Kantianism, ethnology and the political-theological dimension of law. Since these very texts and traditions also shaped Derrida's thought (one of Heidegger's heirs), it is possible to reconnect contemporary poststructuralist and critical debates with their origins and to consider Kelsen's sceptical responses anew. This intellectual tour de force is not merely a refined comparative game of ideas, a kind of *Glass Bead Game*, but leads us directly to the second model of post-foundational thought.

7.2 Debunking foundationalism: Then and now

Given our extensive genealogy – which began with Sappho's riddle, sung before the advent of philosophy, and then took a long route through Plato, Kant and Heidegger – the legalistic outcome might appear unsatisfying. One might even object that it does not belong to the genealogy at all, as it seemingly diverts attention toward a different discipline. However, as a post-foundational account, the earlier philosophical attempts to ground law in absolute principles are, together with their various historical underpinnings, preserved in Kelsen (in the Hegelian sense of *Aufhebung*). As we have seen, philosophical theories often demand existential commitment, like Kant's wager to outlive Frederick William II, and a philosopher's life can, at times, be haunted by their own (misconceived) theories. For this reason, we had to abandon a strictly theoretical perspective at a certain point and take recourse to storytelling.

This survey of the genealogy may raise the suspicion that what has been unveiled is a new, albeit unintentional, form of foundationalist philosophy: one that is critical of narrow accounts of political thinking but open to different modes of thought, including poetic and perhaps even religious reflection. Given such a broad understanding of political thought, a genealogy of cosmopolitanism might easily be rewritten as a success story by relying on 'emancipatory forces' throughout history or recounting the many 'struggles against oppression'. Naturally, suppressed voices across history would thereby gain more prominence. The second model of post-foundational cosmopolitanism responds to such attempts at providing a new foundational narrative. It can be introduced through the work of one of Kelsen's most gifted students: Eric Voegelin.

Voegelin was not a student in the narrow sense of following in Kelsen's footsteps, but rather an *élève*, a thinker of his own stature. During his studies in Vienna, he participated in several private learned societies where topics including philosophy, history, law and economics were discussed. His dissertation was supervised by both Kelsen and the controversial Austrian economist Othmar Spann, and both were also referenced in his later *Habilitation*. In the early years of his academic career, Voegelin broadly embraced the conservative and authoritarian ideas of Spann. His two books on race from 1932[129] were written under the influence of right-wing ideologies.

In his study on the authoritarian state,[130] Voegelin explicitly turned against Kelsen, whom he regarded as an exemplar of ungrounded modernity, a mindset Voegelin retained throughout his life. He criticised Kelsen's pure theory for lacking a true relationship to political reality, arguing that it failed to account for the behaviour of officials who do not obey coercive norms.[131] Voegelin particularly faulted Kelsen for failing to justify the need for a genuine political order, that is, an order rooted in the existence of a real political community. In his view, Kelsen had constructed only an administrative system that, moreover, lent credibility to international law rather than reinforcing national consciousness.[132]

Just as Kelsen's theory was shaped by the precarious modus vivendi of the Austro-Hungarian Empire and the Austrian Republic, Voegelin's ideas drew implicitly on the model of the authoritarian corporate state that governed Austria from 1934 to 1938. After emigrating to the United States, Voegelin reorganised his thought and began studying totalitarianism from a broader, new foundationalist perspective.

In his ground-breaking book *The New Science of Politics*,[133] he explained the rise of totalitarianism as the result of an excessive gnostic tendency in modernity, a response to the loss of genuine religious experience. Nevertheless, his critique of Kelsen, now subsumed under the label of 'destructive positivism', remained consistent. Voegelin blamed modern positivism for dismantling a comprehensive understanding of

[129] Eric Voegelin, *Rasse und Staat*, [*Race and State*] (Tübingen: Mohr Siebeck, 1933) and *Die Rassenidee in der Geistesgeschichte von Ray bis Carus* [The Idea of Race in the History of Ideas from Ray to Carus] (Berlin: Junker und Dünnhaupt, 1933).

[130] Eric Voegelin, *Der autoritäre Staat. Ein Versuch über das österreichische Staatsproblem* [The Authoritarian State. An Essay on the Problem of the Austrian State] (Wien: Springer, 1936).

[131] Ibid., 122–6.

[132] Ibid., 128.

[133] Eric Voegelin, *The New Science of Politics. An Introduction* (Chicago: University of Chicago Press, 1952).

'representation' – in his terms, both descriptive and existential representation, as well as the religiously connoted representation of truth. This, he argued, cleared the way for gnostic, that is, totalitarian fantasies of political damnation and redemption.[134]

Voegelin's far-reaching account of political philosophy is not developed from a cosmopolitan perspective but focuses largely on ancient and early modern intellectual history. Nevertheless, it remains indirectly relevant to contemporary cosmopolitan debates, as it seeks to demonstrate that liberalism is merely another gnostic ideology. In Voegelin's view it lacks a 'representation of truth', which can ultimately be supplied only by religion.[135] As such, Voegelin's project constitutes both a critique of liberalism and an attempt to establish a new foundation for political thought.

Both tendencies can also be observed in some contemporary criticisms of cosmopolitanism, though usually voiced in a different tone. Critical voices point to liberalism's complicity with longstanding structures of domination, articulated in terms of class, gender or race.[136] Others equate liberalism with a specific neoliberal economic order that has triggered financial crises, rising inequality and increased social fragmentation across many Western societies.[137] Conservative critics likewise target liberalism for its role in entrenching structural inequalities and its failure to sustain social cohesion. However, they focus their critique on liberalism's foundational commitments to individual autonomy and procedural neutrality, explicitly advocating for a post-liberal order grounded in substantive visions of the common good.[138] Some commentators who assert that liberalism has been outperformed by an autocratic (notably Chinese) model

134 Ibid., 1–26.

135 Ibid., 75.

136 Dipesh Chakrabarty, *Provincializing Europe. Postcolonial Thought and Historical Difference* (Princeton, NJ: Princeton University Press, 2000); Jennifer Pitts, *A Turn to Empire. The Rise of Imperial Liberalism in Britain and France* (Princeton, NJ: Princeton University Press, 2005).

137 Quinn Slobodian, *Globalists. The End of Empire and the Birth of Neoliberalism* (Cambridge, MA: Harvard University Press, 2018) and his follow-up, *Hayek's Bastards: Race, Gold, IQ, and the Capitalism of the Far Right* (Princeton: Zone Books, 2025).

138 See Deneen, *Regime Change*; Vermeule, *Common Good Constitutionalism*.

attempt to justify this view by invoking a distinct set of 'Asian values'.[139] Compared to Voegelin's magisterial history of ideas, current criticism is more pluralistic, draws on a broader array of philosophical traditions and engages with a wider historical and geographical scope, including developments outside the Western hemisphere.

However, in four respects, they remain comparable to Voegelin's approach. First, they adopt a higher, critical vantage point from which liberalism appears as just one ideology, or what Voegelin would call a 'Gnostic formation'. Second, they attribute destructive tendencies to liberalism (or individualism). Third, they frame cosmopolitanism or international law as extensions of structural domination. And fourth, they seek an alternative foundation or anchoring for their critique. These parallels help explain why Kelsen's response to Voegelin can be seen as the second model of a post-foundational cosmopolitanism.

But why should it be considered a 'model' and not simply another book on Voegelin or one more contribution to intellectual history? Kelsen's commentary on the law of the United Nations was introduced as a model because it is not, like a philosophical treatise, a one-time contribution. It requires, like all juridical commentary, constant revision. Legal technique demands 'maintenance'.[140] The same applies when engaging with philosophical challenges such as Voegelin's *New Science of Politics*.

A puzzling feature of Kelsen's book on Voegelin is that it was published only posthumously.[141] Kelsen withdrew the manuscript from the publisher without explanation. One can only speculate as to whether he was dissatisfied with aspects of the argument (perhaps especially his hypothesis that all

139 Daniel A. Bell, *The China Model. Political Meritocracy and the Limits of Democracy* (Princeton, NJ: Princeton University Press, 2015); Tingyang Zhao, *All Under Heaven: The Tianxia System for a Possible World Order*, trans. Joseph E. Harroff (Berkeley, CA: University of California Press, 2019).

140 'Maintenance' has previously been singled out as missing in Heidegger's critique of technology.

141 Hans Kelsen, *A New Science of Politics: Hans Kelsen's Reply to Eric Voegelin's "New Science of Politics": A Contribution to the Critique of Ideology*, ed. Eckhart Arnold (Frankfurt am Main: Ontos, 2004).

religions require a concept of God) or whether he intended to situate the manuscript in a broader project. However, its unpublished – or, so to speak, spoken but not definitively written – character may itself reflect the nature of the criticism Kelsen aimed to deliver, and also point to the limits of his thinking.

While Kelsen followed Voegelin's intellectual trajectory closely, observing how his ideas adapted to both authoritarian and liberal contexts, he did not historically contextualise Voegelin's argument. His critique remained at a strictly conceptual level. Much like an extended review essay, Kelsen's analysis traces the steps of Voegelin's reasoning, beginning with his mischaracterisation of 'positivism', and proceeding to expose inconsistencies in terminology, questionable translations and unfounded historical associations. He objects in particular to Voegelin's theory of gnosis, arguing that it is an overly broad and insufficiently nuanced account of modernity that lacks real descriptive power.

Despite its detailed focus, Kelsen's critique remains one of the most rigorous and instructive responses to Voegelin, not because it treats Voegelin's work as a canonical statement within a political theory tradition, but because it assesses his claims independently and analytically. In the context of our search for models of post-foundational cosmopolitanism, three features of Kelsen's critique are especially relevant. First, it targets a comprehensive doctrine that seeks to explain a wide range of phenomena, from myths and symbols to discursive transformation. It is this kind of theory that Kelsen believes must be critically examined. From a *longue durée* perspective, Kelsen's effort can be read as continuing the task Kant assigns to philosophy in the age of perpetual peace: to serve as a censor of naïve enthusiasts.[142] Second, in methodological terms, Kelsen does not reject comprehensive doctrines in the abstract. Rather, he demonstrates in detail which specific claims are mistaken, unfounded or poorly reasoned. As with his critique of Carl Schmitt, Kelsen plays on the same intellectual field, always taking the risk of losing

[142] This is what Kant identifies as the eternal task of philosophy once dogmatic quarrels have subsided. See VNAEF, AA 8:421.

a move or even an argument. Third, for any comprehensive, materialist or ideology-critical account, international law is a particularly significant target. Like any legal system, it is a coercive structure embedded within existing power relations. Without that coercive capacity, law could not function effectively.

This strand of thinking is also evident in Voegelin, who equates the movement for peace, disarmament and world order with Gnosticism. He holds that:

> Gnostic dream assumptions about the nature of man, about a mysterious evolution of mankind toward peace and world order, about the possibility of establishing an international order in the abstract without relation to the structure of the field of existential forces, about armies being the cause of war and not the forces and constellations which build them and set them into motion, etc.[143]

As Voegelin had previously characterised the core problem of the Gnostic dream, he believed it relied on 'magic operations in the dream world, such as disapproval, moral condemnation, declarations of intention, resolutions, appeals to the opinion of mankind, branding of enemies as aggressors, outlawing of war, propaganda for world peace and world government, etc.'[144] It is clear that he is referring to a cosmopolitan mindset. At this point, Kelsen delivers his most explicit defence of cosmopolitanism, though not as a fundamental moral principle that everyone, or every 'reasonable' person, must endorse. Rather, he defends it as a principle of realpolitik, one that can be pursued without illusions about its difficulty, and with full awareness of the opposing forces it faces.

He notes that the democratic politicians and liberal intellectuals whom Voegelin ridicules as Gnostic dreamers 'do not believe in a predestined evolution of mankind, but try to bring about peace and world order, without having any illusions about the difficulties involved in such policy, because

143 Voegelin, *The New Science of Politics*, 172.

144 Kelsen, *A New Science of Politics*, 170.

they are fully aware of the forces operating against it'.[145] Moreover, Kelsen maintains that democratic politicians

> suggest disarmament or reduction of armament not because they are so stupid to assume that armies are 'the' cause of war, but because they know – what nobody can deny – that the existence of an army makes war possible and that the militaristic mentality, which is inevitably connected with the maintenance of armies is an additional motive for a policy which uses war as its instrument.[146]

Finally, Kelsen reveals that the term 'Gnostic', as Voegelin applies it to Western politics in general – and to the Democratic Party of the United States and liberal intellectuals in particular – is effectively a code word for communist propaganda. 'It means exactly the same as what is meant when on the lowest level of propaganda those who do not conform with one's own opinion are smeared as communists.'[147]

Kelsen's mode of critique might be seen as a guideline for how to engage in political theory. One might therefore ask why such a critique would remain suspended between the spoken and the written word. After all, Kelsen did not shy away from controversy and continued to publish actively in legal, political and social philosophy. However, he was also aware that the most revolutionary and radical philosophical projects were often grounded in an unwritten doctrine or expressed an immediate awareness of the limits of conceptual articulation. Here, we reach a limit of Kelsen's approach.

As a scholar, he maintained critical distance from mystical experiences, or, generally speaking, any form of transcendent philosophy. This does not mean that he denied such experiences occurred, or that they were widely shared, or even that they might point to something real. But he firmly believed they could not be formulated in scientific terms. For this reason, Voegelin's *New Science of Politics* appeared to Kelsen to be nothing new at all, but rather an old tactic:

145 Ibid., 107.
146 Ibid.
147 Ibid.

the pseudoscientific use of metaphysics and theology in the service of political power.[148] But what about the distinction itself? Even if it cannot be theorised, might it still be symbolised in another way? Kelsen remained silent on this point – as he did not dance.

148 Ibid., 13.

Coda
Hölderlin's Response

Faced with a scholarly book, Nietzsche did not ask about its value, but rather: does it dance?[1] Sappho's dance has sunk into oblivion, but we could hear her song – and maybe we have, through the genealogy, forced some ossified conditions to dance by singing their own melody back to them.[2] We will end with a fragment of a song, but one that contains, upon closer inspection, the entire reflection expounded in the genealogy. A century after Sappho, Pindar rhymed about the all-embracing law (*nomos*), rhymes taken up and translated more than two millennia later by Friedrich Hölderlin.[3]

Νόμος ὁ πάντων βασιλεὺς
θνατῶν τε καὶ ἀθανάτων
ἄγει δικαιῶν τὸ βιαιότατον
ὑπερτάτᾳ χειρί· τεκμαίρομαι

Das Gesetz,
Von allen der König, Sterblichen und
Unsterblichen; das führt eben

[1] Friedrich Nietzsche, *The Gay Science: With a Prelude in Rhymes and an Appendix of Songs*, trans. Walter Kaufmann (New York: Vintage Books, 1974), § 366.

[2] Karl Marx, *Critique of Hegel's Philosophy of Right*, trans. Annette Jolin and Joseph O'Malley (Cambridge: Cambridge University Press, 1970), 134.

[3] Pindar, Fragment 169a and Friedrich Hölderlin, *Sämtliche Werke und Briefe*, ed. Friedrich Beissner (Stuttgart: Kohlhammer, 1952), vol. 5, 285 and Scott Horton, 'Hölderlin on Pindar's Nomos', *Harper's Magazine*, 4 February 2008, 6 June 2025, https://harpers.org/2008/02/holderlin-on-pindars-nomos/.

Darum gewaltig
Das gerechteste Recht mit allerhöchster Hand.

The law is
The king of all, mortal and
Immortal; and thus it guides powerfully
The most just law with a hand from above.

Why should a poem, and why these lines, mark the end of the genealogy? At a first reading – and indeed in a first strand of interpretations and adaptations – the words sound anything but cosmopolitan-minded.[4] Carl Schmitt quotes Hölderlin's Pindar translation and an excerpt of Hölderlin's explanation in 1933 approvingly, bolstering his view that a true nomos is not a system of abstract norms but a concrete legal order based on an understanding of normal types.[5] He explains, in an explicitly political, National Socialist-minded essay, that it is an 'epistemological truth' that only those who belong existentially to the same 'race' can apprehend and adjudicate such types properly.[6] Schmitt bases his conclusion on the second part of Hölderlin's comment in his Pindar translation, which, in Schmitt's compressed account, reads as follows: 'Nomos, the law, is here discipline (*Zucht*), in so far as it is the form within which man encounters himself and God. It is the church and the law of the land and inherited rules that, more firmly than art, embody the living relations within which a people encounters itself and others in time.'[7]

Is Pindar's fragment and Hölderlin's appropriation a celebration of a totalitarian Führer state that is bound up with

[4] In the twentieth century, these lines were interpreted by Heidegger, Derrida and Agamben, among others. For a detailed hermeneutic analysis of this line of reception, see Thomas Schestag, *Parerga: Friedrich Hölderlin, Carl Schmitt, Franz Kafka, Platon, Friedrich Schleiermacher, Walter Benjamin, Jacques Derrida: Zur Literarischen Hermeneutik* (München: Klaus Boer, 1991).

[5] Carl Schmitt, *On the Three Types of Juristic Thought*, trans. Joseph W. Bendersky (Westport, CT: Praeger, 2004), 51.

[6] Carl Schmitt, *State, Movement, People: The Triadic Structure of the Political Unity* 1933, trans. Simona Draghici (Corvallis, OR: Plutarch, 2001), 51, [45].

[7] Schmitt, *On the Three Types*, 51.

eliminative antisemitism? Schmitt does not quote the crucial first part of Hölderlin's comment, which includes the lines: 'The human being, as a creature of reason, must differentiate between ... different worlds, because recognition is possible only through a process of juxtaposition.'[8] The crucial 'methodological' idea that explains Hölderlin's poetic thinking is confined in the expression 'recognition is possible only through a process of juxtaposition.'[9] It is precisely through the juxtaposition to an eliminative, totalitarian reading that a different meaning can be gleaned. Through some reflections that roam through Hölderlin's Pindar fragments, the relation to the present genealogy of cosmopolitan thought can be traced among the various layers.

So why end the genealogy not with a claim, a summary, but with poetry, and Hölderlin in particular? According to Heidegger, Hölderlin is a poet's poet as 'his poetry is sustained by his whole poetic mission: to make poems solely about the essence of poetry.'[10] This claim can be backed up by a more detailed, contextualised interpretation. Hölderlin's translation is part of a collection of nine Pindar fragments, one of the last pieces Hölderlin prepared for publication before his mental breakdown. In Hölderlin's rendering, each fragment has a title and is followed by a remark or interpretation so that the Pindar fragments, when taken together, are Hölderlin's last statement on poetry.[11] This contextualisation takes out some of the belligerent furore Schmitt tries to give them, as the fragment on the nomos is ostensibly related to very different ones. It follows, for instance, on from a short fragment celebrating the dancing dolphin.

[8] Horton, 'Hölderlin on Pindar's Nomos'.

[9] Ibid.

[10] Martin Heidegger, *Elucidations of Hölderlin's Poetry*, trans. Keith Hoeller (Amherst, NY: Humanity Books, 2000), 52; idem, *Erläuterungen zu Hölderlins Dichtung*, ed. Friedrich-Wilhelm von Herrmann (Frankfurt am Main: Vittorio Klostermann, 1981), 34.

[11] On the social and literary context see Michael Franz, *'... und anderes denk in anderer Zeit...' Hölderlins letzte Gedanken zu Recht und Politik in den Pindarfragmenten* (Stuttgart: J.B. Metzler, 2020).

Which in the waveless sea's deep of flutes
The song delightfully has moved.[12]

Hölderlin explains that it is 'the song of nature, fair weather for the Muses.' However, bringing up the context of Hölderlin's thinking about nomos is not meant as a refutation of Schmitt's reading. The strength of Hölderlin's poetry is that it is not a theory that aims to denounce some statements or interpretations, such as Schmitt's, as wrong or mistaken. Instead, for Hölderlin, in poetic thinking recognition is possible only through a process. It is not a Hegelian dialectic, as the aim is not absolute knowledge and as previous formations of thought are not merely temporarily true. Pindar is present in the translation, and thus the Orient, in which the free world is grounded, is brought into a living relationship with the Occident, and antiquity with the Hesperides (Hölderlin's notion of modernity).[13] These are the juxtapositions Hölderlin moulds as 'the immediate is just as impossible for the mortals as for the immortals.'[14]

We started the genealogy with an invocation of Sappho and later saw how proto-cosmopolitan thoughts were silenced by Plato through the invention of metaphysics and the narrative of myths, spectres that still haunted Kant. In Hölderlin we encounter a way of dealing with the past without having to 'deconstruct' the Western tradition in the first place.[15] But how is such an encounter possible without throwing out the philosophy and historical consciousness we reached with Kant in the first place, and what are the connections

12 Friedrich Hölderlin, *Poems and Fragments*, trans. Michael Hamburger (London: Anvil, 2004), 711; Hölderlin, *Sämtliche Werke*, vol. 5, 285.

13 This reading finds support in Thanos Zartaloudis's genealogy of nomos. Through a detailed textual reconstruction of Pindar's fragment and its Platonic reception, he argues that nomos does not denote supreme (sovereign) power but rather serves to mediate what is the highest or ground of knowledge, which he tentatively names 'cosmonomy'. See Zartaloudis, *The Birth of Nomos*, 246–54.

14 Horton, 'Hölderlin on Pindar's Nomos'; Hölderlin, *Sämtliche Werke*, 321.

15 The master narrative of the poststructuralist tradition usually singles out Fichte's seizure of subjectivity as the apogee of oblivion of being or difference but misses out that in Hölderlin (and Schelling), subjectivity depends on nature, the other of subjectivity.

to cosmopolitan thought? Hölderlin is not a 'lyrically naïve enthusiast' (*Schwärmer*) but gives a pointed explanation:

> The immediate is, taken strictly, impossible for the mortals to obtain, just as it is for the immortals. God must differentiate the different worlds according to his nature because heavenly goodness must for its own sake remain holy, and unmixed. The human being, as a creature of reason, must differentiate between these different worlds, because recognition is possible only through a process of juxtaposition. And for that reason, the immediate is just as impossible for the mortals as for the immortals.[16]

Thus, 'the highest', Hölderlin's title for the fragment (which is omitted by Schmitt and Horton's translation), is not the law, let alone a positive law given by a sovereign, but the reflection on the immediate, which neither mortals nor immortals can obtain. In Kant's terms: the noumenal world is unknowable. Hölderlin picks up Kant's idea of the noumenal world, whose *ratio cognoscendi* is the moral law. 'However, law is strict communicability. This is why it powerfully guides the most just law with the highest hand.'[17]

Since we have previously reconstructed the genesis of the categorical imperative, its imperfect realisation in the *Doctrine of Right*, and Kant's critique of historical religion through the idea of an ethical community, Hölderlin's brief allusion to the two disciplines of church and state (positive law and historical religion) is no surprise for Kantians. Here is Hölderlin's explanation again, to which Schmitt referred, now after the brief remembrance, in a different tone: 'Discipline, to the extent that it is the form in which man encounters himself and God, constitutes the laws and inherited regulations of the church and state.'[18]

However, if Hölderlin's prose is not proto-fascist, is it then merely a dense introduction to thoughts we have already encountered in Kant and maybe less visionary and even less poetic, as the following sentence suggests? '[T]hey [church,

16 Horton, 'Hölderlin on Pindar's Nomos'.
17 Ibid.
18 Ibid.

state, and inherited rules] powerfully guide the most just law with the highest hand, they grip the conditions of life which a people has and will encounter in the course of life more firmly than art.'[19]

Even though Hölderlin hardly outlived Kant (in full possession of his mind), he travelled further, both historically and politically. From his early days as a schoolboy he venerated the Oriental, pre-Socratic part of ancient civilisation as a genuine alternative to the established Platonic-Christian tradition. In his formative years he witnessed not only the French Revolution and the subsequent Terror but also its official end (declared by Napoleon in December 1799) and the reestablishment of a modern, post-revolutionary monarchy under Napoleon. In his homeland of Württemberg he was, together with his friend Hegel, involved in envisioning a mixed form of liberal government.

This wide-ranging and deeply felt spirit is expressed in the first of the Pindar fragments, 'Unfaithfulness of Wisdom',[20] where we hear:

> Join all cities
> Praising the present
> Good-willed,
> And think different in different times.

Hölderlin's genealogy of cosmopolitan thought is not a theory but the poetic practice of 'praising the present ... and think different in different times'. Unlike the biblical saying, 'To everything there is a season, / A time for every purpose under heaven' (Ecclesiastes 3:1), Hölderlin's expression about shifting alliances is not an adage but captures the art of prudence. Hölderlin explains: 'Prudence is the art of remaining faithful under different circumstances, knowledge the art of being sure in one's understanding in the midst of positive errors.'[21]

Right from the beginning, Hölderlin's genealogy also traces the tragedy of cosmopolitanism we have witnessed

[19] Ibid.

[20] Hölderlin, *Poems and Fragments*, 704; Hölderlin, *Sämtliche Werke und Briefe*, vol. 5, 281.

[21] Ibid.

and experienced. The first fragment is entitled 'Unfaithfulness of Wisdom', as no wise saying can save us from the maelstrom of intellectual and psychological collapse. Again, it is not far from Kant, who singled out the duty of truthfulness as – perhaps – the only wisdom he had ever produced,[22] the wisdom only the few, among them Franz Jägerstätter, retained while the intellectual, political and moral system around them crumbled. Let us hear Hölderlin's translation and the first sentence of his comment again.

> The law is
> The king of all, mortal and
> Immortal; and thus it guides powerfully
> The most just law with a hand from above
>
> 'King' means in this case the superlative, it is but a sign for the highest stage of recognition, not for the highest power.

Hölderlin speaks of discipline, which constitutes the laws and inherited regulations of church and state. We have encountered it as 'legal discipline' in the state (or, as Kant would say, condition of public law as such, comprising state, international and cosmopolitan law) and intellectual discipline, when dissecting the metaphysical temptations of saying more than one can prove, either in terms of positive religion (censored by Kant) or foundationalist philosophy (censored by Kelsen).

Yet it can be the form in which man encounters himself and God if the law – and the fragment – is not taken as a solitary centre but bends back to reflect its condition in nature and a cosmopolitan truthfulness. The poetic practice is not a firm discipline like the law, but it can celebrate its reflections, like in Hölderlin's *Celebration of Peace*.

As an introduction to this poem, he writes: 'On a fine day – they should consider – almost every mode of song makes itself heard; and Nature, whence it originates, also receives it again. The author intends to offer the public an entire

[22] Cf. Kant, VNAEF 8: 422.

collection of such pieces, and this one should be regarded as a kind of sample.'[23] Let us end with a sample of this sample:

> Viel hat von Morgen an,
> Seit ein Gespräch wir sind und hören voneinander,
> Erfahren der Mensch; bald sind wir aber Gesang.
>
> Much, from the morning onwards,
> Since we have been a discourse and have heard from one
>   another,
> Has human kind learnt; but soon we shall be song.

[23] Friedrich Hölderlin, *Hyperion and Selected Poems*, ed. Eric L. Santner, trans. Michael Hamburger (New York: Continuum, 1990), 234–35.

Postscript

The protests at the United States Capitol on 6 January 2021 were not just riots but a genuine political act, opening up the possibility for a coup d'état in an established Western democracy. Since then, we have become accustomed to the unsettling fact that all forms of political life once thought confined to the musings of ancient authors or to the distant past are yet again on the table. As all ground-breaking political acts dare to do something unprecedented, we can picture dystopian outcomes only through fiction, as a way of grasping the complexity of reality. However, the images of masked and heavily armed protesters occupying the US Capitol will remain in the collective consciousness and confirm the perception that liberalism – with cosmopolitanism as its spearhead – is in retreat. It is as if we were allowed a glimpse of the grotesque mythical masks usually hidden beneath well-fitted suits.

The populist, authoritarian assault on its foundations is not the only danger liberalism has to face today. It is also under attack from the left. The 'new orthodoxy' or 'successor ideology' to liberalism sees America as, in its essence, not about freedom but oppression. In a sweeping condemnation, it sees liberalism's core values and institutions such as individual liberty, religious freedom, limited government and the equality of all human beings as nothing but an ideological veil to cover and justify the enslavement of human beings under the fiction of race. Due to the double attack from the left and the right in the midst of pressing global problems, many commentators have diagnosed a global 'Weimar Moment'. The ongoing wars in Ukraine and the Middle East, with conflicts between the great powers looming in the background, are in this perspective only one more step towards an abyss.

A genealogy of cosmopolitan thought does not attempt to suggest solutions to the polymorphic crises. Instead, it seeks, like in psychoanalytic therapy, the origin of the conflict. The imaginary meeting in Vienna's City Park, where Kelsen could have met fellow colleagues, intellectuals and artists (to name but a few: Sigmund Freud, Oskar Kokoschka, Alma Mahler, Arnold Schoenberg, Ludwig von Mises and Ludwig Wittgenstein but also Adolf Hitler, Joseph Stalin and Leon Trotsky) might still incite new avenues for the future but also call for a more thorough and comparative study of the past. In other words, the 'circumstances of modernity', in all its splendour and the abysses that later resonated across the entire globe, were assembled in a specific historical moment.

Instead of recapitulating the argument, some vertices might suffice to remind the reader of their journey. The prelude resumed Sappho's calling, which was answered millennia later by Hölderlin in an attempt to mediate the Orient and Occident, the Ancients and the Moderns, kineo (dance-) centrism and logocentrism. For the more sober-minded: Plato's challenge to cosmopolitanism, culminating in Heidegger, is still virulent, though it can be met through 'deep play': a more contextualised reading of Kant and Kelsen.

The reason we had to embark on this journey mirrors, on a philosophical level, the political crisis just mentioned. Heidegger's thinking continues to influence – throughout myriad transformations in French philosophy – identity and postcolonial politics. At the same time, he is a favourite point of reference among pretentious nationalistic theoreticians and, in yet another volte, *en vogue* among politically disillusioned Chinese officials.

At the genealogy level, however, Heidegger's challenge could be countered. At each turning point we have passed through in our contextualised reading of Plato and Kant, we have encountered historically situated alternatives. Even Heidegger's existentialist reinterpretation of the categorical imperative could be given a different twist by invoking the example of Franz Jägerstätter. Moreover, the law as the structure of modernity turned out to be, in Kelsen's rendering, a different answer to the circumstances of modernity.

At no point have we encountered a high road to contemporary cosmopolitanism but were instead captured in ever-more-fundamental ways of questioning ourselves. Only after we passed through the night of the twentieth century and gave up the last stronghold of theoretical self-certainty by reflecting on how scholarship can be drawn into the vertigo as well did we discover two models of post-foundational cosmopolitan thought. My hope is that the attentive reader then needs no more 'ladder' or 'normative guidance' but can simply scramble on.

Bibliography

I. Translations Used

I have made use of the following translations; minor modifications are my own.

Kant

Anthropology, History, and Education. Edited by Günter Zöller and Robert B. Louden. Translated by Mary Gregor. Cambridge: Cambridge University Press, 2007.

Correspondence. Edited and translated by Arnulf Zweig. Cambridge: Cambridge University Press, 1999.

Critique of the Power of Judgment. Edited and translated by Paul Guyer and Eric Matthews. Cambridge: Cambridge University Press, 2000.

Critique of Pure Reason. Edited and translated by Paul Guyer and Allen W. Wood. Cambridge: Cambridge University Press, 1998.

The Metaphysics of Morals. Edited and translated by Mary Gregor. Cambridge: Cambridge University Press, 1996.

Political Writings. 2nd ed. Edited by Hans Reiss. Translated by H. B. Nisbet. Cambridge: Cambridge University Press, 1991.

Practical Philosophy. Edited and translated by Mary J. Gregor. Cambridge: Cambridge University Press, 1996.

Religion and Rational Theology. Edited and translated by Allen W. Wood and George di Giovanni. Cambridge: Cambridge University Press, 1996.

Theoretical Philosophy, 1755–1770. Edited and translated by David Walford and Ralf Meerbote. Cambridge: Cambridge University Press, 1992.

Theoretical Philosophy after 1781. Edited by Henry Allison and Peter Heath. Translated by Gary Hatfield et al. Cambridge: Cambridge University Press, 2002.

Classical Works

Athenaeus. *The Deipnosophists (The Learned Banqueters)*. Edited and translated by S. Douglas Olson. Cambridge, MA: Harvard University Press, 2006.

Diogenes Laertius. *Vitae philosophorum*, vol. 1. Edited by Miroslav Marcovich. Stuttgart: Teubner, 1999–2002.

Herodotus. *Histories*. Translated by A. D. Godley. Loeb Classical Library. Cambridge, MA: Harvard University Press, 1926.

Isocrates. *Isocrates*. Edited and translated by George Norlin. Loeb Classical Library. 2 vols. Cambridge, MA: Harvard University Press, 1928.

Plato. *Epistles*. Translated by R. G. Bury. Loeb Classical Library 7. Cambridge, MA: Harvard University Press, 1929.

Plato. *Laws*. Translated by R. G. Bury. Loeb Classical Library. Cambridge, MA, 1926.

Plato. *Republic*. 2nd ed. Translated by Allan Bloom, with notes and an interpretive essay. New York: Basic Books, 1991.

Sappho. *If Not, Winter: Fragments of Sappho*. Translated by Anne Carson. New York: Vintage Books, 2002.

Thucydides. *History of the Peloponnesian War*. Translated by Rex Warner. London: Penguin Books, 1954.

Xenophon. *Hellenica, Books I–V*. Translated by Carleton L. Brownson. Loeb Classical Library 88. Cambridge, MA: Harvard University Press, 1918.

Xenophon. *Memorabilia*. Translated by E. C. Marchant. Loeb Classical Library 168. Cambridge, MA: Harvard University Press, 1923.

II. Secondary Literature

Adam, Rudolf. 'Über die Echtheit der platonischen Briefe'. *Wissenschaftliche Beilage zum Jahresbericht des Falk-Realgymnasiums zu Berlin* 110 (1906): 3–29.

Adorno, Theodor W., Else Frenkel-Brunswik, Daniel J. Levinson and R. Nevitt Sanford. *The Authoritarian Personality*. New York: Harper, 1950.

Allison, Henry E. *Kant's Theory of Freedom.* Cambridge: Cambridge University Press, 1990.

Andrea, Alfred J. and James H. Overfield, eds. *The Human Record: Sources of Global History, Vol. 2: Since 1500.* Boston: Cengage Learning, 2011.

Appiah, Kwame Anthony. *Cosmopolitanism: Ethics in a World of Strangers.* London: Allen Lane, 2006.

Arendt, Hannah. *Ich will verstehen. Selbstauskünfte zu Leben und Werk.* Edited by Ursula Ludz. München: Piper, 1996.

Assmann, Jan. *Cultural Memory and Early Civilization: Writing, Remembrance, and Political Imagination.* Cambridge: Cambridge University Press, 2011.

Badian, Ernst. 'Alexander the Great and the Unity of Mankind'. *Historia* 7, no. 4 (1958): 425–44.

Balot, Ryan K., *Greek Political Thought.* Malden, MA: Wiley-Blackwell, 2006.

Balot, Ryan K., ed. *A Companion to Greek and Roman Political Thought.* Malden, MA: Wiley-Blackwell, 2009.

Barjonet, Aurélie and Liran Razinsky, eds. *Writing the Holocaust Today: Critical Perspectives on Jonathan Littell's 'The Kindly Ones'.* Amsterdam: Rodopi, 2012.

Barry, Brian. 'Equality'. In *Encyclopedia of Ethics.* Edited by Lawrence C. Becker and Charlotte B. Becker, 324–27. New York: Garland, 1992.

Beck, Hans. *Polis und Koinon: Untersuchungen zur Geschichte und Struktur der griechischen Bundesstaaten im 4. Jahrhundert v. Chr.* Stuttgart: Franz Steiner, 1997.

Beck, Hans. *Polis and Koinon: Federalism and the Ancient Greek City-State.* Cambridge: Cambridge University Press, 2020.

Beck, Hans and John Buckler, eds. *Central Greece and the Politics of Power in the Fourth Century BC.* Cambridge: Cambridge University Press, 2008.

Beck, Lewis White. *A Commentary on Kant's Critique of Practical Reason.* Chicago: University of Chicago Press, 1960.

Bell, Daniel A. *The China Model: Political Meritocracy and the Limits of Democracy.* Princeton, NJ: Princeton University Press, 2015.

Bellah, Robert N. and Hans Joas, eds. *The Axial Age and Its Consequences.* Cambridge, MA: Harvard University Press, 2012.

Benjamin, Walter. *Illuminations*. Edited by Hannah Arendt. Translated by Harry Zohn. New York: Schocken Books, 1968.
Berlin, Isaiah. 'Equality'. In *Concepts and Categories*. Edited by Henry Hardy, 102–18. London: Hogarth Press, 1978.
Berman, Paul Schiff. 'Global Legal Pluralism'. *Southern California Law Review* 80, no. 6 (2007): 1155–237.
Besson, Samantha. 'Sovereignty'. In *Max Planck Encyclopedia of Public International Law*. Edited by Rüdiger Wolfrum (online edn).
Bierl, Anton. 'Ich aber (sage), das Schönste ist, was einer liebt!' Eine pragmatische Deutung von Sappho Fr. 16 LP/V'. *Quaderni Urbinati di Cultura Classica* 74, no. 2 (2003): 91–124.
Blau, Adrian, ed. *Meaning and Understanding in the History of Ideas and Beyond. Proceedings of the British Academy*. Liverpool: Liverpool University Press, 2026.
Bloom, Allan. 'Response to Hall'. *Political Theory* 5, no. 3 (1977): 315–30.
Blumenberg, Hans. *Schiffbruch mit Zuschauer: Paradigma einer Daseinsmetapher*. Frankfurt am Main: Suhrkamp, 1979.
Blumenberg, Hans. *Höhlenausgänge*. Frankfurt am Main: Suhrkamp, 1989.
Bobonich, Christopher, ed. *Plato's Laws: A Critical Guide*. Cambridge: Cambridge University Press, 2010.
Borowski, Ludwig Ernst. *Darstellung des Lebens und Charakters Immanuel Kants*. Königsberg: Friedrich Nicolovius, 1804.
Brandom, Robert. *Tales of the Mighty Dead*. Cambridge, MA: Harvard University Press, 2002.
Brandt, Reinhard. 'Das Erlaubnisgesetz, oder Vernunft und Geschichte in Kants Rechtslehre'. In *Rechtsphilosophie der Aufklärung: Symposium Wolfenbüttel 1981*. Edited by Reinhard Brandt, 233–85. Berlin: Walter de Gruyter, 1982.
Brandt, Reinhard. 'Ausgewählte Probleme der Kantischen Anthropologie'. In *Der ganze Mensch: Anthropologie und Literatur im 18. Jahrhundert. DFG-Symposion 1992*. Edited by Hans-Jürgen Schings, 14–32. Stuttgart: J. B. Metzler, 1994.
Brecht, Arnold. *Preußen contra Reich vor dem Staatsgerichtshof*. Berlin: J. H. W. Dietz, 1933.
Brock, Gillian. *Cosmopolitanism versus Non-Cosmopolitanism: Critiques, Defenses, Reconceptualizations*. Oxford: Oxford University Press, 2013.

Brock, Gillian. 'Global Justice'. In *The Stanford Encyclopedia of Philosophy* (Spring 2017 edition). Edited by Edward N. Zalta. Accessed 20 June 2025. https://plato.stanford.edu/archives/spr2017/entries/justice-global.

Brown, Eric. 'Die Erfindung kosmopolitaner Politik durch die Stoiker'. In *Kosmopolitanismus: Zur Geschichte und Zukunft eines umstrittenen Ideals*. Edited by Matthias Lutz-Bachmann, Andreas Niederberger and Philipp Schink, 9–24. Weilerswist: Velbrück, 2010.

Brown, Garrett Wallace and David Held, eds. *The Cosmopolitanism Reader*. Cambridge: Polity Press, 2010.

Brown, Stuart M. 'Has Kant a Philosophy of Law?' *The Philosophical Review* 71, no. 1 (1962): 33–48.

Browning, Christopher R. *Ordinary Men: Reserve Police Battalion 101 and the Final Solution in Poland*. London: Penguin, 1998.

Buchanan, Allen. 'Equality and Human Rights'. *Philosophy, Politics, and Economics* 4, no. 1 (2005): 69–90.

Buchanan, Allen. *The Heart of Human Rights*. New York: Oxford University Press, 2014.

Burckhardt, Jacob. *Griechische Kulturgeschichte*, vol. 1. Edited by Felix Stähelin. Stuttgart: Deutsche Verlags-Anstalt, 1930.

Burnyeat, Myles and Michael Frede, eds. *The Pseudo-Platonic Seventh Letter*. Oxford: Oxford University Press, 2015.

Byrd, B. Sharon and Joachim Hruschka. *Kant's Doctrine of Right: A Commentary*. Cambridge: Cambridge University Press, 2010.

Calame, Claude. 'Sappho's Group: An Initiation into Womanhood'. In *Reading Sappho: Contemporary Approaches*. Edited by Ellen Greene, 113–24. Berkeley, CA: University of California Press, 1996.

Caney, Simon. *Justice Beyond Borders: A Global Political Theory*. Oxford: Oxford University Press, 2005.

Carens, Joseph. 'Aliens and Citizens: The Case for Open Borders'. *The Review of Politics* 49, no. 2 (1987): 251–73.

Carsten, Francis Ludwig. *The Origins of Prussia*. Oxford: Clarendon Press, 1968.

Carsten, Francis Ludwig. *Essays in German History*. London: Hambledon, 1985.

Cavallar, Georg. *Pax Kantiana: Systematisch-historische Untersuchung des Entwurfs 'Zum ewigen Frieden' (1795) von Immanuel Kant*. Wien: Böhlau, 1992.

Cavallar, Georg. *The Rights of Strangers: Theories of International Hospitality, the Global Community and Political Justice since Vitoria.* Aldershot: Ashgate, 2002.

Cavallar, Georg. 'Kant's Embedded Cosmopolitanism'. *History of Political Thought* 31, no. 3 (2010): 494–515.

Chakrabarty, Dipesh. *Provincializing Europe: Postcolonial Thought and Historical Difference.* Princeton, NJ: Princeton University Press, 2000.

Clark, Christopher M. *Iron Kingdom: The Rise and Downfall of Prussia, 1600–1947.* Cambridge, MA: Harvard University Press, 2006.

Collingwood, R. G. *An Autobiography.* Oxford: Oxford University Press, 1939.

Cover, Robert M. 'The Supreme Court, 1982 Term – Foreword: Nomos and Narrative'. *Harvard Law Review* 97, no. 4 (1983): 4–68.

von Daniels, Detlef. *The Concept of Law from a Transnational Perspective.* Aldershot: Ashgate, 2010.

von Daniels, Detlef. 'How Plato Overcame the Cosmopolitans'. *History of Political Thought* 35, no. 4 (2014): 595–631.

von Daniels, Detlef. 'Normativity and the Sources of International Law'. In *The Oxford Handbook on the Sources of International Law.* Edited by Samantha Besson and Jean d'Aspremont, 661–79. Oxford: Oxford University Press, 2017.

von Daniels, Detlef. 'Realism, Power-Loops, and Re-Entry: An Imaginary Conversation with Glen Newey over the Gaps of Time and Traditions'. *Biblioteca della libertà* 56, nos. 225–26 (2019): 177–92.

von Daniels, Detlef. 'Legal Pluralism and the Problem of Evil'. In *The Oxford Handbook of Legal Pluralism.* Edited by Paul Schiff Berman, 383–403. Oxford: Oxford University Press, 2020.

von Daniels, Detlef. 'A Youthful Tone in Philosophy? On Schlosser's Critique of Kant'. In *The Court of Reason: Proceedings of the 13th International Kant Congress.* Edited by Camilla Serck-Hanssen and Beatrix Himmelmann, 1727–36. Berlin and Boston: De Gruyter, 2021.

Deneen, Patrick J. *Regime Change: Toward a Postliberal Future.* New York: Sentinel, 2023.

Derrida, Jacques. *Of Grammatology.* Translated by Gayatri Chakravorty Spivak. Baltimore: Johns Hopkins University Press, 1976.

Derrida, Jacques. *Politiques de l'amitié*. Paris: Éditions Galilée, 1994.

Derrida, Jacques. *Politics of Friendship*. Translated by George Collins. London: Verso, 1997.

Derrida, Jacques. 'The Last of the Rogue States: The "Democracy to Come"', Opening in Two Turns'. *South Atlantic Quarterly* 103, nos. 2–3 (2004): 323–41.

Dewey, John. *German Philosophy and Politics*. New York: G. P. Putnam's Sons, 1915.

Dillery, John. *Xenophon and the History of His Times*. London: Routledge, 1995.

Doyle, Michael W. 'Kant, Liberal Legacies and Foreign Affairs'. *Philosophy and Public Affairs* 12, nos. 3–4 (1983): 205–35 and 323–53.

Due, Bodil. *Isocrates: His Educational and Political Ideal*. Copenhagen: Museum Tusculanum Press, 1989.

Dugin, Alexander. *The Theory of a Multipolar World Order*. London: Arktos, 2021.

Dworkin, Ronald. 'Comment on Narveson: In Defense of Equality'. *Social Philosophy and Policy* 1, no. 1 (Autumn 1983): 25–40.

Dworkin, Ronald. *Law's Empire*. Cambridge, MA: Harvard University Press, 1986.

Dworkin, Ronald. *Justice for Hedgehogs*. Cambridge, MA: Harvard University Press, 2011.

Ebbinghaus, Julius. 'Das Kantische System der Rechte des Menschen und Bürgers in seiner geschichtlichen und aktuellen Bedeutung'. In *Gesammelte Aufsätze, Vorträge und Reden*, 161–93. Darmstadt: Wissenschaftliche Buchgesellschaft, 1968.

Eberl, Oliver. 'Kant on Race and Barbarism: Towards a More Complex View on Racism and Anti-Colonialism in Kant'. *Kantian Review* 24, no. 3 (2019): 385–413.

Edelstein, Ludwig. *Plato's Seventh Letter*. Leiden: Brill, 1966.

Ehrlich, Eugen. *The National Problems in Austria*. The Hague: Martinus Nijhoff, 1917.

Ehrlich, Eugen. *Fundamental Principles of the Sociology of Law*. Translated by Walter L. Moll. Cambridge, MA: Harvard University Press, 1936.

Ehrlich, Eugen. 'Das lebende Recht der Völker der

Bukowina'. In *Recht und Leben: Gesammelte Schriften zur Rechtstatsachenforschung und zur Freirechtslehre*. Edited by Manfred Rehbinder, 43–64. Berlin: Duncker & Humblot, 1967.

Ehrlich, Eugen. 'Bismarck und der Weltkrieg'. In *Politische Schriften*. Edited by Manfred Rehbinder, 105–20. Berlin: Duncker & Humblot, 2007.

Ehrlich, Eugen. 'Das Ende eines großen Reiches'. In *Politische Schriften*. Edited by Manfred Rehbinder, 19–80. Berlin: Duncker & Humblot, 2007.

Ehrlich, Eugen. 'Die Aufgaben der Sozialpolitik im österreichischen Osten (Juden- und Bauernfrage)'. In *Politische Schriften*. Edited by Manfred Rehbinder, 131–52. Berlin: Duncker & Humblot, 2007.

Ehrlich, Eugen. 'Von der Zukunft des Völkerbundes'. In *Politische Schriften*. Edited by Manfred Rehbinder, 183–90. Berlin: Duncker & Humblot, 2007.

Ehs, Tamara, ed. *Hans Kelsen und die Europäische Union*. Baden-Baden: Nomos, 2008.

Eppinger, Monica. 'Governing in the Vernacular: Eugen Ehrlich and Late Habsburg Ethnography'. In *Living Law: Reconsidering Eugen Ehrlich*. Edited by Marc Hertogh, 21–47. Oxford: Hart, 2009.

Fehér, István. 'Heidegger und Kant – Heidegger und die Demokratie'. In *Europa und die Philosophie*. Edited by Hans-Helmuth Gander, 105–28. Frankfurt am Main: Vittorio Klostermann, 1993.

Fillafer, Franz Leander. 'Imperial Diversity, Fractured Sovereignty, and Legal Universals: Hans Kelsen and Eugen Ehrlich in Their Habsburg Context'. *Modern Intellectual History* 19, no. 2 (2022): 421–43.

Fine, Sarah and Lea Ypi, eds. *Migration in Political Theory: The Ethics of Movement and Membership*. Oxford: Oxford University Press, 2016.

Finley, Moses I. 'Athenian Demagogues'. In *Studies in Ancient Society*. Edited by Moses I. Finley, 9–35. London: Routledge, 1974.

Finnis, John. *Natural Law and Natural Rights*. Oxford: Oxford University Press, 1980.

Flikschuh, Katrin. *Kant and Modern Political Philosophy*. Cambridge: Cambridge University Press, 2000.

Flikschuh, Katrin. 'Kant's Sovereignty Dilemma: A Contemporary Analysis'. *Journal of Political Philosophy* 18, no. 4 (2010): 469–93.

Flikschuh, Katrin and Lea Ypi, eds. *Kant and Colonialism: Historical and Critical Perspectives.* Oxford: Oxford University Press, 2014.

Forrester, Katrina. *In the Shadow of Justice: Postwar Liberalism and the Remaking of Political Philosophy.* Princeton, NJ: Princeton University Press, 2019.

Förster, Eckart. *The Twenty-Five Years of Philosophy: A Systematic Reconstruction.* Translated by Brady Bowman. Cambridge, MA: Harvard University Press, 2012.

Foucault, Michel. *Introduction to Kant's Anthropology.* Edited by Roberto Nigro. Translated by Roberto Nigro and Kate Briggs. Cambridge, MA: MIT Press, 2007.

Fraenkel, Hermann. *Early Greek Poetry and Philosophy: A History of Greek Epic, Lyric, and Prose to the Middle of the Fifth Century.* Translated by Moses Hadas and James Willis. Oxford: Blackwell, 1975.

Franz, Michael. *... und anderes Denk in anderer Zeit: Hölderlins letzte Gedanken zu Recht und Politik in den Pindarfragmenten.* Stuttgart: J. B. Metzler, 2020.

Freud, Sigmund. *Civilization, Society and Religion.* Translated by Albert Dickson. Harmondsworth: Penguin, 1985.

Freud, Sigmund. *Jokes and Their Relation to the Unconscious.* Translated by James Strachey. London: Routledge & Kegan Paul, 1960.

Friedensburg, Walter, ed. *Kurmärkische Ständeakten aus der Regierungszeit Kurfürst Joachims II,* vol. 1. München: Duncker & Humblot, 1913.

Fugate, Courtney D. 'On a Supposed Solution to the Reinhold/Sidgwick Problem in Kant's Metaphysics of Morals'. *European Journal of Philosophy* 23, no. 3 (2015): 349–73.

Fuks, Alexander. 'Isocrates and the Social-Economic Situation in Greece'. *Ancient Society* 3 (1972): 17–44.

Fukuyama, Francis. 'The End of History?' *The National Interest*, no. 16 (Summer 1989): 3–18.

Fukuyama, Francis. *The End of History and the Last Man.* New York: Free Press, 1992.

Fukuyama, Francis. 'Against Identity Politics: The New

Tribalism and the Crisis of Democracy'. *Foreign Affairs* 97, no. 5 (2018): 90–115.

Fukuyama, Francis. *Liberalism and Its Discontents.* London: Profile Books, 2022.

Gadamer, Hans-Georg. *Truth and Method.* 2nd ed. Translated by Joel Weinsheimer and Donald G. Marshall. New York: Continuum, 1997.

Garve, Christian and Johann Georg Heinrich Feder. 'Critik der reinen Vernunft. Von Immanuel Kant (Review)'. *Göttingische Anzeigen von gelehrten Sachen* (1782), Zugabe, vol. 1: 40–48.

Gause, Fritz. *Die Geschichte der Stadt Königsberg in Preußen,* 3 vols. Köln: Böhlau, 1965–71.

Geismann, Georg. 'Nachlese zum Jahr des "Ewigen Friedens"'. *Logos* 29, no. 3 (1996): 317–45.

Geismann, Georg. 'World Peace: Rational Idea and Reality: On the Principles of Kant's Political Philosophy'. In *Kant: Analysen – Probleme – Kritik*, vol. 2. Edited by Hariolf Oberer, 265–319. Würzburg: Königshausen & Neumann, 1996.

von Gierke, Otto. *The German Law of Fellowship.* Edited by Anthony Black. Translated by Mary Fischer. Cambridge: Cambridge University Press, 1990.

Gigante, Marcello. *Nomos basileus.* New York: Arno, 1979.

Glendon, Mary Ann. *A World Made New: Eleanor Roosevelt and the Universal Declaration of Human Rights.* New York: Random House, 2002.

von Goethe, Johann Wolfgang. *Truth and Poetry: From My Own Life.* Translated by John Oxenford. London: George Bell & Sons, 1884.

Goody, Jack. *The Logic of Writing and the Organization of Society.* Cambridge: Cambridge University Press, 1986.

Goody, Jack and Ian Watt. 'The Consequences of Literacy'. *Comparative Studies in Society and History* 5, no. 3 (1963): 304–45.

Gottlieb, Michah. *Faith and Freedom: Moses Mendelssohn's Theological-Political Thought.* Oxford: Oxford University Press, 2011.

Graeber, David. *Debt: The First 5,000 Years.* Brooklyn, NY: Melville House, 2011.

Graeser, Andreas. *Philosophische Erkenntnis und begriffliche Darstellung: Bemerkungen zum erkenntnistheoretischen Exkurs des VII. Briefs*. Sitzungsberichte der Mainzer Akademie der Wissenschaften und der Literatur. Stuttgart: Franz Steiner, 1989.

Gragl, Paul. *Legal Monism: Law, Philosophy, and Politics*. Oxford: Oxford University Press, 2018.

Gray, Vivienne J. *Xenophon's Mirror of Princes: Reading the Reflections*. Oxford: Oxford University Press, 2011.

Great Soviet Encyclopedia. vol. 13. Translation of the Third Edition. New York: Macmillan, 1973.

Grimm, Jacob and Wilhelm Grimm. 'Willkür'. In *Grimms Deutsches Wörterbuch*. Edited by Jacob Grimm and Wilhelm Grimm. Stuttgart: S. Hirzel, 1854–1971.

Guthrie, W. K. C. *The Sophists: A History of Greek Philosophy*, vol. 1. Cambridge: Cambridge University Press, 1969.

Guyer, Paul. *Kant on Freedom, Law, and Happiness*. Cambridge: Cambridge University Press, 2000.

Guyer, Paul. 'Kant's Deductions of the Principles of Right'. *Kantian Review* 10 (2005): 118–46.

Haasis, Hellmut G. *Gebt der Freiheit Flügel: Die Zeit der deutschen Jakobiner 1789–1805*. Reinbek bei Hamburg: Rowohlt, 1988.

Habermas, Jürgen. 'Mit Heidegger gegen Heidegger denken: Zur Veröffentlichung von Vorlesungen aus dem Jahr 1935'. In *Philosophisch-politische Profile*. Frankfurt am Main: Suhrkamp, 1971.

Habermas, Jürgen. *The Philosophical Discourse of Modernity: Twelve Lectures*. Translated by Frederick G. Lawrence. Cambridge, MA: MIT Press, 1987.

Habermas, Jürgen. *The Structural Transformation of the Public Sphere: An Inquiry into a Category of Bourgeois Society*. Translated by Thomas Burger and Frederick Lawrence. Cambridge: Polity Press, 1989.

Habermas, Jürgen. 'Work and Weltanschauung: The Heidegger Controversy from a German Perspective'. *Critical Inquiry* 15, no. 2 (1989): 431–56.

Habermas, Jürgen. *The Inclusion of the Other: Studies in Political Theory*. Translated by Ciaran Cronin and Pablo De Greiff. Cambridge, MA: MIT Press, 1999.

Hansen, Frank-Peter. *Das älteste Systemprogramm des deutschen Idealismus: Rezeptionsgeschichte und Interpretation*. Berlin: Walter de Gruyter, 1989.

Hansen, Mogens H. 'Solonian Democracy in Fourth-Century Athens'. *Classica et Mediaevalia* 40 (1989): 71–99.

Hansen, Mogens H. *The Athenian Democracy in the Age of Demosthenes: Structure, Principles, and Ideology*. Norman, OK: University of Oklahoma Press, 1991.

Hansen, Mogens H. 'The Autonomous City-State: Ancient Fact or Modern Fiction?' In *Studies in the Ancient Greek Polis*. Edited by Mogens H. Hansen and Kurt A. Raaflaub, 21–43. Stuttgart: Franz Steiner, 1995.

Hart, H. L. A. *The Concept of Law*. 2nd ed. Oxford: Clarendon Press, 1994.

Hausleitner, Mariana. *Die Rumänisierung der Bukowina. Die Durchsetzung des nationalstaatlichen Anspruchs Grossrumäniens 1918–1944*. München: Oldenbourg, 2001.

Havelock, Eric A. *The Literate Revolution in Greece and Its Cultural Consequences*. Princeton, NJ: Princeton University Press, 1982.

Hegel, Georg W. F. *Philosophy of Nature (Part Two of Hegel's Encyclopaedia of the Philosophical Sciences)*. Translated by Arnold V. Miller. Oxford: Clarendon Press, 1970.

Hegel, Georg W. F. *Vorlesungen über die Geschichte der Philosophie*. Collected Works, vol. 18. Frankfurt am Main: Suhrkamp, 1971.

Heidegger, Martin. *Sein und Zeit*. Edited by Friedrich-Wilhelm von Herrmann. Frankfurt am Main: Vittorio Klostermann, 1977 (1st ed. 1927).

Heidegger, Martin. *Being and Time*. Translated by John MacQuarrie and Edward Robinson. Oxford: Blackwell, 1962.

Heidegger, Martin. 'Brief über den Humanismus'. In *Wegmarken*. Edited by Friedrich-Wilhelm von Herrmann, 313–64. Frankfurt am Main: Vittorio Klostermann, 1976.

Heidegger, Martin. 'Science and Reflection'. In *The Question Concerning Technology and Other Essays*. Translated by William Lovitt. New York: Harper & Row, 1977.

Heidegger, Martin. *Erläuterungen zu Hölderlins Dichtung*. Edited by Friedrich-Wilhelm von Herrmann. Frankfurt am Main: Vittorio Klostermann, 1981.

Heidegger, Martin. *Vom Wesen der menschlichen Freiheit. Einleitung in die Philosophie*. Freiburger Vorlesung Sommersemester 1930. Edited by Hartmut Tietjen. Frankfurt am Main: Vittorio Klostermann, 1982.

Heidegger, Martin. *Einführung in die Metaphysik.* Freiburger Vorlesung Sommersemester 1935. Edited by Petra Jaeger. Frankfurt am Main: Vittorio Klostermann, 1983.

Heidegger, Martin. *Kant and the Problem of Metaphysics.* 5th ed. Translated by James S. Churchill. Bloomington: Indiana University Press, 1990.

Heidegger, Martin. *Kant und das Problem der Metaphysik.* Edited by Friedrich-Wilhelm von Herrmann. Frankfurt am Main: Vittorio Klostermann, 1991 (1st ed. 1929).

Heidegger, Martin. 'The Self-Assertion of the German University'. In *The Heidegger Controversy: A Critical Reader.* Edited by Richard Wolin, 29–39. Cambridge, MA: MIT Press, 1993.

Heidegger, Martin. 'Letter on Humanism'. In *Pathmarks.* Edited by William McNeill. Translated by Frank A. Capuzzi, 239–76. Cambridge: Cambridge University Press, 1998.

Heidegger, Martin. 'Die Selbstbehauptung der deutschen Universität'. In *Reden und andere Zeugnisse eines Lebensweges 1910–1976.* Edited by Hermann Heidegger, 107–17. Frankfurt am Main: Vittorio Klostermann, 2000.

Heidegger, Martin. *Elucidations of Hölderlin's Poetry.* Translated by Keith Hoeller. Amherst, NY: Humanity Books, 2000.

Heidegger, Martin. *Introduction to Metaphysics.* Translated by Gregory Fried and Richard Polt. New Haven, CT: Yale University Press, 2000.

Heidegger, Martin. 'Wissenschaft und Besinnung'. In *Vorträge und Aufsätze 1936–1953.* Edited by Friedrich-Wilhelm von Herrmann, 37–66. Frankfurt am Main: Vittorio Klostermann, 2000.

Heidegger, Martin. *The Essence of Human Freedom: An Introduction to Philosophy.* Edited by Ted Sadler. London and New York: Continuum, 2002.

Heidegger, Martin. *Seminare Hegel – Schelling.* Edited by Peter Trawny. Frankfurt am Main: Vittorio Klostermann, 2011.

Heidegger, Martin. *Ponderings II–VI: Black Notebooks 1931–1938.* Translated by Richard Rojcewicz. Bloomington: Indiana University Press, 2014.

Heidegger, Martin. *Überlegungen II–VI (Schwarze Hefte 1931–1938).* Edited by Peter Trawny. Frankfurt am Main: Vittorio Klostermann, 2014.

Heidegger, Martin. *Überlegungen XII–XV (Schwarze Hefte 1939–1941)*. Edited by Peter Trawny. Frankfurt am Main: Vittorio Klostermann, 2014.

Heidegger, Martin. 'Brief an Fritz Heidegger vom 2. März 1932'. In *Heidegger und der Antisemitismus: Positionen im Widerstreit. Mit Briefen von Martin und Fritz Heidegger*. Edited by Walter Homolka and Arnulf Heidegger, 26–27. Freiburg: Herder, 2016.

Heidegger, Martin. *Ponderings XII–XV. Black Notebooks 1939–1941*. Translated by Richard Rojcewicz. Bloomington: Indiana University Press, 2017.

Heine, Heinrich. *On the History of Religion and Philosophy in Germany and Other Writings*. Edited by Terry Pinkard. Translated by Howard Pollack-Milgate. Cambridge: Cambridge University Press, 2007 (1st ed. 1835).

Held, David and Pietro Maffettone, eds. *Global Political Theory*. Cambridge: Polity Press, 2016.

Herodotus. *Histories*. Translated by A. D. Godley. Cambridge, MA: Harvard University Press, 1926.

Hildebrandt, Kurt. *Platon: Der Kampf des Geistes um die Macht*. Berlin: Georg Bondi, 1933.

Hill, Thomas E. *Virtue, Rules, and Justice: Kantian Aspirations*. Oxford: Oxford University Press, 2012.

von Hippel, Theodor Gottlieb. *Biographie des Königl. Preuß. Geheimenkriegsraths zu Königsberg, Theodor Gottlieb von Hippel, zum Theil von ihm selbst verfasst*. Edited by Friedrich Schlichtegroll and Justus Perthes. Gotha: Perthes, 1801.

von Hippel, Theodor Gottlieb. *Nachricht die v. K—sche Untersuchung betreffend. Ein Beytrag über Verbrechen und Strafen*. Edited by Matthias Luserke. St. Ingbert: Röhrig, 2000 (1st ed. 1792).

Höffe, Otfried. 'Zur Analogie von Individuum und Polis'. In *Platon. Politeia*. Edited by Otfried Höffe, 84–93. Berlin: Akademie, 1997.

Höffe, Otfried. *Königliche Völker: Zu Kants kosmopolitischer Rechts- und Friedenstheorie*. Frankfurt am Main: Suhrkamp, 2001.

Hölderlin, Friedrich. *Sämtliche Werke und Briefe*. vol. 5. Edited by Friedrich Beissner. Stuttgart: Kohlhammer, 1952.

Hölderlin, Friedrich. 'The Oldest System-Program of German Idealism'. In *Essays and Letters on Theory*. Translated by

Thomas Pfau, 154–56. New York: State University of New York Press, 1988.

Hölderlin, Friedrich. *Hyperion and Selected Poems.* Edited by Eric L. Santner. Translated by Michael Hamburger. New York: Continuum, 1990.

Hölderlin, Friedrich. *Poems and Fragments.* Translated by Michael Hamburger. London: Anvil, 2004.

Horn, Christoph. *Nichtideale Normativität. Ein neuer Blick auf Kants politische Philosophie.* Frankfurt am Main: Suhrkamp, 2014.

Horton, Scott. 'Hölderlin on Pindar's Nomos'. *Harper's Magazine*, 4 February 2008. Accessed 5 May 2025. https://harpers.org/2008/02/holderlin-on-pindars-nomos/

Hösle, Vittorio. *Platon interpretieren.* In *Platon interpretieren*, edited by Otfried Höffe, 138–43. Paderborn: Schöningh, 2004.

Hruschka, Joachim. 'The Permissive Law: Kant on Freedom and Right'. *Archiv für Rechts- und Sozialphilosophie* 84 (1998): 29–42.

Huntington, Samuel P. *The Clash of Civilizations and the Remaking of World Order.* London: Touchstone, 1998.

Husserl, Edmund. *The Crisis of European Sciences and Transcendental Phenomenology: An Introduction to Phenomenological Philosophy.* Translated by David Carr. Evanston, IL: Northwestern University Press, 1970.

Invernizzi Accetti, Carlo. 'The Temporality of Normativity: Hans Kelsen's Overcoming of the Problem of the Foundation for Legal Validity'. *Philosophy and Social Criticism* 42, no. 1 (2015): 25–43.

Jabloner, Clemens. *Reine Rechtslehre und Rechtswirklichkeit: Aufsätze zur Wissenschaftstheorie und Rechtstheorie.* Wien: Manz, 2019.

Jaeger, Werner. *Paideia: The Ideals of Greek Culture*, vol. 2. *In Search of the Divine Center.* Translated by Gilbert Highet. Oxford: Oxford University Press, 1947.

Jahandarie, Khosrow. *Spoken and Written Discourse: A Multidisciplinary Perspective.* Stamford, CT: Ablex Publishing Company, 1999.

Jaspers, Karl. *The Origin and Goal of History.* Translated by Michael Bullock. London: Routledge & Kegan Paul, 1953.

Joas, Hans. *The Genesis of Values.* Translated by Gregory Moore. Cambridge: Polity Press, 2000.

Joas, Hans and Robert N. Bellah, eds. *The Axial Age and Its Consequences.* Cambridge, MA: Harvard University Press, 2012.

Kagan, Donald. *The Fall of the Athenian Empire.* Ithaca, NY: Cornell University Press, 1991.

Kammerhofer, Jörg. 'Kelsen – Which Kelsen? A Reapplication of the Pure Theory to International Law'. *Leiden Journal of International Law* 22, no. 2 (2009): 225–49.

Kammerhofer, Jörg. 'Hans Kelsen's Place in International Legal Theory'. In *Research Handbook on the Theory and History of International Law.* Edited by Alexander Orakhelashvili, 143–67. Cheltenham: Edward Elgar, 2011.

Kant, Immanuel. *Metaphysische Anfangsgründe der Rechtslehre.* Edited by Bernd Ludwig. Hamburg: Felix Meiner, 1986.

Kant, Immanuel. *Prolegomena zu einer jeden künftigen Metaphysik, die als Wissenschaft wird auftreten können.* Edited by Rudolf Malter. Stuttgart: Reclam, 1989.

Kapitza, Peter K. *Ein bürgerlicher Krieg in der gelehrten Welt. Zur Geschichte der Querelle des Anciens et des Modernes in Deutschland.* München: Fink, 1981.

Kekes, John. 'A Reasonable Alternative to Egalitarianism'. In *Contemporary Debates in Political Philosophy.* Edited by Thomas Christiano and John Christman, 179–94. Oxford: Blackwell, 2009.

Kelsen, Hans. 'Reichsgesetz und Landesgesetz nach österreichischer Verfassung'. *Archiv des öffentlichen Rechts* 32, nos. 1–2, 3–4 (1914): 202–45, 390–438.

Kelsen, Hans. *Allgemeine Staatslehre.* Berlin: Springer, 1925.

Kelsen, Hans. 'Diskussionsbeitrag'. *Veröffentlichungen der Vereinigung der Deutschen Staatsrechtslehrer* 3 (1927): 54–55.

Kelsen, Hans. 'Die Technik des Völkerrechts und die Organisation des Friedens'. *Zeitschrift für öffentliches Recht* 2 (1934): 240–55.

Kelsen, Hans. *The Legal Process and International Order.* Translated by William Horsfall Carter. New Commonwealth Institute Monographs 1 (1935): 2–27.

Kelsen, Hans. *Zur Reform des Völkerbundes.* Prag: Internationale Kulturliga, 1938.

Kelsen, Hans. *Society and Nature: A Sociological Inquiry.* Chicago: University of Chicago Press, 1943.

Kelsen, Hans. *General Theory of Law and State.* Cambridge, MA: Harvard University Press, 1949.

Kelsen, Hans. *The Law of the United Nations: A Critical Analysis of Its Fundamental Problems.* London: Stevens & Sons, 1951.

Kelsen, Hans. *Reine Rechtslehre.* 2nd ed. Wien: Franz Deuticke, 1960.

Kelsen, Hans. *Pure Theory of Law.* Translated from the 2nd ed. by Max Knight. Berkeley, CA: University of California Press, 1967.

Kelsen, Hans. *Die Illusion der Gerechtigkeit. Eine kritische Untersuchung der Sozialphilosophie Platons.* Edited by Kurt Ringhofer and Robert Walter. Wien: Manz, 1985.

Kelsen, Hans. 'On the Essence and Value of Democracy (1929)'. In *Weimar: A Jurisprudence of Crisis.* Edited by Arthur Jacobson and Bernard Schlink. Translated by Belinda Cooper, 89–93. Berkeley, CA: University of California Press, 2000.

Kelsen, Hans. *A New Science of Politics: Hans Kelsen's Reply to Eric Voegelin's "New Science of Politics": A Contribution to the Critique of Ideology.* Edited by Eckhart Arnold. Frankfurt am Main: Ontos, 2004.

Kelsen, Hans. 'Vom Wesen und Wert der Demokratie (1929)'. In *Verteidigung der Demokratie: Abhandlungen zur Demokratietheorie.* Edited by Matthias Jestaedt and Oliver Lepsius, 208–10. Tübingen: Mohr Siebeck, 2006.

Kelsen, Hans. *Werke*, vol. 1, *Veröffentlichte Schriften 1905–1910 und Selbstzeugnisse*, Edited by Matthias Jestaedt. Tübingen: Mohr Siebeck, 2007.

Kelsen, Hans. *Wer soll Hüter der Verfassung sein?* Edited by Robert Chr. van Ooyen. Tübingen: Mohr Siebeck, 2008 (1st ed. 1931).

Kelsen, Hans. *Secular Religion: A Polemic Against the Misinterpretation of Modern Social Philosophy, Science and Politics as 'New Religions'.* Edited by Robert Walter. Wien: Springer, 2011.

Kelsen, Hans. 'Who Ought to Be the Guardian of the Constitution? Kelsen's Reply to Schmitt'. In *The Guardian of the Constitution: Hans Kelsen and Carl Schmitt on the Limits of Constitutional Law*. Edited and translated by Lars Vinx, 174–221. Cambridge: Cambridge University Press, 2015.

Kerferd, G. B. *The Sophistic Movement*. Cambridge: Cambridge University Press, 1981.

Kerstein, Samuel J. *Kant's Search for the Supreme Principle of Morality*. Cambridge: Cambridge University Press, 2002.

Kittler, Friedrich. *Musik und Mathematik*, vol. 1: *Hellas*. München: Fink, 2006.

Kleingeld, Pauline. *Kant and Cosmopolitanism: The Philosophical Ideal of World Citizenship*. Cambridge: Cambridge University Press, 2012.

Kleingeld, Pauline and Eric Brown. 'Cosmopolitanism'. In *The Stanford Encyclopedia of Philosophy* (Winter 2019 edition). Edited by Edward N. Zalta. Accessed 20 June, 2025. https://plato.stanford.edu/archives/win2019/entries/cosmopolitanism.

Kletzer, Christoph. 'Kelsen and Blumenberg: The Legitimacy of the Modern Age'. *King's Law Journal* 25, no. 1 (2014): 19–33.

Klippel, Diethelm, Dieter Hüning, and Jens Eisfeld, eds. *Die Rezensionen zu Kants Metaphysischen Anfangsgründen der Rechtslehre. Die zeitgenössische Rezeption von Kants Rechtsphilosophie*. Berlin: De Gruyter, 2021.

Klosko, George. *The Development of Plato's Political Theory*. 2nd ed. Oxford: Oxford University Press, 2006.

Kohnen, Joseph and Theodor Gottlieb von Hippel. *Eine zentrale Persönlichkeit der Königsberger Geistesgeschichte: Biographie und Bibliographie*. Lüneburg: Verlag Nordostdeutsches Kulturwerk, 1987.

Konstan, David. 'Cosmopolitan Traditions'. In *A Companion to Greek and Roman Political Thought*. Edited by Ryan K. Balot, 473–84. Malden, MA: Wiley-Blackwell, 2009.

Korsgaard, Christine M. *Creating the Kingdom of Ends*. Cambridge: Cambridge University Press, 1996.

Koskenniemi, Martti. *The Gentle Civilizer of Nations: The Rise and Fall of International Law 1870–1960*. Cambridge: Cambridge University Press, 2002.

Kuehn, Manfred. *Kant: A Biography*. Cambridge: Cambridge University Press, 2001.

Kuzmany, Börries. *Vom Umgang mit nationaler Vielfalt. Eine Geschichte der nicht-territorialen Autonomie in Europa*. Berlin: De Gruyter, 2024.

Kymlicka, Will. *Contemporary Political Philosophy: An Introduction.* Oxford: Clarendon Press, 1990.

Längin, Hartmut. 'Erzählkunst und Philosophie in den Platon-Briefen'. *Grazer Beiträge* 22 (1998): 101–44.

de La Rochefoucauld, François. *Réflexions, ou Sentences et Maximes morales.* Paris: Claude Barbin, 1678.

Larsen, J. A. O. *Greek Federal States: Their Institutions and History.* Oxford: Clarendon Press, 1968.

Laski, Harold. *A Grammar of Politics.* 4th ed. London: George Allen & Unwin, 1938.

Lévi-Strauss, Claude. *The Raw and the Cooked: Introduction to a Science of Mythology I.* Translated by John and Doreen Weightman. London: Jonathan Cape, 1970.

Lilla, Mark. 'What Heidegger Wrought'. *Commentary* 89, no. 1 (January 1990): 33–38.

Lilla, Mark. *The Reckless Mind: Intellectuals in Politics.* New York: New York Review of Books, 2001.

Lilla, Mark. *The Once and Future Liberal: After Identity Politics.* New York: HarperCollins, 2017.

Littell, Jonathan. *The Kindly Ones.* Translated by Charlotte Mandell. London: Vintage, 2010.

Livingstone, Niall and Ephraim Lytle, eds. *Ancient Education and the Formation of Hellenic Identity: Isocrates and the Panhellenic Project.* Cambridge: Cambridge University Press, 2023.

Llewellyn, Karl N. 'The Normative, the Legal, and the Law-Jobs: The Problem of Juristic Method'. *Yale Law Journal* 49, no. 8 (1940): 1355–400.

Llewellyn, Karl N. *Jurisprudence: Realism in Theory and Practice.* Chicago: University of Chicago Press, 1962.

Locke, John. *Two Treatises of Government.* Edited by Peter Laslett. Cambridge: Cambridge University Press, 1967.

Loraux, Nicole. 'La cité comme cuisine et comme partage'. *Annales. Économies, Sociétés, Civilisations* 36, no. 6 (1981): 614–22.

Louden, Robert B. *Kant's Impure Ethics: From Rational Beings to Human Beings.* Oxford: Oxford University Press, 2000.

Löwith, Karl. 'My Last Meeting with Heidegger in Rome 1936'. In *The Heidegger Controversy: A Critical Reader*. Edited and translated by Richard Wolin, 141–43. Cambridge, MA: MIT Press, 1993.

Lu-Adler, Huaping. *Kant, Race, and Racism: Views from Somewhere.* New York: Oxford University Press, 2023.

Ludwig, Bernd. 'Kommentar zum Staatsrecht (II)'. In *Klassiker auslegen: Kants Metaphysische Anfangsgründe der Rechtslehre.* Edited by Otfried Höffe, 173–94. Berlin: Akademie, 1999.

Luhmann, Niklas. *Die Gesellschaft der Gesellschaft.* Frankfurt am Main: Suhrkamp, 1997.

Luhmann, Niklas. *Theory of Society*, 2 vols. Translated by Rhodes Barrett. Stanford, CA: Stanford University Press, 2012.

Maliks, Reidar. *Kant's Politics in Context.* Oxford: Oxford University Press, 2014.

Mallmann, Marion. *Das Innere Reich: Analyse einer konservativen Kulturzeitschrift im Dritten Reich.* Bonn: Bouvier, 1978.

Malter, Rudolf. 'Zeitgenössische Reaktionen auf die Religionsphilosophie: Eine Skizze zur Wirkungsgeschichte des Kantischen und des reformatorischen Denkens'. In *Bewusst sein. Gerhard Funke zu eigen.* Edited by Alexius J. Bucher, Hermann Drüe, and Thomas M. Seebohm, 145–67. Bonn: Bouvier, 1975.

Manthey, Jürgen. *Königsberg: Geschichte einer Weltbürgerrepublik.* München: Hanser, 2005.

Marchart, Oliver. *Post-Foundational Political Thought: Political Difference in Nancy, Lefort, Badiou and Laclau.* Edinburgh: Edinburgh University Press, 2007.

Marx, Karl. *Critique of Hegel's Philosophy of Right.* Translated by Annette Jolin and Joseph O'Malley. Cambridge: Cambridge University Press, 1970.

Maus, Ingeborg. *Zur Aufklärung der Demokratietheorie: Rechts- und demokratietheoretische Überlegungen im Anschluss an Kant.* Frankfurt am Main: Suhrkamp, 1992.

Medicus, Fritz. 'Kants Philosophie der Geschichte'. *Kant-Studien* 4, nos. 1–3 (1900): 61–67.

Mehring, Reinhard. *Carl Schmitt und Hans Kelsen: Der Kampf um die 'Hüter der Verfassung'*. Tübingen: Mohr Siebeck, 2011.

Merle, Jean-Christophe. *German Idealism and the Concept of Punishment.* Cambridge: Cambridge University Press, 2009.

Merle, Robert. *Death Is My Trade.* Translated by Alan Ross. London: Derek Verschoyle, 1954.

Métall, Rudolf Aldár. *Hans Kelsen: Leben und Werk.* Wien: Franz Deuticke, 1969.

Miller, David. *Strangers in Our Midst.* Cambridge, MA: Harvard University Press, 2016.

Millerman, Michael. *Beginning with Heidegger: Strauss, Rorty, Derrida, Dugin, and the Philosophical Constitution of the Political.* London: Arktos, 2020.

Molloy, Seán. *Kant's International Relations: The Political Theology of Perpetual Peace.* Ann Arbor: University of Michigan Press, 2017.

Mommsen, Hans. *Aufstieg und Untergang der Republik von Weimar 1918–1933*. Berlin: Ullstein, 2009.

Nagl-Docekal, Herta. *Innere Freiheit: Grenzen der nachmetaphysischen Moralkonzeptionen.* Berlin and Boston: De Gruyter, 2014.

Nancy, Jean-Luc. *After Politics: The Rejection of Politics in Contemporary Liberal Philosophy.* Basingstoke: Palgrave Macmillan, 2001.

von Neurath, Konstantin. *Deutsche Wissenschaft: Arbeit und Aufgabe. Dem Führer und Reichskanzler legt die Deutsche Wissenschaft zu seinem 50. Geburtstag Rechenschaft ab über ihre Arbeit im Rahmen der ihr gestellten Aufgabe.* Leipzig: Hirzel, 1939.

Nietzsche, Friedrich. *The Gay Science: With a Prelude in Rhymes and an Appendix of Songs.* Translated by Walter Kaufmann. New York: Vintage Books, 1974.

Nietzsche, Friedrich. 'Plato amicus sed. Einleitung in das Studium der platonischen Dialoge'. In *Werke. Kritische Gesamtausgabe,* part 2, vol. 4. Edited by Franco Bornmann and Michele Carpitella. Berlin: Walter de Gruyter, 1995.

Nussbaum, Martha. 'Kant and Stoic Cosmopolitanism'. *The Journal of Political Philosophy* 5, no. 1 (1997): 1–25.

Nussbaum, Martha. *Frontiers of Justice: Disability, Nationality, Species Membership.* Cambridge, MA: Harvard University Press, 2006.

Nussbaum, Martha. *The Cosmopolitan Tradition: A Noble but Flawed Ideal.* Cambridge, MA: Harvard University Press, 2019.

Olechowski, Thomas. *Hans Kelsen: Biographie eines Rechtswissenschaftlers*. Tübingen: Mohr Siebeck, 2020.

Ott, Hugo. *Martin Heidegger: A Political Life.* Translated by Allan Blunden. London: HarperCollins, 1993.

Pahlow, Louis. '"Ich verüble dem Verf. weniger einzelne juristische Fehler als das Versagen des Rechtsgefühls". Juristische Staatsprüfungen im Dritten Reich (1934–1945)'. In *Von den Leges Barbarorum bis zum ius barbarum des Nationalsozialismus. Festschrift für Hermann Nehlsen zum 70. Geburtstag*. Edited by Thomas Gutmann, Hans-Georg Hermann, Joachim Rückert, Mathias Schmoeckel and Harald Siems, 399–420. Köln: Böhlau, 2008.

Paulson, Stanley L., ed. *Hans Kelsen und die Rechtssoziologie: Auseinandersetzungen mit Hermann U. Kantorowicz, Eugen Ehrlich und Max Weber*. Aalen: Scientia, 1992.

Paulson, Stanley L. 'The Neo-Kantian Dimension of Kelsen's Pure Theory of Law'. *Oxford Journal of Legal Studies* 12, no. 3 (1992): 311–32.

Paulson, Stanley L. *Kelsen, Positivism, and the Critique of Pure Theory*. Oxford: Oxford University Press, 2013.

Penrose, Roger. *Shadows of the Mind*. Oxford: Oxford University Press, 1994.

Pettit, Philip. *Republicanism: A Theory of Freedom and Government*. Oxford: Oxford University Press, 1997.

Pettit, Philip. *Just Freedom: A Moral Compass for a Complex World*. New York: W. W. Norton, 2014.

Pettit, Philip. 'The Globalized Republican Ideal'. *Global Justice: Theory, Practice, Rhetoric* 9, no. 1 (2016): 47–68.

Pettit, Philip and José Luis Martí. *A Political Philosophy in Public Life: Civic Republicanism in Zapatero's Spain*. Princeton, NJ: Princeton University Press, 2010.

Pfefferkorn, Julia. *Platons tanzende Stadt*. Leiden: Brill, 2023.

Pinker, Steven. *The Better Angels of Our Nature: Why Violence Has Declined*. New York: Viking, 2011.

Pippin, Robert B. *The Culmination: Heidegger, German Idealism, and the Fate of Philosophy*. Chicago: University of Chicago Press, 2024.

Pippin, Robert B. *Robert Bresson: Cinematic Style as Philosophy*. Chicago: University of Chicago Press, 2026.

Pirsig, Robert M. *Zen and the Art of Motorcycle Maintenance: An Inquiry into Values*. London: Bodley Head, 1975.

Pitts, Jennifer. *A Turn to Empire: The Rise of Imperial Liberalism in Britain and France*. Princeton, NJ: Princeton University Press, 2005.

Pluckrose, Helen and James Lindsay. *Cynical Theories: How Universities Made Everything about Race, Gender, and Identity – and Why This Harms Everybody.* Durham, NC: Pitchstone, 2020.

Pogge, Thomas. 'Cosmopolitanism and Sovereignty'. *Ethics* 103, no. 1 (1992): 48–75.

Pogge, Thomas. *John Rawls.* München: C. H. Beck, 1994.

Pogge, Thomas. 'Is Kant's Rechtslehre Comprehensive?' *Southern Journal of Philosophy* 36, no. 1 (1998): 161–87.

Popper, Karl. *The Open Society and Its Enemies*, 2nd ed. London: Routledge, 1995 (1st ed. 1945).

Postema, Gerald J. 'The Normativity of Law'. In *Issues in Contemporary Legal Philosophy: The Influence of H. L. A. Hart. Edited by* Ruth Gavison, 81–104. Oxford: Clarendon Press, 1987.

Prauss, Gerold. *Erkennen und Handeln in Heideggers Sein und Zeit.* Freiburg: Karl Alber, 1977.

Prauss, Gerold. 'Kants Problem der Einheit theoretischer und praktischer Vernunft'. *Kant-Studien* 72, nos. 1–4 (1981): 286–303.

Prauss, Gerold. *Kant über Freiheit als Autonomie.* Frankfurt am Main: Vittorio Klostermann, 1983.

Quint, Peter E. 'Judging the Past: The Prosecution of East German Border Guards and the GDR Chain of Command'. *The Review of Politics* 61, no. 2 (1999): 303–29.

Raaflaub, Kurt A. 'Contemporary Perceptions of Democracy in Fifth-Century Athens'. *Classica et Mediaevalia* 40 (1989): 33–70.

Raaflaub, Kurt A. 'Learning from the Enemy'. In *Interpreting the Athenian Empire*. Edited by John Ma, Nikolas Papazarkadas and Robert Parker, 89–124. London: Duckworth, 2009.

Raffoul, François, and David Pettigrew, eds. *Heidegger and Practical Philosophy.* Albany, NY: State University of New York Press, 2002.

von Ranke, Leopold. *Fürsten und Völker. Geschichten der romanischen und germanischen Völker von 1494–1514.* Edited by Willy Andreas. Wiesbaden: Emil Vollmer, 1957 (1st ed. 1824).

von Ranke, Leopold. 'Über die Epochen der neueren Geschichte'. In *Werk und Nachlass*, vol. 2. Edited by Walther Peter. München: Oldenbourg, 1971.

Rawls, John. *The Law of Peoples: With 'The Idea of Public Reason Revisited'*. Cambridge, MA: Harvard University Press, 1999.

Rawls, John. 'Justice as Fairness: Political not Metaphysical'. In *Collected Papers*. Edited by Samuel Freeman, 388–414. Cambridge, MA: Harvard University Press, 2001.

Rawls, John. 'A Kantian Conception of Equality'. In *Collected Papers*. Edited by Samuel Freeman, 254–66. Cambridge, MA: Harvard University Press, 2001.

Rawls, John. *Justice as Fairness: A Restatement*. Edited by Erin Kelly. Cambridge, MA: Harvard University Press, 2001.

Rawls, John. *Lectures on the History of Political Philosophy*. Edited by Samuel Freeman. Cambridge, MA: Harvard University Press, 2007.

Raz, Joseph. 'Kelsen's Theory of the Basic Norm'. *The American Journal of Jurisprudence* 19 (1974): 94–111.

Raz, Joseph. 'On the Nature of Law'. *Archiv für Rechts- und Sozialphilosophie* 82, no. 1 (1996): 1–25.

Rehbinder, Manfred. 'Die rechts- und staatswissenschaftliche Fakultät der Franz-Josephs-Universität Czernowitz: Ihr Beitrag zur Erforschung des Rechts in einer multikulturellen Gesellschaft'. In *Festschrift für Hans Stoll zum 75. Geburtstag*. Edited by Gerhard Holoch, Rainer Frank and Peter Schlechtriem, 327–44. Tübingen: Mohr Siebeck, 2001.

Rehbinder, Manfred. 'Aus den letzten Jahren im Leben und Schaffen von Eugen Ehrlich'. In *Festschrift Ernst-Joachim Lampe*. Edited by Dieter Dölling, 199–210. Berlin: Duncker & Humblot, 2003.

Reimann, Matthias. 'Nineteenth-Century German Legal Science'. *Boston College Law Review* 31, no. 4 (1990): 837–97.

Reinhard, Wolfgang. *Geschichte der Staatsgewalt: Eine vergleichende Verfassungsgeschichte Europas von den Anfängen bis zur Gegenwart*. München: C. H. Beck, 1999.

Rhodes, P. J. *A History of the Classical Greek World: 478–323 BC*. Oxford: Blackwell, 2006.

Riley, Patrick. *Leibniz' Universal Jurisprudence: Justice as the Charity of the Wise*. Cambridge, MA: Harvard University Press, 1996.

Ripstein, Arthur. *Force and Freedom: Kant's Legal and Political Philosophy*. Cambridge, MA: Harvard University Press, 2009.

Rissmann, Leah. *Love as War: Homeric Allusion in the Poetry of Sappho*. *Beiträge zur klassischen Philologie* 157. Königstein: Hain, 1983.

Rousseau, Jean-Jacques. *A Discourse on Inequality*. Translated by Maurice Cranston. London: Penguin Books, 1984.

Rückert, Joachim. 'Kant-Rezeption in juristischer und politischer Theorie (Naturrecht, Rechtsphilosophie, Staatslehre, Politik) des 19. Jahrhunderts'. In *John Locke and Immanuel Kant: Historical Reception and Contemporary Relevance*. Edited by Martyn P. Thompson, 144–215. Berlin: Duncker & Humblot, 1991.

Russett, Bruce. *Grasping the Democratic Peace: Principles for a Post–Cold War World*. Princeton, NJ: Princeton University Press, 1993.

Rüthers, Bernd. *Die unbegrenzte Auslegung: Zum Wandel der Privatrechtsordnung im Nationalsozialismus*. 7th ed. Tübingen: Mohr Siebeck, 2012.

Ryan, Alan. *On Politics: A History of Political Thought from Herodotus to the Present*. London: Allen Lane, 2012.

Salkever, Stephen G. and Ryan K. Balot, eds. *The Cambridge Companion to Ancient Greek Political Thought*. Cambridge: Cambridge University Press, 2009.

Sandel, Michael J. *Liberalism and the Limits of Justice*. Cambridge: Cambridge University Press, 1982.

Sauter, Michael J. 'The Enlightenment on Trial: State Service and Social Discipline in Eighteenth-Century Germany's Public Sphere'. *Modern Intellectual History* 5, no. 2 (2008): 195–223.

Scheffler, Samuel. 'Conceptions of Cosmopolitanism'. *Utilitas* 11, no. 3 (1999): 250–73.

von Schelling, Friedrich Wilhelm Joseph. 'Nachruf Immanuel Kant'. In *Sämtliche Werke*, I, 6:3–10. Stuttgart and Augsburg: J. G. Cotta, 1860.

Schestag, Thomas. *Parerga: Friedrich Hölderlin, Carl Schmitt, Franz Kafka, Platon, Friedrich Schleiermacher, Walter Benjamin, Jacques Derrida. Zur literarischen Hermeneutik*. München: Klaus Boer, 1991.

Schlosser, Johann Georg. *Platons Briefe nebst einer historischen Einleitung und Anmerkungen*. Königsberg: Friedrich Nicolovius, 1795.

Schlosser, Johann Georg. *Schreiben an einen jungen Mann, der die kritische Philosophie studieren wollte*. Lübeck: bey Friedrich Bohn, 1797.

Schmitt, Carl. *Der Begriff des Politischen*. Hamburg: Hanseatische Verlagsanstalt, 1933.

Schmitt, Carl. *Der Begriff des Politischen: Text von 1932 mit einem Vorwort und drei Corollarien*. 2nd ed. Berlin: Duncker & Humblot, 1963.

Schmitt, Carl. *Völkerrechtliche Großraumordnung mit Interventionsverbot für raumfremde Mächte: Ein Beitrag zum Reichsbegriff im Völkerrecht*. Berlin: Duncker & Humblot, 1991 (1st ed. 1941).

Schmitt, Carl. 'Der Führer schützt das Recht'. In *Positionen und Begriffe im Kampf um Weimar – Genf – Versailles 1923–1939*, 227–32. 3rd ed. Berlin: Duncker & Humblot, 1994 (first published 1934).

Schmitt, Carl. *The Concept of the Political*. Expanded ed. Translated by George Schwab. Chicago: University of Chicago Press, 1996.

Schmitt, Carl. *Der Hüter der Verfassung*. 4th ed. Berlin: Duncker & Humblot, 1996 (1st ed. 1931).

Schmitt, Carl. *State, Movement, People: The Triadic Structure of Political Unity (1933)*. Translated by Simona Draghici. Corvallis, OR: Plutarch Press, 2001.

Schmitt, Carl. *The Nomos of the Earth in the International Law of the Jus Publicum Europaeum*. Translated by Gary L. Ulmen. New York: Telos Press, 2003.

Schmitt, Carl. *On the Three Types of Juristic Thought*. Translated by Joseph W. Bendersky. Westport, CT: Praeger, 2004.

Schmitt, Carl. 'The Guardian of the Constitution'. In *The Guardian of the Constitution: Hans Kelsen and Carl Schmitt on the Limits of Constitutional Law*. Edited and translated by Lars Vinx, 79–124. Cambridge: Cambridge University Press, 2015.

Schofield, Malcolm. 'Plato and Practical Politics'. In *The Cambridge History of Greek and Roman Political Thought*. Edited by Christopher J. Rowe and Malcolm Schofield, 291–312. Cambridge: Cambridge University Press, 2000.

Schofield, Malcolm. *Plato: Political Philosophy*. Oxford: Oxford University Press, 2006.

Schopenhauer, Arthur. *The World as Will and Representation*, vol. 1. Edited and translated by Judith Norman, Alistair Welchman and Christopher Janaway. Cambridge: Cambridge University Press, 2010.

Schorske, Carl E. *Fin-de-Siècle Vienna: Politics and Culture.* New York: Alfred A. Knopf, 1980.

Seel, Gerhard. 'How Does Kant Justify the Universal Objective Validity of the Law of Right?' *International Journal of Philosophical Studies* 17, no. 1 (2009): 49–70.

Seol, Min. 'Ethical Lessons from Heidegger's Phenomenological Reading of Kant's Practical Philosophy: A Heideggerian Revision of Kant's Justification of Morality'. *Journal of the British Society for Phenomenology* 51, no. 1 (2019): 1–17.

Shapiro, Scott J. *Legality.* Cambridge, MA: Harvard University Press, 2011.

Sigmund, Karl. *Exact Thinking in Demented Times: The Vienna Circle and the Epic Quest for the Foundations of Science.* New York: Basic Books, 2017.

Simmons, A. John. *Justification and Legitimacy: Essays on Rights and Obligations.* Cambridge: Cambridge University Press, 2000.

Singer, Peter. 'Famine, Affluence, and Morality'. *Philosophy and Public Affairs* 1, no. 3 (1972): 229–43.

Skinner, Quentin. 'Meaning and Understanding in the History of Ideas'. *History and Theory* 8, no. 1 (1969): 3–53.

Skinner, Quentin. *The Foundations of Modern Political Thought,* 2 vols. Cambridge: Cambridge University Press, 1978.

Skinner, Quentin. 'An Interview with Quentin Skinner'. *Cogito* 11, no. 2 (1979): 69–76.

Skinner, Quentin. 'A Reply to My Critics'. In *Meaning and Context: Quentin Skinner and His Critics.* Edited by James Tully, 231–88. Cambridge: Polity, 1988.

Skinner, Quentin. 'Who Are 'We'? Ambiguities of the Modern Self'. *Inquiry* 34, no. 2 (1991): 133–53.

Skinner, Quentin. *Liberty Before Liberalism.* Cambridge: Cambridge University Press, 1998.

Skinner, Quentin. *Visions of Politics,* 3 vols. Cambridge: Cambridge University Press, 2002.

Skinner, Quentin. *Hobbes and Republican Liberty.* Cambridge: Cambridge University Press, 2008.

Skinner, Quentin. 'A Genealogy of the Modern State'. *Proceedings of the British Academy* 162 (2009): 325–70.

Slobodian, Quinn. *Globalists: The End of Empire and the Birth of Neoliberalism.* Cambridge, MA: Harvard University Press, 2018.

Slobodian, Quinn. *Hayek's Bastards: Race, Gold, IQ, and the Capitalism of the Far Right*. New York: Zone Books, 2025.

Solmsen, Friedrich. Review of *Plato's Seventh Letter*, by Ludwig Edelstein. *Gnomon* 41, no. 1 (1969): 29–34.

Stein, Eric. 'Lawyers, Judges, and the Making of a Transnational Constitution'. *American Journal of International Law* 75, no. 1 (1981): 1–27.

Stekeler-Weithofer, Pirmin. 'Autonome Vernunft und Normbefolgung des Verstandes: Wie Hegel eine Unterscheidung Kants präzisiert'. *Hegel-Studien* 48 (2015): 13–36.

Strauss, Leo. *On Tyranny*. London: Collier-Macmillan, 1963.

Stray, Christopher. *Classics Transformed: Schools, Universities, and Society in England, 1830–1960*. Oxford: Clarendon Press, 1991.

Svenbro, Jesper. *Phrasikleia: An Anthropology of Reading in Ancient Greece*. Translated by Janet Lloyd. Ithaca, NY: Cornell University Press, 1993.

Szlezák, Thomas A. *Platon und die Schriftlichkeit der Philosophie: Interpretation zu den frühen und mittleren Dialogen*. Berlin: Walter de Gruyter, 1985.

Szlezák, Thomas A. *Platon lesen*. Stuttgart: Frommann-Holzboog, 1993.

Tamanaha, Brian Z. *A General Jurisprudence of Law and Society*. Oxford: Oxford University Press, 2001.

Tamanaha, Brian Z. 'Understanding Legal Pluralism: Past to Present, Local to Global'. *Sydney Law Review* 30, no. 3 (2008): 375–411.

Tarn, William Woodthorpe. 'Alexander the Great and the Unity of Mankind'. *Proceedings of the British Academy* 19 (1933): 123–66.

Thielking, Sigrid. *Weltbürgertum: Kosmopolitische Ideen in Literatur und politischer Publizistik seit dem achtzehnten Jahrhundert*. München: Fink, 2000.

Tigerstedt, E. N. *Interpreting Plato*. Uppsala: Almquist & Wiksell, 1977.

Toynbee, Arnold J. *A Study of History*, vol. 3. Oxford: Oxford University Press, 1934.

Trampedach, Kai. *Platon, die Akademie und die zeitgenössische Politik*. Stuttgart: Franz Steiner, 1994.

Tully, James, ed. *Meaning and Context: Quentin Skinner and His Critics*. Cambridge: Polity, 1988.

Turner, Frank M. *The Greek Heritage in Victorian Britain*. New Haven, CT: Yale University Press, 1981.

von Ungern-Sternberg, Jürgen. *Griechische Studien*. Berlin and New York: Walter de Gruyter, 2009.

Vermeule, Adrian. *Common Good Constitutionalism*. Cambridge: Polity Press, 2022.

Vinx, Lars. *Hans Kelsen's Pure Theory of Law: Legality and Legitimacy*. Oxford: Oxford University Press, 2008.

Vinx, Lars. *The Guardian of the Constitution: Hans Kelsen and Carl Schmitt on the Limits of Constitutional Law*. Edited and translated by Lars Vinx. Cambridge: Cambridge University Press, 2015.

Voegelin, Eric. *Die Rassenidee in der Geistesgeschichte von Ray bis Carus*. Berlin: Junker und Dünnhaupt, 1933.

Voegelin, Eric. *Rasse und Staat*. Tübingen: Mohr Siebeck, 1933.

Voegelin, Eric. *Der autoritäre Staat: Ein Versuch über das österreichische Staatsproblem*. Wien: Springer, 1936.

Voegelin, Eric. *The New Science of Politics: An Introduction*. Chicago: University of Chicago Press, 1952.

Vogl, Stefan. *Soziale Gesetzgebungspolitik, freie Rechtsfindung und soziologische Rechtswissenschaft bei Eugen Ehrlich*. Baden-Baden: Nomos, 2002.

Weber, Max. *Gesammelte Aufsätze zur Wissenschaftslehre*. Edited by Johannes Winckelmann. 6th ed. Tübingen: Mohr Siebeck, 1985.

Weber, Max. *The Vocation Lectures*. Translated by Rodney Livingstone. Indianapolis: Hackett Publishing, 2004.

Wehler, Hans-Ulrich. *Vom Feudalismus des Alten Reiches bis zur defensiven Modernisierung der Reformära 1700–1815*. München: C. H. Beck, 1997.

Wehler, Hans-Ulrich. *Deutsche Gesellschaftsgeschichte*, vol. 4: *Vom Beginn des Ersten Weltkriegs bis zur Gründung der beiden deutschen Staaten 1914–1949*. München: C. H. Beck, 2003.

Wertheim, Stephen. 'The League That Wasn't: American Designs for a Legalist-Sanctionist League of Nations and the Intellectual Origins of International Organization, 1914–1920'. *Diplomatic History* 35, no. 5 (2011): 797–836.

Widerquist, Karl, and Grant McCall. 'Myths about the State of Nature and the Reality of Stateless Societies'. *Analyse & Kritik* 37, nos. 1–2 (2015): 233–57.

von Wilamowitz-Moellendorff, Ulrich. *Platon*, vol. 2. Berlin: Weidmann, 1919.

Willaschek, Marcus. 'The Structure of Normative Space According to Kant'. In *The Court of Reason: Proceedings of the 13th International Kant Congress*. Edited by Camilla Serck-Hanssen and Beatrix Himmelmann, 45–63. Berlin and Boston: De Gruyter, 2021.

Williams, Bernard. 'The Analogy of City and Soul in Plato's Republic'. In *Exegesis and Argument: Studies in Greek Philosophy Presented to Gregory Vlastos*. Edited by Edward N. Lee, Alexander P. D. Mourelatos and Richard Rorty, 196–206. Assen: Van Gorcum, 1973.

Winspear, Alban Dewes. *The Genesis of Plato's Thought*. 2nd ed. New York: Russell, 1956.

Wolff, Christian. *Oratio de Sinarum philosophia practica / Rede über die praktische Philosophie der Chinesen*. Edited by Michael Albrecht. Hamburg: Meiner, 1985.

Wolin, Richard. *Heidegger in Ruins: Between Philosophy and Ideology*. New Haven, CT: Yale University Press, 2022.

Wood, Allen W. 'Unsocial Sociability: The Anthropological Basis of Kantian Ethics'. *Philosophical Topics* 19, no. 1 (1991): 325–51.

Wood, Allen W. *Kant and Religion*. Cambridge: Cambridge University Press, 2020.

Yost, Benjamin S. 'Kant's Justification of the Death Penalty Reconsidered'. *Kantian Review* 15, no. 2 (2010): 1–27.

Zartaloudis, Thanos. *The Birth of Nomos*. Edinburgh: Edinburgh University Press, 2019.

Zhao, Tingyang. *Redefining a Philosophy for World Governance*. Translated by Liqing Tao. Basingstoke and New York: Palgrave Macmillan, 2019.

Zhao, Tingyang. *All Under Heaven: The Tianxia System for a Possible World Order*. Translated by Joseph E. Harroff. Berkeley, CA: University of California Press, 2021.

Zotta, Franco. *Immanuel Kant: Legitimität und Recht. Eine Kritik seiner Eigentumslehre, Staatslehre und seiner Geschichtsphilosophie*. Freiburg: Alber, 2000.

Index

Introductory Note

References such as '178–9' indicate (not necessarily continuous) discussion of a topic across a range of pages. Where topics occur frequently, references have been divided into subtopics or indicate the main passages of discussion. Key terms such as 'genealogy' or 'cosmopolitanism' are not treated as single, uniform concepts, but are indexed according to their development across different historical and theoretical contexts. Some entries bring together terms that suggest implicit connections without presupposing a fully articulated argument. Cross-references guide the reader between related entries and help to trace these connections. The index thus forms a secondary network that complements the argumentative structure of the book.

abyss
  of history, 213, 231, 252–3
  of theory, 62, 150, 162
  see also civilisation
academia
  autonomy of, 183, 221
  degeneration of, 202, 211–12, 221
  see also jurisprudence
anthropology *see* Kant, Immanuel; legal pluralism
Arendt, Hannah, 211, 231; *see also* academia, degeneration of
Aristotle, 29, 35, 43, 62, 77
Athens, 2, 24–6, 29, 31–2, 36–9, 46, 68, 177; *see also* classical Greece
Auschwitz, 227, 231
Austria
  Austro-Hungarian Empire, 180–1, 183–4, 214, 216–21, 224, 237
  Bukovina as multicultural region, 215–19, 224
  Habsburg Empire, 69–70
  Republic of Austria, 180–3, 237
  see also constitution
authentic decision, 165, 172
  Kant, Immanuel, 139–41
  Heidegger, Martin, 163–6
  Jägerstätter, Franz, 169–70
  Kelsen, Hans, 212
  Schmitt, Carl, 207–8
authority
  absolute (god), 116, 119
  legal, 217, 234
  moral law, 86, 145
  see also Kant, Immanuel; Kelsen, Hans
autonomy
  of ancient cities, 22
  of Königsberg, 68–70
  see also Kant, Immanuel, freedom as autonomy

barbarians vs. Hellenes, 23, 33, 49
barbarism vs. civil condition, 75, 81, 134

biopolitics, 141; *see also* Kant, Immanuel, censorship controversy
borders
  case of East German border guards, 198
  communication across borders, see Sappho; Hölderlin, Friedrich
  fall of Berlin wall, vii
  open borders, xiii–xiv
bureaucracy
  Austro-Hungarian Empire, 181–3, 221
  degeneration of in National Socialism, 211–12, 229–30
  Prussia, 68–71

Cambridge School
  Austro-Hungarian Empire, 180–1, 183–4, 214, 216–21, 224, 237
  Greece, fourth century BCE, xxii, 29, 61, 65–6, 74
  Königsberg, 65–72, 88–90
  method, x–xii, xxii, 61, 63, 65–8
  Weimar Republic, 201, 208–12
  see also genealogical method; politics, intervention; Skinner, Quentin
censorship, 137, 140, 156, 227
  of conscience (church), 153–7
  implicit, 155
  of Kant, 138–40
  under totalitarian regimes, 227
Chrysippus, 20; *see also* cosmopolitanism, ancient
church, 114, 137, 153, 156, 169, 245, 248, 250
  Catholic, 169, 180, 225
  Protestant, 135–6
  see also Kant, Immanuel
citizenship
  Bukowina, 225
  change of citizenship (Prussia), 70
  dual (ancient Greece), 26–7
  stateless, vii
civil strife, 24, 33; *see also* classical Greece, fourth century BCE
civilisation, 5, 9, 105, 123–4, 149, 214, 232, 249
  Kant, 123–4, 149–59
  Rousseau, 103–4
  rupture under National Socialism, 214, 232
  Western vs. non-Western, viii, 124–5, 158
classical Greece
  fourth century BCE, xxii, 3, 13, 22–5, 27, 35, 46, 61
    civil strife, 25, 33
    Panhellenic federalism, 22, 25–7, 61
  proto-cosmopolitanism (Sophists), 28–9
closed societies, 43, 46–7, 53, 142; *see also* Plato; Rawls, John
coercion, 100, 102, 123, 151–2, 204–5, 215, 234–5
  in international law, 234–5
  in Kant, 100, 102, 123, 151–2
  as legal force (Kelsen), 204–5
  in legal pluralism, 215
  see also law; politics; power
colonialism, viii, 72–3, 115
community, 4, 26, 36, 47, 108–9, 125, 169, 215–16
  ethical (Kant), 150–4, 248
  formation see Plato, *Politeia*
  mystical (Heidegger, Jägerstätter), 166, 169
  of women (Sappho), 7
  see also legal pluralism
comprehensive doctrines, xx, 143, 157, 240–1
constitution
  of the European Union, 195
  Republic of Austria, 180–3, 233
  Weimar Republic, 206–10
contextual reading *see* Cambridge School
cosmopolitanism
  ancient
    anti-cosmopolitan (Plato), 49–50
    Panhellenic federalism, 22–3, 25–6, 61

proto-cosmopolitanism (Sophists), 43–50
Stoic cosmopolitanism, xix, 15, 21, 66, 167
anti-cosmopolitan positions, xi, 13, 15, 21, 49–50, 178, 202, 213, 238
before and beyond, 1–11, 244–51
civic
as ethical community (Kant), 100, 131, 150–4, 156, 248
contemporary
characterization, xix–xx, 66, 73, 90–130, 151
critique of, left- and right-wing, viii
legal
as legal requirement (Kant), 90–130
as unity of law (Kelsen), 185, 199, 217
post-foundational, 179, 231–41, 254
critical legal analysis, 232–6
debunking foundationalism, 236–43
relation to liberalism, 132–3, 145, 154, 232, 238–9, 252
traditional history of, 19–21
transformation of political philosophy into, 14–15
courts, 117, 195, 198, 206, 210, 235
Staatsgerichtshof (Weimar Republic), 210

death, xiii–xiv, 38, 61, 117, 140–1
penalty, 118, 120, 169
deconstruction, xiv, 1, 11, 13, 177, 180, 247
democracy, 2, 71, 152, 188, 212
agonistic, 201
constitutional, 207
legal institutionalist theory of, 203–6
Solonian, 30
Derrida, Jacques, 4, 10, 13, 180, 235; *see also* Sappho; Kelsen, Hans; Hölderlin, Friedrich
dialectics, 11, 123, 127, 152, 154–6, 227, 247
dialectical method, 53, 76, 83; *see also* Plato
discourse, xxii, 60, 62, 65, 79, 103, 155–7, 164
analysis, 156
public, 75–6, 136–7, 146, 155, 205
religious, 157, 177
see also Foucault, Michel; Cambridge School
domination, 146, 150, 153, 216, 238; *see also* Kant, Immanuel, manias
Dugin, Alexander, xvi
Dworkin, Ronald, xviii, 188, 190
method, 206, 226, 233; *see also* jurisprudence, degeneration under National Socialism

education (*paideia*), 2, 27, 47
dialectical, 53
philosophical, 57–77
see Plato, education
Ehrlich, Eugen, 215–21, 223
critique of jurisprudence (*Rechtswissenschaft*), 215–19
legal pluralism, 217–18
living law, 215–16
multicultural context, 216–21
see also Austro-Hungarian Empire; Kelsen, Hans, critique of legal pluralism
empires, 4, 15, 46, 111, 126, 181–2, 220, 223; *see also* Austria, Austro-Hungarian Empire
enlightenment, 11, 77, 114, 124, 130, 139, 157, 225
anti-enlightenment, xv–xvii, 135, 138
Greek, 154; *see also* cosmopolitanism, ancient
equality, 17, 32, 41, 47, 61–2, 71, 117, 152, 205
Erinyes, 227–31; *see also* guilt; justice; mythology; National Socialism
ethical community *see* Kant, Immanuel, religion
ethnic groups, ix, 182, 204, 216–18, 220; *see also* Ehrlich, Eugen, living law

evil, 42–4, 55, 94–5, 103–4, 127–8, 134–5, 142, 145–50, 153, 227–30; *see also* Kant, Immanuel, freedom, problem of evil
external goods, 115, 121–2, 126, 134; *see also* Kant, Immanuel, highest good

faith, 19, 135, 153–7, 169, 225; *see also* Kant, Immanuel, religion
false consciousness, xiv, 157; *see also* ideology
federalism, 23, 26–7, 61, 206, 210, 220; *see also* Panhellenic federalism
fiction
  legal, 192, 194, 203–4, 209
  literary, 228–30, 252
Foucault, Michel, x, 213, 235; *see also* genealogical method
Frederick the Great, 68–70, 138–40; *see also* Prussia
Frederick William II, 138–140, 177, 236; *see also* Prussia
freedom
  Greek, 25, 29, 32, 61–2
  see also Kant, freedom; Heidegger, Martin, freedom; Hölderlin, Friedrich
French philosophy, 68, 158, 253
French Revolution, 67, 138, 249
Freud, Sigmund, 180–1, 235, 253; *see also* civilisation; Kelsen, Hans, post-foundationalist perspective
Fukuyama, Francis, viii–ix

genealogical method, x–xii, xxii, 65–8, 141, 177–8, 201, 213; *see also* Cambridge School
German Idealism, 65, 74, 146, 155, 167
  prefigured by Schlosser, 80–1
Germany, vii, 15, 67, 136–8, 152, 180, 183–4, 210, 220
  National Socialist period, 210, 226
  see also Königsberg; National Socialism; Prussia; Weimar Republic
god, vii, 6–7, 54–5, 82–3, 144–5, 151–2, 163, 168, 248; *see also* Kant, Immanuel
Gorgonian head of power, 223; *see also* power
guilt, 118, 173, 197–9, 225, 227–31; *see also* Erinyes; National Socialism

happiness, 84, 87, 112, 114, 143–6, 161
  perfect happiness, 145–56
  see also Kant, Immanuel
Hart, H. L. A., 99, 104, 179, 183, 187; *see also* jurisprudence; officials
Hegel, Georg Wilhelm Friedrich, xxi–xxii, 13, 67, 74, 80, 168, 174, 249
Heidegger, Martin
  authentic decision, 165, 172
  contemporary legacy, xiv–xvii, xxi–xxii, 200–1, 253
  context of reading of Kant, 159–66
  Dasein, xiv, 161, 163, 169–71, 175
  failing, 170–5
  freedom, 159–63
  writings
    Being and Time, 159–61, 165, 171, 177
    Black Notebooks, xiv, xvi, 167, 173–4
    Elucidations of Hölderlin's Poetry, 246
    Essence of Human Freedom, 159–66
    Letter on Humanism, 171, 201
high treason, 113, 116, 130
highest good
  in Plato (*agathon*), 27, 50–2, 58
  in Pinar (Hölderlin), 242–6
  see also Kant, Immanuel, highest good
von Hippel, Theodor Gottlieb, 71–2; *see also* discourse, public, Königsberg
Hitler, Adolf, 169, 181, 210, 232, 253
Hölderlin, Friedrich, xxi, 67, 74, 80, 244–51, 253
Holocaust, 158, 213–14, 228

human rights, xx, 15, 72, 124, 195, 232–5

ideal theory, 25, 47, 121, 127, 134
ideology, viii, xvii, xxiii, 209, 238
critique of, 190, 209, 238–41; *see also* myths
in Kant (religion), 130–1, 155–7
nationalist, xiii, xvi, 17, 184, 224
National Socialist, 212, 227, 229–30; *see also* National Socialism
immoralist, 38–9, 63, 228
immortality, 7, 82, 137
immortals, 245, 247–8, 250; *see also* god; Hölderlin, Friedrich
imperialism, 15, 26, 196, 221
indigenous societies, 108, 124, 127, 149
individualism, xviii, 17, 211, 238
injustices, 40, 45, 72, 111, 116, 124–5, 205, 207; *see also* Kant, problem of evil
intellectuals
circles, 27, 70, 120, 131
public, xiii, xxii, 49, 67–69, 117, 120, 124, 129, 139, 176, 220
intellectual history, x, 238–39; *see also* Voegelin, Eric
international relations, viii, xv, 9, 15, 127; *see also* cosmopolitanism; geopolitics, politics
Isocrates, 23–7, 35, 39, 49; *see also* cosmopolitanism, ancient

Jägerstätter, Franz, xxiii, 169, 201, 231, 250, 253; *see also* authentic decision; National Socialism
Jews, 107, 135, 139, 184, 211, 223–4, 229
Judaism, 155, 156, 174
jurisprudence, 182–83, 217–18, 221
analytical, 179, 185, 187, 214
degeneration under National Socialism, 225–7
German (*Rechtswissenschaft*), 182, 185, 217, 226
purity of, 187, 199
justice, 37–43, 45, 100–1, 117–18, 132–3, 191, 198–200, 219
criminal, 117–20, 198, 200
distributive, xx, 108
critique of, 189–91
see also cosmopolitanism; guilt, law

Kant, Immanuel
anthropology, 87–90, 94, 101, 115, 144, 161–2, 164, 170
manias (for honour, domination and possession), 146, 150, 153
categorical imperative, 85, 117, 122, 164–6, 168–9, 172, 248, 253
freedom
as autonomy, 68, 89, 94, 96–7, 133, 146, 161–2
as choice (*Willkür*), 97, 101, 107, 110, 113
problem of free action, 84–6, 93–5, 97–101, 130, 147–8, 165–6, 195, 197–8
highest good
moral, 50–1, 143, 145
perfect happiness, 146
political, 115, 119, 122, 126
intellectual context
engagement with *Schwärmer* (Schlosser's Plato reception), 74–82, 155
early German Idealism, 80–1
see also Cambridge School
law (*Recht*)
criminal law
punishment, 90, 112, 117–19, 134
obedience to law, 101, 112–13, 140–2, 198
private law
as proto-cosmopolitan, 125
public law
cosmopolitanism as legal requirement, 128–30
republican peace thesis, 126–7, 146
moral law, 83–7, 93–5, 97, 99, 112, 148, 248
political context
censorship controversy, 137, 140, 155

Kant, Immanuel (*cont.*)
political context (*cont.*)
Königsberg and Prussia, 65–72, 80, 88, 135–6, 139, 157
religion
as ideology critique, 130–1, 155–7
ethical community, 100, 131, 150–4, 156, 248
faith (ecclesiastical, pure religious, moral), 153–6
problem of evil, 94–5, 103–4, 127–8, 134–5, 142, 145–50, 153
see also censorship controversy
unity of reason, 66, 83, 87, 89, 161; *see also* freedom; highest good; law; religion
writings
Anthropology, 87–90, 94, 101, 115, 144, 161–2, 164, 170
Critique of Pure Reason, 67, 83–4, 137, 160, 162–3
Doctrine of Right, 90–4, 96–7, 100–19, 128, 130, 140–1, 144
Geography, 87–90, 94, 115
Groundwork of the Metaphysics of Morals, 84–6, 99, 134, 161, 164, 166
Metaphysics of Morals, 82, 91–100, 137, 162
On a Recently Voiced Noble-Minded Tone in Philosophy, 77–8, 155
Religion within the Bounds of Mere Reason, 95–7, 127, 140, 143, 147–57
Towards Perpetual Peace, 119–30
Kelsen, Hans
autonomy of law, 186–91
cosmopolitanism, relation to, 191–200
critique of Gnosticism (vs. Voegelin), 241
critique of justice (vs. Plato), 198–200
critique of legal pluralism (vs. Ehrlich), 214–19
democracy (vs. Schmitt)
legal institutionalist theory of, 203–6
guardian of the constitution, 208–10
hierarchy of norms, 185–6
international law
unity of law, 193–4
critical analysis of Law of United Nations, 232–6
post-foundational perspective, 196–200
pure theory of law, 183–91, 199, 217
sovereignty, as legal fiction, 194–6
see also Austria; authentic decision
Kleingeld, Pauline, 73–4
Königsberg, xxii, 65–72, 80, 88, 92, 106–7, 135–6, 139; *see also* Cambridge School

law
legal register *see* Kelsen, Hans; jurisprudence
philosophical register *see* Kant, Immanuel, unity of reason
poetic register (*nomos basileus*) *see* Hölderlin, Friedrich
social practice *see* constitution; league of nations; legal pluralism
see also guilt
league of nations, 110–11, 223, 233–5
Kant, 110–11
League of Nations, 223
United Nations, 232–5
legal fictions, 192, 194, 203; *see also* Kelsen, Hans
legal pluralism, 106–7, 216–18, 223–4, 228–9
in Bukovina, 215–19
in Königsberg, 106
see also Ehrlich, Eugen
legal positivism, 185, 200, 217; *see also* jurisprudence, analytical
legitimacy, ix, 115, 182
of modernity, 62–3, 65

liberalism, viii, xvi, 132–3, 145, 154, 232, 238–9, 252
  critique of, left- and right-wing, viii
  demise under National Socialism, 208–12
  as ideology (Gnosticism), 241
  political, 12, 111, 157
  traditions, xvi–xvii, 65, 174, 207
  see also cosmopolitanism, relation to liberalism
liberty *see* freedom
Littell, Jonathan, xxiii, 179, 228, 230–1; *see also* Erinyes; guilt; National Socialism
living law, 215–16, 218, 223–4; *see also* Ehrlich, Eugen

Malick, Terrence, xxiii, 169–70; *see also* Jägerstätter, Franz; Heidegger, Martin; authentic decision
Marxism, xxii, 15, 74, 180, 190, 235
metaphysics, xxii, 27, 50–1, 53, 60, 82–3, 160–3, 247
  domesticated, 131, 142
  Occidental (Western), xv, 174
  see also Heidegger, Martin; Kant, Immanuel; Voegelin, Eric
modern law *see* jurisprudence; Kelsen, Hans; modernity
modernity, xiv, xxi, 65, 178, 181, 188–9, 240, 247
  circumstances of, xxiii, 65, 181, 253
  critique of, 237
  legitimacy, 62–3, 65
  principle, 63, 167, 170, 176
modus vivendi, 182, 224
morality
  collectivistic, 18
  critique of justice (vs. Plato), 198–200; *see* Kelsen, Hans
  moral politicians vs. political moralists, 122, 127, 128–9
  see also civilisation; Kant, Immanuel, law; Heidegger, Martin, context of reading of Kant
mythology, 10–11, 80–1, 93, 227–31, 247; *see also* Erinyes; justice, guilt, National Socialism
myths, 53, 63, 213, 240, 247; *see also* ideology, critique of

naïve lyrical enthusiasts (*Schwärmer*), 76, 79, 155; *see also* Schlosser, Johann Georg
nation state, 68, 222, 224; *see also* Austria; Prussia
nation, xviii, 23, 108–9, 111, 127, 133–4, 207
National Socialism, 158, 173, 206, 225, 232
  ideology, 212, 227, 229
  see also bureaucracy; civilisation; Erinyes; guilt; ideology, critique of; jurisprudence; politics
nationalism, xvi, xviii, 17–19, 184, 224, 230
neo-Kantianism, 174, 180, 199, 235
Nietzsche, Friedrich, x, xv–xvi, xxii, 74, 190, 244
norms, 193–4, 197–8, 214, 217
  hierarchy of, 185–6
  legal, 189, 192, 196, 234
  moral, 186, 189, 217
  see also Kelsen, Hans
normativity, 98–9, 179, 186–9; *see also* Kelsen, Hans
Nussbaum, Martha, 16, 18–19, 145

obedience, 58, 101, 112–13, 140–2, 198; *see also* Kant, Immanuel, law; National Socialism
officials, 67, 99, 137, 187, 226, 237
  practice of (Hart), 99, 187, 226; *see also* jurisprudence, analytical; Hart, H. L. A.
Oldest System Program of German Idealism, 10, 80, 93; *see also* German Idealism; mythology
oppression, xxii, 134, 139, 236, 252

Panhellenic federalism *see* cosmopolitanism, ancient
peace, 25–6, 32–3, 61, 78, 207, 241–2
  international, 72
  pastoral, 121
  perpetual peace as legal concept, 66, 90, 111–12, 119–30, 141, 241
  treaties, 78, 122
  see also Kant, Immanuel; league of nations
personal salvation, 37–8, 61–2, 169
Pindar, 244–7
Plato
  city and soul, analogy of, 4, 39, 47, 49
  cosmopolitanism
    anti-cosmopolitan position, 49–50
    proto-cosmopolitan interlocutors (Sophists), 43–50
  education (*paideia*), 51–3, 59, 62
  interpretation (modern) *see* Kelsen, Hans; Popper, Karl; Schofield, Malcolm; Wilamowitz-Moellendorff, Ulrich von
  Platonic Academy, 27, 32, 57
  Politeia
    Cephalus's conservativism, 13, 36–9, 41, 61
    dialectical method, 34–54
    formation of the city, 43–6
    justice
      justice as problem of the soul, 37–45
      Thrasymachus's challenge, 38–41
    opening scene as situated intervention, 36–8
    tragic worldview, 54–6
    über-cosmopolitan turn, 50–1
  reception in early German Idealism *see* Schlosser, Johann Georg
  Seventh Letter, 31–2, 51, 75, 79
  see also Cambridge School; highest good; metaphysics
pluralism
  legal *see* legal pluralism
  value, 209, 211
poetry, theory of, 4, 10, 246; *see also* Heidegger, Martin
Pogge, Thomas, xviii, 16–18
  see cosmopolitanism, contemporary
political liberalism, 12, 111, 157
political philosophy, xii, 13, 15, 65–6, 89–90, 98, 130–1, 144–5, 151–5
  liberal, 114, 197
  transformation into cosmopolitanism, 14–15
political theory *see* Arendt, Hannah; political philosophy
politics, xix–xx, 4, 62, 68, 128–30, 138–9, 141–2, 210
  absence of liberal politics in Kant, 81–90
  as applied legal doctrine in Kant, 121, 128
  degeneration under National Socialism, 206, 214, 225–6, 232
  discourse
    public discourse, xxii, 75–6, 136–7, 146, 155, 205
    religious discourse (Kant), 157, 177
  geopolitics, vii-viii, xv, 33, 69–70
  historical forms see Cambridge School
  ideological confrontation, xii–xiii, 252–4
  intervention
    constitutional intervention *see* Schmitt, Carl, contestation with Kelsen
    indirect intervention (Kant) *see* biopolitics
    situated intervention (Plato) *see* Plato, Politeia
  moral politicians vs. political moralists, 122, 127, 128–9
  see also cosmopolitanism; law
Popper, Karl, 27–8; *see also* cosmopolitanism, ancient

popular sovereignty, 203–5, 209; *see also* Kelsen, Hans; Schmitt, Carl
positivism, 238, 240; *see also* legal positivism
power, 25, 38–41, 69–70, 109–11, 116, 126–7, 213–14, 223
  of eros, 10, 17
  Gorgonian head of (Kelsen), 223
  power politics, 25, 69–70, 126–7
  as relation (Thrasymachus), 38–41
  separation of, 105, 116, 174
  see also coercion; education; empires; geopolitics; violence
Prauss, Gerold, 94–6, 168; *see also* Kant, Immanuel, unity of reason
property, 26, 102, 104, 109, 144, 191; *see also* Kant, Immanuel
Prussia, 67–9, 138–40, 177, 210, 236
  see also Cambridge School; Frederick the Great; Frederick William II; Kant, Immanuel, censorship controversy; Königsberg
public discourse *see* politics, discourse
public goods, 114–15
punishment, 90, 112, 117–19, 134; see also Kant, Immanuel

race, ix, 25, 70, 72, 174, 237–9, 245, 252; *see also* legal pluralism; National Socialism
Rawls, John, 15, 18, 44, 65, 122, 131–5, 142, 145, 225
rebellion, 113, 116, 127, 130, 149; *see also* Kant, Immanuel
reconciliation, viii, 63, 207
refugees, xiii–xiv, 25, 73, 173
religion, 67, 94, 131, 135–45, 150–7, 240; *see also* Kant, Immanuel, religion
republican peace thesis, 126–7, 146; *see also* Kant, Immanuel
revolution
  inner (moral conversion), 150, 152
  political, xxi–xxiii, 67, 72, 113, 129, 139–40, 154, 249
  revolution of thinking (Kant), 72–4, 82–4, 86
right (*Recht*), 101–2; *see also* Kant, Immanuel
Rostropovich, Mstislav, vii
Rousseau, Jean-Jacques, 103–4, 123
Russia, viii, xv, 70, 88, 107, 174

salvation, personal, 37–8, 61–2, 169
sanctions, 192, 195, 197, 204, 234–5
Sappho, xx–xxi, 1–12, 236, 244, 247, 253; *see also* borders, communication across borders; law, poetic register; mythology; power, of love
Schelling, Friedrich Wilhelm Joseph, 67, 74, 80; *see also Oldest System Program of German Idealism*
Schlosser, Johann Georg, 74–82, 120, 132–3, 155, 167; *see also* Plato, reception in early German Idealism; Kant, Immanuel, intellectual context; *Schwärmer*
Schmitt, Carl, xv–xvi, xxi, 178, 192–3, 212–14, 245–8
  contestation with Kelsen, 201–12
  guardian of the constitution, 208–10
  political activist position, 206–8; *see also* Cambridge School
Schofield, Malcolm, 31, 37; *see also* Plato, interpretation (modern)
Schwärmer, *see* naïve lyrical enthusiasts
separation of powers, 105, 116, 174
Skinner, Quentin, x–xi, 71; *see also* Cambridge School
social groups, 216, 219–20, 223; *see also* Ehrlich, Eugen
sophists, 20, 28–30, 34, 38, 48–50, 61–2
  as proto-cosmopolitans, 43–50
  see also cosmopolitanism, ancient; Plato, *Politeia*

soul
in Kant, 81–4, 137, 145, 151
in Plato, 37–9, 47, 49, 53, 55–6
sovereignty, 105, 112, 192, 203
as legal fiction, 194–6; *see also* Kelsen, Hans
popular, 203–5, 209
stoicism, ix, xix, 20–1, 65, 167; *see also* cosmopolitanism, ancient
subjectivity, 63, 167–8, 170–1, 173, 176, 181, 197; *see also* Kant, Immanuel
Syracuse, 32

Thrasymachus, 38–41, 49; *see also* Plato, *Politeia*
totalitarianism, 60, 80, 188, 227, 238, 245–6
high treason, 113, 116, 130; *see also* Kant, Immanuel

Ukraine, viii, xiii, 216, 252
United Nations, 179–80, 232–3, 239; *see also* League of Nations
United States, 71, 237, 242

values, 17–18, 27, 99, 128, 141–2, 204, 207, 209
value-free nature of science, 209
value pluralism, 209, 211
see also Kelsen, Hans
Vienna, xxiii, 176, 180–1, 199–200, 217, 235, 237, 253; *see also* Cambridge School
violence, 88, 103–5, 108–9, 112–15, 121, 154, 164, 223
at the origin of civilisation, 103–5
establishing a rightful condition, 108–9
historical church, 154
manias for domination, honour and possession (Kant), 88
obedience and punishment, 112–15
see also empires; geopolitics; power; National Socialism
Voegelin, Eric, xxiii, 179, 236–43; *see also* liberalism as ideology

wars, 25, 44, 69–70, 89, 110–11, 121–2, 179–80, 241–2
Weimar Republic, 206–10; *see also* Cambridge School
Wilamowitz-Moellendorff, Ulrich von, 30; *see also* Plato, interpretation (modern)
Willkür see Kant, Immanuel, freedom of choice
Wissenschaft (natural sciences and humanities), 46, 48, 50, 52, 62, 155; *see also* Plato; Kant, Immanuel
women, xxii, 2, 18, 47, 71–3, 120, 136, 139
World War I, xi, 183, 218–19, 222–3
World War II, 169

Xenophon, 23–4, 26–7, 35, 39
critique of panhellenic federalism, 26
depiction of Socrates, 27
see also cosmopolitanism, ancient; Socrates

EU Authorised Representative:
Easy Access System Europe Mustamäe tee 50, 10621 Tallinn, Estonia
gpsr.requests@easproject.com

Printed and bound by CPI Group (UK) Ltd, Croydon, CR0 4YY
10/07/2026
02163911-0002